Biographia Literaria

Samuel Taylor Coleridge

Alpha Editions

This edition published in 2024

ISBN : 9789367247198

Design and Setting By
Alpha Editions
www.alphaedis.com
Email - info@alphaedis.com

As per information held with us this book is in Public Domain.
This book is a reproduction of an important historical work. Alpha Editions uses the best technology to reproduce historical work in the same manner it was first published to preserve its original nature. Any marks or number seen are left intentionally to preserve its true form.

Contents

CHAPTER I ....- 1 -

CHAPTER II ....- 12 -

CHAPTER III ....- 20 -

CHAPTER IV ....- 29 -

CHAPTER V ....- 37 -

CHAPTER VI ....- 42 -

CHAPTER VII ....- 47 -

CHAPTER VIII ....- 52 -

CHAPTER IX ....- 56 -

CHAPTER X ....- 65 -

CHAPTER XI ....- 93 -

CHAPTER XII ....- 99 -

CHAPTER XIII ....- 120 -

CHAPTER XIV ....- 126 -

CHAPTER XV ....- 132 -

CHAPTER XVI ....- 138 -

CHAPTER XVII .... - 142 -

CHAPTER XVIII .... - 152 -

CHAPTER XIX .... - 169 -

CHAPTER XX .... - 176 -

CHAPTER XXI .... - 182 -

CHAPTER XXII .... - 189 -

SATYRANE'S LETTERS .... - 217 -

CHAPTER XXIII .... - 249 -

CHAPTER XXIV   CONCLUSION .... - 268 -

FOOTNOTES .... - 276 -

CHAPTER I

Motives to the present work—Reception of the Author's first publication—Discipline of his taste at school—Effect of contemporary writers on youthful minds—Bowles's Sonnets—Comparison between the poets before and since Pope.

It has been my lot to have had my name introduced both in conversation, and in print, more frequently than I find it easy to explain, whether I consider the fewness, unimportance, and limited circulation of my writings, or the retirement and distance, in which I have lived, both from the literary and political world. Most often it has been connected with some charge which I could not acknowledge, or some principle which I had never entertained. Nevertheless, had I had no other motive or incitement, the reader would not have been troubled with this exculpation. What my additional purposes were, will be seen in the following pages. It will be found, that the least of what I have written concerns myself personally. I have used the narration chiefly for the purpose of giving a continuity to the work, in part for the sake of the miscellaneous reflections suggested to me by particular events, but still more as introductory to a statement of my principles in Politics, Religion, and Philosophy, and an application of the rules, deduced from philosophical principles, to poetry and criticism. But of the objects, which I proposed to myself, it was not the least important to effect, as far as possible, a settlement of the long continued controversy concerning the true nature of poetic diction; and at the same time to define with the utmost impartiality the real poetic character of the poet, by whose writings this controversy was first kindled, and has been since fuelled and fanned.

In the spring of 1796, when I had but little passed the verge of manhood, I published a small volume of juvenile poems. They were received with a degree of favour, which, young as I was, I well know was bestowed on them not so much for any positive merit, as because they were considered buds of hope, and promises of better works to come. The critics of that day, the most flattering, equally with the severest, concurred in objecting to them obscurity, a general turgidness of diction, and a profusion of new coined double epithets [1]. The first is the fault which a writer is the least able to detect in his own compositions: and my mind was not then sufficiently disciplined to receive the authority of others, as a substitute for my own conviction. Satisfied that the thoughts, such as they were, could not have been expressed otherwise, or at least more perspicuously, I forgot to inquire, whether the thoughts themselves did not demand a degree of attention unsuitable to the nature and objects of poetry. This remark however applies chiefly, though not exclusively, to the Religious Musings. The remainder of the charge I admitted to its full extent, and not without sincere acknowledgments both to my private and public censors for their friendly admonitions. In the after editions, I pruned the double epithets with no sparing hand, and used my best efforts to tame the swell and glitter both of thought and diction; though in truth, these parasite plants of youthful poetry had insinuated themselves into my longer poems with such intricacy of union, that I was often obliged to omit disentangling the weed, from the fear of snapping the flower. From that period to the date of the present work I have published nothing, with my name, which could by any possibility have come before the board of anonymous criticism. Even the three or four poems, printed with the works of a friend [2], as far as they were censured at all, were charged with the same or similar defects, (though I am persuaded not with equal justice),—with an excess of ornament, in addition to strained and elaborate diction. I must be permitted to add, that, even at the early period of my juvenile poems, I saw and admitted the superiority of an austerer and more natural style, with an insight not less clear, than I at present possess. My judgment was stronger than were my powers of realizing its dictates; and the faults of my language, though indeed partly owing to a wrong choice of subjects, and the desire of giving a poetic colouring to abstract and metaphysical truths, in which a new world then seemed to open upon me, did yet, in part likewise, originate in unfeigned diffidence of my own comparative talent.—During several years of my youth and early manhood, I reverenced those who had re-introduced the manly simplicity of the Greek, and of our own elder poets, with such enthusiasm as made the hope seem presumptuous of writing successfully in the same style. Perhaps a similar process has happened to others; but my earliest poems were marked by an ease and simplicity, which I have studied, perhaps with inferior success, to impress on my later compositions.

At school, (Christ's Hospital,) I enjoyed the inestimable advantage of a very sensible, though at the same time, a very severe master, the Reverend James Bowyer. He early moulded my taste to the preference of Demosthenes to Cicero, of Homer and Theocritus to Virgil, and again of Virgil to Ovid. He habituated me to compare Lucretius, (in such extracts as I then read,) Terence, and above all the chaster poems of Catullus, not only with the Roman poets of the, so called, silver and brazen ages; but with even those of the Augustan aera: and on grounds of plain sense and universal logic to see and assert the superiority of the former in the truth and nativeness both of their thoughts and diction. At the same time that we were studying the Greek tragic poets, he made us read Shakespeare and Milton as lessons: and they were the lessons too, which required most time and trouble to bring up, so as to escape his censure. I learned from him, that poetry, even that of the loftiest and, seemingly, that of the wildest odes, had a logic of its own, as severe as that of science; and more difficult, because more subtle, more complex, and dependent on more, and more fugitive causes. In the truly great poets, he would say, there is a reason assignable, not only for every word, but for the position of every word; and I well remember that, availing himself of the synonymes to the Homer of Didymus, he made us attempt to show, with regard to each, why it would not have answered the same purpose; and wherein consisted the peculiar fitness of the word in the original text.

In our own English compositions, (at least for the last three years of our school education,) he showed no mercy to phrase, metaphor, or image, unsupported by a sound sense, or where the same sense might have been conveyed with equal force and dignity in plainer words [3]. Lute, harp, and lyre, Muse, Muses, and inspirations, Pegasus, Parnassus, and Hippocrene were all an abomination to him. In fancy I can almost hear him now, exclaiming "Harp? Harp? Lyre? Pen and ink, boy, you mean! Muse, boy, Muse? Your nurse's daughter, you mean! Pierian spring? Oh aye! the cloister-pump, I suppose!" Nay certain introductions, similes, and examples, were placed by name on a list of interdiction. Among the similes, there was, I remember, that of the manchineel fruit, as suiting equally well with too many subjects; in which however it yielded the palm at once to the example of Alexander and Clytus, which was equally good and apt, whatever might be the theme. Was it ambition? Alexander and Clytus!—Flattery? Alexander and Clytus!—anger—drunkenness—pride—friendship—ingratitude—late repentance? Still, still Alexander and Clytus! At length, the praises of agriculture having been exemplified in the sagacious observation that, had Alexander been holding the plough, he would not have run his friend Clytus through with a spear, this tried, and serviceable old friend was banished by public edict in saecula saeculorum. I have sometimes ventured to think, that a list of this kind, or an index expurgatorius of certain well-known and ever-returning phrases, both introductory, and transitional, including a large assortment of modest egoisms, and flattering illeisms, and the like, might be hung up in our Law-courts, and both Houses of Parliament, with great advantage to the public, as an important saving of national time, an incalculable relief to his Majesty's ministers, but above all, as insuring the thanks of country attornies, and their clients, who have private bills to carry through the House.

Be this as it may, there was one custom of our master's, which I cannot pass over in silence, because I think it imitable and worthy of imitation. He would often permit our exercises, under some pretext of want of time, to accumulate, till each lad had four or five to be looked over. Then placing the whole number abreast on his desk, he would ask the writer, why this or that sentence might not have found as appropriate a place under this or that other thesis: and if no satisfying answer could be returned, and two faults of the same kind were found in one exercise, the irrevocable verdict followed, the exercise was torn up, and another on the same subject to be produced, in addition to the tasks of the day. The reader will, I trust, excuse this tribute of recollection to a man, whose severities, even now, not seldom furnish the dreams, by which the blind fancy would fain interpret to the mind the painful sensations of distempered sleep; but neither lessen nor dim the deep sense of my moral and intellectual obligations. He sent us to the University excellent Latin and Greek scholars, and tolerable Hebraists. Yet our classical knowledge was the least of the good gifts, which we derived from his zealous and conscientious tutorage. He is now gone to his final reward, full of years, and full of honours, even of those honours, which were dearest to his heart, as gratefully bestowed by that school, and still binding him to the interests of that school, in which he had been himself educated, and to which during his whole life he was a dedicated thing.

From causes, which this is not the place to investigate, no models of past times, however perfect, can have the same vivid effect on the youthful mind, as the productions of contemporary genius. The discipline, my mind had undergone, Ne falleretur rotundo sono et versuum cursu, cincinnis, et floribus; sed ut inspiceret quidnam subesset, quae, sedes, quod firmamentum, quis fundus verbis; an figures essent mera ornatura et orationis fucus; vel sanguinis e materiae ipsius corde effluentis rubor quidam nativus et incalescentia genuina;—removed all obstacles to the appreciation of excellence in style without diminishing my delight. That I was thus prepared for the perusal of Mr. Bowles's sonnets and earlier poems, at once increased their influence, and my enthusiasm. The great works of past ages seem to a young man things of another race, in respect to which his faculties must remain passive and submiss, even as to the stars and mountains. But the writings of a contemporary, perhaps not many years older than himself, surrounded by the same circumstances, and disciplined by the same manners, possess a reality for him, and inspire an actual friendship as of a man for a man. His very admiration is the wind which fans and feeds his hope. The poems themselves assume the properties of flesh and blood. To recite, to extol, to contend for them is but the payment of a debt due to one, who exists to receive it.

There are indeed modes of teaching which have produced, and are producing, youths of a very different stamp; modes of teaching, in comparison with which we have been called on to despise our great public schools, and universities,

in whose halls are hung
Armoury of the invincible knights of old—

modes, by which children are to be metamorphosed into prodigies. And prodigies with a vengeance have I known thus produced; prodigies of self-conceit, shallowness, arrogance, and infidelity! Instead of storing the memory, during the period when the memory is the predominant faculty, with facts for the after exercise of the judgment; and instead of awakening by the noblest models the fond and unmixed love and admiration, which is the natural and graceful temper of early youth; these nurslings of improved pedagogy are taught to dispute and decide; to suspect all but their own and their lecturer's wisdom; and to hold nothing sacred from their contempt, but their own contemptible arrogance; boy-graduates in all the technicals, and in all the dirty passions and impudence of anonymous criticism. To such dispositions alone can the admonition of Pliny be requisite, Neque enim debet operibus ejus obesse, quod vivit. An si inter eos, quos nunquam vidimus, floruisset, non solum libros ejus, verum etiam imagines conquireremus, ejusdem nunc honor prasentis, et gratia quasi satietate languescet? At hoc pravum, malignumque est, non admirari hominem admiratione dignissimum, quia videre, complecti, nec laudare tantum, verum etiam amare contingit.

I had just entered on my seventeenth year, when the sonnets of Mr. Bowles, twenty in number, and just then published in a quarto pamphlet, were first made known and presented to me, by a schoolfellow who had quitted us for the University, and who, during the whole time that he was in our first form (or in our school language a Grecian,) had been my patron and protector. I refer to Dr. Middleton, the truly learned, and every way excellent Bishop of Calcutta:

qui laudibus amplis
Ingenium celebrare meum, calamumque solebat,
Calcar agens animo validum. Non omnia terra
Obruta; vivit amor, vivit dolor; ora negatur
Dulcia conspicere; at flere et meminisse relictum est.

It was a double pleasure to me, and still remains a tender recollection, that I should have received from a friend so revered the first knowledge of a poet, by whose works, year after year, I was so enthusiastically delighted and inspired. My earliest acquaintances will not have forgotten the undisciplined eagerness and impetuous zeal, with which I laboured to make proselytes, not only of my companions, but of all with whom I conversed, of whatever rank, and in whatever place. As my school finances did not permit me to purchase copies, I made, within less than a year and a half, more than forty transcriptions, as the best presents I could offer to those, who had in any way won my regard. And with almost equal delight did I receive the three or four following publications of the same author.

Though I have seen and known enough of mankind to be well aware, that I shall perhaps stand alone in my creed, and that it will be well, if I subject myself to no worse charge than that of singularity; I am not therefore deterred from avowing, that I regard, and ever have regarded the obligations of intellect among the most sacred of the claims of gratitude. A valuable thought, or a particular train of thoughts, gives me additional pleasure, when I can safely refer and attribute it to the conversation or correspondence of another. My obligations to Mr. Bowles were indeed important, and for radical good. At a very premature age, even before my fifteenth year, I had bewildered myself in metaphysics, and in theological controversy. Nothing else pleased me. History, and particular facts, lost all interest in my mind. Poetry—(though for a school-boy of that age, I was above par in English versification, and had already produced two or three compositions which, I may venture to say, without reference to my age, were somewhat above mediocrity, and which had gained me more credit than the sound, good sense of my old master was at all pleased with,)—poetry itself, yea, novels and romances, became insipid to me. In my friendless wanderings on our leave-days [4], (for I was an orphan, and had scarcely any connections in London,) highly was I delighted, if any passenger, especially if he were dressed in black, would enter into conversation with me. For I soon found the means of directing it to my favourite subjects

Of providence, fore-knowledge, will, and fate,
Fixed fate, free will, fore-knowledge absolute,
And found no end in wandering mazes lost.

This preposterous pursuit was, beyond doubt, injurious both to my natural powers, and to the progress of my education. It would perhaps have been destructive, had it been continued; but from this I was auspiciously withdrawn, partly indeed by an accidental introduction to an amiable family, chiefly however, by the genial influence of a style of poetry, so tender and yet so manly, so natural and real, and yet so dignified and harmonious, as the sonnets and other early poems of Mr. Bowles. Well would it have been for me, perhaps, had I never relapsed into the same mental disease; if I had continued to pluck the flower and reap the harvest from the cultivated surface, instead of delving in the unwholesome quicksilver mines of metaphysic lore. And if in after time I have sought a refuge from bodily pain and mismanaged sensibility in abstruse researches, which exercised the strength and subtilty of the understanding without awakening the feelings of the heart; still there was a long and blessed interval, during which my natural faculties were allowed to expand, and my original tendencies to develop themselves;—my fancy, and the love of nature, and the sense of beauty in forms and sounds.

The second advantage, which I owe to my early perusal, and admiration of these poems, (to which let me add,) though known to me at a somewhat later period, the Lewesdon Hill of Mr. Crowe bears more immediately on my present subject. Among those with whom I conversed, there were, of course, very many who had formed their taste, and their notions of poetry, from the writings of Pope and his followers; or to speak more generally, in that school of French poetry, condensed and invigorated by English understanding, which had predominated from the last century. I was not blind to the merits of this school, yet, as from inexperience of the world, and consequent want of sympathy with the general subjects of these poems, they gave me little pleasure, I doubtless undervalued the kind, and with the presumption of youth withheld from its masters the legitimate name of poets. I saw that the excellence of this kind consisted in just and acute observations on men and manners in an artificial state of society, as its matter and substance; and in the logic of wit, conveyed in smooth and strong epigrammatic couplets, as its form: that even when the subject was addressed to the fancy, or the intellect, as in the Rape of the Lock, or the Essay on Man; nay, when it was a consecutive narration, as in that astonishing product of matchless talent and ingenuity Pope's Translation of the Iliad; still a point was looked for at the end of each second line, and the whole was, as it were, a sorites, or, if I may exchange a logical for a grammatical metaphor, a conjunction disjunctive, of epigrams. Meantime the matter and diction seemed to me characterized not so much by poetic thoughts, as by thoughts translated into the language of poetry. On this last point, I had occasion to render my own thoughts gradually more and more plain to myself, by frequent amicable disputes concerning Darwin's Botanic Garden, which, for some years, was greatly extolled, not only by the reading public in general, but even by those, whose genius and natural robustness of understanding enabled them afterwards to act foremost in dissipating these "painted mists" that occasionally rise from the marshes at the foot of Parnassus. During my first Cambridge vacation, I assisted a friend in a contribution for a literary society in Devonshire: and in this I remember to have compared Darwin's work to the Russian palace of ice, glittering, cold and transitory. In the same essay too, I assigned sundry reasons, chiefly drawn from a comparison of passages in the Latin poets with the original Greek, from which they were borrowed, for the preference of Collins's odes to those of Gray; and of the simile in Shakespeare

How like a younker or a prodigal
The scarfed bark puts from her native bay,
Hugg'd and embraced by the strumpet wind!

How like the prodigal doth she return,
With over-weather'd ribs and ragged sails,
Lean, rent, and beggar'd by the strumpet wind!
(Merch. of Ven. Act II. sc. 6.)

to the imitation in the Bard;

Fair laughs the morn, and soft the zephyr blows
While proudly riding o'er the azure realm
In gallant trim the gilded vessel goes,
Youth at the prow and pleasure at the helm;
Regardless of the sweeping whirlwind's sway,
That hush'd in grim repose, expects it's evening prey.

(in which, by the bye, the words "realm" and "sway" are rhymes dearly purchased)—I preferred the original on the ground, that in the imitation it depended wholly on the compositor's putting, or not putting, a small capital, both in this, and in many other passages of the same poet, whether the words should be personifications, or mere abstractions. I mention this, because, in referring various lines in Gray to their original in Shakespeare and Milton, and in the clear perception how completely all the propriety was lost in the transfer, I was, at that early period, led to a conjecture, which, many years afterwards was recalled to me from the same thought having been started in conversation, but far more ably, and developed more fully, by Mr. Wordsworth;—namely, that this style of poetry, which I have characterized above, as translations of prose thoughts into poetic language, had been kept up by, if it did not wholly arise from, the custom of writing Latin verses, and the great importance attached to these exercises, in our public schools. Whatever might have been the case in the fifteenth century, when the use of the Latin tongue was so general among learned men, that Erasmus is said to have forgotten his native language; yet in the present day it is not to be supposed, that a youth can think in Latin, or that he can have any other reliance on the force or fitness of his phrases, but the authority of the writer from whom he has adopted them. Consequently he must first prepare his thoughts, and then pick out, from Virgil, Horace, Ovid, or perhaps more compendiously from his Gradus, halves and quarters of lines, in which to embody them.

I never object to a certain degree of disputatiousness in a young man from the age of seventeen to that of four or five and twenty, provided I find him always arguing on one side of the question. The controversies, occasioned by my unfeigned zeal for the honour of a favourite contemporary, then known to me only by his works, were of great advantage in the formation and establishment of my taste and critical opinions. In my defence of the lines running into each other, instead of closing at each couplet; and of natural language, neither bookish, nor vulgar, neither redolent of the lamp, nor of the kennel, such as I will remember thee; instead of the same thought tricked up in the rag-fair finery of,

————*thy image on her wing*
Before my fancy's eye shall memory bring,—

I had continually to adduce the metre and diction of the Greek poets, from Homer to Theocritus inclusively; and still more of our elder English poets, from Chaucer to Milton. Nor was this all. But as it was my constant reply to authorities brought against me from later poets of great name, that no authority could avail in opposition to Truth, Nature, Logic, and the Laws of Universal Grammar; actuated too by my former passion for metaphysical investigations; I laboured at a solid foundation, on which permanently to ground my opinions, in the component faculties of the human mind itself, and their comparative dignity and importance. According to the faculty or source, from which the pleasure given by any poem or passage was derived, I estimated the merit of such poem or passage. As the result of all my reading and meditation, I abstracted two critical aphorisms, deeming them to comprise the conditions and criteria of poetic style;—first, that not the poem which we have read, but that to which we return, with the greatest pleasure, possesses the genuine power, and claims the name of essential poetry;—secondly, that whatever lines can be translated into other words of the same language, without diminution of their significance, either in sense or association, or in any worthy feeling, are so far vicious in their diction. Be it however observed, that I excluded from the list of worthy feelings, the pleasure derived from mere novelty in the reader, and the desire of exciting wonderment at his powers in the author. Oftentimes since then, in pursuing French tragedies, I have fancied two marks of admiration at the end of each line, as hieroglyphics of the author's own admiration at his own cleverness. Our genuine admiration of a great poet is a continuous undercurrent of feeling! it is everywhere present, but seldom anywhere as a separate excitement. I was wont boldly to affirm, that it would be scarcely more difficult to push a stone out from the Pyramids with the bare hand, than to alter a word, or the position of a word, in Milton or Shakespeare, (in their most important works at least,) without making the poet say something else, or something worse, than he does say. One great distinction, I appeared to myself to see plainly between even the characteristic faults of our elder poets, and the false beauty of the moderns. In the former, from Donne to Cowley, we find the most fantastic out-of-the-way thoughts, but in the most pure and genuine mother English, in the latter the most obvious thoughts, in language the most fantastic and arbitrary. Our faulty elder poets sacrificed the passion and passionate flow of poetry to the subtleties of intellect and to the stars of wit; the moderns to the glare and glitter of a perpetual, yet broken and heterogeneous imagery, or rather to an amphibious something, made up, half of image, and half of abstract [5] meaning. The one sacrificed the heart to the head; the other both heart and head to point and drapery.

The reader must make himself acquainted with the general style of composition that was at that time deemed poetry, in order to understand and account for the effect produced on me by the Sonnets, the Monody at Matlock, and the Hope, of Mr. Bowles; for it is peculiar to original genius to become less and less striking, in proportion to its success in improving the taste and judgment of its contemporaries. The poems of West, indeed, had the merit of chaste and manly diction; but they were cold, and, if I may so express it, only dead-coloured; while in the best of Warton's there is a stiffness, which too often gives them the appearance of imitations from the Greek. Whatever relation, therefore, of cause or impulse Percy's collection of Ballads may bear to the most popular poems of the present day; yet in a more sustained and elevated style, of the then living poets, Cowper and Bowles [6] were, to the best of my knowledge, the first who combined natural thoughts with natural diction; the first who reconciled the heart with the head.

It is true, as I have before mentioned, that from diffidence in my own powers, I for a short time adopted a laborious and florid diction, which I myself deemed, if not absolutely vicious, yet of very inferior worth. Gradually, however, my practice conformed to my better judgment; and the compositions of my twenty-fourth and twenty-fifth years—(for example, the shorter blank verse poems, the lines, which now form the middle and conclusion of the poem entitled the Destiny of Nations, and the tragedy of Remorse)—are not more below my present ideal in respect of the general tissue of the style than those of the latest date. Their faults were at least a remnant of the former leaven, and among the many who have done me the honour of putting my poems in the same class with those of my betters, the one or two, who have pretended to bring examples of affected simplicity from my volume, have been able to adduce but one instance, and that out of a copy of verses half ludicrous, half splenetic, which I intended, and had myself characterized, as sermoni propiora.

Every reform, however necessary, will by weak minds be carried to an excess, which will itself need reforming. The reader will excuse me for noticing, that I myself was the first to expose risu honesto the three sins of poetry, one or the other of which is the most likely to beset a young writer. So long ago as the publication of the second number of the Monthly Magazine, under the name of Nehemiah Higginbottom, I contributed three sonnets, the first of which had for its object to excite a good-natured laugh at the spirit of doleful egotism, and at the recurrence of favourite phrases, with the double defect of being at once trite and licentious;—the second was on low creeping language and thoughts, under the pretence of simplicity; the third, the phrases of which were borrowed entirely from my own poems, on the indiscriminate use of elaborate and swelling language and imagery. The reader will find them in the note [7] below, and will I trust regard them as reprinted for biographical purposes alone, and not for their poetic merits. So general at that time, and so decided was the opinion concerning the characteristic vices of my style, that a celebrated physician (now, alas! no more) speaking of me in other respects with his usual kindness, to a gentleman, who was about to meet me at a dinner party, could not however resist giving him a hint not to mention 'The house that Jack built' in my presence, for "that I was as sore as a boil about that sonnet;" he not knowing that I was myself the author of it.

CHAPTER II

Supposed irritability of men of genius brought to the test of facts—Causes and occasions of the charge—Its injustice.

I have often thought, that it would be neither uninstructive nor unamusing to analyze, and bring forward into distinct consciousness, that complex feeling, with which readers in general take part against the author, in favour of the critic; and the readiness with which they apply to all poets the old sarcasm of Horace upon the scribblers of his time

————*genus irritabile vatum.*

A debility and dimness of the imaginative power, and a consequent necessity of reliance on the immediate impressions of the senses, do, we know well, render the mind liable to superstition and fanaticism. Having a deficient portion of internal and proper warmth, minds of this class seek in the crowd circum fana for a warmth in common, which they do not possess singly. Cold and phlegmatic in their own nature, like damp hay, they heat and inflame by co-acervation; or like bees they become restless and irritable through the increased temperature of collected multitudes. Hence the German word for fanaticism, (such at least was its original import,) is derived from the swarming of bees, namely, schwaermen, schwaermerey. The passion being in an inverse proportion to the insight,—that the more vivid, as this the less distinct—anger is the inevitable consequence. The absense of all foundation within their own minds for that, which they yet believe both true and indispensable to their safety and happiness, cannot but produce an uneasy state of feeling, an involuntary sense of fear from which nature has no means of rescuing herself but by anger. Experience informs us that the first defence of weak minds is to recriminate.

There's no philosopher but sees,
That rage and fear are one disease;
Tho' that may burn, and this may freeze,
They're both alike the ague.

But where the ideas are vivid, and there exists an endless power of combining and modifying them, the feelings and affections blend more easily and intimately with these ideal creations than with the objects of the senses; the mind is affected by thoughts, rather than by things; and only then feels the requisite interest even for the most important events and accidents, when by means of meditation they have passed into thoughts. The sanity of the mind is between superstition with fanaticism on the one hand, and enthusiasm with indifference and a diseased slowness to action on the other. For the conceptions of the mind may be so vivid and adequate, as to preclude that impulse to the realizing of them, which is strongest and most restless in those, who possess more than mere talent, (or the faculty of appropriating and applying the knowledge of others,)— yet still want something of the creative and self-sufficing power of absolute genius. For this reason therefore, they are men of commanding genius. While the former rest content between thought and reality, as it were in an intermundium of which their own living spirit supplies the substance, and their imagination the ever-varying form; the latter must impress their preconceptions on the world without, in order to present them back to their own view with the satisfying degree of clearness, distinctness, and individuality. These in tranquil times are formed to exhibit a perfect poem in palace, or temple, or landscape-garden; or a tale of romance in canals that join sea with sea, or in walls of rock, which, shouldering back the billows, imitate the power, and supply the benevolence of nature to sheltered navies; or in aqueducts that, arching the wide vale from mountain to mountain, give a Palmyra to the desert. But alas! in times of tumult they are the men destined to come forth as the shaping spirit of ruin, to destroy the wisdom of ages in order to substitute the fancies of a day, and to change kings and kingdoms, as the wind shifts and shapes the clouds [8]. The records of biography seem to confirm this theory. The men of the greatest genius, as far as we can judge from their own works or from the accounts of their contemporaries, appear to have been of calm and tranquil temper in all that related to themselves. In the inward assurance of permanent fame, they seem to have been either indifferent or resigned with regard to immediate reputation. Through all the works of Chaucer there reigns a cheerfulness, a manly hilarity which makes it almost impossible to doubt a correspondent habit of feeling in the author himself. Shakespeare's evenness and sweetness of temper were almost proverbial in his own age. That this did not arise from ignorance of his own comparative greatness, we have abundant proof in his Sonnets, which could scarcely have been known to Pope [9], when he asserted, that our great bard--

------*grew immortal in his own despite.*
(Epist. to Augustus.)

Speaking of one whom he had celebrated, and contrasting the duration of his works with that of his personal existence, Shakespeare adds:

Your name from hence immortal life shall have,
Tho' I once gone to all the world must die;
The earth can yield me but a common grave,
When you entombed in men's eyes shall lie.
Your monument shall be my gentle verse,
Which eyes not yet created shall o'er-read;

And tongues to be your being shall rehearse,
When all the breathers of this world are dead;
You still shall live, such virtue hath my pen,
Where breath most breathes, e'en in the mouth of men.
SONNET LXXXI.

I have taken the first that occurred; but Shakespeare's readiness to praise his rivals, ore pleno, and the confidence of his own equality with those whom he deemed most worthy of his praise, are alike manifested in another Sonnet.

Was it the proud full sail of his great verse,
Bound for the praise of all-too-precious you,
That did my ripe thoughts in my brain inhearse,
Making their tomb, the womb wherein they grew?
Was it his spirit, by spirits taught to write
Above a mortal pitch that struck me dead?
No, neither he, nor his compeers by night
Giving him aid, my verse astonished.
He, nor that affable familiar ghost,
Which nightly gulls him with intelligence,
As victors of my silence cannot boast;
I was not sick of any fear from thence!
But when your countenance fill'd up his line,
Then lack'd I matter, that enfeebled mine.
S. LXXXVI.

In Spenser, indeed, we trace a mind constitutionally tender, delicate, and, in comparison with his three great compeers, I had almost said, effeminate; and this additionally saddened by the unjust persecution of Burleigh, and the severe calamities, which overwhelmed his latter days. These causes have diffused over all his compositions "a melancholy grace," and have drawn forth occasional strains, the more pathetic from their gentleness. But no where do we find the least trace of irritability, and still less of quarrelsome or affected contempt of his censurers.

The same calmness, and even greater self-possession, may be affirmed of Milton, as far as his poems, and poetic character are concerned. He reserved his anger for the enemies of religion, freedom, and his country. My mind is not capable of forming a more august conception, than arises from the contemplation of this great man in his latter days;--poor, sick, old, blind, slandered, persecuted,--

Darkness before, and danger's voice behind,--

in an age in which he was as little understood by the party, for whom, as by that against whom, he had contended; and among men before whom he strode so far as to dwarf himself by the distance; yet still listening to the music of his own thoughts, or if additionally cheered, yet cheered only by the prophetic faith of two or three solitary individuals, he did nevertheless

------*argue not*
Against Heaven's hand or will, nor bate a jot
Of heart or hope; but still bore up and steer'd
Right onward.

From others only do we derive our knowledge that Milton, in his latter day, had his scorners and detractors; and even in his day of youth and hope, that he had enemies would have been unknown to us, had they not been likewise the enemies of his country.

I am well aware, that in advanced stages of literature, when there exist many and excellent models, a high degree of talent, combined with taste and judgment, and employed in works of imagination, will acquire for a man the name of a great genius; though even that analogon of genius, which, in certain states of society, may even render his writings more popular than the absolute reality could have done, would be sought for in vain in the mind and temper of the author himself. Yet even in instances of this kind, a close examination will often detect, that the irritability, which has been attributed to the author's genius as its cause, did really originate in an ill conformation of body, obtuse pain, or constitutional defect of pleasurable sensation. What is charged to the author, belongs to the man, who would probably have been still more impatient, but for the humanizing influences of the very pursuit, which yet bears the blame of his irritability.

How then are we to explain the easy credence generally given to this charge, if the charge itself be not, as I have endeavoured to show, supported by experience? This seems to me of no very difficult solution. In whatever country literature is widely diffused, there will be many who mistake an intense desire to possess the reputation of poetic genius, for the actual powers, and original tendencies which constitute it. But men, whose dearest wishes are fixed on objects wholly out of their own power, become in all cases more or less impatient and prone to anger. Besides, though it may be paradoxical to assert, that a man can know one thing and believe the opposite, yet assuredly a vain person may have so habitually indulged the wish, and persevered in the attempt, to appear what he is not, as to become himself one of his own proselytes. Still, as this counterfeit and artificial persuasion must differ, even in the person's own feelings, from a real sense of inward power, what can be more natural, than that this difference should betray itself in suspicious and jealous irritability? Even as the flowery sod, which covers a hollow, may be often detected by its shaking and trembling.

But, alas! the multitude of books and the general diffusion of literature, have produced other and more lamentable effects in the world of letters, and such as are abundant to explain, though by no means to justify, the contempt with which the best grounded complaints of injured genius are rejected as frivolous, or entertained as matter of merriment. In the days of Chaucer and Gower, our language might (with due allowance for the imperfections of a simile) be compared to a wilderness of vocal reeds, from which the favourites only of Pan or Apollo could construct even the rude syrinx; and from this the constructors alone could elicit strains of music. But now, partly by the labours of successive poets, and in part by the more artificial state of society and social intercourse, language, mechanized as it were into a barrel-organ, supplies at once both instrument and tune. Thus even the deaf may play, so as to delight the many. Sometimes (for it is with similes, as it is with jests at a wine table, one is sure to suggest another) I have attempted to illustrate the present state of our language, in its relation to literature, by a press-room of larger and smaller stereotype pieces, which, in the present Anglo-Gallican fashion of unconnected, epigrammatic periods, it requires but an ordinary portion of ingenuity to vary indefinitely, and yet still produce something, which, if not sense, will be so like it as to do as well. Perhaps better: for it spares the reader the trouble of thinking; prevents vacancy, while it indulges indolence; and secures the memory from all danger of an intellectual plethora. Hence of all trades, literature at present demands the least talent or information; and, of all modes of literature, the manufacturing of poems. The difference indeed between these and the works of genius is not less than between an egg and an egg-shell; yet at a distance they both look alike.

Now it is no less remarkable than true, with how little examination works of polite literature are commonly perused, not only by the mass of readers, but by men of first rate ability, till some accident or chance [10] discussion have roused their attention, and put them on their guard. And hence individuals below mediocrity not less in natural power than in acquired knowledge; nay, bunglers who have failed in the lowest mechanic crafts, and whose presumption is in due proportion to their want of sense and sensibility; men, who being first scribblers from idleness and ignorance, next become libellers from envy and malevolence,—have been able to drive a successful trade in the employment of the booksellers, nay, have raised themselves into temporary name and reputation with the public at large, by that most powerful of all adulation, the appeal to the bad and malignant passions of mankind [11]. But as it is the nature of scorn, envy, and all malignant propensities to require a quick change of objects, such writers are sure, sooner or later, to awake from their dream of vanity to disappointment and neglect with embittered and envenomed feelings. Even during their short-lived success, sensible in spite of themselves on what a shifting foundation it rests, they resent the mere refusal of praise as a robbery, and at the justest censures kindle at once into violent and undisciplined abuse; till the acute disease changing into chronical, the more deadly as the less violent, they become the fit instruments of literary detraction and moral slander. They are then no longer to be questioned without exposing the complainant to ridicule, because, forsooth, they are anonymous critics, and authorized, in Andrew Marvell's phrase, as "synodical individuals" to speak of themselves plurali majestatico! As if literature formed a caste, like that of the Paras in Hindostan, who, however maltreated, must not dare to deem themselves wronged! As if that, which in all other cases adds a deeper dye to slander, the circumstance of its being anonymous, here acted only to make the slanderer inviolable! [12] Thus, in part, from the accidental tempers of individuals—(men of undoubted talent, but not men of genius)—tempers rendered yet more irritable by their desire to appear men of genius; but still more effectively by the excesses of the mere counterfeits both of talent and genius; the number too being so incomparably greater of those who are thought to be, than of those who really are men of genius; and in part from the natural, but not therefore the less partial and unjust distinction, made by the public itself between literary and all other property; I believe the prejudice to have arisen, which considers an unusual irascibility concerning the reception of its products as characteristic of genius.

It might correct the moral feelings of a numerous class of readers, to suppose a Review set on foot, the object of which should be to criticise all the chief works presented to the public by our ribbon-weavers, calico-printers, cabinet-makers, and china-manufacturers; which should be conducted in the same spirit, and take the same freedom with personal character, as our literary journals. They would scarcely, I think, deny their belief, not only that the genus irritabile would be found to include many other species besides that of bards; but that the irritability of trade would soon reduce the resentments of poets into mere shadow-fights in the comparison. Or is wealth the only rational object of human interest? Or even if this were admitted, has the poet no property in his works? Or is it a rare, or culpable case, that he who serves at the altar of the Muses, should be compelled to derive his maintenance from the altar, when too he has perhaps deliberately abandoned the fairest prospects of rank and opulence in order to devote himself, an entire and undistracted man, to the instruction or refinement of his fellow-citizens? Or, should we pass by all higher objects and motives, all disinterested benevolence, and even that ambition of lasting praise which is at once the crutch and ornament, which at once supports and betrays, the infirmity of human virtue,—is the character and property of the man, who labours for our intellectual pleasures, less entitled to a share of our fellow feeling, than that of the wine-merchant or milliner? Sensibility indeed, both quick and deep, is not only a characteristic feature, but may be deemed a component part, of genius. But it is not less an essential mark of true genius, that its sensibility is excited by any other cause more powerfully than by its own personal interests; for this plain reason, that the man of genius lives most in the ideal world, in which the present is still constituted by the future or the past; and because his feelings have been habitually associated with thoughts and images, to the number, clearness, and vivacity of which the sensation of self is always in an inverse proportion. And yet, should he perchance have occasion to repel some false charge, or to rectify some erroneous censure, nothing is more common than for the many to mistake the general liveliness of his manner and language, whatever is the subject, for the effects of peculiar irritation from its accidental relation to himself. [13]

For myself, if from my own feelings, or from the less suspicious test of the observations of others, I had been made aware of any literary testiness or jealousy; I trust, that I should have been, however, neither silly nor arrogant enough to have burthened the imperfection on genius. But an experience—(and I should not need documents in abundance to prove my words, if I added)—a tried experience of twenty years, has taught me, that the original sin of my character consists in a careless indifference to public opinion, and to the attacks of those who influence it; that praise and admiration have become yearly less and less desirable, except as marks of sympathy; nay that it is difficult and distressing to me to think with any interest even about the sale and profit of my works, important as, in my present circumstances, such considerations must needs be. Yet it never occurred to me to believe or fancy, that the quantum of intellectual power bestowed on me by nature or education was in any way connected with this habit of my feelings; or that it needed any other parents or fosterers than constitutional indolence, aggravated into languor by ill-health; the accumulating embarrassments of procrastination; the mental cowardice, which is the inseparable companion of procrastination, and which makes us anxious to think and converse on any thing rather than on what concerns ourselves; in fine, all those close vexations, whether chargeable on my faults or my fortunes, which leave me but little grief to spare for evils comparatively distant and alien.

Indignation at literary wrongs I leave to men born under happier stars. I cannot afford it. But so far from condemning those who can, I deem it a writer's duty, and think it creditable to his heart, to feel and express a resentment proportioned to the grossness of the provocation, and the importance of the object. There is no profession on earth, which requires an attention so early, so long, or so unintermitting as that of poetry; and indeed as that of literary composition in general, if it be such as at all satisfies the demands both of taste and of sound logic. How difficult and delicate a task even the mere mechanism of verse is, may be conjectured from the failure of those, who have attempted poetry late in life. Where then a man has, from his earliest youth, devoted his whole being to an object, which by the admission of all civilized nations in all ages is honourable as a pursuit, and glorious as an attainment; what of all that relates to himself and his family, if only we except his moral character, can have fairer claims to his protection, or more authorize acts of self-defence, than the elaborate products of his intellect and intellectual industry? Prudence itself would command us to show, even if defect or diversion of natural sensibility had prevented us from feeling, a due interest and qualified anxiety for the offspring and representatives of our nobler being. I know it, alas! by woful experience. I have laid too many eggs in the hot sands of this wilderness, the world, with ostrich carelessness and ostrich oblivion. The greater part indeed have been trod under foot, and are forgotten; but yet no small number have crept forth into life, some to furnish feathers for the caps of others, and still more to plume the shafts in the quivers of my enemies, of them that unprovoked have lain in wait against my soul.

Sic vos, non vobis, mellificatis, apes!

CHAPTER III

The Author's obligations to critics, and the probable occasion—Principles of modern criticism—Mr. Southey's works and character.

To anonymous critics in reviews, magazines, and news-journals of various name and rank, and to satirists with or without a name in verse or prose, or in verse-text aided by prose-comment, I do seriously believe and profess, that I owe full two-thirds of whatever reputation and publicity I happen to possess. For when the name of an individual has occurred so frequently, in so many works, for so great a length of time, the readers of these works—(which with a shelf or two of beauties, elegant Extracts and Anas, form nine-tenths of the reading of the reading Public [14])—cannot but be familiar with the name, without distinctly remembering whether it was introduced for eulogy or for censure. And this becomes the more likely, if (as I believe) the habit of perusing periodical works may be properly added to Averroes' catalogue of Anti-Mnemonics, or weakeners of the memory [15]. But where this has not been the case, yet the reader will be apt to suspect that there must be something more than usually strong and extensive in a reputation, that could either require or stand so merciless and long-continued a cannonading. Without any feeling of anger therefore—(for which indeed, on my own account, I have no pretext)—I may yet be allowed to express some degree of surprise, that, after having run the critical gauntlet for a certain class of faults which I had, nothing having come before the judgment-seat in the interim, I should, year after year, quarter after quarter, month after month—(not to mention sundry petty periodicals of still quicker revolution, "or weekly or diurnal")—have been, for at least seventeen years consecutively, dragged forth by them into the foremost ranks of the proscribed, and forced to abide the brunt of abuse, for faults directly opposite, and which I certainly had not. How shall I explain this?

Whatever may have been the case with others, I certainly cannot attribute this persecution to personal dislike, or to envy, or to feelings of vindictive animosity. Not to the former, for with the exception of a very few who are my intimate friends, and were so before they were known as authors, I have had little other acquaintance with literary characters, than what may be implied in an accidental introduction, or casual meeting in a mixed company. And as far as words and looks can be trusted, I must believe that, even in these instances, I had excited no unfriendly disposition. Neither by letter, nor in conversation, have I ever had dispute or controversy beyond the common social interchange of opinions. Nay, where I had reason to suppose my convictions fundamentally different, it has been my habit, and I may add, the impulse of my nature, to assign the grounds of my belief, rather than the belief itself; and not to express dissent, till I could establish some points of complete sympathy, some grounds common to both sides, from which to commence its explanation.

Still less can I place these attacks to the charge of envy. The few pages which I have published, are of too distant a date, and the extent of their sale a proof too conclusive against their having been popular at any time, to render probable, I had almost said possible, the excitement of envy on their account; and the man who should envy me on any other, verily he must be envy-mad!

Lastly, with as little semblance of reason, could I suspect any animosity towards me from vindictive feelings as the cause. I have before said, that my acquaintance with literary men has been limited and distant; and that I have had neither dispute nor controversy. From my first entrance into life, I have, with few and short intervals, lived either abroad or in retirement. My different essays on subjects of national interest, published at different times, first in the Morning Post and then in the Courier, with my courses of Lectures on the principles of criticism as applied to Shakespeare and Milton, constitute my whole publicity; the only occasions on which I could offend any member of the republic of letters. With one solitary exception in which my words were first misstated and then wantonly applied to an individual, I could never learn that I had excited the displeasure of any among my literary contemporaries. Having announced my intention to give a course of Lectures on the characteristic merits and defects of English poetry in its different aeras; first, from Chaucer to Milton; second, from Dryden inclusively to Thomson; and third, from Cowper to the present day; I changed my plan, and confined my disquisition to the former two periods, that I might furnish no possible pretext for the unthinking to misconstrue, or the malignant to misapply my words, and having stamped their own meaning on them, to pass them as current coin in the marts of garrulity or detraction.

Praises of the unworthy are felt by ardent minds as robberies of the deserving; and it is too true, and too frequent, that Bacon, Harrington, Machiavel, and Spinoza, are not read, because Hume, Condillac, and Voltaire are. But in promiscuous company no prudent man will oppugn the merits of a contemporary in his own supposed department; contenting himself with praising in his turn those whom he deems excellent. If I should ever deem it my duty at all to oppose the pretensions of individuals, I would oppose them in books which could be weighed and answered, in which I could evolve the whole of my reasons and feelings, with their requisite limits and modifications; not in irrecoverable conversation, where however strong the reasons might be, the feelings that prompted them would assuredly be attributed by some one or other to envy and discontent. Besides I well know, and, I trust, have acted on that knowledge, that it must be the ignorant and injudicious who extol the unworthy; and the eulogies of critics without taste or judgment are the natural reward of authors without feeling or genius. Sint unicuique sua praemia.

How then, dismissing, as I do, these three causes, am I to account for attacks, the long continuance and inveteracy of which it would require all three to explain? The solution seems to be this,—I was in habits of intimacy with Mr. Wordsworth and Mr. Southey! This, however, transfers, rather than removes the difficulty. Be it, that, by an unconscionable extension of the old adage, noscitur a socio, my literary friends are never under the water-fall of criticism, but I must be wet through with the spray; yet how came the torrent to descend upon them?

First then, with regard to Mr. Southey. I well remember the general reception of his earlier publications; namely, the poems published with Mr. Lovell under the names of Moschus and Bion; the two volumes of poems under his own name, and the Joan of Arc. The censures of the critics by profession are extant, and may be easily referred to:—careless lines, inequality in the merit of the different poems, and (in the lighter works) a predilection for the strange and whimsical; in short, such faults as might have been anticipated in a young and rapid writer, were indeed sufficiently enforced. Nor was there at that time wanting a party spirit to aggravate the defects of a poet, who with all the courage of uncorrupted youth had avowed his zeal for a cause, which he deemed that of liberty, and his abhorrence of oppression by whatever name consecrated. But it was as little objected by others, as dreamed of by the poet himself, that he preferred careless and prosaic lines on rule and of forethought, or indeed that he pretended to any other art or theory of poetic diction, except that which we may all learn from Horace, Quinctilian, the admirable dialogue, De Oratoribus, generally attributed to Tacitus, or Strada's Prolusions; if indeed natural good sense and the early study of the best models in his own language had not infused the same maxims more securely, and, if I may venture the expression, more vitally. All that could have been fairly deduced was, that in his taste and estimation of writers Mr. Southey agreed far more with Thomas Warton, than with Dr. Johnson. Nor do I mean to deny, that at all times Mr. Southey was of the same mind with Sir Philip Sidney in preferring an excellent ballad in the humblest style of poetry to twenty indifferent poems that strutted in the highest. And by what have his works, published since then, been characterized, each more strikingly than the preceding, but by greater splendour, a deeper pathos, profounder reflections, and a more sustained dignity of language and of metre? Distant may the period be, but whenever the time shall come, when all his works shall be collected by some editor worthy to be his biographer, I trust that an appendix of excerpta of all the passages, in which his writings, name, and character have been attacked, from the pamphlets and periodical works of the last twenty years, may be an accompaniment. Yet that it would prove medicinal in after times I dare not hope; for as long as there are readers to be delighted with calumny, there will be found reviewers to calumniate. And such readers will become in all probability more numerous, in proportion as a still greater diffusion of literature shall produce an increase of sciolists, and sciolism bring with it petulance and presumption. In times of old, books were as religious oracles; as literature advanced, they next became venerable preceptors; they then descended to the rank of instructive friends; and, as their numbers increased, they sank still lower to that of entertaining companions; and at present they seem degraded into culprits to hold up their hands at the bar of every self-elected, yet not the less peremptory, judge, who chooses to write from humour or interest, from enmity or arrogance, and to abide the decision "of him that reads in malice, or him that reads after dinner."

The same retrograde movement may be traced, in the relation which the authors themselves have assumed towards their readers. From the lofty address of Bacon: "these are the meditations of Francis of Verulam, which that posterity should be possessed of, he deemed their interest:" or from dedication to Monarch or Pontiff, in which the honour given was asserted in equipoise to the patronage acknowledged: from Pindar's

———'*ep' alloi*—
si d'alloi megaloi: to d'eschaton koryphoutai
basilensi. Maeketi
paptaine porsion.
Eiae se te touton
upsou chronon patein, eme
te tossade nikaphorois
omilein, prophanton sophian kath' Ellanas eonta panta.—OLYMP. OD. I.

there was a gradual sinking in the etiquette or allowed style of pretension.

Poets and Philosophers, rendered diffident by their very number, addressed themselves to "learned readers;" then aimed to conciliate the graces of "the candid reader;" till, the critic still rising as the author sank, the amateurs of literature collectively were erected into a municipality of judges, and addressed as the Town! And now, finally, all men being supposed able to read, and all readers able to judge, the multitudinous Public, shaped into personal unity by the magic of abstraction, sits nominal despot on the throne of criticism. But, alas! as in other despotisms, it but echoes the decisions of its invisible ministers, whose intellectual claims to the guardianship of the Muses seem, for the greater part, analogous to the physical qualifications which adapt their oriental brethren for the superintendence of the Harem. Thus it is said, that St. Nepomuc was installed the guardian of bridges, because he had fallen over one, and sunk out of sight; thus too St. Cecilia is said to have been first propitiated by musicians, because, having failed in her own attempts, she had taken a dislike to the art and all its successful professors. But I shall probably have occasion hereafter to deliver my convictions more at large concerning this state of things, and its influences on taste, genius and morality.

In the Thalaba, the Madoc, and still more evidently in the unique [16] Cid, in the Kehama, and, as last, so best, the Roderick; Southey has given abundant proof, se cogitare quam sit magnum dare aliquid in manus hominum: nec persuadere sibi posse, non saepe tractandum quod placere et semper et omnibus cupiat. But on the other hand, I conceive, that Mr. Southey was quite unable to comprehend, wherein could consist the crime or mischief of printing half a dozen or more playful poems; or to speak more generally, compositions which would be enjoyed or passed over, according as the taste and humour of the reader might chance to be; provided they contained nothing immoral. In the present age periturae parcere chartae is emphatically an unreasonable demand. The merest trifle he ever sent abroad had tenfold better claims to its ink and paper than all the silly criticisms on it, which proved no more than that the critic was not one of those, for whom the trifle was written; and than all the grave exhortations to a greater reverence for the public—as if the passive page of a book, by having an epigram or doggerel tale impressed on it, instantly assumed at once loco-motive power and a sort of ubiquity, so as to flutter and buz in the ear of the public to the sore annoyance of the said mysterious personage. But what gives an additional and more ludicrous absurdity to these lamentations is the curious fact, that if in a volume of poetry the critic should find poem or passage which he deems more especially worthless, he is sure to select and reprint it in the review; by which, on his own grounds, he wastes as much more paper than the author, as the copies of a fashionable review are more numerous than those of the original book; in some, and those the most prominent instances, as ten thousand to five hundred. I know nothing that surpasses the vileness of deciding on the merits of a poet or painter,—(not by characteristic defects; for where there is genius, these always point to his characteristic beauties; but)—by accidental failures or faulty passages; except the impudence of defending it, as the proper duty, and most instructive part, of criticism. Omit or pass slightly over the expression, grace, and grouping of Raffael's figures; but ridicule in detail the knitting-needles and broom-twigs, that are to represent trees in his back grounds; and never let him hear the last of his galli-pots! Admit that the Allegro and Penseroso of Milton are not without merit; but repay yourself for this concession, by reprinting at length the two poems on the University Carrier! As a fair specimen of his Sonnets, quote

"A Book was writ of late called Tetrachordon;"

and, as characteristic of his rhythm and metre, cite his literal translation of the first and second Psalm! In order to justify yourself, you need only assert, that had you dwelt chiefly on the beauties and excellencies of the poet, the admiration of these might seduce the attention of future writers from the objects of their love and wonder, to an imitation of the few poems and passages in which the poet was most unlike himself.

But till reviews are conducted on far other principles, and with far other motives; till in the place of arbitrary dictation and petulant sneers, the reviewers support their decisions by reference to fixed canons of criticism, previously established and deduced from the nature of man; reflecting minds will pronounce it arrogance in them thus to announce themselves to men of letters, as the guides of their taste and judgment. To the purchaser and mere reader it is, at all events, an injustice. He who tells me that there are defects in a new work, tells me nothing which I should not have taken for granted without his information. But he, who points out and elucidates the beauties of an original work does indeed give me interesting information, such as experience would not have authorized me in anticipating. And as to compositions which the authors themselves announce with

Haec ipsi novimus esse nihil,

why should we judge by a different rule two printed works, only because the one author is alive, and the other in his grave? What literary man has not regretted the prudery of Spratt in refusing to let his friend Cowley appear in his slippers and dressing gown? I am not perhaps the only one who has derived an innocent amusement from the riddles, conundrums, trisyllable lines, and the like, of Swift and his correspondents, in hours of languor, when to have read his more finished works would have been useless to myself, and, in some sort, an act of injustice to the author. But I am at a loss to conceive by what perversity of judgment, these relaxations of his genius could be employed to diminish his fame as the writer of Gulliver, or the Tale of a Tub. Had Mr. Southey written twice as many poems of inferior merit, or partial interest, as have enlivened the journals of the day, they would have added to his honour with good and wise men, not merely or principally as proving the versatility of his talents, but as evidences of the purity of that mind, which even in its levities never dictated a line which it need regret on any moral account.

I have in imagination transferred to the future biographer the duty of contrasting Southey's fixed and well-earned fame, with the abuse and indefatigable hostility of his anonymous critics from his early youth to his ripest manhood. But I cannot think so ill of human nature as not to believe, that these critics have already taken shame to themselves, whether they consider the object of their abuse in his moral or his literary character. For reflect but on the variety and extent of his acquirements! He stands second to no man, either as an historian or as a bibliographer; and when I regard him as a popular essayist,—(for the articles of his compositions in the reviews are, for the greater part, essays on subjects of deep or curious interest rather than criticisms on particular works)—I look in vain for any writer, who has conveyed so much information, from so many and such recondite sources, with so many just and original reflections, in a style so lively and poignant, yet so uniformly classical and perspicuous; no one, in short, who has combined so much wisdom with so much wit; so much truth and knowledge with so much life and fancy. His prose is always intelligible and always entertaining. In poetry he has attempted almost every species of composition known before, and he has added new ones; and if we except the highest lyric,—(in which how few, how very few even of the greatest minds have been fortunate)—he has attempted every species successfully; from the political song of the day, thrown off in the playful overflow of honest joy and patriotic exultation, to the wild ballad; from epistolary ease and graceful narrative, to austere and impetuous moral declamation; from the pastoral charms and wild streaming lights of the Thalaba, in which sentiment and imagery have given permanence even to the excitement of curiosity; and from the full blaze of the Kehama,—(a gallery of finished pictures in one splendid fancy piece, in which, notwithstanding, the moral grandeur rises gradually above the brilliance of the colouring and the boldness and novelty of the machinery)—to the more sober beauties of the Madoc; and lastly, from the Madoc to his Roderick, in which, retaining all his former excellencies of a poet eminently inventive and picturesque, he has surpassed himself in language and metre, in the construction of the whole, and in the splendour of particular passages.

Here then shall I conclude? No! The characters of the deceased, like the encomia on tombstones, as they are described with religious tenderness, so are they read, with allowing sympathy indeed, but yet with rational deduction. There are men, who deserve a higher record; men with whose characters it is the interest of their contemporaries, no less than that of posterity, to be made acquainted; while it is yet possible for impartial censure, and even for quick-sighted envy, to cross-examine the tale without offence to the courtesies of humanity; and while the eulogist, detected in exaggeration or falsehood, must pay the full penalty of his baseness in the contempt which brands the convicted flatterer. Publicly has Mr. Southey been reviled by men, who, as I would fain hope for the honour of human nature, hurled fire-brands against a figure of their own imagination; publicly have his talents been depreciated, his principles denounced; as publicly do I therefore, who have known him intimately, deem it my duty to leave recorded, that it is Southey's almost unexampled felicity, to possess the best gifts of talent and genius free from all their characteristic defects. To those who remember the state of our public schools and universities some twenty years past, it will appear no ordinary praise in any man to have passed from innocence into virtue, not only free from all vicious habit, but unstained by one act of intemperance, or the degradations akin to intemperance. That scheme of head, heart, and habitual demeanour, which in his early manhood, and first controversial writings, Milton, claiming the privilege of self-defence, asserts of himself, and challenges his calumniators to disprove; this will his school-mates, his fellow-collegians, and his maturer friends, with a confidence proportioned to the intimacy of their knowledge, bear witness to, as again realized in the life of Robert Southey. But still more striking to those, who by biography or by their own experience are familiar with the general habits of genius, will appear the poet's matchless industry and perseverance in his pursuits; the worthiness and dignity of those pursuits; his generous submission to tasks of transitory interest, or such as his genius alone could make otherwise; and that having thus more than satisfied the claims of affection or prudence, he should yet have made for himself time and power, to achieve more, and in more various departments, than almost any other writer has done, though employed wholly on subjects of his own choice and ambition. But as Southey possesses, and is not possessed by, his genius, even so is he master even of his virtues. The regular and methodical tenor of his daily labours, which would be deemed rare in the most mechanical pursuits, and might be envied by the mere man of business, loses all semblance of formality in the dignified simplicity of his manners, in the spring and healthful cheerfulness of his spirits. Always employed, his friends find him always at leisure. No less punctual in trifles, than steadfast in the performance of highest duties, he inflicts none of those small pains and discomforts which irregular men scatter about them, and which in the aggregate so often become formidable obstacles both to happiness and utility; while on the contrary he bestows all the pleasures, and inspires all that ease of mind on those around him or connected with him, which perfect consistency, and (if such a word might be framed) absolute reliability, equally in small as in great concerns, cannot but inspire and bestow; when this too is softened without being weakened by kindness and gentleness. I know few men who so well deserve the character which an antient attributes to Marcus Cato, namely, that he was likest virtue, in as much as he seemed to act aright, not in obedience to any law or outward motive, but by the necessity of a happy nature, which could not act otherwise. As son, brother, husband, father, master, friend, he moves with firm yet light steps, alike unostentatious, and alike exemplary. As a writer, he has uniformly made his talents subservient to the best interests of humanity, of public virtue, and domestic piety; his cause has ever been the cause of pure religion and of liberty, of national independence and of national illumination. When future critics shall weigh out his guerdon of praise and censure, it will be Southey the poet only, that will supply them with the scanty materials for the latter. They will likewise not fail to record, that as no man was ever a more constant friend, never had poet more friends and honourers among the good of all parties; and that quacks in education, quacks in politics, and quacks in criticism were his only enemies. [17]

CHAPTER IV

The Lyrical Ballads with the Preface—Mr. Wordsworth's earlier poems—On fancy and imagination—The investigation of the distinction important to the Fine Arts.

I have wandered far from the object in view, but as I fancied to myself readers who would respect the feelings that had tempted me from the main road; so I dare calculate on not a few, who will warmly sympathize with them. At present it will be sufficient for my purpose, if I have proved, that Mr. Southey's writings no more than my own furnished the original occasion to this fiction of a new school of poetry, and to the clamours against its supposed founders and proselytes.

As little do I believe that Mr. Wordsworth's Lyrical Ballads were in themselves the cause. I speak exclusively of the two volumes so entitled. A careful and repeated examination of these confirms me in the belief, that the omission of less than a hundred lines would have precluded nine-tenths of the criticism on this work. I hazard this declaration, however, on the supposition, that the reader has taken it up, as he would have done any other collection of poems purporting to derive their subjects or interests from the incidents of domestic or ordinary life, intermingled with higher strains of meditation which the poet utters in his own person and character; with the proviso, that these poems were perused without knowledge of, or reference to, the author's peculiar opinions, and that the reader had not had his attention previously directed to those peculiarities. In that case, as actually happened with Mr. Southey's earlier works, the lines and passages which might have offended the general taste, would have been considered as mere inequalities, and attributed to inattention, not to perversity of judgment. The men of business who had passed their lives chiefly in cities, and who might therefore be expected to derive the highest pleasure from acute notices of men and manners conveyed in easy, yet correct and pointed language; and all those who, reading but little poetry, are most stimulated with that species of it, which seems most distant from prose, would probably have passed by the volumes altogether. Others more catholic in their taste, and yet habituated to be most pleased when most excited, would have contented themselves with deciding, that the author had been successful in proportion to the elevation of his style and subject. Not a few, perhaps, might, by their admiration of the Lines written near Tintern Abbey, on revisiting the Wye, those Left upon a Yew Tree Seat, The Old Cumberland Beggar, and Ruth, have been gradually led to peruse with kindred feeling The Brothers, the Hart-leap Well, and whatever other poems in that collection may be described as holding a middle place between those written in the highest and those in the humblest style; as for instance between the Tintern Abbey, and The Thorn, or Simon Lee. Should their taste submit to no further change, and still remain unreconciled to the colloquial phrases, or the imitations of them, that are, more or less, scattered through the class last mentioned; yet even from the small number of the latter, they would have deemed them but an inconsiderable subtraction from the merit of the whole work; or, what is sometimes not unpleasing in the publication of a new writer, as serving to ascertain the natural tendency, and consequently the proper direction of the author's genius.

In the critical remarks, therefore, prefixed and annexed to the Lyrical Ballads, I believe, we may safely rest, as the true origin of the unexampled opposition which Mr. Wordsworth's writings have been since doomed to encounter. The humbler passages in the poems themselves were dwelt on and cited to justify the rejection of the theory. What in and for themselves would have been either forgotten or forgiven as imperfections, or at least comparative failures, provoked direct hostility when announced as intentional, as the result of choice after full deliberation. Thus the poems, admitted by all as excellent, joined with those which had pleased the far greater number, though they formed two-thirds of the whole work, instead of being deemed (as in all right they should have been, even if we take for granted that the reader judged aright) an atonement for the few exceptions, gave wind and fuel to the animosity against both the poems and the poet. In all perplexity there is a portion of fear, which predisposes the mind to anger. Not able to deny that the author possessed both genius and a powerful intellect, they felt very positive,—but yet were not quite certain that he might not be in the right, and they themselves in the wrong; an unquiet state of mind, which seeks alleviation by quarrelling with the occasion of it, and by wondering at the perverseness of the man, who had written a long and argumentative essay to persuade them, that

Fair is foul, and foul is fair;

in other words, that they had been all their lives admiring without judgment, and were now about to censure without reason. [18]

That this conjecture is not wide from the mark, I am induced to believe from the noticeable fact, which I can state on my own knowledge, that the same general censure has been grounded by almost every different person on some different poem. Among those, whose candour and judgment I estimate highly, I distinctly remember six who expressed their objections to the Lyrical Ballads almost in the same words, and altogether to the same purport, at the same time admitting, that several of the poems had given them great pleasure; and, strange as it might seem, the composition which one cited as execrable, another quoted as his favourite. I am indeed convinced in my own mind, that could the same experiment have been tried with these volumes, as was made in the well known story of the picture, the result would have been the same; the parts which had been covered by black spots on the one day, would be found equally *albo lapide notatae* on the succeeding.

However this may be, it was assuredly hard and unjust to fix the attention on a few separate and insulated poems with as much aversion, as if they had been so many plague-spots on the whole work, instead of passing them over in silence, as so much blank paper, or leaves of a bookseller's catalogue; especially, as no one pretended to have found in them any immorality or indelicacy; and the poems, therefore, at the worst, could only be regarded as so many light or inferior coins in a rouleau of gold, not as so much alloy in a weight of bullion. A friend whose talents I hold in the highest respect, but whose judgment and strong sound sense I have had almost continued occasion to revere, making the usual complaints to me concerning both the style and subjects of Mr. Wordsworth's minor poems; I admitted that there were some few of the tales and incidents, in which I could not myself find a sufficient cause for their having been recorded in metre. I mentioned Alice Fell as an instance; "Nay," replied my friend with more than usual quickness of manner, "I cannot agree with you there!—that, I own, does seem to me a remarkably pleasing poem." In the Lyrical Ballads, (for my experience does not enable me to extend the remark equally unqualified to the two subsequent volumes,) I have heard at different times, and from different individuals, every single poem extolled and reprobated, with the exception of those of loftier kind, which as was before observed, seem to have won universal praise. This fact of itself would have made me diffident in my censures, had not a still stronger ground been furnished by the strange contrast of the heat and long continuance of the opposition, with the nature of the faults stated as justifying it. The seductive faults, the *dulcia vitia* of Cowley, Marini, or Darwin might reasonably be thought capable of corrupting the public judgment for half a century, and require a twenty years war, campaign after campaign, in order to dethrone the usurper and re-establish the legitimate taste. But that a downright simpleness, under the affectation of simplicity, prosaic words in feeble metre, silly thoughts in childish phrases, and a preference of mean, degrading, or at best trivial associations and characters, should succeed in forming a school of imitators, a company of almost religious admirers, and this too among young men of ardent minds, liberal education, and not

————*with academic laurels unbestowed;*

and that this bare and bald counterfeit of poetry, which is characterized as below criticism, should for nearly twenty years have well-nigh engrossed criticism, as the main, if not the only, butt of review, magazine, pamphlet, poem, and paragraph; this is indeed matter of wonder. Of yet greater is it, that the contest should still continue as undecided as [19] that between Bacchus and the frogs in Aristophanes; when the former descended to the realms of the departed to bring back the spirit of old and genuine poesy;—

CH. *Brekekekex, koax, koax.*

D. *All' exoloisth' auto koax.*
Ouden gar est' all', hae koax.
Oimozet' ou gar moi melei.

CH. *Alla maen kekraxomestha*
g', oposon hae pharynx an haemon
chandanae di' haemeras, brekekekex, koax, koax!

D. *Touto gar ou nikaesete.*

CH. *Oude men haemas su pantos.*

D. *Oude maen humeis ge dae m'*
oudepote. Kekraxomai gar,
kan me deae, di' haemeras,
eos an humon epikrataeso tou koax!

CH. *Brekekekex, KO'AX, KOAX!*

During the last year of my residence at Cambridge, 1794, I became acquainted with Mr. Wordsworth's first publication entitled Descriptive Sketches; and seldom, if ever, was the emergence of an original poetic genius above the literary horizon more evidently announced. In the form, style, and manner of the whole poem, and in the structure of the particular lines and periods, there is a harshness and acerbity connected and combined with words and images all a-glow, which might recall those products of the vegetable world, where gorgeous blossoms rise out of a hard and thorny rind and shell, within which the rich fruit is elaborating. The language is not only peculiar and strong, but at times knotty and contorted, as by its own impatient strength; while the novelty and struggling crowd of images, acting in conjunction with the difficulties of the style, demands always a greater closeness of attention, than poetry,—at all events, than descriptive poetry—has a right to claim. It not seldom therefore justified the complaint of obscurity. In the following extract I have sometimes fancied, that I saw an emblem of the poem itself, and of the author's genius as it was then displayed.—

'Tis storm; and hid in mist from hour to hour,
All day the floods a deepening murmur pour;
The sky is veiled, and every cheerful sight
Dark is the region as with coming night;
Yet what a sudden burst of overpowering light!
Triumphant on the bosom of the storm,
Glances the fire-clad eagle's wheeling form;
Eastward, in long perspective glittering, shine
The wood-crowned cliffs that o'er the lake recline;
Those Eastern cliffs a hundred streams unfold,
At once to pillars turned that flame with gold;
Behind his sail the peasant strives to shun
The west, that burns like one dilated sun,
Where in a mighty crucible expire
The mountains, glowing hot, like coals of fire.

The poetic Psyche, in its process to full development, undergoes as many changes as its Greek namesake, the butterfly [20]. And it is remarkable how soon genius clears and purifies itself from the faults and errors of its earliest products; faults which, in its earliest compositions, are the more obtrusive and confluent, because as heterogeneous elements, which had only a temporary use, they constitute the very ferment, by which themselves are carried off. Or we may compare them to some diseases, which must work on the humours, and be thrown out on the surface, in order to secure the patient from their future recurrence. I was in my twenty-fourth year, when I had the happiness of knowing Mr. Wordsworth personally, and while memory lasts, I shall hardly forget the sudden effect produced on my mind, by his recitation of a manuscript poem, which still remains unpublished, but of which the stanza and tone of style were the same as those of The Female Vagrant, as originally printed in the first volume of the Lyrical Ballads. There was here no mark of strained thought, or forced diction, no crowd or turbulence of imagery; and, as the poet hath himself well described in his Lines on revisiting the Wye, manly reflection and human associations had given both variety, and an additional interest to natural objects, which, in the passion and appetite of the first love, they had seemed to him neither to need nor permit. The occasional obscurities, which had risen from an imperfect control over the resources of his native language, had almost wholly disappeared, together with that worse defect of arbitrary and illogical phrases, at once hackneyed and fantastic, which hold so distinguished a place in the technique of ordinary poetry, and will, more or less, alloy the earlier poems of the truest genius, unless the attention has been specially directed to their worthlessness and incongruity [21]. I did not perceive anything particular in the mere style of the poem alluded to during its recitation, except indeed such difference as was not separable from the thought and manner; and the Spenserian stanza, which always, more or less, recalls to the reader's mind Spenser's own style, would doubtless have authorized, in my then opinion, a more frequent descent to the phrases of ordinary life, than could without an ill effect have been hazarded in the heroic couplet. It was not however the freedom from false taste, whether as to common defects, or to those more properly his own, which made so unusual an impression on my feelings immediately, and subsequently on my judgment. It was the union of deep feeling with profound thought; the fine balance of truth in observing, with the imaginative faculty in modifying, the objects observed; and above all the original gift of spreading the tone, the atmosphere, and with it the depth and height of the ideal world around forms, incidents, and situations, of which, for the common view, custom had bedimmed all the lustre, had dried up the sparkle and the dew drops.

This excellence, which in all Mr. Wordsworth's writings is more or less predominant, and which constitutes the character of his mind, I no sooner felt, than I sought to understand. Repeated meditations led me first to suspect,--(and a more intimate analysis of the human faculties, their appropriate marks, functions, and effects matured my conjecture into full conviction,)--that Fancy and Imagination were two distinct and widely different faculties, instead of being, according to the general belief, either two names with one meaning, or, at furthest, the lower and higher degree of one and the same power. It is not, I own, easy to conceive a more apposite translation of the Greek phantasia than the Latin imaginatio; but it is equally true that in all societies there exists an instinct of growth, a certain collective, unconscious good sense working progressively to desynonymize [22] those words originally of the same meaning, which the conflux of dialects supplied to the more homogeneous languages, as the Greek and German: and which the same cause, joined with accidents of translation from original works of different countries, occasion in mixed languages like our own. The first and most important point to be proved is, that two conceptions perfectly distinct are confused under one and the same word, and—this done—to appropriate that word exclusively to the one meaning, and the synonyme, should there be one, to the other. But if,—(as will be often the case in the arts and sciences,)—no synonyme exists, we must either invent or borrow a word. In the present instance the appropriation has already begun, and been legitimated in the derivative adjective: Milton had a highly imaginative, Cowley a very fanciful mind. If therefore I should succeed in establishing the actual existence of two faculties generally different, the nomenclature would be at once determined. To the faculty by which I had characterized Milton, we should confine the term 'imagination;' while the other would be contra-distinguished as 'fancy.' Now were it once fully ascertained, that this division is no less grounded in nature than that of delirium from mania, or Otway's

Lutes, laurels, seas of milk, and ships of amber,

from Shakespeare's

What! have his daughters brought him to this pass?

or from the preceding apostrophe to the elements; the theory of the fine arts, and of poetry in particular, could not but derive some additional and important light. It would in its immediate effects furnish a torch of guidance to the philosophical critic; and ultimately to the poet himself. In energetic minds, truth soon changes by domestication into power; and from directing in the discrimination and appraisal of the product, becomes influencive in the production. To admire on principle, is the only way to imitate without loss of originality.

It has been already hinted, that metaphysics and psychology have long been my hobby-horse. But to have a hobby-horse, and to be vain of it, are so commonly found together, that they pass almost for the same. I trust therefore, that there will be more good humour than contempt, in the smile with which the reader chastises my self-complacency, if I confess myself uncertain, whether the satisfaction from the perception of a truth new to myself may not have been rendered more poignant by the conceit, that it would be equally so to the public. There was a time, certainly, in which I took some little credit to myself, in the belief that I had been the first of my countrymen, who had pointed out the diverse meaning of which the two terms were capable, and analyzed the faculties to which they should be appropriated. Mr. W. Taylor's recent volume of synonymes I have not yet seen [23]; but his specification of the terms in question has been clearly shown to be both insufficient and erroneous by Mr. Wordsworth in the Preface added to the late collection of his Poems. The explanation which Mr. Wordsworth has himself given, will be found to differ from mine, chiefly, perhaps as our objects are different. It could scarcely indeed happen otherwise, from the advantage I have enjoyed of frequent conversation with him on a subject to which a poem of his own first directed my attention, and my conclusions concerning which he had made more lucid to myself by many happy instances drawn from the operation of natural objects on the mind. But it was Mr. Wordsworth's purpose to consider the influences of fancy and imagination as they are manifested in poetry, and from the different effects to conclude their diversity in kind; while it is my object to investigate the seminal principle, and then from the kind to deduce the degree. My friend has drawn a masterly sketch of the branches with their poetic fruitage. I wish to add the trunk, and even the roots as far as they lift themselves above ground, and are visible to the naked eye of our common consciousness.

Yet even in this attempt I am aware that I shall be obliged to draw more largely on the reader's attention, than so immethodical a miscellany as this can authorize; when in such a work (the Ecclesiasical Polity) of such a mind as Hooker's, the judicious author, though no less admirable for the perspicuity than for the port and dignity of his language,—and though he wrote for men of learning in a learned age,—saw nevertheless occasion to anticipate and guard against "complaints of obscurity," as often as he was to trace his subject "to the highest well-spring and fountain." Which, (continues he) "because men are not accustomed to, the pains we take are more needful a great deal, than acceptable; and the matters we handle, seem by reason of newness (till the mind grow better acquainted with them) dark and intricate." I would gladly therefore spare both myself and others this labour, if I knew how without it to present an intelligible statement of my poetic creed,—not as my opinions, which weigh for nothing, but as deductions from established premises conveyed in such a form, as is calculated either to effect a fundamental conviction, or to receive a fundamental confutation. If I may dare once more adopt the words of Hooker, "they, unto whom we shall seem tedious, are in no wise injured by us, because it is in their own hands to spare that labour, which they are not willing to endure." Those at least, let me be permitted to add, who have taken so much pains to render me ridiculous for a perversion of taste, and have supported the charge by attributing strange notions to me on no other authority than their own conjectures, owe it to themselves as well as to me not to refuse their attention to my own statement of the theory which I do acknowledge; or shrink from the trouble of examining the grounds on which I rest it, or the arguments which I offer in its justification.

CHAPTER V

On the law of Association—Its history traced from Aristotle to Hartley.

There have been men in all ages, who have been impelled as by an instinct to propose their own nature as a problem, and who devote their attempts to its solution. The first step was to construct a table of distinctions, which they seem to have formed on the principle of the absence or presence of the Will. Our various sensations, perceptions, and movements were classed as active or passive, or as media partaking of both. A still finer distinction was soon established between the voluntary and the spontaneous. In our perceptions we seem to ourselves merely passive to an external power, whether as a mirror reflecting the landscape, or as a blank canvass on which some unknown hand paints it. For it is worthy of notice, that the latter, or the system of Idealism may be traced to sources equally remote with the former, or Materialism; and Berkeley can boast an ancestry at least as venerable as Gassendi or Hobbes. These conjectures, however, concerning the mode in which our perceptions originated, could not alter the natural difference of Things and Thoughts. In the former, the cause appeared wholly external, while in the latter, sometimes our will interfered as the producing or determining cause, and sometimes our nature seemed to act by a mechanism of its own, without any conscious effort of the will, or even against it. Our inward experiences were thus arranged in three separate classes, the passive sense, or what the School-men call the merely receptive quality of the mind; the voluntary; and the spontaneous, which holds the middle place between both. But it is not in human nature to meditate on any mode of action, without inquiring after the law that governs it; and in the explanation of the spontaneous movements of our being, the metaphysician took the lead of the anatomist and natural philosopher. In Egypt, Palestine, Greece, and India the analysis of the mind had reached its noon and manhood, while experimental research was still in its dawn and infancy. For many, very many centuries, it has been difficult to advance a new truth, or even a new error, in the philosophy of the intellect or morals. With regard, however, to the laws that direct the spontaneous movements of thought and the principle of their intellectual mechanism there exists, it has been asserted, an important exception most honourable to the moderns, and in the merit of which our own country claims the largest share. Sir James Mackintosh,—(who, amid the variety of his talents and attainments, is not of less repute for the depth and accuracy of his philosophical inquiries than for the eloquence with which he is said to render their most difficult results perspicuous, and the driest attractive,)—

affirmed in the Lectures, delivered by him in Lincoln's Inn Hall, that the law of association as established in the contemporaneity of the original impressions, formed the basis of all true psychology; and that any ontological or metaphysical science, not contained in such (that is, an empirical) psychology, was but a web of abstractions and generalizations. Of this prolific truth, of this great fundamental law, he declared Hobbes to have been the original discoverer, while its full application to the whole intellectual system we owed to Hartley; who stood in the same relation to Hobbes as Newton to Kepler; the law of association being that to the mind, which gravitation is to matter.

Of the former clause in this assertion, as it respects the comparative merits of the ancient metaphysicians, including their commentators, the Schoolmen, and of the modern and British and French philosophers from Hobbes to Hume, Hartley, and Condillac, this is not the place to speak. So wide indeed is the chasm between Sir James Mackintosh's philosophical creed and mine, that so far from being able to join hands, we could scarcely make our voices intelligible to each other: and to bridge it over would require more time, skill, and power than I believe myself to possess. But the latter clause involves for the greater part a mere question of fact and history, and the accuracy of the statement is to be tried by documents rather than reasoning.

First, then, I deny Hobbes's claim in toto: for he had been anticipated by Des Cartes, whose work De Methodo, preceded Hobbes's De Natura Humana, by more than a year. But what is of much more importance, Hobbes builds nothing on the principle which he had announced. He does not even announce it, as differing in any respect from the general laws of material motion and impact: nor was it, indeed, possible for him so to do, compatibly with his system, which was exclusively material and mechanical. Far otherwise is it with Des Cartes; greatly as he too in his after writings (and still more egregiously his followers De la Forge, and others) obscured the truth by their attempts to explain it on the theory of nervous fluids, and material configurations. But, in his interesting work, De Methodo, Des Cartes relates the circumstance which first led him to meditate on this subject, and which since then has been often noticed and employed as an instance and illustration of the law. A child who with its eyes bandaged had lost several of his fingers by amputation, continued to complain for many days successively of pains, now in this joint and now in that, of the very fingers which had been cut off. Des Cartes was led by this incident to reflect on the uncertainty with which we attribute any particular place to any inward pain or uneasiness, and proceeded after long consideration to establish it as a general law: that contemporaneous impressions, whether images or sensations, recall each other mechanically. On this principle, as a ground work, he built up the whole system of human language, as one continued process of association. He showed in what sense not only general terms, but generic images,—under the name of abstract ideas,—actually existed, and in what consist their nature and power. As one word may become the general exponent of many, so by association a simple image may represent a whole class. But in truth Hobbes himself makes no claims to any discovery, and introduces this law of association, or (in his own language) discursion of mind, as an admitted fact, in the solution alone of which, and this by causes purely physiological, he arrogates any originality. His system is briefly this; whenever the senses are impinged on by external objects, whether by the rays of light reflected from them, or by effluxes of their finer particles, there results a correspondent motion of the innermost and subtlest organs. This motion constitutes a representation, and there remains an impression of the same, or a certain disposition to repeat the same motion. Whenever we feel several objects at the same time, the impressions that are left, (or in the language of Mr. Hume, the ideas,) [24] are linked together. Whenever therefore any one of the movements, which constitute a complex impression, is renewed through the senses, the others succeed mechanically. It follows of necessity, therefore, that Hobbes, as well as Hartley and all others who derive association from the connection and interdependence of the supposed matter, the movements of which constitute our thoughts, must have reduced all its forms to the one law of Time. But even the merit of announcing this law with philosophic precision cannot be fairly conceded to him. For the objects of any two ideas need not have co-existed in the same sensation in order to become mutually associable. The same result will follow when one only of the two ideas has been represented by the senses, and the other by the memory.

Long however before either Hobbes or Des Cartes the law of association had been defined, and its important functions set forth by Ludovicus Vives. Phantasia, it is to be noticed, is employed by Vives to express the mental power of comprehension, or the active function of the mind; and imaginatio for the receptivity (via receptiva) of impressions, or for the passive perception. The power of combination he appropriates to the former: "quae singula et simpliciter acceperat imaginatio, ea conjungit et disjungait phantasia." And the law by which the thoughts are spontaneously presented follows thus: "quae simul sunt a phantasia comprehensa, si alterutrum occurrat, solet secum alterum representare." To time therefore he subordinates all the other exciting causes of association. The soul proceeds "a causa ad effectum, ab hoc ad instrumentum, a parte ad totum;" thence to the place, from place to person, and from this to whatever preceded or followed, all as being parts of a total impression, each of which may recall the other. The apparent springs "saltus vel transitus etiam longissimos," he explains by the same thought having been a component part of two or more total impressions. Thus "ex Scipione venio in cogitationem potentiae Turcicae, propter victorias ejus de Asia, in qua regnabat Antiochus."

But from Vives I pass at once to the source of his doctrines, and (as far as we can judge from the remains yet extant of Greek philosophy) as to the first, so to the fullest and most perfect enunciation of the associative principle, namely, to the writings of Aristotle; and of these in particular to the treatises De Anima, and "De Memoria," which last belongs to the series of essays entitled in the old translations Parva Naturalia. In as much as later writers have either deviated from, or added to his doctrines, they appear to me to have introduced either error or groundless supposition.

In the first place it is to be observed, that Aristotle's positions on this subject are unmixed with fiction. The wise Stagyrite speaks of no successive particles propagating motion like billiard balls, as Hobbes; nor of nervous or animal spirits, where inanimate and irrational solids are thawed down, and distilled, or filtrated by ascension, into living and intelligent fluids, that etch and re-etch engravings on the brain, as the followers of Des Cartes, and the humoral pathologists in general; nor of an oscillating ether which was to effect the same service for the nerves of the brain considered as solid fibres, as the animal spirits perform for them under the notion of hollow tubes, as Hartley teaches—nor finally, (with yet more recent dreamers) of chemical compositions by elective affinity, or of an electric light at once the immediate object and the ultimate organ of inward vision, which rises to the brain like an Aurora Borealis, and there, disporting in various shapes,—as the balance of plus and minus, or negative and positive, is destroyed or re-established,—images out both past and present. Aristotle delivers a just theory without pretending to an hypothesis; or in other words a comprehensive survey of the different facts, and of their relations to each other without supposition, that is, a fact placed under a number of facts, as their common support and explanation; though in the majority of instances these hypotheses or suppositions better deserve the name of upopoiaeseis, or suffictions. He uses indeed the word kinaeseis, to express what we call representations or ideas, but he carefully distinguishes them from material motion, designating the latter always by annexing the words en topo, or kata topon. On the contrary, in his treatise De Anima, he excludes place and motion from all the operations of thought, whether representations or volitions, as attributes utterly and absurdly heterogeneous.

The general law of association, or, more accurately, the common condition under which all exciting causes act, and in which they may be generalized, according to Aristotle is this. Ideas by having been together acquire a power of recalling each other; or every partial representation awakes the total representation of which it had been a part. In the practical determination of this common principle to particular recollections, he admits five agents or occasioning causes: first, connection in time, whether simultaneous, preceding, or successive; second, vicinity or connection in space; third, interdependence or necessary connection, as cause and effect; fourth, likeness; and fifth, contrast. As an additional solution of the occasional seeming chasms in the continuity of reproduction he proves, that movements or ideas possessing one or the other of these five characters had passed through the mind as intermediate links, sufficiently clear to recall other parts of the same total impressions with which they had co-existed, though not vivid enough to excite that degree of attention which is requisite for distinct recollection, or as we may aptly express it, after consciousness. In association then consists the whole mechanism of the reproduction of impressions, in the Aristotelian Psychology. It is the universal law of the passive fancy and mechanical memory; that which supplies to all other faculties their objects, to all thought the elements of its materials.

In consulting the excellent commentary of St. Thomas Aquinas on the Parva Naturalia of Aristotle, I was struck at once with its close resemblance to Hume's Essay on Association. The main thoughts were the same in both, the order of the thoughts was the same, and even the illustrations differed only by Hume's occasional substitution of more modern examples. I mentioned the circumstance to several of my literary acquaintances, who admitted the closeness of the resemblance, and that it seemed too great to be explained by mere coincidence; but they thought it improbable that Hume should have held the pages of the Angelic Doctor worth turning over. But some time after Mr. Payne showed Sir James Mackintosh some odd volumes of St. Thomas Aquinas, partly perhaps from having heard that he had in his Lectures passed a high encomium on this canonized philosopher; but chiefly from the fact, that the volumes had belonged to Mr. Hume, and had here and there marginal marks and notes of reference in his own hand writing. Among these volumes was that which contains the Parva Naturalia, in the old Latin version, swathed and swaddled in the commentary afore mentioned

It remains then for me, first to state wherein Hartley differs from Aristotle; then, to exhibit the grounds of my conviction, that he differed only to err: and next as the result, to show, by what influences of the choice and judgment the associative power becomes either memory or fancy; and, in conclusion, to appropriate the remaining offices of the mind to the reason, and the imagination. With my best efforts to be as perspicuous as the nature of language will permit on such a subject, I earnestly solicit the good wishes and friendly patience of my readers, while I thus go "sounding on my dim and perilous way."

CHAPTER VI

That Hartley's system, as far as it differs from that of Aristotle, is neither tenable in theory, nor founded in facts.

Of Hartley's hypothetical vibrations in his hypothetical oscillating ether of the nerves, which is the first and most obvious distinction between his system and that of Aristotle, I shall say little. This, with all other similar attempts to render that an object of the sight which has no relation to sight, has been already sufficiently exposed by the younger Reimarus, Maasz, and others, as outraging the very axioms of mechanics in a scheme, the merit of which consists in its being mechanical. Whether any other philosophy be possible, but the mechanical; and again, whether the mechanical system can have any claim to be called philosophy; are questions for another place. It is, however, certain, that as long as we deny the former, and affirm the latter, we must bewilder ourselves, whenever we would pierce into the adyta of causation; and all that laborious conjecture can do, is to fill up the gaps of fancy. Under that despotism of the eye (the emancipation from which Pythagoras by his numeral, and Plato by his musical, symbols, and both by geometric discipline, aimed at, as the first propaideuma of the mind)— under this strong sensuous influence, we are restless because invisible things are not the objects of vision; and metaphysical systems, for the most part, become popular, not for their truth, but in proportion as they attribute to causes a susceptibility of being seen, if only our visual organs were sufficiently powerful.

From a hundred possible confutations let one suffice. According to this system the idea or vibration a from the external object A becomes associable with the idea or vibration m from the external object M, because the oscillation a propagated itself so as to re-produce the oscillation m. But the original impression from M was essentially different from the impression A: unless therefore different causes may produce the same effect, the vibration a could never produce the vibration m: and this therefore could never be the means, by which a and m are associated. To understand this, the attentive reader need only be reminded, that the ideas are themselves, in Hartley's system, nothing more than their appropriate configurative vibrations. It is a mere delusion of the fancy to conceive the pre-existence of the ideas, in any chain of association, as so many differently coloured billiard-balls in contact, so that when an object, the billiard-stick, strikes the first or white ball, the same motion propagates itself through the red, green, blue and black, and sets the whole in motion. No! we must suppose the very same force, which constitutes the white ball, to constitute the red or black; or the idea of a circle to constitute the idea of a triangle; which is impossible.

But it may be said, that by the sensations from the objects A and M, the nerves have acquired a disposition to the vibrations a and m, and therefore a need only be repeated in order to re-produce m. Now we will grant, for a moment, the possibility of such a disposition in a material nerve, which yet seems scarcely less absurd than to say, that a weather-cock had acquired a habit of turning to the east, from the wind having been so long in that quarter: for if it be replied, that we must take in the circumstance of life, what then becomes of the mechanical philosophy? And what is the nerve, but the flint which the wag placed in the pot as the first ingredient of his stone broth, requiring only salt, turnips, and mutton, for the remainder! But if we waive this, and pre-suppose the actual existence of such a disposition; two cases are possible. Either, every idea has its own nerve and correspondent oscillation, or this is not the case. If the latter be the truth, we should gain nothing by these dispositions; for then, every nerve having several dispositions, when the motion of any other nerve is propagated into it, there will be no ground or cause present, why exactly the oscillation m should arise, rather than any other to which it was equally pre-disposed. But if we take the former, and let every idea have a nerve of its own, then every nerve must be capable of propagating its motion into many other nerves; and again, there is no reason assignable, why the vibration m should arise, rather than any other ad libitum.

It is fashionable to smile at Hartley's vibrations and vibratiuncles; and his work has been re-edited by Priestley, with the omission of the material hypothesis. But Hartley was too great a man, too coherent a thinker, for this to have been done, either consistently or to any wise purpose. For all other parts of his system, as far as they are peculiar to that system, once removed from their mechanical basis, not only lose their main support, but the very motive which led to their adoption. Thus the principle of contemporaneity, which Aristotle had made the common condition of all the laws of association, Hartley was constrained to represent as being itself the sole law. For to what law can the action of material atoms be subject, but that of proximity in place? And to what law can their motions be subjected but that of time? Again, from this results inevitably, that the will, the reason, the judgment, and the understanding, instead of being the determining causes of association, must needs be represented as its creatures, and among its mechanical effects. Conceive, for instance, a broad stream, winding through a mountainous country with an indefinite number of currents, varying and running into each other according as the gusts chance to blow from the opening of the mountains. The temporary union of several currents in one, so as to form the main current of the moment, would present an accurate image of Hartley's theory of the will.

Had this been really the case, the consequence would have been, that our whole life would be divided between the despotism of outward impressions, and that of senseless and passive memory. Take his law in its highest abstraction and most philosophical form, namely, that every partial representation recalls the total representation of which it was a part; and the law becomes nugatory, were it only for its universality. In practice it would indeed be mere lawlessness. Consider, how immense must be the sphere of a total impression from the top of St. Paul's church; and how rapid and continuous the series of such total impressions. If, therefore, we suppose the absence of all interference of the will, reason, and judgment, one or other of two consequences must result. Either the ideas, or reliques of such impression, will exactly imitate the order of the impression itself, which would be absolute delirium: or any one part of that impression might recall any other part, and—(as from the law of continuity, there must exist in every total impression, some one or more parts, which are components of some other following total impression, and so on ad infinitum)—any part of any impression might recall any part of any other, without a cause present to determine what it should be. For to bring in the will, or reason, as causes of their own cause, that is, as at once causes and effects, can satisfy those only who, in their pretended evidences of a God, having first demanded organization, as the sole cause and ground of intellect, will then coolly demand the pre-existence of intellect, as the cause and ground-work of organization. There is in truth but one state to which this theory applies at all, namely, that of complete light-headedness; and even to this it applies but partially, because the will and reason are perhaps never wholly suspended.

A case of this kind occurred in a Roman Catholic town in Germany a year or two before my arrival at Goettingen, and had not then ceased to be a frequent subject of conversation. A young woman of four or five and twenty, who could neither read, nor write, was seized with a nervous fever; during which, according to the asseverations of all the priests and monks of the neighbourhood, she became possessed, and, as it appeared, by a very learned devil. She continued incessantly talking Latin, Greek, and Hebrew, in very pompous tones and with most distinct enunciation. This possession was rendered more probable by the known fact that she was or had been a heretic. Voltaire humorously advises the devil to decline all acquaintance with medical men; and it would have been more to his reputation, if he had taken this advice in the present instance. The case had attracted the particular attention of a young physician, and by his statement many eminent physiologists and psychologists visited the town, and cross-examined the case on the spot. Sheets full of her ravings were taken down from her own mouth, and were found to consist of sentences, coherent and intelligible each for itself, but with little or no connection with each other. Of the Hebrew, a small portion only could be traced to the Bible; the remainder seemed to be in the Rabbinical dialect. All trick or conspiracy was out of the question. Not only had the young woman ever been a harmless, simple creature; but she was evidently labouring under a nervous fever. In the town, in which she had been resident for many years as a servant in different families, no solution presented itself. The young physician, however, determined to trace her past life step by step; for the patient herself was incapable of returning a rational answer. He at length succeeded in discovering the place, where her parents had lived: travelled thither, found them dead, but an uncle surviving; and from him learned, that the patient had been charitably taken by an old Protestant pastor at nine years old, and had remained with him some years, even till the old man's death. Of this pastor the uncle knew nothing, but that he was a very good man. With great difficulty, and after much search, our young medical philosopher discovered a niece of the pastor's, who had lived with him as his house-keeper, and had inherited his effects. She remembered the girl; related, that her venerable uncle had been too indulgent, and could not bear to hear the girl scolded; that she was willing to have kept her, but that, after her patron's death, the girl herself refused to stay. Anxious inquiries were then, of course, made concerning the pastor's habits; and the solution of the phenomenon was soon obtained. For it appeared, that it had been the old man's custom, for years, to walk up and down a passage of his house into which the kitchen door opened, and to read to himself with a loud voice, out of his favourite books. A considerable number of these were still in the niece's possession. She added, that he was a very learned man and a great Hebraist. Among the books were found a collection of Rabbinical writings, together with several of the Greek and Latin Fathers; and the physician succeeded in identifying so many passages with those taken down at the young woman's bedside, that no doubt could remain in any rational mind concerning the true origin of the impressions made on her nervous system.

This authenticated case furnishes both proof and instance, that reliques of sensation may exist for an indefinite time in a latent state, in the very same order in which they were originally impressed; and as we cannot rationally suppose the feverish state of the brain to act in any other way than as a stimulus, this fact (and it would not be difficult to adduce several of the same kind) contributes to make it even probable, that all thoughts are in themselves imperishable; and, that if the intelligent faculty should be rendered more comprehensive, it would require only a different and apportioned organization,—the body celestial instead of the body terrestrial,—to bring before every human soul the collective experience of its whole past existence. And this, this, perchance, is the dread book of judgment, in the mysterious hieroglyphics of which every idle word is recorded! Yea, in the very nature of a living spirit, it may be more possible that heaven and earth should pass away, than that a single act, a single thought, should be loosened or lost from that living chain of causes, with all the links of which, conscious or unconscious, the free-will, our only absolute Self, is coextensive and co-present. But not now dare I longer discourse of this, waiting for a loftier mood, and a nobler subject, warned from within and from without, that it is profanation to speak of these "mysteries tois maede phantasteisin, os kalon to taes dikaiosynaes kai sophrosynaes prosopon, kai oute hesperos oute eoos outo kala. To gar horon pros to horomenon syngenes kai homoion poiaesamenon dei epiballein tae thea, ou gar an popote eiden ophthalmos haelion, haelioeidaes mae gegenaemenos oude to kalon an idae psychae, mae kagae genomenae—to those to whose imagination it has never been presented, how beautiful is the countenance of justice and wisdom; and that neither the morning nor the evening star are so fair. For in order to direct the view aright, it behoves that the beholder should have made himself congenerous and similar to the object beheld. Never could the eye have beheld the sun, had not its own essence been soliform," (i.e. pre-configured to light by a similarity of essence with that of light) "neither can a soul not beautiful attain to an intuition of beauty."

CHAPTER VII

Of the necessary consequences of the Hartleian Theory—Of the original mistake or equivocation which procured its admission—Memoria technica.

We will pass by the utter incompatibility of such a law—if law it may be called, which would itself be a slave of chances—with even that appearance of rationality forced upon us by the outward phaenomena of human conduct, abstracted from our own consciousness. We will agree to forget this for the moment, in order to fix our attention on that subordination of final to efficient causes in the human being, which flows of necessity from the assumption, that the will and, with the will, all acts of thought and attention are parts and products of this blind mechanism, instead of being distinct powers, the function of which it is to control, determine, and modify the phantasmal chaos of association. The soul becomes a mere ens logicum; for, as a real separable being, it would be more worthless and ludicrous than the Grimalkins in the cat-harpsichord, described in the Spectator. For these did form a part of the process; but, to Hartley's scheme, the soul is present only to be pinched or stroked, while the very squeals or purring are produced by an agency wholly independent and alien. It involves all the difficulties, all the incomprehensibility (if it be not indeed, os emoige dokei, the absurdity), of intercommunion between substances that have no one property in common, without any of the convenient consequences that bribed the judgment to the admission of the Dualistic hypothesis. Accordingly, this caput mortuum of the Hartleian process has been rejected by his followers, and the consciousness considered as a result, as a tune, the common product of the breeze and the harp though this again is the mere remotion of one absurdity to make way for another, equally preposterous. For what is harmony but a mode of relation, the very esse of which is percipi?—an ens rationale, which pre-supposes the power, that by perceiving creates it? The razor's edge becomes a saw to the armed vision; and the delicious melodies of Purcell or Cimarosa might be disjointed stammerings to a hearer, whose partition of time should be a thousand times subtler than ours. But this obstacle too let us imagine ourselves to have surmounted, and "at one bound high overleap all bound." Yet according to this hypothesis the disquisition, to which I am at present soliciting the reader's attention, may be as truly said to be written by Saint Paul's church, as by me: for it is the mere motion of my muscles and nerves; and these again are set in motion from external causes equally passive, which external causes stand themselves in interdependent connection with every thing that exists or has existed. Thus the whole universe co-operates to produce the minutest stroke of every letter, save only that I myself, and I alone, have nothing to do with it, but merely the causeless and effectless beholding of it when it is done. Yet scarcely can it be called a beholding; for it is neither an act nor an effect; but an impossible creation of a something nothing out of its very contrary! It is the mere quick-silver plating behind a looking-glass; and in this alone consists the poor worthless I! The sum total of my moral and intellectual intercourse, dissolved into its elements, is reduced to extension, motion, degrees of velocity, and those diminished copies of configurative motion, which form what we call notions, and notions of notions. Of such philosophy well might Butler say—

The metaphysic's but a puppet motion
That goes with screws, the notion of a notion;
The copy of a copy and lame draught
Unnaturally taken from a thought
That counterfeits all pantomimic tricks,
And turns the eyes, like an old crucifix;
That counterchanges whatsoe'er it calls
By another name, and makes it true or false;
Turns truth to falsehood, falsehood into truth,
By virtue of the Babylonian's tooth.

The inventor of the watch, if this doctrine be true, did not in reality invent it; he only looked on, while the blind causes, the only true artists, were unfolding themselves. So must it have been too with my friend Allston, when he sketched his picture of the dead man revived by the bones of the prophet Elijah. So must it have been with Mr. Southey and Lord Byron, when the one fancied himself composing his Roderick, and the other his Childe Harold. The same must hold good of all systems of philosophy; of all arts, governments, wars by sea and by land; in short, of all things that ever have been or that ever will be produced. For, according to this system, it is not the affections and passions that are at work, in as far as they are sensations or thoughts. We only fancy, that we act from rational resolves, or prudent motives, or from impulses of anger, love, or generosity. In all these cases the real agent is a something-nothing-everything, which does all of which we know, and knows nothing of all that itself does.

The existence of an infinite spirit, of an intelligent and holy will, must, on this system, be mere articulated motions of the air. For as the function of the human understanding is no other than merely to appear to itself to combine and to apply the phaenomena of the association; and as these derive all their reality from the primary sensations; and the sensations again all their reality from the impressions ab extra; a God not visible, audible, or tangible, can exist only in the sounds and letters that form his name and attributes. If in ourselves there be no such faculties as those of the will, and the scientific reason, we must either have an innate idea of them, which would overthrow the whole system; or we can have no idea at all. The process, by which Hume degraded the notion of cause and effect into a blind product of delusion and habit, into the mere sensation of proceeding life (nisus vitalis) associated with the images of the memory; this same process must be repeated to the equal degradation of every fundamental idea in ethics or theology.

Far, very far am I from burthening with the odium of these consequences the moral characters of those who first formed, or have since adopted the system! It is most noticeable of the excellent and pious Hartley, that, in the proofs of the existence and attributes of God, with which his second volume commences, he makes no reference to the principle or results of the first. Nay, he assumes, as his foundations, ideas which, if we embrace the doctrines of his first volume, can exist no where but in the vibrations of the ethereal medium common to the nerves and to the atmosphere. Indeed the whole of the second volume is, with the fewest possible exceptions, independent of his peculiar system. So true is it, that the faith, which saves and sanctifies, is a collective energy, a total act of the whole moral being; that its living sensorium is in the heart; and that no errors of the understanding can be morally arraigned unless they have proceeded from the heart. But whether they be such, no man can be certain in the case of another, scarcely perhaps even in his own. Hence it follows by inevitable consequence, that man may perchance determine what is a heresy; but God only can know who is a heretic. It does not, however, by any means follow that opinions fundamentally false are harmless. A hundred causes may co-exist to form one complex antidote. Yet the sting of the adder remains venomous, though there are many who have taken up the evil thing, and it hurted them not. Some indeed there seem to have been, in an unfortunate neighbour nation at least, who have embraced this system with a full view of all its moral and religious consequences; some—

————*who deem themselves most free,*
When they within this gross and visible sphere
Chain down the winged thought, scoffing ascent,
Proud in their meanness; and themselves they cheat
With noisy emptiness of learned phrase,
Their subtle fluids, impacts, essences,
Self-working tools, uncaus'd effects, and all
Those blind omniscients, those almighty slaves,
Untenanting creation of its God!

Such men need discipline, not argument; they must be made better men, before they can become wiser.

The attention will be more profitably employed in attempting to discover and expose the paralogisms, by the magic of which such a faith could find admission into minds framed for a nobler creed. These, it appears to me, may be all reduced to one sophism as their common genus; the mistaking the conditions of a thing for its causes and essence; and the process, by which we arrive at the knowledge of a faculty, for the faculty itself. The air I breathe is the condition of my life, not its cause. We could never have learned that we had eyes but by the process of seeing; yet having seen we know that the eyes must have pre-existed in order to render the process of sight possible. Let us cross-examine Hartley's scheme under the guidance of this distinction; and we shall discover, that contemporaneity, (Leibnitz's Lex Continui,) is the limit and condition of the laws of mind, itself being rather a law of matter, at least of phaenomena considered as material. At the utmost, it is to thought the same, as the law of gravitation is to locomotion. In every voluntary movement we first counteract gravitation, in order to avail ourselves of it. It must exist, that there may be a something to be counteracted, and which, by its re-action, may aid the force that is exerted to resist it. Let us consider what we do when we leap. We first resist the gravitating power by an act purely voluntary, and then by another act, voluntary in part, we yield to it in order to alight on the spot, which we had previously proposed to ourselves. Now let a man watch his mind while he is composing; or, to take a still more common case, while he is trying to recollect a name; and he will find the process completely analogous. Most of my readers will have observed a small water-insect on the surface of rivulets, which throws a cinque-spotted shadow fringed with prismatic colours on the sunny bottom of the brook; and will have noticed, how the little animal wins its way up against the stream, by alternate pulses of active and passive motion, now resisting the current, and now yielding to it in order to gather strength and a momentary fulcrum for a further propulsion. This is no unapt emblem of the mind's self-experience in the act of thinking. There are evidently two powers at work, which relatively to each other are active and passive; and this is not possible without an intermediate faculty, which is at once both active and passive. In philosophical language, we must denominate this intermediate faculty in all its degrees and determinations, the IMAGINATION. But, in common language, and especially on the subject of poetry, we appropriate the name to a superior degree of the faculty, joined to a superior voluntary control over it.

Contemporaneity, then, being the common condition of all the laws of association, and a component element in the materia subjecta, the parts of which are to be associated, must needs be co-present with all. Nothing, therefore, can be more easy than to pass off on an incautious mind this constant companion of each, for the essential substance of all. But if we appeal to our own consciousness, we shall find that even time itself, as the cause of a particular act of association, is distinct from contemporaneity, as the condition of all association. Seeing a mackerel, it may happen, that I immediately think of gooseberries, because I at the same time ate mackerel with gooseberries as the sauce. The first syllable of the latter word, being that which had coexisted with the image of the bird so called, I may then think of a goose. In the next moment the image of a swan may arise before me, though I had never seen the two birds together. In the first two instances, I am conscious that their co-existence in time was the circumstance, that enabled me to recollect them; and equally conscious am I that the latter was recalled to me by the joint operation of likeness and contrast. So it is with cause and effect: so too with order. So I am able to distinguish whether it was proximity in time, or continuity in space, that occasioned me to recall B on the mention of A. They cannot be indeed separated from contemporaneity; for that would be to separate them from the mind itself. The act of consciousness is indeed identical with time considered in its essence. I mean time per se, as contra-distinguished from our notion of time; for this is always blended with the idea of space, which, as the opposite of time, is therefore its measure. Nevertheless the accident of seeing two objects at the same moment, and the accident of seeing them in the same place are two distinct or distinguishable causes: and the true practical general law of association is this; that whatever makes certain parts of a total impression more vivid or distinct than the rest, will determine the mind to recall these in preference to others equally linked together by the common condition of contemporaneity, or (what I deem a more appropriate and philosophical term) of continuity. But the will itself by confining and intensifying [25] the attention may arbitrarily give vividness or distinctness to any object whatsoever; and from hence we may deduce the uselessness, if not the absurdity, of certain recent schemes which promise an artificial memory, but which in reality can only produce a confusion and debasement of the fancy. Sound logic, as the habitual subordination of the individual to the species, and of the species to the genus; philosophical knowledge of facts under the relation of cause and effect; a cheerful and communicative temper disposing us to notice the similarities and contrasts of things, that we may be able to illustrate the one by the other; a quiet conscience; a condition free from anxieties; sound health, and above all (as far as relates to passive remembrance) a healthy digestion; these are the best, these are the only Arts of Memory.

CHAPTER VIII

The system of Dualism introduced by Des Cartes—Refined first by Spinoza and afterwards by Leibnitz into the doctrine of Harmonia praestabilita—Hylozoism—Materialism—None of these systems, or any possible theory of association, supplies or supersedes a theory of perception, or explains the formation of the associable.

To the best of my knowledge Des Cartes was the first philosopher who introduced the absolute and essential heterogenity of the soul as intelligence, and the body as matter. The assumption, and the form of speaking have remained, though the denial of all other properties to matter but that of extension, on which denial the whole system of Dualism is grounded, has been long exploded. For since impenetrability is intelligible only as a mode of resistance; its admission places the essence of matter in an act or power, which it possesses in common with spirit; and body and spirit are therefore no longer absolutely heterogeneous, but may without any absurdity be supposed to be different modes, or degrees in perfection, of a common substratum. To this possibility, however, it was not the fashion to advert. The soul was a thinking substance, and body a space-filling substance. Yet the apparent action of each on the other pressed heavy on the philosopher on the one hand; and no less heavily on the other hand pressed the evident truth, that the law of causality holds only between homogeneous things, that is, things having some common property; and cannot extend from one world into another, its contrary. A close analysis evinced it to be no less absurd than the question whether a man's affection for his wife lay North-east, or South-west of the love he bore towards his child. Leibnitz's doctrine of a pre-established harmony; which he certainly borrowed from Spinoza, who had himself taken the hint from Des Cartes's animal machines, was in its common interpretation too strange to survive the inventor—too repugnant to our common sense; which is not indeed entitled to a judicial voice in the courts of scientific philosophy; but whose whispers still exert a strong secret influence. Even Wolf, the admirer and illustrious systematizer of the Leibnitzian doctrine, contents himself with defending the possibility of the idea, but does not adopt it as a part of the edifice.

The hypothesis of Hylozoism, on the other side, is the death of all rational physiology, and indeed of all physical science; for that requires a limitation of terms, and cannot consist with the arbitrary power of multiplying attributes by occult qualities. Besides, it answers no purpose; unless, indeed, a difficulty can be solved by multiplying it, or we can acquire a clearer notion of our soul by being told that we have a million of souls, and that every atom of our bodies has a soul of its own. Far more prudent is it to admit the difficulty once for all, and then let it lie at rest. There is a sediment indeed at the bottom of the vessel, but all the water above it is clear and transparent. The Hylozoist only shakes it up, and renders the whole turbid.

But it is not either the nature of man, or the duty of the philosopher to despair concerning any important problem until, as in the squaring of the circle, the impossibility of a solution has been demonstrated. How the esse assumed as originally distinct from the scire, can ever unite itself with it; how being can transform itself into a knowing, becomes conceivable on one only condition; namely, if it can be shown that the vis representativa, or the Sentient, is itself a species of being; that is, either as a property or attribute, or as an hypostasis or self subsistence. The former—that thinking is a property of matter under particular conditions,—is, indeed, the assumption of materialism; a system which could not but be patronized by the philosopher, if only it actually performed what it promises. But how any affection from without can metamorphose itself into perception or will, the materialist has hitherto left, not only as incomprehensible as he found it, but has aggravated it into a comprehensible absurdity. For, grant that an object from without could act upon the conscious self, as on a consubstantial object; yet such an affection could only engender something homogeneous with itself. Motion could only propagate motion. Matter has no Inward. We remove one surface, but to meet with another. We can but divide a particle into particles; and each atom comprehends in itself the properties of the material universe. Let any reflecting mind make the experiment of explaining to itself the evidence of our sensuous intuitions, from the hypothesis that in any given perception there is a something which has been communicated to it by an impact, or an impression ab extra. In the first place, by the impact on the percipient, or ens representans, not the object itself, but only its action or effect, will pass into the same. Not the iron tongue, but its vibrations, pass into the metal of the bell. Now in our immediate perception, it is not the mere power or act of the object, but the object itself, which is immediately present. We might indeed attempt to explain this result by a chain of deductions and conclusions; but that, first, the very faculty of deducing and concluding would equally demand an explanation; and secondly, that there exists in fact no such intermediation by logical notions, such as those of cause and effect. It is the object itself, not the product of a syllogism, which is present to our consciousness. Or would we explain this supervention of the object to the sensation, by a productive faculty set in motion by an impulse; still the transition, into the percipient, of the object itself, from which the impulse proceeded, assumes a power that can permeate and wholly possess the soul,

And like a God by spiritual art,
Be all in all, and all in every part.

And how came the percipient here? And what is become of the wonder-promising Matter, that was to perform all these marvels by force of mere figure, weight and motion? The most consistent proceeding of the dogmatic materialist is to fall back into the common rank of soul-and-bodyists; to affect the mysterious, and declare the whole process a revelation given, and not to be understood, which it would be profane to examine too closely. Datur non intelligitur. But a revelation unconfirmed by miracles, and a faith not commanded by the conscience, a philosopher may venture to pass by, without suspecting himself of any irreligious tendency.

Thus, as materialism has been generally taught, it is utterly unintelligible, and owes all its proselytes to the propensity so common among men, to mistake distinct images for clear conceptions; and vice versa, to reject as inconceivable whatever from its own nature is unimaginable. But as soon as it becomes intelligible, it ceases to be materialism. In order to explain thinking, as a material phaenomenon, it is necessary to refine matter into a mere modification of intelligence, with the two-fold function of appearing and perceiving. Even so did Priestley in his controversy with Price. He stripped matter of all its material properties; substituted spiritual powers; and when we expected to find a body, behold! we had nothing but its ghost—the apparition of a defunct substance!

I shall not dilate further on this subject; because it will, (if God grant health and permission), be treated of at large and systematically in a work, which I have many years been preparing, on the Productive Logos human and divine; with, and as the introduction to, a full commentary on the Gospel of St. John. To make myself intelligible as far as my present subject requires, it will be sufficient briefly to observe.—1. That all association demands and presupposes the existence of the thoughts and images to be associated.—2. That the hypothesis of an external world exactly correspondent to those images or modifications of our own being, which alone, according to this system, we actually behold, is as thorough idealism as Berkeley's, inasmuch as it equally, perhaps in a more perfect degree, removes all reality and immediateness of perception, and places us in a dream-world of phantoms and spectres, the inexplicable swarm and equivocal generation of motions in our own brains.—3. That this hypothesis neither involves the explanation, nor precludes the necessity, of a mechanism and co-adequate forces in the percipient, which at the more than magic touch of the impulse from without is to create anew for itself the correspondent object. The formation of a copy is not solved by the mere pre-existence of an original; the copyist of Raffael's Transfiguration must repeat more or less perfectly the process of Raffael. It would be easy to explain a thought from the image on the retina, and that from the geometry of light, if this very light did not present the very same difficulty. We might as rationally chant the Brahim creed of the tortoise that supported the bear, that supported the elephant, that supported the world, to the tune of "This is the house that Jack built." The sic Deo placitum est we all admit as the sufficient cause, and the divine goodness as the sufficient reason; but an answer to the Whence and Why is no answer to the How, which alone is the physiologist's concern. It is a sophisma pigrum, and (as Bacon hath said) the arrogance of pusillanimity, which lifts up the idol of a mortal's fancy and commands us to fall down and worship it, as a work of divine wisdom, an ancile or palladium fallen from heaven. By the very same argument the supporters of the Ptolemaic system might have rebuffed the Newtonian, and pointing to the sky with self-complacent grin [26] have appealed to common sense, whether the sun did not move and the earth stand still.

CHAPTER IX

Is Philosophy possible as a science, and what are its conditions?—Giordano Bruno—Literary Aristocracy, or the existence of a tacit compact among the learned as a privileged order—The Author's obligations to the Mystics—to Immanuel Kant—The difference between the letter and the spirit of Kant's writings, and a vindication of prudence in the teaching of Philosophy—Fichte's attempt to complete the Critical system—Its partial success and ultimate failure—Obligations to Schelling; and among English writers to Saumarez.

After I had successively studied in the schools of Locke, Berkeley, Leibnitz, and Hartley, and could find in none of them an abiding place for my reason, I began to ask myself; is a system of philosophy; as different from mere history and historic classification, possible? If possible, what are its necessary conditions? I was for a while disposed to answer the first question in the negative, and to admit that the sole practicable employment for the human mind was to observe, to collect, and to classify. But I soon felt, that human nature itself fought up against this wilful resignation of intellect; and as soon did I find, that the scheme, taken with all its consequences and cleared of all inconsistencies, was not less impracticable than contranatural. Assume in its full extent the position, nihil in intellectu quod non prius in sensu, assume it without Leibnitz's qualifying praeter ipsum intellectum, and in the same sense, in which the position was understood by Hartley and Condillac: and then what Hume had demonstratively deduced from this concession concerning cause and effect, will apply with equal and crushing force to all the other eleven categorical forms [27], and the logical functions corresponding to them. How can we make bricks without straw;--or build without cement? We learn all things indeed by occasion of experience; but the very facts so learned force us inward on the antecedents, that must be presupposed in order to render experience itself possible. The first book of Locke's Essay, (if the supposed error, which it labours to subvert, be not a mere thing of straw, an absurdity which, no man ever did, or indeed ever could, believe,) is formed on a sophisma heterozaetaeseos, and involves the old mistake of Cum hoc: ergo, propter hoc.

The term, Philosophy, defines itself as an affectionate seeking after the truth; but Truth is the correlative of Being. This again is no way conceivable, but by assuming as a postulate, that both are ab initio, identical and coinherent; that intelligence and being are reciprocally each other's substrate. I presumed that this was a possible conception, (i.e. that it involved no logical inconsonance,) from the length of time during which the scholastic definition of the Supreme Being, as actus purissimus sine ulla potentialitate, was received in the schools of Theology, both by the Pontifician and the Reformed divines. The early study of Plato and Plotinus, with the commentaries and the THEOLOGIA PLATONICA of the illustrious Florentine; of Proclus, and Gemistius Pletho; and at a later period of the De Immenso et Innumerabili and the "De la causa, principio et uno," of the philosopher of Nola, who could boast of a Sir Philip Sidney and Fulke Greville among his patrons, and whom the idolaters of Rome burnt as an atheist in the year 1600; had all contributed to prepare my mind for the reception and welcoming of the Cogito quia Sum, et Sum quia Cogito; a philosophy of seeming hardihood, but certainly the most ancient, and therefore presumptively the most natural.

Why need I be afraid? Say rather how dare I be ashamed of the Teutonic theosophist, Jacob Behmen? Many, indeed, and gross were his delusions; and such as furnish frequent and ample occasion for the triumph of the learned over the poor ignorant shoemaker, who had dared think for himself. But while we remember that these delusions were such, as might be anticipated from his utter want of all intellectual discipline, and from his ignorance of rational psychology, let it not be forgotten that the latter defect he had in common with the most learned theologians of his age. Neither with books, nor with book-learned men was he conversant. A meek and shy quietest, his intellectual powers were never stimulated into feverous energy by crowds of proselytes, or by the ambition of proselyting. Jacob Behmen was an enthusiast, in the strictest sense, as not merely distinguished, but as contra-distinguished, from a fanatic. While I in part translate the following observations from a contemporary writer of the Continent, let me be permitted to premise, that I might have transcribed the substance from memoranda of my own, which were written many years before his pamphlet was given to the world; and that I prefer another's words to my own, partly as a tribute due to priority of publication; but still more from the pleasure of sympathy in a case where coincidence only was possible.

Whoever is acquainted with the history of philosophy, during the last two or three centuries, cannot but admit that there appears to have existed a sort of secret and tacit compact among the learned, not to pass beyond a certain limit in speculative science. The privilege of free thought, so highly extolled, has at no time been held valid in actual practice, except within this limit; and not a single stride beyond it has ever been ventured without bringing obloquy on the transgressor. The few men of genius among the learned class, who actually did overstep this boundary, anxiously avoided the appearance of having so done. Therefore the true depth of science, and the penetration to the inmost centre, from which all the lines of knowledge diverge to their ever distant circumference, was abandoned to the illiterate and the simple, whom unstilled yearning, and an original ebulliency of spirit, had urged to the investigation of the indwelling and living ground of all things. These, then, because their names had never been enrolled in the guilds of the learned, were persecuted by the registered livery-men as interlopers on their rights and privileges. All without distinction were branded as fanatics and phantasts; not only those, whose wild and exorbitant imaginations had actually engendered only extravagant and grotesque phantasms, and whose productions were, for the most part, poor copies and gross caricatures of genuine inspiration; but the truly inspired likewise, the originals themselves. And this for no other reason, but because they were the unlearned, men of humble and obscure occupations. When, and from whom among the literati by profession, have we ever heard the divine doxology repeated, I thank thee, O Father! Lord of Heaven and Earth! because thou hast hid these things from the wise and prudent, and hast revealed them unto babes [28]. No; the haughty priests of learning not only banished from the schools and marts of science all who had dared draw living waters from the fountain, but drove them out of the very Temple, which mean time the buyers, and sellers, and money-changers were suffered to make a den of thieves.

And yet it would not be easy to discover any substantial ground for this contemptuous pride in those literati, who have most distinguished themselves by their scorn of Behmen, Thaulerus, George Fox, and others; unless it be, that they could write orthographically, make smooth periods, and had the fashions of authorship almost literally at their fingers' ends, while the latter, in simplicity of soul, made their words immediate echoes of their feelings. Hence the frequency of those phrases among them, which have been mistaken for pretences to immediate inspiration; as for instance, "It was delivered unto me;"—"I strove not to speak;"-"I said, I will be silent;"—"But the word was in my heart as a burning fire;"—"and I could not forbear." Hence too the unwillingness to give offence; hence the foresight, and the dread of the clamours, which would be raised against them, so frequently avowed in the writings of these men, and expressed, as was natural, in the words of the only book, with which they were familiar [29]. "Woe is me that I am become a man of strife, and a man of contention,--I love peace: the souls of men are dear unto me: yet because I seek for light every one of them doth curse me!" O! it requires deeper feeling, and a stronger imagination, than belong to most of those, to whom reasoning and fluent expression have been as a trade learnt in boyhood, to conceive with what might, with what inward strivings and commotion, the perception of a new and vital truth takes possession of an uneducated man of genius. His meditations are almost inevitably employed on the eternal, or the everlasting; for "the world is not his friend, nor the world's law." Need we then be surprised, that, under an excitement at once so strong and so unusual, the man's body should sympathize with the struggles of his mind; or that he should at times be so far deluded, as to mistake the tumultuous sensations of his nerves, and the co-existing spectres of his fancy, as parts or symbols of the truths which were opening on him? It has indeed been plausibly observed, that in order to derive any advantage, or to collect any intelligible meaning, from the writings of these ignorant Mystics, the reader must bring with him a spirit and judgment superior to that of the writers themselves:

And what he brings, what needs he elsewhere seek?

—a sophism, which I fully agree with Warburton, is unworthy of Milton; how much more so of the awful Person, in whose mouth he has placed it? One assertion I will venture to make, as suggested by my own experience, that there exist folios on the human understanding, and the nature of man, which would have a far juster claim to their high rank and celebrity, if in the whole huge volume there could be found as much fulness of heart and intellect, as burst forth in many a simple page of George Fox, Jacob Behmen, and even of Behmen's commentator, the pious and fervid William Law.

The feeling of gratitude, which I cherish toward these men, has caused me to digress further than I had foreseen or proposed; but to have passed them over in an historical sketch of my literary life and opinions, would have seemed to me like the denial of a debt, the concealment of a boon. For the writings of these Mystics acted in no slight degree to prevent my mind from being imprisoned within the outline of any single dogmatic system. They contributed to keep alive the heart in the head; gave me an indistinct, yet stirring and working presentiment, that all the products of the mere reflective faculty partook of death, and were as the rattling twigs and sprays in winter, into which a sap was yet to be propelled from some root to which I had not penetrated, if they were to afford my soul either food or shelter. If they were too often a moving cloud of smoke to me by day, yet they were always a pillar of fire throughout the night, during my wanderings through the wilderness of doubt, and enabled me to skirt, without crossing, the sandy deserts of utter unbelief. That the system is capable of being converted into an irreligious Pantheism, I well know. The Ethics of Spinoza, may, or may not, be an instance. But at no time could I believe, that in itself and essentially it is incompatible with religion, natural or revealed: and now I am most thoroughly persuaded of the contrary. The writings of the illustrious sage of Koenigsberg, the founder of the Critical Philosophy, more than any other work, at once invigorated and disciplined my understanding. The originality, the depth, and the compression of the thoughts; the novelty and subtlety, yet solidity and importance of the distinctions; the adamantine chain of the logic; and I will venture to add—(paradox as it will appear to those who have taken their notion of Immanuel Kant from Reviewers and Frenchmen)—the clearness and evidence, of the Critique of the Pure Reason; and Critique of the Judgment; of the Metaphysical Elements of Natural Philosophy; and of his Religion within the bounds of Pure Reason, took possession of me as with the giant's hand. After fifteen years' familiarity with them, I still read these and all his other productions with undiminished delight and increasing admiration. The few passages that remained obscure to me, after due efforts of thought, (as the chapter on original apperception,) and the apparent contradictions which occur, I soon found were hints and insinuations referring to ideas, which KANT either did not think it prudent to avow, or which he considered as consistently left behind in a pure analysis, not of human nature in toto, but of the speculative intellect alone. Here therefore he was constrained to commence at the point of reflection, or natural consciousness: while in his moral system he was permitted to assume a higher ground (the autonomy of the will) as a postulate deducible from the unconditional command, or (in the technical language of his school) the categorical imperative, of the conscience. He had been in imminent danger of persecution during the reign of the late king of Prussia, that strange compound of lawless debauchery and priest-ridden superstition: and it is probable that he had little inclination, in his old age, to act over again the fortunes, and hair-breadth escapes of Wolf. The expulsion of the first among Kant's disciples, who attempted to complete his system, from the University of Jena, with the confiscation and prohibition of the obnoxious work by the joint efforts of the courts of Saxony and Hanover, supplied experimental proof, that the venerable old man's caution was not groundless. In spite therefore of his own declarations, I could never believe, that it was possible for him to have meant no more by his Noumenon, or Thing in itself, than his mere words express; or that in his own conception he confined the whole plastic power to the forms of the intellect, leaving for the external cause, for the materiale of our sensations, a matter without form, which is doubtless inconceivable. I entertained doubts likewise, whether, in his own mind, he even laid all the stress, which he appears to do, on the moral postulates.

An idea, in the highest sense of that word, cannot be conveyed but by a symbol; and, except in geometry, all symbols of necessity involve an apparent contradiction. Phonaese synetoisin: and for those who could not pierce through this symbolic husk, his writings were not intended. Questions which cannot be fully answered without exposing the respondent to personal danger, are not entitled to a fair answer; and yet to say this openly, would in many cases furnish the very advantage which the adversary is insidiously seeking after. Veracity does not consist in saying, but in the intention of communicating, truth; and the philosopher who cannot utter the whole truth without conveying falsehood, and at the same time, perhaps, exciting the most malignant passions, is constrained to express himself either mythically or equivocally. When Kant therefore was importuned to settle the disputes of his commentators himself, by declaring what he meant, how could he decline the honours of martyrdom with less offence, than by simply replying, "I meant what I said, and at the age of near fourscore, I have something else, and more important to do, than to write a commentary on my own works."

Fichte's Wissenschaftslehre, or Lore of Ultimate Science, was to add the key-stone of the arch: and by commencing with an act, instead of a thing or substance, Fichte assuredly gave the first mortal blow to Spinozism, as taught by Spinoza himself; and supplied the idea of a system truly metaphysical, and of a metaphysique truly systematic: (i.e. having its spring and principle within itself). But this fundamental idea he overbuilt with a heavy mass of mere notions, and psychological acts of arbitrary reflection. Thus his theory degenerated into a crude [30] egoismus, a boastful and hyperstoic hostility to Nature, as lifeless, godless, and altogether unholy: while his religion consisted in the assumption of a mere Ordo ordinans, which we were permitted exoterice to call GOD; and his ethics in an ascetic, and almost monkish, mortification of the natural passions and desires. In Schelling's Natur-Philosophie, and the System des transcendentalen Idealismus, I first found a genial coincidence with much that I had toiled out for myself, and a powerful assistance in what I had yet to do.

I have introduced this statement, as appropriate to the narrative nature of this sketch; yet rather in reference to the work which I have announced in a preceding page, than to my present subject. It would be but a mere act of justice to myself, were I to warn my future readers, than an identity of thought, or even similarity of phrase, will not be at all times a certain proof that the passage has been borrowed from Schelling, or that the conceptions were originally learnt from him. In this instance, as in the dramatic lectures of Schlegel to which I have before alluded, from the same motive of self-defence against the charge of plagiarism, many of the most striking resemblances, indeed all the main and fundamental ideas, were born and matured in my mind before I had ever seen a single page of the German Philosopher; and I might indeed affirm with truth, before the more important works of Schelling had been written, or at least made public. Nor is this coincidence at all to be wondered at. We had studied in the same school; been disciplined by the same preparatory philosophy, namely, the writings of Kant; we had both equal obligations to the polar logic and dynamic philosophy of Giordano Bruno; and Schelling has lately, and, as of recent acquisition, avowed that same affectionate reverence for the labours of Behmen, and other mystics, which I had formed at a much earlier period. The coincidence of Schelling's system with certain general ideas of Behmen, he declares to have been mere coincidence; while my obligations have been more direct. He needs give to Behmen only feelings of sympathy; while I owe him a debt of gratitude. God forbid! that I should be suspected of a wish to enter into a rivalry with Schelling for the honours so unequivocally his right, not only as a great and original genius, but as the founder of the Philosophy of Nature, and as the most successful improver of the Dynamic System [31] which, begun by Bruno, was re-introduced (in a more philosophical form, and freed from all its impurities and visionary accompaniments) by Kant; in whom it was the native and necessary growth of his own system. Kant's followers, however, on whom (for the greater part) their master's cloak had fallen without, or with a very scanty portion of, his spirit, had adopted his dynamic ideas, only as a more refined species of mechanics. With exception of one or two fundamental ideas, which cannot be withheld from Fichte, to Schelling we owe the completion, and the most important victories, of this revolution in philosophy. To me it will be happiness and honour enough, should I succeed in rendering the system itself intelligible to my countrymen, and in the application of it to the most awful of subjects for the most important of purposes. Whether a work is the offspring of a man's own spirit, and the product of original thinking, will be discovered by those who are its sole legitimate judges, by better tests than the mere reference to dates. For readers in general, let whatever shall be found in this or any future work of mine, that resembles, or coincides with, the doctrines of my German predecessor, though contemporary, be wholly attributed to him: provided, that the absence of distinct references to his books, which I could not at all times make with truth as designating citations or thoughts actually derived from him; and which, I trust, would, after this general acknowledgment be superfluous; be not charged on me as an ungenerous concealment or intentional plagiarism. I have not indeed (eheu! res angusta domi!) been hitherto able to procure more than two of his books, viz. the first volume of his collected Tracts, and his System of Transcendental Idealism; to which, however, I must add a small pamphlet against Fichte, the spirit of which was to my feelings painfully incongruous with the principles, and which (with the usual allowance afforded to an antithesis) displayed the love of wisdom rather than the wisdom of love. I regard truth as a divine ventriloquist: I care not from whose mouth the sounds are supposed to proceed, if only the words are audible and intelligible. "Albeit, I must confess to be half in doubt, whether I should bring it forth or no, it being so contrary to the eye of the world, and the world so potent in most men's hearts, that I shall endanger either not to be regarded or not to be understood."

And to conclude the subject of citation, with a cluster of citations, which as taken from books, not in common use, may contribute to the reader's amusement, as a voluntary before a sermon: "Dolet mihi quidem deliciis literarum inescatos subito jam homines adeo esse, praesertim qui Christianos se profitentur, et legere nisi quod ad delectationem facit, sustineant nihil: unde et disciplinae severiores et philosophia ipsa jam fere prorsus etiam a doctis negliguntur. Quod quidem propositum studiorum, nisi mature corrigitur, tam magnum rebus incommodum dabit, quam dedit barbaries olim. Pertinax res barbaries est, fateor: sed minus potent tamen, quam illa mollities et persuasa prudentia literarum, si ratione caret, sapientiae virtutisque specie mortales misere circumducens. Succedet igitur, ut arbitror, haud ita multo post, pro rusticana seculi nostri ruditate captatrix illa communi-loquentia robur animi virilis omne, omnem virtutem masculam, profligatura nisi cavetur."

A too prophetic remark, which has been in fulfilment from the year 1680, to the present 1815. By persuasa prudentia, Grynaeus means self-complacent common sense as opposed to science and philosophic reason.

Est medius ordo, et velut equestris, ingeniorum quidem sagacium, et commodorum rebus humanis, non tamen in primam magnitudinem patentium. Eorum hominum, ut sic dicam, major annona est. Sedulum esse, nihil temere loqui, assuescere labori, et imagine prudentiae et modistiae tegere angustiores partes captus, dum exercitationem ac usum, quo isti in civilibus rebus pollent, pro natura et magnitudine ingenii plerique accipiunt.

"As therefore physicians are many times forced to leave such methods of curing as themselves know to be the fittest, and being overruled by the patient's impatiency, are fain to try the best they can: in like sort, considering how the case doth stand with this present age, full of tongue and weak of brain, behold we would (if our subject permitted it) yield to the stream thereof. That way we would be contented to prove our thesis, which being the worse in itself, is notwithstanding now by reason of common imbecility the fitter and likelier to be brooked."

If this fear could be rationally entertained in the controversial age of Hooker, under the then robust discipline of the scholastic logic, pardonably may a writer of the present times anticipate a scanty audience for abstrusest themes, and truths that can neither be communicated nor received without effort of thought, as well as patience of attention.

"Che s'io non erro al calcolar de' punti,
Par ch' Asinina Stella a noi predomini,
E 'l Somaro e 'l Castron si sian congiunti.
Il tempo d'Apuleio piu non si nomini:
Che se allora un sol huom sembrava un Asino,
Mille Asini a' miei di rassembran huomini!"

CHAPTER X

A chapter of digression and anecdotes, as an interlude preceding that on the nature and genesis of the Imagination or Plastic Power—On pedantry and pedantic expressions—Advice to young authors respecting publication—Various anecdotes of the Author's literary life, and the progress of his opinions in Religion and Politics.

"Esemplastic. The word is not in Johnson, nor have I met with it elsewhere." Neither have, I. I constructed it myself from the Greek words, eis en plattein, to shape into one; because, having to convey a new sense, I thought that a new term would both aid the recollection of my meaning, and prevent its being confounded with the usual import of the word, imagination. "But this is pedantry!" Not necessarily so, I hope. If I am not misinformed, pedantry consists in the use of words unsuitable to the time, place, and company. The language of the market would be in the schools as pedantic, though it might not be reprobated by that name, as the language of the schools in the market. The mere man of the world, who insists that no other terms but such as occur in common conversation should be employed in a scientific disquisition, and with no greater precision, is as truly a pedant as the man of letters, who either over-rating the acquirements of his auditors, or misled by his own familiarity with technical or scholastic terms, converses at the wine-table with his mind fixed on his museum or laboratory; even though the latter pedant instead of desiring his wife to make the tea should bid her add to the quant. suff. of thea Sinensis the oxyd of hydrogen saturated with caloric. To use the colloquial (and in truth somewhat vulgar) metaphor, if the pedant of the cloister, and the pedant of the lobby, both smell equally of the shop, yet the odour from the Russian binding of good old authentic-looking folios and quartos is less annoying than the steams from the tavern or bagnio. Nay, though the pedantry of the scholar should betray a little ostentation, yet a well-conditioned mind would more easily, methinks, tolerate the fox brush of learned vanity, than the sans culotterie of a contemptuous ignorance, that assumes a merit from mutilation in the self-consoling sneer at the pompous incumbrance of tails.

The first lesson of philosophic discipline is to wean the student's attention from the degrees of things, which alone form the vocabulary of common life, and to direct it to the kind abstracted from degree. Thus the chemical student is taught not to be startled at disquisitions on the heat in ice, or on latent and fixible light. In such discourse the instructor has no other alternative than either to use old words with new meanings (the plan adopted by Darwin in his Zoonomia;) or to introduce new terms, after the example of Linnaeus, and the framers of the present chemical nomenclature. The latter mode is evidently preferable, were it only that the former demands a twofold exertion of thought in one and the same act. For the reader, or hearer, is required not only to learn and bear in mind the new definition; but to unlearn, and keep out of his view, the old and habitual meaning; a far more difficult and perplexing task, and for which the mere semblance of eschewing pedantry seems to me an inadequate compensation. Where, indeed, it is in our power to recall an unappropriate term that had without sufficient reason become obsolete, it is doubtless a less evil to restore than to coin anew. Thus to express in one word all that appertains to the perception, considered as passive and merely recipient, I have adopted from our elder classics the word sensuous; because sensual is not at present used, except in a bad sense, or at least as a moral distinction; while sensitive and sensible would each convey a different meaning. Thus too have I followed Hooker, Sanderson, Milton and others, in designating the immediateness of any act or object of knowledge by the word intuition, used sometimes subjectively, sometimes objectively, even as we use the word, thought; now as the thought, or act of thinking, and now as a thought, or the object of our reflection; and we do this without confusion or obscurity. The very words, objective and subjective, of such constant recurrence in the schools of yore, I have ventured to re-introduce, because I could not so briefly or conveniently by any more familiar terms distinguish the percipere from the percipi. Lastly, I have cautiously discriminated the terms, the reason, and the understanding, encouraged and confirmed by the authority of our genuine divines and philosophers, before the Revolution.

————both life, and sense,
Fancy and understanding; whence the soul
Reason receives, and reason is her bring,
Discursive or intuitive: discourse [32]
Is oftest yours, the latter most is ours,
Differing but in degree, in kind the same.

I say, that I was confirmed by authority so venerable: for I had previous and higher motives in my own conviction of the importance, nay, of the necessity of the distinction, as both an indispensable condition and a vital part of all sound speculation in metaphysics, ethical or theological. To establish this distinction was one main object of The Friend; if even in a biography of my own literary life I can with propriety refer to a work, which was printed rather than published, or so published that it had been well for the unfortunate author, if it had remained in manuscript. I have even at this time bitter cause for remembering that, which a number of my subscribers have but a trifling motive for forgetting. This effusion might have been spared; but I would fain flatter myself, that the reader will be less austere than an oriental professor of the bastinado, who during an attempt to extort per argumentum baculinum a full confession from a culprit, interrupted his outcry of pain by reminding him, that it was "a mere digression!" "All this noise, Sir! is nothing to the point, and no sort of answer to my questions!" "Ah! but," (replied the sufferer,) "it is the most pertinent reply in nature to your blows."

An imprudent man of common goodness of heart cannot but wish to turn even his imprudences to the benefit of others, as far as this is possible. If therefore any one of the readers of this semi-narrative should be preparing or intending a periodical work, I warn him, in the first place, against trusting in the number of names on his subscription list. For he cannot be certain that the names were put down by sufficient authority; or, should that be ascertained, it still remains to be known, whether they were not extorted by some over zealous friend's importunity; whether the subscriber had not yielded his name, merely from want of courage to answer, no; and with the intention of dropping the work as soon as possible. One gentleman procured me nearly a hundred names for THE FRIEND, and not only took frequent opportunity to remind me of his success in his canvass, but laboured to impress my mind with the sense of the obligation, I was under to the subscribers; for, (as he very pertinently admonished me,) "fifty-two shillings a year was a large sum to be bestowed on one individual, where there were so many objects of charity with strong claims to the assistance of the benevolent." Of these hundred patrons ninety threw up the publication before the fourth number, without any notice; though it was well known to them, that in consequence of the distance, and the slowness and irregularity of the conveyance, I was compelled to lay in a stock of stamped paper for at least eight weeks beforehand; each sheet of which stood me in five pence previously to its arrival at my printer's; though the subscription money was not to be received till the twenty-first week after the commencement of the work; and lastly, though it was in nine cases out of ten impracticable for me to receive the money for two or three numbers without paying an equal sum for the postage.

In confirmation of my first caveat, I will select one fact among many. On my list of subscribers, among a considerable number of names equally flattering, was that of an Earl of Cork, with his address. He might as well have been an Earl of Bottle, for aught I knew of him, who had been content to reverence the peerage in abstracto, rather than in concretis. Of course THE FRIEND was regularly sent as far, if I remember right, as the eighteenth number; that is, till a fortnight before the subscription was to be paid. And lo! just at this time I received a letter from his Lordship, reproving me in language far more lordly than courteous for my impudence in directing my pamphlets to him, who knew nothing of me or my work! Seventeen or eighteen numbers of which, however, his Lordship was pleased to retain, probably for the culinary or post-culinary conveniences of his servants.

Secondly, I warn all others from the attempt to deviate from the ordinary mode of publishing a work by the trade. I thought indeed, that to the purchaser it was indifferent, whether thirty per cent of the purchase-money went to the booksellers or to the government; and that the convenience of receiving the work by the post at his own door would give the preference to the latter. It is hard, I own, to have been labouring for years, in collecting and arranging the materials; to have spent every shilling that could be spared after the necessaries of life had been furnished, in buying books, or in journeys for the purpose of consulting them or of acquiring facts at the fountain head; then to buy the paper, pay for the printing, and the like, all at least fifteen per cent beyond what the trade would have paid; and then after all to give thirty per cent not of the net profits, but of the gross results of the sale, to a man who has merely to give the books shelf or warehouse room, and permit his apprentice to hand them over the counter to those who may ask for them; and this too copy by copy, although, if the work be on any philosophical or scientific subject, it may be years before the edition is sold off. All this, I confess, must seem a hardship, and one, to which the products of industry in no other mode of exertion are subject. Yet even this is better, far better, than to attempt in any way to unite the functions of author and publisher. But the most prudent mode is to sell the copy-right, at least of one or more editions, for the most that the trade will offer. By few only can a large remuneration be expected; but fifty pounds and ease of mind are of more real advantage to a literary man, than the chance of five hundred with the certainty of insult and degrading anxieties. I shall have been grievously misunderstood, if this statement should be interpreted as written with the desire of detracting from the character of booksellers or publishers. The individuals did not make the laws and customs of their trade, but, as in every other trade, take them as they find them. Till the evil can be proved to be removable, and without the substitution of an equal or greater inconvenience, it were neither wise nor manly even to complain of it. But to use it as a pretext for speaking, or even for thinking, or feeling, unkindly or opprobriously of the tradesmen, as individuals, would be something worse than unwise or even than unmanly; it would be immoral and calumnious. My motives point in a far different direction and to far other objects, as will be seen in the conclusion of the chapter.

A learned and exemplary old clergyman, who many years ago went to his reward followed by the regrets and blessings of his flock, published at his own expense two volumes octavo, entitled, A NEW THEORY OF

REDEMPTION. The work was most severely handled in THE MONTHLY or CRITICAL REVIEW, I forget which; and this unprovoked hostility became the good old man's favourite topic of conversation among his friends. "Well!" (he used to exclaim,) "in the second edition, I shall have an opportunity of exposing both the ignorance and the malignity of the anonymous critic." Two or three years however passed by without any tidings from the bookseller, who had undertaken the printing and publication of the work, and who was perfectly at his ease, as the author was known to be a man of large property. At length the accounts were written for; and in the course of a few weeks they were presented by the rider for the house, in person. My old friend put on his spectacles, and holding the scroll with no very firm hand, began—"Paper, so much: O moderate enough—not at all beyond my expectation! Printing, so much: well! moderate enough! Stitching, covers, advertisements, carriage, and so forth, so much."—Still nothing amiss. Selleridge (for orthography is no necessary part of a bookseller's literary acquirements) L3. 3s. "Bless me! only three guineas for the what d'ye call it—the selleridge?" "No more, Sir!" replied the rider. "Nay, but that is too moderate!" rejoined my old friend. "Only three guineas for selling a thousand copies of a work in two volumes?" "O Sir!" (cries the young traveller) "you have mistaken the word. There have been none of them sold; they have been sent back from London long ago; and this L3. 3s. is for the cellaridge, or warehouse-room in our book cellar." The work was in consequence preferred from the ominous cellar of the publisher's to the author's garret; and, on presenting a copy to an acquaintance, the old gentleman used to tell the anecdote with great humour and still greater good nature.

With equal lack of worldly knowledge, I was a far more than equal sufferer for it, at the very outset of my authorship. Toward the close of the first year from the time, that in an inauspicious hour I left the friendly cloisters, and the happy grove of quiet, ever honoured Jesus College, Cambridge, I was persuaded by sundry philanthropists and Anti-polemists to set on foot a periodical work, entitled THE WATCHMAN, that, according to the general motto of the work, all might know the truth, and that the truth might make us free! In order to exempt it from the stamp-tax, and likewise to contribute as little as possible to the supposed guilt of a war against freedom, it was to be published on every eighth day, thirty-two pages, large octavo, closely printed, and price only four-pence. Accordingly with a flaming prospectus,—"Knowledge is Power," "To cry the state of the political atmosphere,"—and so forth, I set off on a tour to the North, from Bristol to Sheffield, for the purpose of procuring customers, preaching by the way in most of the great towns, as an hireless volunteer, in a blue coat and white waistcoat, that not a rag of the woman of Babylon might be seen on me. For I was at that time and long after, though a Trinitarian (that is ad normam Platonis) in philosophy, yet a zealous Unitarian in religion; more accurately, I was a Psilanthropist, one of those who believe our Lord to have been the real son of Joseph, and who lay the main stress on the resurrection rather than on the crucifixion. O! never can I remember those days with either shame or regret. For I was most sincere, most disinterested. My opinions were indeed in many and most important points erroneous; but my heart was single. Wealth, rank, life itself then seemed cheap to me, compared with the interests of what I believed to be the truth, and the will of my Maker. I cannot even accuse myself of having been actuated by vanity; for in the expansion of my enthusiasm I did not think of myself at all.

My campaign commenced at Birmingham; and my first attack was on a rigid Calvinist, a tallow-chandler by trade. He was a tall dingy man, in whom length was so predominant over breadth, that he might almost have been borrowed for a foundery poker. O that face! a face kat' emphasin! I have it before me at this moment. The lank, black, twine-like hair, pinguinitescent, cut in a straight line along the black stubble of his thin gunpowder eye-brows, that looked like a scorched after-math from a last week's shaving. His coat collar behind in perfect unison, both of colour and lustre, with the coarse yet glib cordage, which I suppose he called his hair, and which with a bend inward at the nape of the neck,—the only approach to flexure in his whole figure,—slunk in behind his waistcoat; while the countenance lank, dark, very hard, and with strong perpendicular furrows, gave me a dim notion of some one looking at me through a used gridiron, all soot, grease, and iron! But he was one of the thorough-bred, a true lover of liberty, and, as I was informed, had proved to the satisfaction of many, that Mr. Pitt was one of the horns of the second beast in THE REVELATIONS, that spake as a dragon. A person, to whom one of my letters of recommendation had been addressed, was my introducer. It was a new event in my life, my first stroke in the new business I had undertaken of an author, yea, and of an author trading on his own account. My companion after some imperfect sentences and a multitude of hums and has abandoned the cause to his client; and I commenced an harangue of half an hour to Phileleutheros, the tallow-chandler, varying my notes, through the whole gamut of eloquence, from the ratiocinative to the declamatory, and in the latter from the pathetic to the indignant. I argued, I described, I promised, I prophesied; and beginning with the captivity of nations I ended with the near approach of the millennium, finishing the whole with some of my own verses describing that glorious state out of the Religious Musings:

———*Such delights*
As float to earth, permitted visitants!

When in some hour of solemn jubilee
The massive gates of Paradise are thrown
Wide open, and forth come in fragments wild
Sweet echoes of unearthly melodies,
And odours snatched from beds of amaranth,
And they, that from the crystal river of life
Spring up on freshened wing, ambrosial gales!

My taper man of lights listened with perseverant and praiseworthy patience, though, as I was afterwards told, on complaining of certain gales that were not altogether ambrosial, it was a melting day with him. "And what, Sir," he said, after a short pause, "might the cost be?" "Only four-pence,"—(O! how I felt the anti-climax, the abysmal bathos of that four-pence!)—"only four-pence, Sir, each number, to be published on every eighth day."—"That comes to a deal of money at the end of a year. And how much, did you say, there was to be for the money?"—"Thirty-two pages, Sir, large octavo, closely printed."—"Thirty and two pages? Bless me! why except what I does in a family way on the Sabbath, that's more than I ever reads, Sir! all the year round. I am as great a one, as any man in Brummagem, Sir! for liberty and truth and all them sort of things, but as to this,—no offence, I hope, Sir,—I must beg to be excused."

So ended my first canvass: from causes that I shall presently mention, I made but one other application in person. This took place at Manchester to a stately and opulent wholesale dealer in cottons. He took my letter of introduction, and, having perused it, measured me from head to foot and again from foot to head, and then asked if I had any bill or invoice of the thing. I presented my prospectus to him. He rapidly skimmed and hummed over the first side, and still more rapidly the second and concluding page; crushed it within his fingers and the palm of his hand; then most deliberately and significantly rubbed and smoothed one part against the other; and lastly putting it into his pocket turned his back on me with an "over-run with these articles!" and so without another syllable retired into his counting house. And, I can truly say, to my unspeakable amusement.

This, I have said, was my second and last attempt. On returning baffled from the first, in which I had vainly essayed to repeat the miracle of Orpheus with the Brummagem patriot, I dined with the tradesman who had introduced me to him. After dinner he importuned me to smoke a pipe with him, and two or three other illuminati of the same rank. I objected, both because I was engaged to spend the evening with a minister and his friends, and because I had never smoked except once or twice in my lifetime, and then it was herb tobacco mixed with Oronooko. On the assurance, however, that the tobacco was equally mild, and seeing too that it was of a yellow colour; not forgetting the lamentable difficulty, I have always experienced, in saying, "No," and in abstaining from what the people about me were doing,—I took half a pipe, filling the lower half of the bowl with salt. I was soon however compelled to resign it, in consequence of a giddiness and distressful feeling in my eyes, which, as I had drunk but a single glass of ale, must, I knew, have been the effect of the tobacco. Soon after, deeming myself recovered, I sallied forth to my engagement; but the walk and the fresh air brought on all the symptoms again, and, I had scarcely entered the minister's drawing-room, and opened a small pacquet of letters, which he had received from Bristol for me; ere I sank back on the sofa in a sort of swoon rather than sleep. Fortunately I had found just time enough to inform him of the confused state of my feelings, and of the occasion. For here and thus I lay, my face like a wall that is white-washing, deathly pale and with the cold drops of perspiration running down it from my forehead, while one after another there dropped in the different gentlemen, who had been invited to meet, and spend the evening with me, to the number of from fifteen to twenty. As the poison of tobacco acts but for a short time, I at length awoke from insensibility, and looked round on the party, my eyes dazzled by the candles which had been lighted in the interim. By way of relieving my embarrassment one of the gentlemen began the conversation, with "Have you seen a paper to-day, Mr. Coleridge?" "Sir!" I replied, rubbing my eyes, "I am far from convinced, that a Christian is permitted to read either newspapers or any other works of merely political and temporary interest." This remark, so ludicrously inapposite to, or rather, incongruous with, the purpose, for which I was known to have visited Birmingham, and to assist me in which they were all then met, produced an involuntary and general burst of laughter; and seldom indeed have I passed so many delightful hours, as I enjoyed in that room from the moment of that laugh till an early hour the next morning. Never, perhaps, in so mixed and numerous a party have I since heard conversation, sustained with such animation, enriched with such variety of information and enlivened with such a flow of anecdote. Both then and afterwards they all joined in dissuading me from proceeding with my scheme; assured me in the most friendly and yet most flattering expressions, that neither was the employment fit for me, nor I fit for the employment. Yet, if I determined on persevering in it, they promised to exert themselves to the utmost to procure subscribers, and insisted that I should make no more applications in person, but carry on the canvass by proxy. The same hospitable reception, the same dissuasion, and, that failing, the same kind exertions in my behalf, I met with at Manchester, Derby, Nottingham, Sheffield,—indeed, at every place in which I took up my sojourn. I often recall with affectionate pleasure the many respectable men who interested themselves for me, a perfect stranger to them, not a few of whom I can still name among my friends. They will bear witness for me how opposite even then my principles were to those of Jacobinism or even of democracy, and can attest the strict accuracy of the statement which I have left on record in the tenth and eleventh numbers of THE FRIEND.

From this rememberable tour I returned with nearly a thousand names on the subscription list of THE WATCHMAN; yet more than half convinced, that prudence dictated the abandonment of the scheme. But for this very reason I persevered in it; for I was at that period of my life so completely hag-ridden by the fear of being influenced by selfish motives, that to know a mode of conduct to be the dictate of prudence was a sort of presumptive proof to my feelings, that the contrary was the dictate of duty. Accordingly, I commenced the work, which was announced in London by long bills in letters larger than had ever been seen before, and which, I have been informed, for I did not see them myself, eclipsed the glories even of the lottery puffs. But alas! the publication of the very first number was delayed beyond the day announced for its appearance. In the second number an essay against fast days, with a most censurable application of a text from Isaiah for its motto, lost me near five hundred of my subscribers at one blow. In the two following numbers I made enemies of all my Jacobin and democratic patrons; for, disgusted by their infidelity, and their adoption of French morals with French psilosophy; and perhaps thinking, that charity ought to begin nearest home; Instead of abusing the government and the Aristocrats chiefly or entirely, as had been expected of me, I levelled my attacks at "modern patriotism," and even ventured to declare my belief, that whatever the motives of ministers might have been for the sedition, or as it was then the fashion to call them, the gagging bills, yet the bills themselves would produce an effect to be desired by all the true friends of freedom, as far as they should contribute to deter men from openly declaiming on subjects, the principles of which they had never bottomed and from "pleading to the poor and ignorant, instead of pleading for them." At the same time I avowed my conviction, that national education and a concurring spread of the Gospel were the indispensable condition of any true political melioration. Thus by the time the seventh number was published, I had the mortification—(but why should I say this, when in truth I cared too little for any thing that concerned my worldly interests to be at all mortified about it?)—of seeing the preceding numbers exposed in sundry old iron shops for a penny a piece. At the ninth number I dropt the work. But from the London publisher I could not obtain a shilling; he was a ———— and set me at defiance. From other places I procured but little, and after such delays as rendered that little worth nothing; and I should have been inevitably thrown into jail by my Bristol printer, who refused to wait even for a month, for a sum between eighty and ninety pounds, if the money had not been paid for me by a man by no means affluent, a dear friend, who attached himself to me from my first arrival at Bristol, who has continued my friend with a fidelity unconquered by time or even by my own apparent neglect; a friend from whom I never received an advice that was not wise, nor a remonstrance that was not gentle and affectionate.

Conscientiously an opponent of the first revolutionary war, yet with my eyes thoroughly opened to the true character and impotence of the favourers of revolutionary principles in England, principles which I held in abhorrence,—(for it was part of my political creed, that whoever ceased to act as an individual by making himself a member of any society not sanctioned by his Government, forfeited the rights of a citizen)—a vehement Anti-Ministerialist, but after the invasion of Switzerland, a more vehement Anti-Gallican, and still more intensely an Anti-Jacobin, I retired to a cottage at Stowey, and provided for my scanty maintenance by writing verses for a London Morning Paper. I saw plainly, that literature was not a profession, by which I could expect to live; for I could not disguise from myself, that, whatever my talents might or might not be in other respects, yet they were not of the sort that could enable me to become a popular writer; and that whatever my opinions might be in themselves, they were almost equi-distant from all the three prominent parties, the Pittites, the Foxites, and the Democrats. Of the unsaleable nature of my writings I had an amusing memento one morning from our own servant girl. For happening to rise at an earlier hour than usual, I observed her putting an extravagant quantity of paper into the grate in order to light the fire, and mildly checked her for her wastefulness; "La, Sir!" (replied poor Nanny) "why, it is only Watchmen."

I now devoted myself to poetry and to the study of ethics and psychology; and so profound was my admiration at this time of Hartley's ESSAY ON MAN, that I gave his name to my first-born. In addition to the gentleman, my neighbour, whose garden joined on to my little orchard, and the cultivation of whose friendship had been my sole motive in choosing Stowey for my residence, I was so fortunate as to acquire, shortly after my settlement there, an invaluable blessing in the society and neighbourhood of one, to whom I could look up with equal reverence, whether I regarded him as a poet, a philosopher, or a man. His conversation extended to almost all subjects, except physics and politics; with the latter he never troubled himself. Yet neither my retirement nor my utter abstraction from all the disputes of the day could secure me in those jealous times from suspicion and obloquy, which did not stop at me, but extended to my excellent friend, whose perfect innocence was even adduced as a proof of his guilt. One of the many busy sycophants of that day,—(I here use the word sycophant in its original sense, as a wretch who flatters the prevailing party by informing against his neighbours, under pretence that they are exporters of prohibited figs or fancies,—for the moral application of the term it matters not which)—one of these sycophantic law-mongrels, discoursing on the politics of the neighbourhood, uttered the following deep remark: "As to Coleridge, there is not so much harm in him, for he is a whirl-brain that talks whatever comes uppermost; but that ———! he is the dark traitor. You never hear HIM say a syllable on the subject."

Now that the hand of Providence has disciplined all Europe into sobriety, as men tame wild elephants, by alternate blows and caresses; now that Englishmen of all classes are restored to their old English notions and feelings; it will with difficulty be credited, how great an influence was at that time possessed and exerted by the spirit of secret defamation,—(the too constant attendant on party-zeal)—during the restless interim from 1793 to the commencement of the Addington administration, or the year before the truce of Amiens. For by the latter period the minds of the partizans, exhausted by excess of stimulation and humbled by mutual disappointment, had become languid. The same causes, that inclined the nation to peace, disposed the individuals to reconciliation. Both parties had found themselves in the wrong. The one had confessedly mistaken the moral character of the revolution, and the other had miscalculated both its moral and its physical resources. The experiment was made at the price of great, almost, we may say, of humiliating sacrifices; and wise men foresaw that it would fail, at least in its direct and ostensible object. Yet it was purchased cheaply, and realized an object of equal value, and, if possible, of still more vital importance. For it brought about a national unanimity unexampled in our history since the reign of Elizabeth; and Providence, never wanting to a good work when men have done their parts, soon provided a common focus in the cause of Spain, which made us all once more Englishmen by at once gratifying and correcting the predilections of both parties. The sincere reverers of the throne felt the cause of loyalty ennobled by its alliance with that of freedom; while the honest zealots of the people could not but admit, that freedom itself assumed a more winning form, humanized by loyalty and consecrated by religious principle. The youthful enthusiasts who, flattered by the morning rainbow of the French revolution, had made a boast of expatriating their hopes and fears, now, disciplined by the succeeding storms and sobered by increase of years, had been taught to prize and honour the spirit of nationality as the best safeguard of national independence, and this again as the absolute pre-requisite and necessary basis of popular rights.

If in Spain too disappointment has nipped our too forward expectations, yet all is not destroyed that is checked. The crop was perhaps springing up too rank in the stalk to kern well; and there were, doubtless, symptoms of the Gallican blight on it. If superstition and despotism have been suffered to let in their wolvish sheep to trample and eat it down even to the surface, yet the roots remain alive, and the second growth may prove the stronger and healthier for the temporary interruption. At all events, to us heaven has been just and gracious. The people of England did their best, and have received their rewards. Long may we continue to deserve it! Causes, which it had been too generally the habit of former statesmen to regard as belonging to another world, are now admitted by all ranks to have been the main agents of our success. "We fought from heaven; the stars in their courses fought against Sisera." If then unanimity grounded on moral feelings has been among the least equivocal sources of our national glory, that man deserves the esteem of his countrymen, even as patriots, who devotes his life and the utmost efforts of his intellect to the preservation and continuance of that unanimity by the disclosure and establishment of principles. For by these all opinions must be ultimately tried; and, (as the feelings of men are worthy of regard only as far as they are the representatives of their fixed opinions,) on the knowledge of these all unanimity, not accidental and fleeting, must be grounded. Let the scholar, who doubts this assertion, refer only to the speeches and writings of Edmund Burke at the commencement of the American war and compare them with his speeches and writings at the commencement of the French revolution. He will find the principles exactly the same and the deductions the same; but the practical inferences almost opposite in the one case from those drawn in the other; yet in both equally legitimate and in both equally confirmed by the results. Whence gained he the superiority of foresight? Whence arose the striking difference, and in most instances even, the discrepancy between the grounds assigned by him and by those who voted with him, on the same questions? How are we to explain the notorious fact, that the speeches and writings of Edmund Burke are more interesting at the present day than they were found at the time of their first publication; while those of his illustrious confederates are either forgotten, or exist only to furnish proofs, that the same conclusion, which one man had deduced scientifically, may be brought out by another in consequence of errors that luckily chanced to neutralize each other. It would be unhandsome as a conjecture, even were it not, as it actually is, false in point of fact to attribute this difference to the deficiency of talent on the part of Burke's friends, or of experience, or of historical knowledge. The satisfactory solution is, that Edmund Burke possessed and had sedulously sharpened that eye, which sees all things, actions, and events, in relation to the laws that determine their existence and circumscribe their possibility. He referred habitually to principles. He was a scientific statesman; and therefore a seer. For every principle contains in itself the germs of a prophecy; and, as the prophetic power is the essential privilege of science, so the fulfilment of its oracles supplies the outward and, (to men in general,) the only test of its claim to the title. Wearisome as Burke's refinements appeared to his parliamentary auditors, yet the cultivated classes throughout Europe have reason to be thankful, that he

―――――*went on refining,*
And thought of convincing, while they thought of dining.

Our very sign-boards, (said an illustrious friend to me,) give evidence, that there has been a Titian in the world. In like manner, not only the debates in parliament, not only our proclamations and state papers, but the essays and leading paragraphs of our journals are so many remembrancers of Edmund Burke. Of this the reader may easily convince himself, if either by recollection or reference he will compare the opposition newspapers at the commencement and during the five or six following years of the French revolution with the sentiments, and grounds of argument assumed in the same class of journals at present, and for some years past.

Whether the spirit of jacobinism, which the writings of Burke exorcised from the higher and from the literary classes, may not, like the ghost in Hamlet, be heard moving and mining in the underground chambers with an activity the more dangerous because less noisy, may admit of a question. I have given my opinions on this point, and the grounds of them, in my letters to judge Fletcher occasioned by his charge to the Wexford grand jury, and published in the Courier. Be this as it may, the evil spirit of jealousy, and with it the Cerberean whelps of feud and slander, no longer walk their rounds, in cultivated society.

Far different were the days to which these anecdotes have carried me back. The dark guesses of some zealous Quidnunc met with so congenial a soil in the grave alarm of a titled Dogberry of our neighbourhood, that a spy was actually sent down from the government pour surveillance of myself and friend. There must have been not only abundance, but variety of these "honourable men" at the disposal of Ministers: for this proved a very honest fellow. After three weeks' truly Indian perseverance in tracking us, (for we were commonly together,) during all which time seldom were we out of doors, but he contrived to be within hearing,—(and all the while utterly unsuspected; how indeed could such a suspicion enter our fancies?)—he not only rejected Sir Dogberry's request that he would try yet a little longer, but declared to him his belief, that both my friend and myself were as good subjects, for aught he could discover to the contrary, as any in His Majesty's dominions. He had repeatedly hid himself, he said, for hours together behind a bank at the sea-side, (our favourite seat,) and overheard our conversation. At first he fancied, that we were aware of our danger; for he often heard me talk of one Spy Nozy, which he was inclined to interpret of himself, and of a remarkable feature belonging to him; but he was speedily convinced that it was the name of a man who had made a book and lived long ago. Our talk ran most upon books, and we were perpetually desiring each other to look at this, and to listen to that; but he could not catch a word about politics. Once he had joined me on the road; (this occurred, as I was returning home alone from my friend's house, which was about three miles from my own cottage,) and, passing himself off as a traveller, he had entered into conversation with me, and talked of purpose in a democrat way in order to draw me out. The result, it appears, not only convinced him that I was no friend of jacobinism; but, (he added,) I had "plainly made it out to be such a silly as well as wicked thing, that he felt ashamed though he had only put it on." I distinctly remembered the occurrence, and had mentioned it immediately on my return, repeating what the traveller with his Bardolph nose had said, with my own answer; and so little did I suspect the true object of my "tempter ere accuser," that I expressed with no small pleasure my hope and belief, that the conversation had been of some service to the poor misled malcontent. This incident therefore prevented all doubt as to the truth of the report, which through a friendly medium came to me from the master of the village inn, who had been ordered to entertain the Government gentleman in his best manner, but above all to be silent concerning such a person being in his house. At length he received Sir Dogberry's commands to accompany his guest at the final interview; and, after the absolving suffrage of the gentleman honoured with the confidence of Ministers, answered, as follows, to the following queries: D. "Well, landlord! and what do you know of the person in question? L. I see him often pass by with maister ——, my landlord, (that is, the owner of the house,) and sometimes with the new-comers at Holford; but I never said a word to him or he to me. D. But do you not know, that he has distributed papers and hand-bills of a seditious nature among the common people? L. No, your Honour! I never heard of such a thing. D. Have you not seen this Mr. Coleridge, or heard of, his haranguing and talking to knots and clusters of the inhabitants?—What are you grinning at, Sir? L. Beg your Honour's pardon! but I was only thinking, how they'd have stared at him. If what I have heard be true, your Honour! they would not have understood a word he said. When our Vicar was here, Dr. L. the master of the great school and Canon of Windsor, there was a great dinner party at maister's; and one of the farmers, that was there, told us that he and the Doctor talked real Hebrew Greek at each other for an hour together after dinner. D. Answer the question, Sir! does he ever harangue the people? L. I hope your Honour an't angry with me. I can say no more than I know. I never saw him talking with any one, but my landlord, and our curate, and the strange gentleman. D. Has he not been seen wandering on the hills towards the Channel, and along the shore, with books and papers in his hand, taking charts and maps of the country? L. Why, as to that, your Honour! I own, I have heard; I am sure, I would not wish to say ill of any body; but it is certain, that I have heard—D. Speak out, man! don't be afraid, you are doing your duty to your King and Government. What have you heard? L. Why, folks do say, your Honour! as how that he is a Poet, and that he is going to put Quantock and all about here in print; and as they be so much together, I suppose that the strange gentleman has some consarn in the business."—So ended this formidable inquisition, the latter part of which alone requires explanation, and at the same time entitles the anecdote to a place in my literary life. I had considered it as a defect in the admirable poem of THE TASK, that the subject, which gives the title to the work, was not, and indeed could not be, carried on beyond the three or four first pages, and that, throughout the poem, the connections are frequently awkward, and the transitions abrupt and arbitrary. I sought for a subject, that should give equal room and freedom for description, incident, and impassioned reflections on men, nature, and society, yet supply in itself a natural connection to the parts, and unity to the whole. Such a subject I conceived myself to have found in a stream, traced from its source in the hills among the yellow-red moss and conical glass-shaped tufts of bent, to the first break or fall, where its drops become audible, and it begins to form a channel; thence to the peat and turf barn, itself built of the same dark squares as it sheltered; to the sheepfold; to the first cultivated plot of ground; to the lonely cottage and its bleak garden won from the heath; to the hamlet, the villages, the market-town, the manufactories, and the seaport. My walks therefore were almost daily on the top of Quantock, and among its sloping coombes. With my pencil and memorandum-book in my hand, I was making studies, as the artists call them, and often moulding my thoughts into verse, with the objects and imagery immediately before my senses. Many circumstances, evil and good, intervened to prevent the completion of the poem, which was to have been entitled THE BROOK. Had I finished the work, it was my purpose in the heat of the moment to have dedicated it to our then committee of public safety as containing the charts and maps, with which I was to have supplied the French Government in aid of their plans of invasion. And these too for a tract of coast that, from Clevedon to Minehead, scarcely permits the approach of a fishing-boat!

All my experience from my first entrance into life to the present hour is in favour of the warning maxim, that the man, who opposes in toto the political or religious zealots of his age, is safer from their obloquy than he who differs from them but in one or two points, or perhaps only in degree. By that transfer of the feelings of private life into the discussion of public questions, which is the queen bee in the hive of party fanaticism, the partisan has more sympathy with an intemperate opposite than with a moderate friend. We now enjoy an intermission, and long may it continue! In addition to far higher and more important merits, our present Bible societies and other numerous associations for national or charitable objects, may serve perhaps to carry off the superfluous activity and fervour of stirring minds in innocent hyperboles and the bustle of management. But the poison-tree is not dead, though the sap may for a season have subsided to its roots. At least let us not be lulled into such a notion of our entire security, as not to keep watch and ward, even on our best feelings. I have seen gross intolerance shown in support of toleration; sectarian antipathy most obtrusively displayed in the promotion of an undistinguishing comprehension of sects: and acts of cruelty, (I had almost said,) of treachery, committed in furtherance of an object vitally important to the cause of humanity; and all this by men too of naturally kind dispositions and exemplary conduct.

The magic rod of fanaticism is preserved in the very adyta of human nature; and needs only the re-exciting warmth of a master hand to bud forth afresh and produce the old fruits. The horror of the Peasants' war in Germany, and the direful effects of the Anabaptists' tenets, (which differed only from those of jacobinism by the substitution of theological for philosophical jargon,) struck all Europe for a time with affright. Yet little more than a century was sufficient to obliterate all effective memory of these events. The same principles with similar though less dreadful consequences were again at work from the imprisonment of the first Charles to the restoration of his son. The fanatic maxim of extirpating fanaticism by persecution produced a civil war. The war ended in the victory of the insurgents; but the temper survived, and Milton had abundant grounds for asserting, that "Presbyter was but OLD PRIEST writ large!" One good result, thank heaven! of this zealotry was the re-establishment of the church. And now it might have been hoped, that the mischievous spirit would have been bound for a season, "and a seal set upon him, that he should deceive the nation no more." [33] But no! The ball of persecution was taken up with undiminished vigour by the persecuted. The same fanatic principle that, under the solemn oath and covenant, had turned cathedrals into stables, destroyed the rarest trophies of art and ancestral piety, and hunted the brightest ornaments of learning and religion into holes and corners, now marched under episcopal banners, and, having first crowded the prisons of England, emptied its whole vial of wrath on the miserable Covenanters of Scotland [34]. A merciful providence at length constrained both parties to join against a common enemy. A wise government followed; and the established church became, and now is, not only the brightest example, but our best and only sure bulwark, of toleration!—the true and indispensable bank against a new inundation of persecuting zeal—Esto perpetua!

A long interval of quiet succeeded; or rather, the exhaustion had produced a cold fit of the ague which was symptomatized by indifference among the many, and a tendency to infidelity or scepticism in the educated classes. At length those feelings of disgust and hatred, which for a brief while the multitude had attached to the crimes and absurdities of sectarian and democratic fanaticism, were transferred to the oppressive privileges of the noblesse, and the luxury; intrigues and favouritism of the continental courts. The same principles, dressed in the ostentatious garb of a fashionable philosophy, once more rose triumphant and effected the French revolution. And have we not within the last three or four years had reason to apprehend, that the detestable maxims and correspondent measures of the late French despotism had already bedimmed the public recollections of democratic phrensy; had drawn off to other objects the electric force of the feelings which had massed and upheld those recollections; and that a favourable concurrence of occasions was alone wanting to awaken the thunder and precipitate the lightning from the opposite quarter of the political heaven?

In part from constitutional indolence, which in the very hey-day of hope had kept my enthusiasm in check, but still more from the habits and influences of a classical education and academic pursuits, scarcely had a year elapsed from the commencement of my literary and political adventures before my mind sank into a state of thorough disgust and despondency, both with regard to the disputes and the parties disputant. With more than poetic feeling I exclaimed:

The sensual and the dark rebel in vain,
Slaves by their own compulsion! In mad game
They break their manacles, to wear the name
Of freedom, graven on a heavier chain.
O Liberty! with profitless endeavour
Have I pursued thee many a weary hour;
But thou nor swell'st the victor's pomp, nor ever
Didst breathe thy soul in forms of human power!
Alike from all, howe'er they praise thee,
(Nor prayer nor boastful name delays thee)
From Superstition's harpy minions
And factious Blasphemy's obscener slaves,
Thou speedest on thy cherub pinions,
The guide of homeless winds and playmate of the waves!

I retired to a cottage in Somersetshire at the foot of Quantock, and devoted my thoughts and studies to the foundations of religion and morals. Here I found myself all afloat. Doubts rushed in; broke upon me "from the fountains of the great deep," and fell "from the windows of heaven." The fontal truths of natural religion and the books of Revelation alike contributed to the flood; and it was long ere my ark touched on an Ararat, and rested. The idea of the Supreme Being appeared to me to be as necessarily implied in all particular modes of being as the idea of infinite space in all the geometrical figures by which space is limited. I was pleased with the Cartesian opinion, that the idea of God is distinguished from all other ideas by involving its reality; but I was not wholly satisfied. I began then to ask myself, what proof I had of the outward existence of anything? Of this sheet of paper for instance, as a thing in itself, separate from the phaenomenon or image in my perception. I saw, that in the nature of things such proof is impossible; and that of all modes of being, that are not objects of the senses, the existence is assumed by a logical necessity arising from the constitution of the mind itself,—by the absence of all motive to doubt it, not from any absolute contradiction in the supposition of the contrary. Still the existence of a Being, the ground of all existence, was not yet the existence of a moral creator, and governour. "In the position, that all reality is either contained in the necessary being as an attribute, or exists through him, as its ground, it remains undecided whether the properties of intelligence and will are to be referred to the Supreme Being in the former or only in the latter sense; as inherent attributes, or only as consequences that have existence in other things through him [35]. Were the latter the truth, then notwithstanding all the pre-eminence which must be assigned to the Eternal First from the sufficiency, unity, and independence of his being, as the dread ground of the universe, his nature would yet fall far short of that, which we are bound to comprehend in the idea of GOD. For, without any knowledge or determining resolve of its own, it would only be a blind necessary ground of other things and other spirits; and thus would be distinguished from the FATE of certain ancient philosophers in no respect, but that of being more definitely and intelligibly described."

For a very long time, indeed, I could not reconcile personality with infinity; and my head was with Spinoza, though my whole heart remained with Paul and John. Yet there had dawned upon me, even before I had met with the CRITIQUE OF THE PURE REASON, a certain guiding light. If the mere intellect could make no certain discovery of a holy and intelligent first cause, it might yet supply a demonstration, that no legitimate argument could be drawn from the intellect against its truth. And what is this more than St. Paul's assertion, that by wisdom,—(more properly translated by the powers of reasoning)—no man ever arrived at the knowledge of God? What more than the sublimest, and probably the oldest, book on earth has taught us,

Silver and gold man searcheth out:
Bringeth the ore out of the earth, and darkness into light.

But where findeth he wisdom?

Where is the place of understanding?

The abyss crieth; it is not in me!
Ocean echoeth back; not in me!

Whence then cometh wisdom?
Where dwelleth understanding?

Hidden from the eyes of the living
Kept secret from the fowls of heaven!

Hell and death answer;
We have heard the rumour thereof from afar!

GOD marketh out the road to it;
GOD knoweth its abiding place!

He beholdeth the ends of the earth;
He surveyeth what is beneath the heavens!

And as he weighed out the winds, and measured the sea,
And appointed laws to the rain,
And a path to the thunder,
A path to the flashes of the lightning!

Then did he see it,
And he counted it;
He searched into the depth thereof,
And with a line did he compass it round!

But to man he said,
The fear of the Lord is wisdom for thee!
And to avoid evil,
That is thy understanding. [36]

I become convinced, that religion, as both the cornerstone and the keystone of morality, must have a moral origin; so far at least, that the evidence of its doctrines could not, like the truths of abstract science, be wholly independent of the will. It were therefore to be expected, that its fundamental truth would be such as might be denied; though only, by the fool, and even by the fool from the madness of the heart alone!

The question then concerning our faith in the existence of a God, not only as the ground of the universe by his essence, but as its maker and judge by his wisdom and holy will, appeared to stand thus. The sciential reason, the objects of which are purely theoretical, remains neutral, as long as its name and semblance are not usurped by the opponents of the doctrine. But it then becomes an effective ally by exposing the false show of demonstration, or by evincing the equal demonstrability of the contrary from premises equally logical [37]. The understanding meantime suggests, the analogy of experience facilitates, the belief. Nature excites and recalls it, as by a perpetual revelation. Our feelings almost necessitate it; and the law of conscience peremptorily commands it. The arguments, that at all apply to it, are in its favour; and there is nothing against it, but its own sublimity. It could not be intellectually more evident without becoming morally less effective; without counteracting its own end by sacrificing the life of faith to the cold mechanism of a worth less because compulsory assent. The belief of a God and a future state, (if a passive acquiescence may be flattered with the name of belief,) does not indeed always beget a good heart; but a good heart so naturally begets the belief, that the very few exceptions must be regarded as strange anomalies from strange and unfortunate circumstances.

From these premises I proceeded to draw the following conclusions. First, that having once fully admitted the existence of an infinite yet self-conscious Creator, we are not allowed to ground the irrationality of any other article of faith on arguments which would equally prove that to be irrational, which we had allowed to be real. Secondly, that whatever is deducible from the admission of a self-comprehending and creative spirit may be legitimately used in proof of the possibility of any further mystery concerning the divine nature. Possibilitatem mysteriorum, (Trinitatis, etc.) contra insultus Infidelium et Haereticorum a contradictionibus vindico; haud quidem veritatem, quae revelatione sola stabiliri possit; says Leibnitz in a letter to his Duke. He then adds the following just and important remark. "In vain will tradition or texts of scripture be adduced in support of a doctrine, donec clava impossibilitatis et contradictionis e manibus horum Herculum extorta fuerit. For the heretic will still reply, that texts, the literal sense of which is not so much above as directly against all reason, must be understood figuratively, as Herod is a fox, and so forth."

These principles I held, philosophically, while in respect of revealed religion I remained a zealous Unitarian. I considered the idea of the Trinity a fair scholastic inference from the being of God, as a creative intelligence; and that it was therefore entitled to the rank of an esoteric doctrine of natural religion. But seeing in the same no practical or moral bearing, I confined it to the schools of philosophy. The admission of the Logos, as hypostasized (that is, neither a mere attribute, nor a personification) in no respect removed my doubts concerning the Incarnation and the Redemption by the cross; which I could neither reconcile in reason with the impassiveness of the Divine Being, nor in my moral feelings with the sacred distinction between things and persons, the vicarious payment of a debt and the vicarious expiation of guilt. A more thorough revolution in my philosophic principles, and a deeper insight into my own heart, were yet wanting. Nevertheless, I cannot doubt, that the difference of my metaphysical notions from those of Unitarians in general contributed to my final reconversion to the whole truth in Christ; even as according to his own confession the books of certain Platonic philosophers (libri quorundam Platonicorum) commenced the rescue of St. Augustine's faith from the same error aggravated by the far darker accompaniment of the Manichaean heresy.

While my mind was thus perplexed, by a gracious providence for which I can never be sufficiently grateful, the generous and munificent patronage of Mr. Josiah, and Mr. Thomas Wedgwood enabled me to finish my education in Germany. Instead of troubling others with my own crude notions and juvenile compositions, I was thenceforward better employed in attempting to store my own head with the wisdom of others. I made the best use of my time and means; and there is therefore no period of my life on which I can look back with such unmingled satisfaction. After acquiring a tolerable sufficiency in the German language [38] at Ratzeburg, which with my voyage and journey thither I have described in The Friend, I proceeded through Hanover to Goettingen.

Here I regularly attended the lectures on physiology in the morning, and on natural history in the evening, under Blumenbach, a name as dear to every Englishman who has studied at that university, as it is venerable to men of science throughout Europe! Eichhorn's lectures on the New Testament were repeated to me from notes by a student from Ratzeburg, a young man of sound learning and indefatigable industry, who is now, I believe, a professor of the oriental languages at Heidelberg. But my chief efforts were directed towards a grounded knowledge of the German language and literature. From professor Tychsen I received as many lessons in the Gothic of Ulphilas as sufficed to make me acquainted with its grammar, and the radical words of most frequent occurrence; and with the occasional assistance of the same philosophical linguist, I read through [39] Ottfried's metrical paraphrase of the gospel, and the most important remains of the Theotiscan, or the transitional state of the Teutonic language from the Gothic to the old German of the Swabian period. Of this period—(the polished dialect of which is analogous to that of our Chaucer, and which leaves the philosophic student in doubt, whether the language has not since then lost more in sweetness and flexibility, than it has gained in condensation and copiousness)—I read with sedulous accuracy the

Minnesinger (or singers of love, the Provencal poets of the Swabian court) and the metrical romances; and then laboured through sufficient specimens of the master singers, their degenerate successors; not however without occasional pleasure from the rude, yet interesting strains of Hans Sachs, the cobbler of Nuremberg. Of this man's genius five folio volumes with double columns are extant in print, and nearly an equal number in manuscript; yet the indefatigable bard takes care to inform his readers, that he never made a shoe the less, but had virtuously reared a large family by the labour of his hands.

In Pindar, Chaucer, Dante, Milton, and many more, we have instances of the close connection of poetic genius with the love of liberty and of genuine reformation. The moral sense at least will not be outraged, if I add to the list the name of this honest shoemaker, (a trade by the by remarkable for the production of philosophers and poets).

His poem entitled THE MORNING STAR, was the very first publication that appeared in praise and support of Luther; and an excellent hymn of Hans Sachs, which has been deservedly translated into almost all the European languages, was commonly sung in the Protestant churches, whenever the heroic reformer visited them.

In Luther's own German writings, and eminently in his translation of the Bible, the German language commenced. I mean the language as it is at present written; that which is called the High-German, as contra-distinguished from the Platt-Teutsch, the dialect on the flat or northern countries, and from the Ober-Teutsch, the language of the middle and Southern Germany. The High German is indeed a lingua communis, not actually the native language of any province, but the choice and fragrancy of all the dialects. From this cause it is at once the most copious and the most grammatical of all the European tongues.

Within less than a century after Luther's death the German was inundated with pedantic barbarisms. A few volumes of this period I read through from motives of curiosity; for it is not easy to imagine any thing more fantastic, than the very appearance of their pages. Almost every third word is a Latin word with a Germanized ending, the Latin portion being always printed in Roman letters, while in the last syllable the German character is retained.

At length, about the year 1620, Opitz arose, whose genius more nearly resembled that of Dryden than any other poet, who at present occurs to my recollection. In the opinion of Lessing, the most acute of critics, and of Adelung, the first of Lexicographers, Opitz, and the Silesian poets, his followers, not only restored the language, but still remain the models of pure diction. A stranger has no vote on such a question; but after repeated perusal of the works of Opitz my feelings justified the verdict, and I seemed to have acquired from them a sort of tact for what is genuine in the style of later writers.

Of the splendid aera, which commenced with Gellert, Klopstock, Ramler, Lessing, and their compeers, I need not speak. With the opportunities which I enjoyed, it would have been disgraceful not to have been familiar with their writings; and I have already said as much as the present biographical sketch requires concerning the German philosophers, whose works, for the greater part, I became acquainted with at a far later period.

Soon after my return from Germany I was solicited to undertake the literary and political department in the Morning Post; and I acceded to the proposal on the condition that the paper should thenceforwards be conducted on certain fixed and announced principles, and that I should neither be obliged nor requested to deviate from them in favour of any party or any event. In consequence, that journal became and for many years continued anti-ministerial indeed, yet with a very qualified approbation of the opposition, and with far greater earnestness and zeal both anti-Jacobin and anti-Gallican. To this hour I cannot find reason to approve of the first war either in its commencement or its conduct. Nor can I understand, with what reason either Mr. Perceval, (whom I am singular enough to regard as the best and wisest minister of this reign,) nor the present Administration, can be said to have pursued the plans of Mr. Pitt. The love of their country, and perseverant hostility to French principles and French ambition are indeed honourable qualities common to them and to their predecessor. But it appears to me as clear as the evidence of the facts can render any question of history, that the successes of the Perceval and of the existing ministry have been owing to their having pursued measures the direct contrary to Mr. Pitt's. Such for instance are the concentration of the national force to one object; the abandonment of the subsidizing policy, so far at least as neither to goad nor bribe the continental courts into war, till the convictions of their subjects had rendered it a war of their own seeking; and above all, in their manly and generous reliance on the good sense of the English people, and on that loyalty which is linked to the very [40] heart of the nation by the system of credit and the interdependence of property.

Be this as it may, I am persuaded that the Morning Post proved a far more useful ally to the Government in its most important objects, in consequence of its being generally considered as moderately anti-ministerial, than if it had been the avowed eulogist of Mr. Pitt. The few, whose curiosity or fancy should lead them to turn over the journals of that date, may find a small proof of this in the frequent charges made by the Morning Chronicle, that such and such essays or leading paragraphs had been sent from the Treasury. The rapid and unusual increase in the sale of the Morning Post is a sufficient pledge, that genuine impartiality with a respectable portion of literary talent will secure the success of a newspaper without the aid of party or ministerial patronage. But by impartiality I mean an honest and enlightened adherence to a code of intelligible principles previously announced, and faithfully referred to in support of every judgment on men and events; not indiscriminate abuse, not the indulgence of an editor's own malignant passions, and still less, if that be possible, a determination to make money by flattering the envy and cupidity, the vindictive restlessness and self-conceit of the half-witted vulgar; a determination almost fiendish, but which, I have been informed, has been boastfully avowed by one man, the most notorious of these mob-sycophants! From the commencement of the Addington administration to the present day, whatever I have written in THE MORNING POST, or (after that paper was transferred to other proprietors) in THE COURIER, has been in defence or furtherance of the measures of Government.

Things of this nature scarce survive that night
That gives them birth; they perish in the sight;
Cast by so far from after-life, that there
Can scarcely aught be said, but that they were!

Yet in these labours I employed, and, in the belief of partial friends wasted, the prime and manhood of my intellect. Most assuredly, they added nothing to my fortune or my reputation. The industry of the week supplied the necessities of the week. From government or the friends of government I not only never received remuneration, nor ever expected it; but I was never honoured with a single acknowledgment, or expression of satisfaction. Yet the retrospect is far from painful or matter of regret. I am not indeed silly enough to take as any thing more than a violent hyperbole of party debate, Mr. Fox's assertion that the late war (I trust that the epithet is not prematurely applied) was a war produced by the Morning Post; or I should be proud to have the words inscribed on my tomb. As little do I regard the circumstance, that I was a specified object of Buonaparte's resentment during my residence in Italy in consequence of those essays in the Morning Post during the peace of Amiens. Of this I was warned, directly, by Baron Von Humboldt, the Prussian Plenipotentiary, who at that time was the minister of the Prussian court at Rome; and indirectly, through his secretary, by Cardinal Fesch himself. Nor do I lay any greater weight on the confirming fact, that an order for my arrest was sent from Paris, from which danger I was rescued by the kindness of a noble Benedictine, and the gracious connivance of that good old man, the present Pope. For the late tyrant's vindictive appetite was omnivorous, and preyed equally on a Duc d'Enghien [41], and the writer of a newspaper paragraph. Like a true vulture [42], Napoleon with an eye not less telescopic, and with a taste equally coarse in his ravin, could descend from the most dazzling heights to pounce on the leveret in the brake, or even on the field mouse amid the grass. But I do derive a gratification from the knowledge, that my essays contributed to introduce the practice of placing the questions and events of the day in a moral point of view; in giving a dignity to particular measures by tracing their policy or impolicy to permanent principles, and an interest to principles by the application of them to individual measures. In Mr. Burke's writings indeed the germs of almost all political truths may be found. But I dare assume to myself the merit of having first explicitly defined and analyzed the nature of Jacobinism; and that in distinguishing the Jacobin from the republican, the democrat, and the mere demagogue, I both rescued the word from remaining a mere term of abuse, and put on their guard many honest minds, who even in their heat of zeal against Jacobinism, admitted or supported principles from which the worst parts of that system may be legitimately deduced. That these are not necessary practical results of such principles, we owe to that fortunate inconsequence of our nature, which permits the heart to rectify the errors of the understanding. The detailed examination of the consular Government and its pretended constitution, and the proof given by me, that it was a consummate despotism in masquerade, extorted a recantation even from the Morning Chronicle, which had previously extolled this constitution as the perfection of a wise and regulated liberty. On every great occurrence I endeavoured to discover in past history the event, that most nearly resembled it. I procured, wherever it was possible, the contemporary historians, memorialists, and pamphleteers. Then fairly subtracting the points of difference from those of likeness, as the balance favoured the former or the latter, I conjectured that the result would be the same or different. In the series of essays entitled "A comparison of France under Napoleon with Rome under the first Caesars," and in those which followed "On the probable final restoration of the Bourbons," I feel myself authorized to affirm, by the effect produced on many intelligent men, that, were the dates wanting, it might have been suspected that the essays had been written within the last twelve months. The same plan I pursued at the commencement of the Spanish revolution, and with the same success, taking the war of the United Provinces with Philip II as the ground work of the comparison. I have mentioned this from no motives of vanity, nor even from motives of self defence, which would justify a certain degree of egotism, especially if it be considered, how often and grossly I have been attacked for sentiments, which I have exerted my best powers to confute and expose, and how grievously these charges acted to my disadvantage while I was in Malta. Or rather they would have done so, if my own feelings had not precluded the wish of a settled establishment in that island. But I have mentioned it from the full persuasion that, armed with the two-fold knowledge of history and the human mind, a man will scarcely err in his judgment concerning the sum total of any future national event, if he have been able to procure the original documents of the past, together with authentic accounts of the present, and if he have a philosophic tact for what is truly important in facts, and in most instances therefore for such facts as the dignity of history has excluded from the volumes of our modern compilers, by the courtesy of the age entitled historians.

To have lived in vain must be a painful thought to any man, and especially so to him who has made literature his profession. I should therefore rather condole than be angry with the mind, which could attribute to no worthier feelings than those of vanity or self-love, the satisfaction which I acknowledged myself to have enjoyed from the republication of my political essays (either whole or as extracts) not only in many of our own provincial papers, but in the federal journals throughout America. I regarded it as some proof of my not having laboured altogether in vain, that from the articles written by me shortly before and at the commencement of the late unhappy war with America, not only the sentiments were adopted, but in some instances the very language, in several of the Massachusetts state papers.

But no one of these motives nor all conjointly would have impelled me to a statement so uncomfortable to my own feelings, had not my character been repeatedly attacked, by an unjustifiable intrusion on private life, as of a man incorrigibly idle, and who intrusted not only with ample talents, but favoured with unusual opportunities of improving them, had nevertheless suffered them to rust away without any efficient exertion, either for his own good or that of his fellow creatures. Even if the compositions, which I have made public, and that too in a form the most certain of an extensive circulation, though the least flattering to an author's self-love, had been published in books, they would have filled a respectable number of volumes, though every passage of merely temporary interest were omitted. My prose writings have been charged with a disproportionate demand on the attention; with an excess of refinement in the mode of arriving at truths; with beating the ground for that which might have been run down by the eye; with the length and laborious construction of my periods; in short with obscurity and the love of paradox. But my severest critics have not pretended to have found in my compositions triviality, or traces of a mind that shrunk from the toil of thinking. No one has charged me with tricking out in other words the thoughts of others, or with hashing up anew the cramben jam decies coctam of English literature or philosophy. Seldom have I written that in a day, the acquisition or investigation of which had not cost me the previous labour of a month.

But are books the only channel through which the stream of intellectual usefulness can flow? Is the diffusion of truth to be estimated by publications; or publications by the truth, which they diffuse or at least contain? I speak it in the excusable warmth of a mind stung by an accusation, which has not only been advanced in reviews of the widest circulation, not only registered in the bulkiest works of periodical literature, but by frequency of repetition has become an admitted fact in private literary circles, and thoughtlessly repeated by too many who call themselves my friends, and whose own recollections ought to have suggested a contrary testimony. Would that the criterion of a scholar's utility were the number and moral value of the truths, which he has been the means of throwing into the general circulation; or the number and value of the minds, whom by his conversation or letters, he has excited into activity, and supplied with the germs of their after-growth! A distinguished rank might not indeed, even then, be awarded to my exertions; but I should dare look forward with confidence to an honourable acquittal. I should dare appeal to the numerous and respectable audiences, which at different times and in different places honoured my lecture rooms with their attendance, whether the points of view from which the subjects treated of were surveyed,— whether the grounds of my reasoning were such, as they had heard or read elsewhere, or have since found in previous publications. I can conscientiously declare, that the complete success of the REMORSE on the first night of its representation did not give me as great or as heart-felt a pleasure, as the observation that the pit and boxes were crowded with faces familiar to me, though of individuals whose names I did not know, and of whom I knew nothing, but that they had attended one or other of my courses of lectures. It is an excellent though perhaps somewhat vulgar proverb, that there are cases where a man may be as well "in for a pound as for a penny." To those, who from ignorance of the serious injury I have received from this rumour of having dreamed away my life to no purpose, injuries which I unwillingly remember at all, much less am disposed to record in a sketch of my literary life; or to those, who from their own feelings, or the gratification they derive from thinking contemptuously of others, would like job's comforters attribute these complaints, extorted from me by the sense of wrong, to self conceit or presumptuous vanity, I have already furnished such ample materials, that I shall gain nothing by withholding the remainder. I will not therefore hesitate to ask the consciences of those, who from their long acquaintance with me and with the circumstances are best qualified to decide or be my judges, whether the restitution of the suum cuique would increase or detract from my literary reputation. In this exculpation I hope to be understood as speaking of myself comparatively, and in proportion to the claims, which others are entitled to make on my time or my talents. By what I have effected, am I to be judged by my fellow men; what I could have done, is a question for my own conscience. On my own account I may perhaps have had sufficient reason to lament my deficiency in self-control, and the neglect of concentering my powers to the realization of some permanent work. But to verse rather than to prose, if to either, belongs the voice of mourning for

Keen pangs of Love, awakening as a babe
Turbulent, with an outcry in the heart;
And fears self-willed that shunned the eye of hope;
And hope that scarce would know itself from fear;
Sense of past youth, and manhood come in vain,
And genius given and knowledge won in vain;
And all which I had culled in wood-walks wild,
And all which patient toil had reared, and all,
Commune with thee had opened out—but flowers
Strewed on my corpse, and borne upon my bier,
In the same coffin, for the self-same grave!

These will exist, for the future, I trust, only in the poetic strains, which the feelings at the time called forth. In those only, gentle reader,

Affectus animi varios, bellumque sequacis
Perlegis invidiae, curasque revolvis inanes,
Quas humilis tenero stylus olim effudit in aevo.
Perlegis et lacrymas, et quod pharetratus acuta
Ille puer puero fecit mihi cuspide vulnus.
Omnia paulatim consumit longior aetas,
Vivendoque simul morimur, rapimurque manendo.
Ipse mihi collatus enim non ille videbor;
Frons alia est, moresque alii, nova mentis imago,
Vox aliudque sonat—Jamque observatio vitae
Multa dedit—lugere nihil, ferre omnia; jamque
Paulatim lacrymas rerum experientia tersit.

CHAPTER XI

An affectionate exhortation to those who in early life feel themselves disposed to become authors.

It was a favourite remark of the late Mr. Whitbread's, that no man does any thing from a single motive. The separate motives, or rather moods of mind, which produced the preceding reflections and anecdotes have been laid open to the reader in each separate instance. But an interest in the welfare of those, who at the present time may be in circumstances not dissimilar to my own at my first entrance into life, has been the constant accompaniment, and (as it were) the under-song of all my feelings. Whitehead exerting the prerogative of his laureateship addressed to youthful poets a poetic Charge, which is perhaps the best, and certainly the most interesting, of his works. With no other privilege than that of sympathy and sincere good wishes, I would address an affectionate exhortation to the youthful literati, grounded on my own experience. It will be but short; for the beginning, middle, and end converge to one charge: never pursue literature as a trade. With the exception of one extraordinary man, I have never known an individual, least of all an individual of genius, healthy or happy without a profession, that is, some regular employment, which does not depend on the will of the moment, and which can be carried on so far mechanically that an average quantum only of health, spirits, and intellectual exertion are requisite to its faithful discharge. Three hours of leisure, unannoyed by any alien anxiety, and looked forward to with delight as a change and recreation, will suffice to realize in literature a larger product of what is truly genial, than weeks of compulsion. Money, and immediate reputation form only an arbitrary and accidental end of literary labour. The hope of increasing them by any given exertion will often prove a stimulant to industry; but the necessity of acquiring them will in all works of genius convert the stimulant into a narcotic. Motives by excess reverse their very nature, and instead of exciting, stun and stupify the mind. For it is one contradistinction of genius from talent, that its predominant end is always comprised in the means; and this is one of the many points, which establish an analogy between genius and virtue. Now though talents may exist without genius, yet as genius cannot exist, certainly not manifest itself, without talents, I would advise every scholar, who feels the genial power working within him, so far to make a division between the two, as that he should devote his talents to the acquirement of competence in some known trade or profession, and his genius to objects of his tranquil and unbiassed choice; while the consciousness of being actuated in both alike by the sincere desire to perform his duty, will alike ennoble both. "My dear young friend," (I would say) "suppose yourself established in any honourable occupation. From the manufactory or counting house, from the law-court, or from having visited your last patient, you return at evening,

Dear tranquil time, when the sweet sense of Home
Is sweetest———

to your family, prepared for its social enjoyments, with the very countenances of your wife and children brightened, and their voice of welcome made doubly welcome, by the knowledge that, as far as they are concerned, you have satisfied the demands of the day by the labour of the day. Then, when you retire into your study, in the books on your shelves you revisit so many venerable friends with whom you can converse. Your own spirit scarcely less free from personal anxieties than the great minds, that in those books are still living for you! Even your writing desk with its blank paper and all its other implements will appear as a chain of flowers, capable of linking your feelings as well as thoughts to events and characters past or to come; not a chain of iron, which binds you down to think of the future and the remote by recalling the claims and feelings of the peremptory present. But why should I say retire? The habits of active life and daily intercourse with the stir of the world will tend to give you such self-command, that the presence of your family will be no interruption. Nay, the social silence, or undisturbing voices of a wife or sister will be like a restorative atmosphere, or soft music which moulds a dream without becoming its object. If facts are required to prove the possibility of combining weighty performances in literature with full and independent employment, the works of Cicero and Xenophon among the ancients; of Sir Thomas More, Bacon, Baxter, or to refer at once to later and contemporary instances, Darwin and Roscoe, are at once decisive of the question."

But all men may not dare promise themselves a sufficiency of self- control for the imitation of those examples: though strict scrutiny should always be made, whether indolence, restlessness, or a vanity impatient for immediate gratification, have not tampered with the judgment and assumed the vizard of humility for the purposes of self- delusion. Still the Church presents to every man of learning and genius a profession, in which he may cherish a rational hope of being able to unite the widest schemes of literary utility with the strictest performance of professional duties. Among the numerous blessings of Christianity, the introduction of an established Church makes an especial claim on the gratitude of scholars and philosophers; in England, at least, where the principles of Protestantism have conspired with the freedom of the government to double all its salutary powers by the removal of its abuses.

That not only the maxims, but the grounds of a pure morality, the mere fragments of which

————*the lofty grave tragedians taught*
In chorus or iambic, teachers best
Of moral prudence, with delight received
In brief sententious precepts; [43]

and that the sublime truths of the divine unity and attributes, which a Plato found most hard to learn and deemed it still more difficult to reveal; that these should have become the almost hereditary property of childhood and poverty, of the hovel and the workshop; that even to the unlettered they sound as common place, is a phaenomenon, which must withhold all but minds of the most vulgar cast from undervaluing the services even of the pulpit and the reading desk. Yet those, who confine the efficiency of an established Church to its public offices, can hardly be placed in a much higher rank of intellect. That to every parish throughout the kingdom there is transplanted a germ of civilization; that in the remotest villages there is a nucleus, round which the capabilities of the place may crystallize and brighten; a model sufficiently superior to excite, yet sufficiently near to encourage and facilitate, imitation; this, the unobtrusive, continuous agency of a protestant church establishment, this it is, which the patriot, and the philanthropist, who would fain unite the love of peace with the faith in the progressive melioration of mankind, cannot estimate at too high a price. It cannot be valued with the gold of Ophir, with the precious onyx, or the sapphire. No mention shall be made of coral, or of pearls: for the price of wisdom is above rubies. The clergyman is with his parishioners and among them; he is neither in the cloistered cell, nor in the wilderness, but a neighbour and a family-man, whose education and rank admit him to the mansion of the rich landholder, while his duties make him the frequent visitor of the farmhouse and the cottage. He is, or he may become, connected, with the families of his parish or its vicinity by marriage. And among the instances of the blindness, or at best of the short-sightedness, which it is the nature of cupidity to inflict, I know few more striking than the clamours of the farmers against Church property. Whatever was not paid to the clergyman would inevitably at the next lease be paid to the landholder, while, as the case at present stands, the revenues of the Church are in some sort the reversionary property of every family, that may have a member educated for the Church, or a daughter that may marry a clergyman. Instead of being foreclosed and immovable, it is in fact the only species of landed property, that is essentially moving and circulative. That there exist no inconveniences, who will pretend to assert? But I have yet to expect the proof, that the inconveniences are greater in this than in any other species; or that either the farmers or the clergy would be benefited by forcing the latter to become either Trullibers or salaried placemen. Nay, I do not hesitate to declare my firm persuasion, that whatever reason of discontent the farmers may assign, the true cause is this; that they may cheat the parson, but cannot cheat the steward; and that they are disappointed, if they should have been able to withhold only two pounds less than the legal claim, having expected to withhold five. At all events, considered relatively to the encouragement of learning and genius, the establishment presents a patronage at once so effective and unburdensome, that it would be impossible to afford the like or equal in any but a Christian and Protestant country. There is scarce a department of human knowledge without some bearing on the various critical, historical, philosophical and moral truths, in which the scholar must be interested as a clergyman; no one pursuit worthy of a man of genius, which may not be followed without incongruity. To give the history of the Bible as a book, would be little less than to relate the origin or first excitement of all the literature and science, that we now possess. The very decorum, which the profession imposes, is favourable to the best purposes of genius, and tends to counteract its most frequent defects. Finally, that man must be deficient in sensibility, who would not find an incentive to emulation in the great and burning lights, which in a long series have illustrated the church of England; who would not hear from within an echo to the voice from their sacred shrines,

Et Pater Aeneas et avunculus excitat Hector.

But, whatever be the profession or trade chosen, the advantages are many and important, compared with the state of a mere literary man, who in any degree depends on the sale of his works for the necessaries and comforts of life. In the former a man lives in sympathy with the world, in which he lives. At least he acquires a better and quicker tact for the knowledge of that, with which men in general can sympathize. He learns to manage his genius more prudently and efficaciously. His powers and acquirements gain him likewise more real admiration; for they surpass the legitimate expectations of others. He is something besides an author, and is not therefore considered merely as an author. The hearts of men are open to him, as to one of their own class; and whether he exerts himself or not in the conversational circles of his acquaintance, his silence is not attributed to pride, nor his communicativeness to vanity. To these advantages I will venture to add a superior chance of happiness in domestic life, were it only that it is as natural for the man to be out of the circle of his household during the day, as it is meritorious for the woman to remain for the most part within it. But this subject involves points of consideration so numerous and so delicate, and would not only permit, but require such ample documents from the biography of literary men, that I now merely allude to it in transitu. When the same circumstance has occurred at very different times to very different persons, all of whom have some one thing in common; there is reason to suppose that such circumstance is not merely attributable to the persons concerned, but is in some measure occasioned by the one point in common to them all. Instead of the vehement and almost slanderous dehortation from marriage, which the Misogyne, Boccaccio[44] addresses to literary men, I would substitute the simple advice: be not merely a man of letters! Let literature be an honourable augmentation to your arms; but not constitute the coat, or fill the escutcheon!

To objections from conscience I can of course answer in no other way, than by requesting the youthful objector (as I have already done on a former occasion) to ascertain with strict self-examination, whether other influences may not be at work; whether spirits, "not of health," and with whispers "not from heaven," may not be walking in the twilight of his consciousness. Let him catalogue his scruples, and reduce them to a distinct intelligible form; let him be certain, that he has read with a docile mind and favourable dispositions the best and most fundamental works on the subject; that he has had both mind and heart opened to the great and illustrious qualities of the many renowned characters, who had doubted like himself, and whose researches had ended in the clear conviction, that their doubts had been groundless, or at least in no proportion to the counter-weight. Happy will it be for such a man, if among his contemporaries elder than himself he should meet with one, who, with similar powers and feelings as acute as his own, had entertained the same scruples; had acted upon them; and who by after-research (when the step was, alas! irretrievable, but for that very reason his research undeniably disinterested) had discovered himself to have quarrelled with received opinions only to embrace errors, to have left the direction tracked out for him on the high road of honourable exertion, only to deviate into a labyrinth, where when he had wandered till his head was giddy, his best good fortune was finally to have found his way out again, too late for prudence though not too late for conscience or for truth! Time spent in such delay is time won: for manhood in the meantime is advancing, and with it increase of knowledge, strength of judgment, and above all, temperance of feelings. And even if these should effect no change, yet the delay will at least prevent the final approval of the decision from being alloyed by the inward censure of the rashness and vanity, by which it had been precipitated. It would be a sort of irreligion, and scarcely less than a libel on human nature to believe, that there is any established and reputable profession or employment, in which a man may not continue to act with honesty and honour; and doubtless there is likewise none, which may not at times present temptations to the contrary. But wofully will that man find himself mistaken, who imagines that the profession of literature, or (to speak more plainly) the trade of authorship, besets its members with fewer or with less insidious temptations, than the Church, the law, or the different branches of commerce. But I have treated sufficiently on this unpleasant subject in an early chapter of this volume. I will conclude the present therefore with a short extract from Herder, whose name I might have added to the illustrious list of those, who have combined the successful pursuit of the Muses, not only with the faithful discharge, but with the highest honours and honourable emoluments of an established profession. The translation the reader will find in a note below [45]. "Am sorgfaeltigsten, meiden sie die Autorschaft. Zu frueh oder unmaessig gebraucht, macht sie den Kopf wueste und das Herz leer; wenn sie auch sonst keine ueble Folgen gaebe. Ein Mensch, der nur lieset um zu druecken, lieset wahrscheinlich uebel; und wer jeden Gedanken, der ihm aufstosst, durch Feder and Presse versendet, hat sie in kurzer Zeit alle versandt, und wird bald ein blosser Diener der Druckerey, ein Buchstabensetzer werden."

CHAPTER XII

A chapter of requests and premonitions concerning the perusal or omission of the chapter that follows.

In the perusal of philosophical works I have been greatly benefited by a resolve, which, in the antithetic form and with the allowed quaintness of an adage or maxim, I have been accustomed to word thus: until you understand a writer's ignorance, presume yourself ignorant of his understanding. This golden rule of mine does, I own, resemble those of Pythagoras in its obscurity rather than in its depth. If however the reader will permit me to be my own Hierocles, I trust, that he will find its meaning fully explained by the following instances. I have now before me a treatise of a religious fanatic, full of dreams and supernatural experiences. I see clearly the writer's grounds, and their hollowness. I have a complete insight into the causes, which through the medium of his body has acted on his mind; and by application of received and ascertained laws I can satisfactorily explain to my own reason all the strange incidents, which the writer records of himself. And this I can do without suspecting him of any intentional falsehood. As when in broad day-light a man tracks the steps of a traveller, who had lost his way in a fog or by a treacherous moonshine, even so, and with the same tranquil sense of certainty, can I follow the traces of this bewildered visionary. I understand his ignorance.

On the other hand, I have been re-perusing with the best energies of my mind the TIMAEUS of Plato. Whatever I comprehend, impresses me with a reverential sense of the author's genius; but there is a considerable portion of the work, to which I can attach no consistent meaning. In other treatises of the same philosopher, intended for the average comprehensions of men, I have been delighted with the masterly good sense, with the perspicuity of the language, and the aptness of the inductions. I recollect likewise, that numerous passages in this author, which I thoroughly comprehend, were formerly no less unintelligible to me, than the passages now in question. It would, I am aware, be quite fashionable to dismiss them at once as Platonic jargon. But this I cannot do with satisfaction to my own mind, because I have sought in vain for causes adequate to the solution of the assumed inconsistency. I have no insight into the possibility of a man so eminently wise, using words with such half-meanings to himself, as must perforce pass into no meaning to his readers. When in addition to the motives thus suggested by my own reason, I bring into distinct remembrance the number and the series of great men, who, after long and zealous study of these works had joined in honouring the name of Plato with epithets, that almost transcend humanity, I feel, that a contemptuous verdict on my part might argue want of modesty, but would hardly be received by the judicious, as evidence of superior penetration. Therefore, utterly baffled in all my attempts to understand the ignorance of Plato, I conclude myself ignorant of his understanding.

In lieu of the various requests which the anxiety of authorship addresses to the unknown reader, I advance but this one; that he will either pass over the following chapter altogether, or read the whole connectedly. The fairest part of the most beautiful body will appear deformed and monstrous, if dissevered from its place in the organic whole. Nay, on delicate subjects, where a seemingly trifling difference of more or less may constitute a difference in kind, even a faithful display of the main and supporting ideas, if yet they are separated from the forms by which they are at once clothed and modified, may perchance present a skeleton indeed; but a skeleton to alarm and deter. Though I might find numerous precedents, I shall not desire the reader to strip his mind of all prejudices, nor to keep all prior systems out of view during his examination of the present. For in truth, such requests appear to me not much unlike the advice given to hypochondriacal patients in Dr. Buchan's domestic medicine; videlicet, to preserve themselves uniformly tranquil and in good spirits. Till I had discovered the art of destroying the memory a parte post, without injury to its future operations, and without detriment to the judgment, I should suppress the request as premature; and therefore, however much I may wish to be read with an unprejudiced mind, I do not presume to state it as a necessary condition.

The extent of my daring is to suggest one criterion, by which it may be rationally conjectured beforehand, whether or no a reader would lose his time, and perhaps his temper, in the perusal of this, or any other treatise constructed on similar principles. But it would be cruelly misinterpreted, as implying the least disrespect either for the moral or intellectual qualities of the individuals thereby precluded. The criterion is this: if a man receives as fundamental facts, and therefore of course indemonstrable and incapable of further analysis, the general notions of matter, spirit, soul, body, action, passiveness, time, space, cause and effect, consciousness, perception, memory and habit; if he feels his mind completely at rest concerning all these, and is satisfied, if only he can analyse all other notions into some one or more of these supposed elements with plausible subordination and apt arrangement: to such a mind I would as courteously as possible convey the hint, that for him the chapter was not written.

Vir bonus es, doctus, prudens; ast haud tibi spiro.

For these terms do in truth include all the difficulties, which the human mind can propose for solution. Taking them therefore in mass, and unexamined, it required only a decent apprenticeship in logic, to draw forth their contents in all forms and colours, as the professors of legerdemain at our village fairs pull out ribbon after ribbon from their mouths. And not more difficult is it to reduce them back again to their different genera. But though this analysis is highly useful in rendering our knowledge more distinct, it does not really add to it. It does not increase, though it gives us a greater mastery over, the wealth which we before possessed. For forensic purposes, for all the established professions of society, this is sufficient. But for philosophy in its highest sense as the science of ultimate truths, and therefore scientia scientiarum, this mere analysis of terms is preparative only, though as a preparative discipline indispensable.

Still less dare a favourable perusal be anticipated from the proselytes of that compendious philosophy, which talking of mind but thinking of brick and mortar, or other images equally abstracted from body, contrives a theory of spirit by nicknaming matter, and in a few hours can qualify its dullest disciples to explain the omne scibile by reducing all things to impressions, ideas, and sensations.

But it is time to tell the truth; though it requires some courage to avow it in an age and country, in which disquisitions on all subjects, not privileged to adopt technical terms or scientific symbols, must be addressed to the Public. I say then, that it is neither possible nor necessary for all men, nor for many, to be philosophers. There is a philosophic (and inasmuch as it is actualized by an effort of freedom, an artificial) consciousness, which lies beneath or (as it were) behind the spontaneous consciousness natural to all reflecting beings. As the elder Romans distinguished their northern provinces into Cis-Alpine and Trans-Alpine, so may we divide all the objects of human knowledge into those on this side, and those on the other side of the spontaneous consciousness; citra et trans conscientiam communem. The latter is exclusively the domain of pure philosophy, which is therefore properly entitled transcendental, in order to discriminate it at once, both from mere reflection and representation on the one hand, and on the other from those flights of lawless speculation which, abandoned by all distinct consciousness, because transgressing the bounds and purposes of our intellectual faculties, are justly condemned, as transcendent [46]. The first range of hills, that encircles the scanty vale of human life, is the horizon for the majority of its inhabitants. On its ridges the common sun is born and departs. From them the stars rise, and touching them they vanish. By the many, even this range, the natural limit and bulwark of the vale, is but imperfectly known. Its higher ascents are too often hidden by mists and clouds from uncultivated swamps, which few have courage or curiosity to penetrate. To the multitude below these vapours appear, now as the dark haunts of terrific agents, on which none may intrude with impunity; and now all aglow, with colours not their own, they are gazed at as the splendid palaces of happiness and power. But in all ages there have been a few, who measuring and sounding the rivers of the vale at the feet of their furthest inaccessible falls have learned, that the sources must be far higher and far inward; a few, who even in the level streams have detected elements, which neither the vale itself nor the surrounding mountains contained or could supply [47]. How and whence to these thoughts, these strong probabilities, the ascertaining vision, the intuitive knowledge may finally supervene, can be learnt only by the fact. I might oppose to the question the words with which [48] Plotinus supposes Nature to answer a similar difficulty. "Should any one interrogate her, how she works, if graciously she vouchsafe to listen and speak, she will reply, it behoves thee not to disquiet me with interrogatories, but to understand in silence, even as I am silent, and work without words."

Likewise in the fifth book of the fifth Ennead, speaking of the highest and intuitive knowledge as distinguished from the discursive, or in the language of Wordsworth,

"The vision and the faculty divine;"

he says: "it is not lawful to inquire from whence it sprang, as if it were a thing subject to place and motion, for it neither approached hither, nor again departs from hence to some other place; but it either appears to us or it does not appear. So that we ought not to pursue it with a view of detecting its secret source, but to watch in quiet till it suddenly shines upon us; preparing ourselves for the blessed spectacle as the eye waits patiently for the rising sun." They and they only can acquire the philosophic imagination, the sacred power of self-intuition, who within themselves can interpret and understand the symbol, that the wings of the air-sylph are forming within the skin of the caterpillar; those only, who feel in their own spirits the same instinct, which impels the chrysalis of the horned fly to leave room in its involucrum for antenna, yet to come. They know and feel, that the potential works in them, even as the actual works on them! In short, all the organs of sense are framed for a corresponding world of sense; and we have it. All the organs of spirit are framed for a correspondent world of spirit: though the latter organs are not developed in all alike. But they exist in all, and their first appearance discloses itself in the moral being. How else could it be, that even worldlings, not wholly debased, will contemplate the man of simple and disinterested goodness with contradictory feelings of pity and respect? "Poor man! he is not made for this world." Oh! herein they utter a prophecy of universal fulfilment; for man must either rise or sink.

It is the essential mark of the true philosopher to rest satisfied with no imperfect light, as long as the impossibility of attaining a fuller knowledge has not been demonstrated. That the common consciousness itself will furnish proofs by its own direction, that it is connected with master-currents below the surface, I shall merely assume as a postulate pro tempore. This having been granted, though but in expectation of the argument, I can safely deduce from it the equal truth of my former assertion, that philosophy cannot be intelligible to all, even of the most learned and cultivated classes. A system, the first principle of which it is to render the mind intuitive of the spiritual in man (i.e. of that which lies on the other side of our natural consciousness) must needs have a great obscurity for those, who have never disciplined and strengthened this ulterior consciousness. It must in truth be a land of darkness, a perfect Anti-Goshen, for men to whom the noblest treasures of their own being are reported only through the imperfect translation of lifeless and sightless motions. Perhaps, in great part, through words which are but the shadows of notions; even as the notional understanding itself is but the shadowy abstraction of living and actual truth. On the IMMEDIATE, which dwells in every man, and on the original intuition, or absolute affirmation of it, (which is likewise in every man, but does not in every man rise into consciousness) all the certainty of our knowledge depends; and this becomes intelligible to no man by the ministry of mere words from without. The medium, by which spirits understand each other, is not the surrounding air; but the freedom which they possess in common, as the common ethereal element of their being, the tremulous reciprocations of which propagate themselves even to the inmost of the soul. Where the spirit of a man is not filled with the consciousness of freedom (were it only from its restlessness, as of one still struggling in bondage) all spiritual intercourse is interrupted, not only with others, but even with himself. No wonder then, that he remains incomprehensible to himself as well as to others. No wonder, that, in the fearful desert of his consciousness, he wearies himself out with empty words, to which no friendly echo answers, either from his own heart, or the heart of a fellow being; or bewilders himself in the pursuit of notional phantoms, the mere refractions from unseen and distant truths through the distorting medium of his own unenlivened and stagnant understanding! To remain unintelligible to such a mind, exclaims Schelling on a like occasion, is honour and a good name before God and man.

The history of philosophy (the same writer observes) contains instances of systems, which for successive generations have remained enigmatic. Such he deems the system of Leibnitz, whom another writer (rashly I think, and invidiously) extols as the only philosopher, who was himself deeply convinced of his own doctrines. As hitherto interpreted, however, they have not produced the effect, which Leibnitz himself, in a most instructive passage, describes as the criterion of a true philosophy; namely, that it would at once explain and collect the fragments of truth scattered through systems apparently the most incongruous. The truth, says he, is diffused more widely than is commonly believed; but it is often painted, yet oftener masked, and is sometimes mutilated and sometimes, alas! in close alliance with mischievous errors. The deeper, however, we penetrate into the ground of things, the more truth we discover in the doctrines of the greater number of the philosophical sects. The want of substantial reality in the objects of the senses, according to the sceptics; the harmonies or numbers, the prototypes and ideas, to which the Pythagoreans and Platonists reduced all things: the ONE and ALL of Parmenides and Plotinus, without [49] Spinozism; the necessary connection of things according to the Stoics, reconcilable with the spontaneity of the other schools; the vital-philosophy of the Cabalists and Hermetists, who assumed the universality of sensation; the substantial forms and entelechies of Aristotle and the schoolmen, together with the mechanical solution of all particular phaenomena according to Democritus and the recent philosophers—all these we shall find united in one perspective central point, which shows regularity and a coincidence of all the parts in the very object, which from every other point of view must appear confused and distorted. The spirit of sectarianism has been hitherto our fault, and the cause of our failures. We have imprisoned our own conceptions by the lines, which we have drawn, in order to exclude the conceptions of others. J'ai trouve que la plupart des Sectes ont raison dans une bonne partie de ce qu'elles avancent, mais non pas tant en ce qu'elles nient.

A system, which aims to deduce the memory with all the other functions of intelligence, must of course place its first position from beyond the memory, and anterior to it, otherwise the principle of solution would be itself a part of the problem to be solved. Such a position therefore must, in the first instance be demanded, and the first question will be, by what right is it demanded? On this account I think it expedient to make some preliminary remarks on the introduction of Postulates in philosophy. The word postulate is borrowed from the science of mathematics [50]. In geometry the primary construction is not demonstrated, but postulated. This first and most simple construction in space is the point in motion, or the line. Whether the point is moved in one and the same direction, or whether its direction is continually changed, remains as yet undetermined. But if the direction of the point have been determined, it is either by a point without it, and then there arises the straight line which incloses no space; or the direction of the point is not determined by a point without it, and then it must flow back again on itself, that is, there arises a cyclical line, which does enclose a space. If the straight line be assumed as the positive, the cyclical is then the negation of the straight. It is a line, which at no point strikes out into the straight, but changes its direction continuously. But if the primary line be conceived as undetermined, and the straight line as determined throughout, then the cyclical is the third compounded of both. It is at once undetermined and determined; undetermined through any point without, and determined through itself. Geometry therefore supplies philosophy with the example of a primary intuition, from which every science that lays claim to evidence must take its commencement. The mathematician does not begin with a demonstrable proposition, but with an intuition, a practical idea.

But here an important distinction presents itself. Philosophy is employed on objects of the inner SENSE, and cannot, like geometry, appropriate to every construction a correspondent outward intuition. Nevertheless, philosophy, if it is to arrive at evidence, must proceed from the most original construction, and the question then is, what is the most original construction or first productive act for the inner sense. The answer to this question depends on the direction which is given to the inner sense. But in philosophy the inner sense cannot have its direction determined by an outward object. To the original construction of the line I can be compelled by a line drawn before me on the slate or on sand. The stroke thus drawn is indeed not the line itself, but only the image or picture of the line. It is not from it, that we first learn to know the line; but, on the contrary, we bring this stroke to the original line generated by the act of the imagination; otherwise we could not define it as without breadth or thickness. Still however this stroke is the sensuous image of the original or ideal line, and an efficient mean to excite every imagination to the intuition of it.

It is demanded then, whether there be found any means in philosophy to determine the direction of the inner sense, as in mathematics it is determinable by its specific image or outward picture. Now the inner sense has its direction determined for the greater part only by an act of freedom. One man's consciousness extends only to the pleasant or unpleasant sensations caused in him by external impressions; another enlarges his inner sense to a consciousness of forms and quantity; a third in addition to the image is conscious of the conception or notion of the thing; a fourth attains to a notion of his notions—he reflects on his own reflections; and thus we may say without impropriety, that the one possesses more or less inner sense, than the other. This more or less betrays already, that philosophy in its first principles must have a practical or moral, as well as a theoretical or speculative side. This difference in degree does not exist in the mathematics. Socrates in Plato shows, that an ignorant slave may be brought to understand and of himself to solve the most difficult geometrical problem. Socrates drew the figures for the slave in the sand.

The disciples of the critical philosophy could likewise (as was indeed actually done by La Forge and some other followers of Des Cartes) represent the origin of our representations in copper-plates; but no one has yet attempted it, and it would be utterly useless. To an Esquimaux or New Zealander our most popular philosophy would be wholly unintelligible. The sense, the inward organ, for it is not yet born in him. So is there many a one among us, yes, and some who think themselves philosophers too, to whom the philosophic organ is entirely wanting. To such a man philosophy is a mere play of words and notions, like a theory of music to the deaf, or like the geometry of light to the blind. The connection of the parts and their logical dependencies may be seen and remembered; but the whole is groundless and hollow, unsustained by living contact, unaccompanied with any realizing intuition which exists by and in the act that affirms its existence, which is known, because it is, and is, because it is known. The words of Plotinus, in the assumed person of Nature, hold true of the philosophic energy. To theoroun mou, theoraema poiei, osper oi geometrai theorountes graphousin; all' emon mae graphousaes, theorousaes de, uphistantai ai ton somaton grammai. With me the act of contemplation makes the thing contemplated, as the geometricians contemplating describe lines correspondent; but I not describing lines, but simply contemplating, the representative forms of things rise up into existence.

The postulate of philosophy and at the same time the test of philosophic capacity, is no other than the heaven-descended KNOW THYSELF! (E coelo descendit, Gnothi seauton). And this at once practically and speculatively. For as philosophy is neither a science of the reason or understanding only, nor merely a science of morals, but the science of BEING altogether, its primary ground can be neither merely speculative nor merely practical, but both in one. All knowledge rests on the coincidence of an object with a subject. (My readers have been warned in a former chapter that, for their convenience as well as the writer's, the term, subject, is used by me in its scholastic sense as equivalent to mind or sentient being, and as the necessary correlative of object or quicquid objicitur menti.) For we can know that only which is true: and the truth is universally placed in the coincidence of the thought with the thing, of the representation with the object represented.

Now the sum of all that is merely OBJECTIVE, we will henceforth call NATURE, confining the term to its passive and material sense, as comprising all the phaenomena by which its existence is made known to us. On the other hand the sum of all that is SUBJECTIVE, we may comprehend in the name of the SELF or INTELLIGENCE. Both conceptions are in necessary antithesis. Intelligence is conceived of as exclusively representative, nature as exclusively represented; the one as conscious, the other as without consciousness. Now in all acts of positive knowledge there is required a reciprocal concurrence of both, namely of the conscious being, and of that which is in itself unconscious. Our problem is to explain this concurrence, its possibility and its necessity.

During the act of knowledge itself, the objective and subjective are so instantly united, that we cannot determine to which of the two the priority belongs. There is here no first, and no second; both are coinstantaneous and one. While I am attempting to explain this intimate coalition, I must suppose it dissolved. I must necessarily set out from the one, to which therefore I give hypothetical antecedence, in order to arrive at the other. But as there are but two factors or elements in the problem, subject and object, and as it is left indeterminate from which of them I should commence, there are two cases equally possible.

1. EITHER THE OBJECTIVE IS TAKEN AS THE FIRST, AND THEN WE HAVE TO ACCOUNT FOR THE SUPERVENTION OF THE SUBJECTIVE, WHICH COALESCES WITH IT.

The notion of the subjective is not contained in the notion of the objective. On the contrary they mutually exclude each other. The subjective therefore must supervene to the objective. The conception of nature does not apparently involve the co-presence of an intelligence making an ideal duplicate of it, that is, representing it. This desk for instance would (according to our natural notions) be, though there should exist no sentient being to look at it. This then is the problem of natural philosophy. It assumes the objective or unconscious nature as the first, and as therefore to explain how intelligence can supervene to it, or how itself can grow into intelligence. If it should appear, that all enlightened naturalists, without having distinctly proposed the problem to themselves, have yet constantly moved in the line of its solution, it must afford a strong presumption that the problem itself is founded in nature. For if all knowledge has, as it were, two poles reciprocally required and presupposed, all sciences must proceed from the one or the other, and must tend toward the opposite as far as the equatorial point in which both are reconciled and become identical. The necessary tendency therefore of all natural philosophy is from nature to intelligence; and this, and no other is the true ground and occasion of the instinctive striving to introduce theory into our views of natural phaenomena. The highest perfection of natural philosophy would consist in the perfect spiritualization of all the laws of nature into laws of intuition and intellect. The phaenomena (the material) most wholly disappear, and the laws alone (the formal) must remain. Thence it comes, that in nature itself the more the principle of law breaks forth, the more does the husk drop off, the phaenomena themselves become more spiritual and at length cease altogether in our consciousness. The optical phaenomena are but a geometry, the lines of which are drawn by light, and the materiality of this light itself has already become matter of doubt. In the appearances of magnetism all trace of matter is lost, and of the phaenomena of gravitation, which not a few among the most illustrious Newtonians have declared no otherwise comprehensible than as an immediate spiritual influence, there remains nothing but its law, the execution of which on a vast scale is the mechanism of the heavenly motions. The theory of natural philosophy would then be completed, when all nature was demonstrated to be identical in essence with that, which in its highest known power exists in man as intelligence and self-consciousness; when the heavens and the earth shall declare not only the power of their maker, but the glory and the presence of their God, even as he appeared to the great prophet during the vision of the mount in the skirts of his divinity.

This may suffice to show, that even natural science, which commences with the material phaenomenon as the reality and substance of things existing, does yet by the necessity of theorizing unconsciously, and as it were instinctively, end in nature as an intelligence; and by this tendency the science of nature becomes finally natural philosophy, the one of the two poles of fundamental science.

2. OR THE SUBJECTIVE IS TAKEN AS THE FIRST, AND THE PROBLEM THEN IS, HOW THERE SUPERVENES TO IT A COINCIDENT OBJECTIVE.

In the pursuit of these sciences, our success in each, depends on an austere and faithful adherence to its own principles, with a careful separation and exclusion of those, which appertain to the opposite science. As the natural philosopher, who directs his views to the objective, avoids above all things the intermixture of the subjective in his knowledge, as for instance, arbitrary suppositions or rather suflictions, occult qualities, spiritual agents, and the substitution of final for efficient causes; so on the other hand, the transcendental or intelligential philosopher is equally anxious to preclude all interpellation of the objective into the subjective principles of his science, as for instance the assumption of impresses or configurations in the brain, correspondent to miniature pictures on the retina painted by rays of light from supposed originals, which are not the immediate and real objects of vision, but deductions from it for the purposes of explanation. This purification of the mind is effected by an absolute and scientific scepticism, to which the mind voluntarily determines itself for the specific purpose of future certainty. Des Cartes who (in his meditations) himself first, at least of the moderns, gave a beautiful example of this voluntary doubt, this self-determined indetermination, happily expresses its utter difference from the scepticism of vanity or irreligion: *Nec tamen in Scepticos imitabar, qui dubitant tantum ut dubitent, et praeter incertitudinem ipsam nihil quaerunt.*

Nam contra totus in eo eram ut aliquid certi reperirem [51]. Nor is it less distinct in its motives and final aim, than in its proper objects, which are not as in ordinary scepticism the prejudices of education and circumstance, but those original and innate prejudices which nature herself has planted in all men, and which to all but the philosopher are the first principles of knowledge, and the final test of truth.

Now these essential prejudices are all reducible to the one fundamental presumption, THAT THERE EXIST THINGS WITHOUT US. As this on the one hand originates, neither in grounds nor arguments, and yet on the other hand remains proof against all attempts to remove it by grounds or arguments (naturam furca expellas tamen usque redibit;) on the one hand lays claim to IMMEDIATE certainty as a position at once indemonstrable and irresistible, and yet on the other hand, inasmuch as it refers to something essentially different from ourselves, nay even in opposition to ourselves, leaves it inconceivable how it could possibly become a part of our immediate consciousness; (in other words how that, which ex hypothesi is and continues to be extrinsic and alien to our being, should become a modification of our being) the philosopher therefore compels himself to treat this faith as nothing more than a prejudice, innate indeed and connatural, but still a prejudice.

The other position, which not only claims but necessitates the admission of its immediate certainty, equally for the scientific reason of the philosopher as for the common sense of mankind at large, namely, I AM, cannot so properly be entitled a prejudice. It is groundless indeed; but then in the very idea it precludes all ground, and separated from the immediate consciousness loses its whole sense and import. It is groundless; but only because it is itself the ground of all other certainty. Now the apparent contradiction, that the former position, namely, the existence of things without us, which from its nature cannot be immediately certain, should be received as blindly and as independently of all grounds as the existence of our own being, the Transcendental philosopher can solve only by the supposition, that the former is unconsciously involved in the latter; that it is not only coherent but identical, and one and the same thing with our own immediate self consciousness. To demonstrate this identity is the office and object of his philosophy.

If it be said, that this is idealism, let it be remembered that it is only so far idealism, as it is at the same time, and on that very account, the truest and most binding realism. For wherein does the realism of mankind properly consist? In the assertion that there exists a something without them, what, or how, or where they know not, which occasions the objects of their perception? Oh no! This is neither connatural nor universal. It is what a few have taught and learned in the schools, and which the many repeat without asking themselves concerning their own meaning. The realism common to all mankind is far elder and lies infinitely deeper than this hypothetical explanation of the origin of our perceptions, an explanation skimmed from the mere surface of mechanical philosophy. It is the table itself, which the man of common sense believes himself to see, not the phantom of a table, from which he may argumentatively deduce the reality of a table, which he does not see. If to destroy the reality of all, that we actually behold, be idealism, what can be more egregiously so, than the system of modern metaphysics, which banishes us to a land of shadows, surrounds us with apparitions, and distinguishes truth from illusion only by the majority of those who dream the same dream? "I asserted that the world was mad," exclaimed poor Lee, "and the world said, that I was mad, and confound them, they outvoted me."

It is to the true and original realism, that I would direct the attention. This believes and requires neither more nor less, than the object which it beholds or presents to itself, is the real and very object. In this sense, however much we may strive against it, we are all collectively born idealists, and therefore and only therefore are we at the same time realists. But of this the philosophers of the schools know nothing, or despise the faith as the prejudice of the ignorant vulgar, because they live and move in a crowd of phrases and notions from which human nature has long ago vanished. Oh, ye that reverence yourselves, and walk humbly with the divinity in your own hearts, ye are worthy of a better philosophy! Let the dead bury the dead, but do you preserve your human nature, the depth of which was never yet fathomed by a philosophy made up of notions and mere logical entities.

In the third treatise of my Logosophia, announced at the end of this volume, I shall give (Deo volente) the demonstrations and constructions of the Dynamic Philosophy scientifically arranged. It is, according to my conviction, no other than the system of Pythagoras and of Plato revived and purified from impure mixtures. Doctrina per tot manus tradita tandem in vappam desiit! The science of arithmetic furnishes instances, that a rule may be useful in practical application, and for the particular purpose may be sufficiently authenticated by the result, before it has itself been fully demonstrated. It is enough, if only it be rendered intelligible. This will, I trust, have been effected in the following Theses for those of my readers, who are willing to accompany me through the following chapter, in which the results will be applied to the deduction of the Imagination, and with it the principles of production and of genial criticism in the fine arts.

THESIS I

Truth is correlative to being. Knowledge without a correspondent reality is no knowledge; if we know, there must be somewhat known by us. To know is in its very essence a verb active.

THESIS II

All truth is either mediate, that is, derived from some other truth or truths; or immediate and original. The latter is absolute, and its formula A. A.; the former is of dependent or conditional certainty, and represented in the formula B. A. The certainty, which adheres in A, is attributable to B.

SCHOLIUM. A chain without a staple, from which all the links derived their stability, or a series without a first, has been not inaptly allegorized, as a string of blind men, each holding the skirt of the man before him, reaching far out of sight, but all moving without the least deviation in one straight line. It would be naturally taken for granted, that there was a guide at the head of the file: what if it were answered, No! Sir, the men are without number, and infinite blindness supplies the place of sight?

Equally inconceivable is a cycle of equal truths without a common and central principle, which prescribes to each its proper sphere in the system of science. That the absurdity does not so immediately strike us, that it does not seem equally unimaginable, is owing to a surreptitious act of the imagination, which, instinctively and without our noticing the same, not only fills up the intervening spaces, and contemplates the cycle (of B. C. D. E. F. etc.) as a continuous circle (A.) giving to all collectively the unity of their common orbit; but likewise supplies, by a sort of subintelligitur, the one central power, which renders the movement harmonious and cyclical.

THESIS III

We are to seek therefore for some absolute truth capable of communicating to other positions a certainty, which it has not itself borrowed; a truth self-grounded, unconditional and known by its own light. In short, we have to find a somewhat which is, simply because it is. In order to be such, it must be one which is its own predicate, so far at least that all other nominal predicates must be modes and repetitions of itself. Its existence too must be such, as to preclude the possibility of requiring a cause or antecedent without an absurdity.

THESIS IV

That there can be but one such principle, may be proved a priori; for were there two or more, each must refer to some other, by which its equality is affirmed; consequently neither would be self-established, as the hypothesis demands. And a posteriori, it will be proved by the principle itself when it is discovered, as involving universal antecedence in its very conception.

SCHOLIUM. If we affirm of a board that it is blue, the predicate (blue) is accidental, and not implied in the subject, board. If we affirm of a circle that it is equi-radial, the predicate indeed is implied in the definition of the subject; but the existence of the subject itself is contingent, and supposes both a cause and a percipient. The same reasoning will apply to the indefinite number of supposed indemonstrable truths exempted from the profane approach of philosophic investigation by the amiable Beattie, and other less eloquent and not more profound inaugurators of common sense on the throne of philosophy; a fruitless attempt, were it only that it is the two-fold function of philosophy to reconcile reason with common sense, and to elevate common sense into reason.

THESIS V

Such a principle cannot be any THING or OBJECT. Each thing is what it is in consequence of some other thing. An infinite, independent [52] thing, is no less a contradiction, than an infinite circle or a sideless triangle. Besides a thing is that, which is capable of being an object which itself is not the sole percipient. But an object is inconceivable without a subject as its antithesis. Omne perceptum percipientem supponit.

But neither can the principle be found in a subject as a subject, contra-distinguished from an object: for unicuique percipienti aliquid objicitur perceptum. It is to be found therefore neither in object nor subject taken separately, and consequently, as no other third is conceivable, it must be found in that which is neither subject nor object exclusively, but which is the identity of both.

THESIS VI

This principle, and so characterised manifests itself in the SUM or I AM; which I shall hereafter indiscriminately express by the words spirit, self, and self-consciousness. In this, and in this alone, object and subject, being and knowing, are identical, each involving and supposing the other. In other words, it is a subject which becomes a subject by the act of constructing itself objectively to itself; but which never is an object except for itself, and only so far as by the very same act it becomes a subject. It may be described therefore as a perpetual self-duplication of one and the same power into object and subject, which presuppose each other, and can exist only as antitheses.

SCHOLIUM. If a man be asked how he knows that he is? he can only answer, sum quia sum. But if (the absoluteness of this certainty having been admitted) he be again asked, how he, the individual person, came to be, then in relation to the ground of his existence, not to the ground of his knowledge of that existence, he might reply, sum quia Deus est, or still more philosophically, sum quia in Deo sum.

But if we elevate our conception to the absolute self, the great eternal I AM, then the principle of being, and of knowledge, of idea, and of reality; the ground of existence, and the ground of the knowledge of existence, are absolutely identical, Sum quia sum [53]; I am, because I affirm myself to be; I affirm myself to be, because I am.

THESIS VII

If then I know myself only through myself, it is contradictory to require any other predicate of self, but that of self-consciousness. Only in the self-consciousness of a spirit is there the required identity of object and of representation; for herein consists the essence of a spirit, that it is self-representative. If therefore this be the one only immediate truth, in the certainty of which the reality of our collective knowledge is grounded, it must follow that the spirit in all the objects which it views, views only itself. If this could be proved, the immediate reality of all intuitive knowledge would be assured. It has been shown, that a spirit is that, which is its own object, yet not originally an object, but an absolute subject for which all, itself included, may become an object. It must therefore be an ACT; for every object is, as an object, dead, fixed, incapable in itself of any action, and necessarily finite. Again the spirit (originally the identity of object and subject) must in some sense dissolve this identity, in order to be conscious of it; fit alter et idem. But this implies an act, and it follows therefore that intelligence or self-consciousness is impossible, except by and in a will. The self-conscious spirit therefore is a will; and freedom must be assumed as a ground of philosophy, and can never be deduced from it.

THESIS VIII

Whatever in its origin is objective, is likewise as such necessarily finite. Therefore, since the spirit is not originally an object, and as the subject exists in antithesis to an object, the spirit cannot originally be finite. But neither can it be a subject without becoming an object, and, as it is originally the identity of both, it can be conceived neither as infinite nor finite exclusively, but as the most original union of both. In the existence, in the reconciling, and the recurrence of this contradiction consists the process and mystery of production and life.

THESIS IX

This principium commune essendi et cognoscendi, as subsisting in a WILL, or primary ACT of self-duplication, is the mediate or indirect principle of every science; but it is the immediate and direct principle of the ultimate science alone, i.e. of transcendental philosophy alone. For it must be remembered, that all these Theses refer solely to one of the two Polar Sciences, namely, to that which commences with, and rigidly confines itself within, the subjective, leaving the objective (as far as it is exclusively objective) to natural philosophy, which is its opposite pole. In its very idea therefore as a systematic knowledge of our collective KNOWING, (scientia scientiae) it involves the necessity of some one highest principle of knowing, as at once the source and accompanying form in all particular acts of intellect and perception. This, it has been shown, can be found only in the act and evolution of self-consciousness. We are not investigating an absolute principium essendi; for then, I admit, many valid objections might be started against our theory; but an absolute principium cognoscendi. The result of both the sciences, or their equatorial point, would be the principle of a total and undivided philosophy, as, for prudential reasons, I have chosen to anticipate in the Scholium to Thesis VI and the note subjoined. In other words, philosophy would pass into religion, and religion become inclusive of philosophy. We begin with the I KNOW MYSELF, in order to end with the absolute I AM. We proceed from the SELF, in order to lose and find all self in GOD.

THESIS X

The transcendental philosopher does not inquire, what ultimate ground of our knowledge there may lie out of our knowing, but what is the last in our knowing itself, beyond which we cannot pass. The principle of our knowing is sought within the sphere of our knowing. It must be some thing therefore, which can itself be known. It is asserted only, that the act of self-consciousness is for us the source and principle of all our possible knowledge. Whether abstracted from us there exists any thing higher and beyond this primary self-knowing, which is for us the form of all our knowing must be decided by the result.

That the self-consciousness is the fixed point, to which for us all is mortised and annexed, needs no further proof. But that the self-consciousness may be the modification of a higher form of being, perhaps of a higher consciousness, and this again of a yet higher, and so on in an infinite regressus; in short, that self-consciousness may be itself something explicable into something, which must lie beyond the possibility of our knowledge, because the whole synthesis of our intelligence is first formed in and through the self-consciousness, does not at all concern us as transcendental philosophers. For to us, self-consciousness is not a kind of being, but a kind of knowing, and that too the highest and farthest that exists for us. It may however be shown, and has in part already been shown earlier, that even when the Objective is assumed as the first, we yet can never pass beyond the principle of self-consciousness. Should we attempt it, we must be driven back from ground to ground, each of which would cease to be a ground the moment we pressed on it. We must be whirled down the gulf of an infinite series. But this would make our reason baffle the end and purpose of all reason, namely, unity and system. Or we must break off the series arbitrarily, and affirm an absolute something that is in and of itself at once cause and effect (causa sui), subject and object, or rather the absolute identity of both. But as this is inconceivable, except in a self-consciousness, it follows, that even as natural philosophers we must arrive at the same principle from which as transcendental philosophers we set out; that is, in a self-consciousness in which the principium essendi does not stand to the principlum cognoscende in the relation of cause to effect, but both the one and the other are co-inherent and identical. Thus the true system of natural philosophy places the sole reality of things in an ABSOLUTE, which is at once causa sui et effectus, pataer autopator, uios heautou—in the absolute identity of subject and object, which it calls nature, and which in its highest power is nothing else than self-conscious will or intelligence. In this sense the position of Malebranche, that we see all things in God, is a strict philosophical truth; and equally true is the assertion of Hobbes, of Hartley, and of their masters in ancient Greece, that all real knowledge supposes a prior sensation. For sensation itself is but vision nascent, not the cause of intelligence, but intelligence itself revealed as an earlier power in the process of self-construction.

Makar, ilathi moi;
Pater, ilathi moi
Ei para kosmon,
Ei para moiran
Ton son ethigon!

Bearing then this in mind, that intelligence is a self-development, not a quality supervening to a substance, we may abstract from all degree, and for the purpose of philosophic construction reduce it to kind, under the idea of an indestructible power with two opposite and counteracting forces, which by a metaphor borrowed from astronomy, we may call the centrifugal and centripetal forces. The intelligence in the one tends to objectize itself, and in the other to know itself in the object. It will be hereafter my business to construct by a series of intuitions the progressive schemes, that must follow from such a power with such forces, till I arrive at the fulness of the human intelligence. For my present purpose, I assume such a power as my principle, in order to deduce from it a faculty, the generation, agency, and application of which form the contents of the ensuing chapter.

In a preceding page I have justified the use of technical terms in philosophy, whenever they tend to preclude confusion of thought, and when they assist the memory by the exclusive singleness of their meaning more than they may, for a short time, bewilder the attention by their strangeness. I trust, that I have not extended this privilege beyond the grounds on which I have claimed it; namely, the conveniency of the scholastic phrase to distinguish the kind from all degrees, or rather to express the kind with the abstraction of degree, as for instance multeity instead of multitude; or secondly, for the sake of correspondence in sound in interdependent or antithetical terms, as subject and object; or lastly, to avoid the wearying recurrence of circumlocutions and definitions. Thus I shall venture to use potence, in order to express a specific degree of a power, in imitation of the Algebraists. I have even hazarded the new verb potenziate, with its derivatives, in order to express the combination or transfer of powers. It is with new or unusual terms, as with privileges in courts of justice or legislature; there can be no legitimate privilege, where there already exists a positive law adequate to the purpose; and when there is no law in existence, the privilege is to be justified by its accordance with the end, or final cause, of all law. Unusual and new-coined words are doubtless an evil; but vagueness, confusion, and imperfect conveyance of our thoughts, are a far greater. Every system, which is under the necessity of using terms not familiarized by the metaphysics in fashion, will be described as written in an unintelligible style, and the author must expect the charge of having substituted learned jargon for clear conception; while, according to the creed of our modern philosophers, nothing is deemed a clear conception, but what is representable by a distinct image. Thus the conceivable is reduced within the bounds of the picturable. Hinc patet, qui fiat, ut cum irrepraesentabile et impossibile vulgo ejusdem significatus habeantur, conceptus tam continui, quam infiniti, a plurimis rejiciantur, quippe quorum, secundum leges cognitionis intuitivae, repraesentatio est impossibilis. Quanquam autem harum e non paucis scholis explosarum notionum, praesertim prioris, causam hic non gero, maximi tamen momendi erit monuisse. gravissimo illos errore labi, qui tam perverse argumentandi ratione utuntur. Quicquid enim repugnat legibus intellectus et rationis, utique est impossibile; quod autem, cum rationis purae sit objectum, legibus cognitionis intuitivae tantummodo non subest, non item. Nam hic dissensus inter facultatem sensitivam et intellectualem, (quarum indolem mox exponam,) nihil indigitat, nisi, quas mens ab intellectu acceptas fert ideas abstractas, illas in concreto exsequi et in intuitus commutare saepenumero non posse. Haec autem reluctantia subjectiva mentitur, ut plurimum, repugnantiam aliquam objectivam, et incautos facile fallit, limitibus, quibus mens humana circumscribitur, pro iis habitis, quibus ipsa rerum essentia continetur. [54]

Critics, who are most ready to bring this charge of pedantry and unintelligibility, are the most apt to overlook the important fact, that, besides the language of words, there is a language of spirits—(sermo interior)—and that the former is only the vehicle of the latter. Consequently their assurance, that they do not understand the philosophic writer, instead of proving any thing against the philosophy, may furnish an equal, and (caeteris paribus) even a stronger presumption against their own philosophic talent.

Great indeed are the obstacles which an English metaphysician has to encounter. Amongst his most respectable and intelligent judges, there will be many who have devoted their attention exclusively to the concerns and interests of human life, and who bring with them to the perusal of a philosophic system an habitual aversion to all speculations, the utility and application of which are not evident and immediate. To these I would in the first instance merely oppose an authority, which they themselves hold venerable, that of Lord Bacon: non inutiles Scientiae existimandae sunt, quarum in se nullus est usus, si ingenia acuant et ordinent.

There are others, whose prejudices are still more formidable, inasmuch as they are grounded in their moral feelings and religious principles, which had been alarmed and shocked by the impious and pernicious tenets defended by Hume, Priestley, and the French fatalists or necessitarians; some of whom had perverted metaphysical reasonings to the denial of the mysteries and indeed of all the peculiar doctrines of Christianity; and others even to the subversion of all distinction between right and wrong. I would request such men to consider what an eminent and successful defender of the Christian faith has observed, that true metaphysics are nothing else but true divinity, and that in fact the writers, who have given them such just offence, were sophists, who had taken advantage of the general neglect into which the science of logic has unhappily fallen, rather than metaphysicians, a name indeed which those writers were the first to explode as unmeaning. Secondly, I would remind them, that as long as there are men in the world to whom the Gnothi seauton is an instinct and a command from their own nature, so long will there be metaphysicians and metaphysical speculations; that false metaphysics can be effectually counteracted by true metaphysics alone; and that if the reasoning be clear, solid and pertinent, the truth deduced can never be the less valuable on account of the depth from which it may have been drawn.

A third class profess themselves friendly to metaphysics, and believe that they are themselves metaphysicians. They have no objection to system or terminology, provided it be the method and the nomenclature to which they have been familiarized in the writings of Locke, Hume, Hartley, Condillac, or perhaps Dr. Reid, and Professor Stewart. To objections from this cause, it is a sufficient answer, that one main object of my attempt was to demonstrate the vagueness or insufficiency of the terms used in the metaphysical schools of France and Great Britain since the revolution, and that the errors which I propose to attack cannot subsist, except as they are concealed behind the mask of a plausible and indefinite nomenclature.

But the worst and widest impediment still remains. It is the predominance of a popular philosophy, at once the counterfeit and the mortal enemy of all true and manly metaphysical research. It is that corruption, introduced by certain immethodical aphorisming eclectics, who, dismissing not only all system, but all logical connection, pick and choose whatever is most plausible and showy; who select, whatever words can have some semblance of sense attached to them without the least expenditure of thought; in short whatever may enable men to talk of what they do not understand, with a careful avoidance of every thing that might awaken them to a moment's suspicion of their ignorance. This alas! is an irremediable disease, for it brings with it, not so much an indisposition to any particular system, but an utter loss of taste and faculty for all system and for all philosophy. Like echoes that beget each other amongst the mountains, the praise or blame of such men rolls in volleys long after the report from the original blunderbuss. Sequacitas est potius et coitio quam consensus: et tamen (quod pessimum est) pusillanimitas ista non sine arrogantia et fastidio se offert. [55]

I shall now proceed to the nature and genesis of the Imagination; but I must first take leave to notice, that after a more accurate perusal of Mr. Wordsworth's remarks on the Imagination, in his preface to the new edition of his poems, I find that my conclusions are not so consentient with his as, I confess, I had taken for granted. In an article contributed by me to Mr. Southey's Omniana, On the soul and its organs of sense, are the following sentences. "These (the human faculties) I would arrange under the different senses and powers: as the eye, the ear, the touch, etc.; the imitative power, voluntary and automatic; the imagination, or shaping and modifying power; the fancy, or the aggregative and associative power; the understanding, or the regulative, substantiating and realizing power; the speculative reason, vis theoretica et scientifica, or the power by which we produce or aim to produce unity, necessity, and universality in all our knowledge by means of principles a priori [56]; the will, or practical reason; the faculty of choice (Germanice, Willkuehr) and (distinct both from the moral will and the choice,) the sensation of volition, which I have found reason to include under the head of single and double touch." To this, as far as it relates to the subject in question, namely the words (the aggregative and associative power) Mr. Wordsworth's "objection is only that the definition is too general. To aggregate and to associate, to evoke and to combine, belong as well to the Imagination as to the Fancy." I reply, that if, by the power of evoking and combining, Mr. Wordsworth means the same as, and no more than, I meant by the aggregative and associative, I continue to deny, that it belongs at all to the Imagination; and I am disposed to conjecture, that he has mistaken the copresence of Fancy with Imagination for the operation of the latter singly. A man may work with two very different tools at the same moment; each has its share in the work, but the work effected by each is distinct and different. But it will probably appear in the next chapter, that deeming it necessary to go back much further than Mr. Wordsworth's subject required or permitted, I have attached a meaning to both Fancy and Imagination, which he had not in view, at least while he was writing that preface. He will judge. Would to Heaven, I might meet with many such readers! I will conclude with the words of Bishop Jeremy Taylor: "He to whom all things are one, who draweth all things to one, and seeth all things in one, may enjoy true peace and rest of spirit." [57]

CHAPTER XIII

On the imagination, or esemplastic power

O Adam, One Almighty is, from whom
All things proceed, and up to him return,
If not deprav'd from good, created all
Such to perfection, one first matter all,
Endued with various forms, various degrees
Of substance, and, in things that live, of life;
But more refin'd, more spiritous and pure,
As nearer to him plac'd, or nearer tending,
Each in their several active spheres assigu'd,
Till body up to spirit work, in bounds
Proportion'd to each kind. So from the root
Springs lighter the green stalk, from thence the leaves
More aery: last the bright consummate flower
Spirits odorous breathes: flowers and their fruit,
Man's nourishment, by gradual scale sublim'd,
To vital spirits aspire: to animal:
To intellectual!—give both life and sense,
Fancy and understanding; whence the soul
REASON receives, and reason is her being,
Discursive or intuitive. [58]

"Sane dicerentur si res corporales nil nisi materiale continerent, verissime in fluxu consistere, neque habere substantiale quicquam, quemadmodum et Platonici olim recte agnovere."

"Hinc igitur, praeter pure mathematica et phantasiae subjecta, collegi quaedam metaphysica solaque mente perceptibilia, esse admittenda et massae materiali principium quoddam superius et, ut sic dicam, formale addendum: quandoquidem omnes veritates rerum corporearum ex solis axiomatibus logisticis et geometricis, nempe de magno et parvo, toto et parte, figura et situ, colligi non possint; sed alia de causa et effectu, actioneque et passione, accedere debeant, quibus ordinis rerum rationes salventur. Id principium rerum, an entelecheian an vim appellemus, non refert, modo meminerimus, per solam Virium notionem intelligibiliter explicari." [59]

Sebomai noeron
Kruphian taxin

Chorei TI MESON
Ou katachuthen. [60]

Des Cartes, speaking as a naturalist, and in imitation of Archimedes, said, give me matter and motion and I will construct you the universe. We must of course understand him to have meant; I will render the construction of the universe intelligible. In the same sense the transcendental philosopher says; grant me a nature having two contrary forces, the one of which tends to expand infinitely, while the other strives to apprehend or find itself in this infinity, and I will cause the world of intelllgences with the whole system of their representations to rise up before you. Every other science presupposes intelligence as already existing and complete: the philosopher contemplates it in its growth, and as it were represents its history to the mind from its birth to its maturity.

The venerable sage of Koenigsberg has preceded the march of this master-thought as an effective pioneer in his essay on the introduction of negative quantities into philosophy, published 1763. In this he has shown, that instead of assailing the science of mathematics by metaphysics, as Berkeley did in his ANALYST, or of sophisticating it, as Wolf did, by the vain attempt of deducing the first principles of geometry from supposed deeper grounds of ontology, it behoved the metaphysician rather to examine whether the only province of knowledge, which man has succeeded in erecting into a pure science, might not furnish materials, or at least hints, for establishing and pacifying the unsettled, warring, and embroiled domain of philosophy. An imitation of the mathematical method had indeed been attempted with no better success than attended the essay of David to wear the armour of Saul. Another use however is possible and of far greater promise, namely, the actual application of the positions which had so wonderfully enlarged the discoveries of geometry, mutatis mutandis, to philosophical subjects. Kant having briefly illustrated the utility of such an attempt in the questions of space, motion, and infinitely small quantities, as employed by the mathematician, proceeds to the idea of negative quantities and the transfer of them to metaphysical investigation. Opposites, he well observes, are of two kinds, either logical, that is, such as are absolutely incompatible; or real, without being contradictory. The former he denominates Nihil negativum irrepraesentabile, the connection of which produces nonsense. A body in motion is something--Aliquid cogitabile; but a body, at one and the same time in motion and not in motion, is nothing, or, at most, air articulated into nonsense. But a motory force of a body in one direction, and an equal force of the same body in an opposite direction is not incompatible, and the result, namely, rest, is real and representable. For the purposes of mathematical calculus it is indifferent which force we term negative, and which positive, and consequently we appropriate the latter to that, which happens to be the principal object in our thoughts. Thus if a man's capital be ten and his debts eight, the subtraction will be the same, whether we call the capital negative debt, or the debt negative capital. But in as much as the latter stands practically in reference to the former, we of course represent the sum as 10-8. It is equally clear that two equal forces acting in opposite directions, both being finite and each distinguished from the other by its direction only, must neutralize or reduce each other to inaction. Now the transcendental philosophy demands; first, that two forces should be conceived which counteract each other by their essential nature; not only not in consequence of the accidental direction of each, but as prior to all direction, nay, as the primary forces from which the conditions of all possible directions are derivative and deducible: secondly, that these forces should be assumed to be both alike infinite, both alike indestructible. The problem will then be to discover the result or product of two such forces, as distinguished from the result of those forces which are finite, and derive their difference solely from the circumstance of their direction. When we have formed a scheme or outline of these two different kinds of force, and of their different results, by the process of discursive reasoning, it will then remain for us to elevate the thesis from notional to actual, by contemplating intuitively this one power with its two inherent indestructible yet counteracting forces, and the results or generations to which their inter-penetration gives existence, in the living principle and in the process of our own self-consciousness. By what instrument this is possible the solution itself will discover, at the same time that it will reveal to and for whom it is possible. Non omnia possumus omnes. There is a philosophic no less than a poetic genius, which is differenced from the highest perfection of talent, not by degree but by kind.

The counteraction then of the two assumed forces does not depend on their meeting from opposite directions; the power which acts in them is indestructible; it is therefore inexhaustibly re-ebullient; and as something must be the result of these two forces, both alike infinite, and both alike indestructible; and as rest or neutralization cannot be this result; no other conception is possible, but that the product must be a tertium aliquid, or finite generation. Consequently this conception is necessary. Now this tertium aliquid can be no other than an inter-penetration of the counteracting powers, partaking of both.

* * * * * *

Thus far had the work been transcribed for the press, when I received the following letter from a friend, whose practical judgment I have had ample reason to estimate and revere, and whose taste and sensibility preclude all the excuses which my self-love might possibly have prompted me to set up in plea against the decision of advisers of equal good sense, but with less tact and feeling.

"Dear C.

"You ask my opinion concerning your Chapter on the Imagination, both as to the impressions it made on myself, and as to those which I think it will make on the Public, i.e. that part of the public, who, from the title of the work and from its forming a sort of introduction to a volume of poems, are likely to constitute the great majority of your readers.

"As to myself, and stating in the first place the effect on my understanding, your opinions and method of argument were not only so new to me, but so directly the reverse of all I had ever been accustomed to consider as truth, that even if I had comprehended your premises sufficiently to have admitted them, and had seen the necessity of your conclusions, I should still have been in that state of mind, which in your note in Chap. IV you have so ingeniously evolved, as the antithesis to that in which a man is, when he makes a bull. In your own words, I should have felt as if I had been standing on my head.

"The effect on my feelings, on the other hand, I cannot better represent, than by supposing myself to have known only our light airy modern chapels of ease, and then for the first time to have been placed, and left alone, in one of our largest Gothic cathedrals in a gusty moonlight night of autumn. 'Now in glimmer, and now in gloom;' often in palpable darkness not without a chilly sensation of terror; then suddenly emerging into broad yet visionary lights with coloured shadows of fantastic shapes, yet all decked with holy insignia and mystic symbols; and ever and anon coming out full upon pictures and stone-work images of great men, with whose names I was familiar, but which looked upon me with countenances and an expression, the most dissimilar to all I had been in the habit of connecting with those names. Those whom I had been taught to venerate as almost super-human in magnitude of intellect, I found perched in little fret-work niches, as grotesque dwarfs; while the grotesques, in my hitherto belief, stood guarding the high altar with all the characters of apotheosis. In short, what I had supposed substances were thinned away into shadows, while everywhere shadows were deepened into substances:

If substance might be call'd that shadow seem'd,
For each seem'd either!

"Yet after all, I could not but repeat the lines which you had quoted from a MS. poem of your own in the FRIEND, and applied to a work of Mr. Wordsworth's though with a few of the words altered:

------An Orphic tale indeed,
A tale obscure of high and passionate thoughts
To a strange music chanted!

"Be assured, however, that I look forward anxiously to your great book on the CONSTRUCTIVE PHILOSOPHY, which you have promised and announced: and that I will do my best to understand it. Only I will not promise to descend into the dark cave of Trophonius with you, there to rub my own eyes, in order to make the sparks and figured flashes, which I am required to see.

"So much for myself. But as for the Public I do not hesitate a moment in advising and urging you to withdraw the Chapter from the present work, and to reserve it for your announced treatises on the Logos or communicative intellect in Man and Deity. First, because imperfectly as I understand the present Chapter, I see clearly that you have done too much, and yet not enough. You have been obliged to omit so many links, from the necessity of compression, that what remains, looks (if I may recur to my former illustration) like the fragments of the winding steps of an old ruined tower. Secondly, a still stronger argument (at least one that I am sure will be more forcible with you) is, that your readers will have both right and reason to complain of you. This Chapter, which cannot, when it is printed, amount to so little as an hundred pages, will of necessity greatly increase the expense of the work; and every reader who, like myself, is neither prepared nor perhaps calculated for the study of so abstruse a subject so abstrusely treated, will, as I have before hinted, be almost entitled to accuse you of a sort of imposition on him. For who, he might truly observe, could from your title-page, to wit, "My Literary Life and Opinions," published too as introductory to a volume of miscellaneous poems, have anticipated, or even conjectured, a long treatise on Ideal Realism which holds the same relation in abstruseness to Plotinus, as Plotinus does to Plato. It will be well, if already you have not too much of metaphysical disquisition in your work, though as the larger part of the disquisition is historical, it will doubtless be both interesting and instructive to many to whose unprepared minds your speculations on the esemplastic power would be utterly unintelligible. Be assured, if you do publish this Chapter in the present work, you will be reminded of Bishop Berkeley's Siris, announced as an Essay on Tar-water, which beginning with Tar ends with the Trinity, the omne scibile forming the interspace. I say in the present work. In that greater work to which you have devoted so many years, and study so intense and various, it will be in its proper place. Your prospectus will have described and announced both its contents and their nature; and if any persons purchase it, who feel no interest in the subjects of which it treats, they will have themselves only to blame.

"I could add to these arguments one derived from pecuniary motives, and particularly from the probable effects on the sale of your present publication; but they would weigh little with you compared with the preceding. Besides, I have long observed, that arguments drawn from your own personal interests more often act on you as narcotics than as stimulants, and that in money concerns you have some small portion of pig-nature in your moral idiosyncrasy, and, like these amiable creatures, must occasionally be pulled backward from the boat in order to make you enter it. All success attend you, for if hard thinking and hard reading are merits, you have deserved it.

"Your affectionate, etc."

In consequence of this very judicious letter, which produced complete conviction on my mind, I shall content myself for the present with stating the main result of the chapter, which I have reserved for that future publication, a detailed prospectus of which the reader will find at the close of the second volume.

The Imagination then I consider either as primary, or secondary. The primary Imagination I hold to be the living power and prime agent of all human perception, and as a repetition in the finite mind of the eternal act of creation in the infinite I AM. The secondary Imagination I consider as an echo of the former, co-existing with the conscious will, yet still as identical with the primary in the kind of its agency, and differing only in degree, and in the mode of its operation. It dissolves, diffuses, dissipates, in order to recreate: or where this process is rendered impossible, yet still at all events it struggles to idealize and to unify. It is essentially vital, even as all objects (as objects) are essentially fixed and dead.

FANCY, on the contrary, has no other counters to play with, but fixities and definites. The fancy is indeed no other than a mode of memory emancipated from the order of time and space; while it is blended with, and modified by that empirical phaenomenon of the will, which we express by the word Choice. But equally with the ordinary memory the Fancy must receive all its materials ready made from the law of association.

CHAPTER XIV

Occasion of the Lyrical Ballads, and the objects originally proposed—Preface to the second edition—The ensuing controversy, its causes and acrimony—Philosophic definitions of a Poem and Poetry with scholia.

During the first year that Mr. Wordsworth and I were neighbours, our conversations turned frequently on the two cardinal points of poetry, the power of exciting the sympathy of the reader by a faithful adherence to the truth of nature, and the power of giving the interest of novelty by the modifying colours of imagination. The sudden charm, which accidents of light and shade, which moon-light or sunset diffused over a known and familiar landscape, appeared to represent the practicability of combining both. These are the poetry of nature. The thought suggested itself—(to which of us I do not recollect)—that a series of poems might be composed of two sorts. In the one, the incidents and agents were to be, in part at least, supernatural; and the excellence aimed at was to consist in the interesting of the affections by the dramatic truth of such emotions, as would naturally accompany such situations, supposing them real. And real in this sense they have been to every human being who, from whatever source of delusion, has at any time believed himself under supernatural agency. For the second class, subjects were to be chosen from ordinary life; the characters and incidents were to be such as will be found in every village and its vicinity, where there is a meditative and feeling mind to seek after them, or to notice them, when they present themselves.

In this idea originated the plan of the LYRICAL BALLADS; in which it was agreed, that my endeavours should be directed to persons and characters supernatural, or at least romantic; yet so as to transfer from our inward nature a human interest and a semblance of truth sufficient to procure for these shadows of imagination that willing suspension of disbelief for the moment, which constitutes poetic faith. Mr. Wordsworth, on the other hand, was to propose to himself as his object, to give the charm of novelty to things of every day, and to excite a feeling analogous to the supernatural, by awakening the mind's attention to the lethargy of custom, and directing it to the loveliness and the wonders of the world before us; an inexhaustible treasure, but for which, in consequence of the film of familiarity and selfish solicitude, we have eyes, yet see not, ears that hear not, and hearts that neither feel nor understand.

With this view I wrote THE ANCIENT MARINER, and was preparing among other poems, THE DARK LADIE, and the CHRISTABEL, in which I should have more nearly realized my ideal, than I had done in my first attempt. But Mr. Wordsworth's industry had proved so much more successful, and the number of his poems so much greater, that my compositions, instead of forming a balance, appeared rather an interpolation of heterogeneous matter. Mr. Wordsworth added two or three poems written in his own character, in the impassioned, lofty, and sustained diction, which is characteristic of his genius. In this form the LYRICAL BALLADS were published; and were presented by him, as an experiment, whether subjects, which from their nature rejected the usual ornaments and extra-colloquial style of poems in general, might not be so managed in the language of ordinary life as to produce the pleasurable interest, which it is the peculiar business of poetry to impart. To the second edition he added a preface of considerable length; in which, notwithstanding some passages of apparently a contrary import, he was understood to contend for the extension of this style to poetry of all kinds, and to reject as vicious and indefensible all phrases and forms of speech that were not included in what he (unfortunately, I think, adopting an equivocal expression) called the language of real life. From this preface, prefixed to poems in which it was impossible to deny the presence of original genius, however mistaken its direction might be deemed, arose the whole long-continued controversy. For from the conjunction of perceived power with supposed heresy I explain the inveteracy and in some instances, I grieve to say, the acrimonious passions, with which the controversy has been conducted by the assailants.

Had Mr. Wordsworth's poems been the silly, the childish things, which they were for a long time described as being had they been really distinguished from the compositions of other poets merely by meanness of language and inanity of thought; had they indeed contained nothing more than what is found in the parodies and pretended imitations of them; they must have sunk at once, a dead weight, into the slough of oblivion, and have dragged the preface along with them. But year after year increased the number of Mr. Wordsworth's admirers. They were found too not in the lower classes of the reading public, but chiefly among young men of strong sensibility and meditative minds; and their admiration (inflamed perhaps in some degree by opposition) was distinguished by its intensity, I might almost say, by its religious fervour. These facts, and the intellectual energy of the author, which was more or less consciously felt, where it was outwardly and even boisterously denied, meeting with sentiments of aversion to his opinions, and of alarm at their consequences, produced an eddy of criticism, which would of itself have borne up the poems by the violence with which it whirled them round and round. With many parts of this preface in the sense attributed to them and which the words undoubtedly seem to authorize, I never concurred; but on the contrary objected to them as erroneous in principle, and as contradictory (in appearance at least) both to other parts of the same preface, and to the author's own practice in the greater part of the poems themselves. Mr. Wordsworth in his recent collection has, I find, degraded this prefatory disquisition to the end of his second volume, to be read or not at the reader's choice. But he has not, as far as I can discover, announced any change in his poetic creed. At all events, considering it as the source of a controversy, in which I have been honoured more than I deserve by the frequent conjunction of my name with his, I think it expedient to declare once for all, in what points I coincide with the opinions supported in that preface, and in what points I altogether differ. But in order to render myself intelligible I must previously, in as few words as possible, explain my views, first, of a Poem; and secondly, of Poetry itself, in kind, and in essence.

The office of philosophical disquisition consists in just distinction; while it is the privilege of the philosopher to preserve himself constantly aware, that distinction is not division. In order to obtain adequate notions of any truth, we must intellectually separate its distinguishable parts; and this is the technical process of philosophy. But having so done, we must then restore them in our conceptions to the unity, in which they actually co-exist; and this is the result of philosophy. A poem contains the same elements as a prose composition; the difference therefore must consist in a different combination of them, in consequence of a different object being proposed. According to the difference of the object will be the difference of the combination. It is possible, that the object may be merely to facilitate the recollection of any given facts or observations by artificial arrangement; and the composition will be a poem, merely because it is distinguished from prose by metre, or by rhyme, or by both conjointly. In this, the lowest sense, a man might attribute the name of a poem to the well-known enumeration of the days in the several months;

"Thirty days hath September,
April, June, and November," etc.

and others of the same class and purpose. And as a particular pleasure is found in anticipating the recurrence of sounds and quantities, all compositions that have this charm super-added, whatever be their contents, may be entitled poems.

So much for the superficial form. A difference of object and contents supplies an additional ground of distinction. The immediate purpose may be the communication of truths; either of truth absolute and demonstrable, as in works of science; or of facts experienced and recorded, as in history. Pleasure, and that of the highest and most permanent kind, may result from the attainment of the end; but it is not itself the immediate end. In other works the communication of pleasure may be the immediate purpose; and though truth, either moral or intellectual, ought to be the ultimate end, yet this will distinguish the character of the author, not the class to which the work belongs. Blest indeed is that state of society, in which the immediate purpose would be baffled by the perversion of the proper ultimate end; in which no charm of diction or imagery could exempt the BATHYLLUS even of an Anacreon, or the ALEXIS of Virgil, from disgust and aversion!

But the communication of pleasure may be the immediate object of a work not metrically composed; and that object may have been in a high degree attained, as in novels and romances. Would then the mere superaddition of metre, with or without rhyme, entitle these to the name of poems? The answer is, that nothing can permanently please, which does not contain in itself the reason why it is so, and not otherwise. If metre be superadded, all other parts must be made consonant with it. They must be such, as to justify the perpetual and distinct attention to each part, which an exact correspondent recurrence of accent and sound are calculated to excite. The final definition then, so deduced, may be thus worded. A poem is that species of composition, which is opposed to works of science, by proposing for its immediate object pleasure, not truth; and from all other species—(having this object in common with it)—it is discriminated by proposing to itself such delight from the whole, as is compatible with a distinct gratification from each component part.

Controversy is not seldom excited in consequence of the disputants attaching each a different meaning to the same word; and in few instances has this been more striking, than in disputes concerning the present subject. If a man chooses to call every composition a poem, which is rhyme, or measure, or both, I must leave his opinion uncontroverted. The distinction is at least competent to characterize the writer's intention. If it were subjoined, that the whole is likewise entertaining or affecting, as a tale, or as a series of interesting reflections; I of course admit this as another fit ingredient of a poem, and an additional merit. But if the definition sought for be that of a legitimate poem, I answer, it must be one, the parts of which mutually support and explain each other; all in their proportion harmonizing with, and supporting the purpose and known influences of metrical arrangement. The philosophic critics of all ages coincide with the ultimate judgment of all countries, in equally denying the praises of a just poem, on the one hand, to a series of striking lines or distiches, each of which, absorbing the whole attention of the reader to itself, becomes disjoined from its context, and forms a separate whole, instead of a harmonizing part; and on the other hand, to an unsustained composition, from which the reader collects rapidly the general result unattracted by the component parts. The reader should be carried forward, not merely or chiefly by the mechanical impulse of curiosity, or by a restless desire to arrive at the final solution; but by the pleasureable activity of mind excited by the attractions of the journey itself. Like the motion of a serpent, which the Egyptians made the emblem of intellectual power; or like the path of sound through the air;—at every step he pauses and half recedes; and from the retrogressive movement collects the force which again carries him onward. Praecipitandus est liber spiritus, says Petronius most happily. The epithet, liber, here balances the preceding verb; and it is not easy to conceive more meaning condensed in fewer words.

But if this should be admitted as a satisfactory character of a poem, we have still to seek for a definition of poetry. The writings of Plato, and Jeremy Taylor, and Burnet's Theory of the Earth, furnish undeniable proofs that poetry of the highest kind may exist without metre, and even without the contradistringuishing objects of a poem. The first chapter of Isaiah— (indeed a very large portion of the whole book)—is poetry in the most emphatic sense; yet it would be not less irrational than strange to assert, that pleasure, and not truth was the immediate object of the prophet. In short, whatever specific import we attach to the word, Poetry, there will be found involved in it, as a necessary consequence, that a poem of any length neither can be, nor ought to be, all poetry. Yet if an harmonious whole is to be produced, the remaining parts must be preserved in keeping with the poetry; and this can be no otherwise effected than by such a studied selection and artificial arrangement, as will partake of one, though not a peculiar property of poetry. And this again can be no other than the property of exciting a more continuous and equal attention than the language of prose aims at, whether colloquial or written.

My own conclusions on the nature of poetry, in the strictest use of the word, have been in part anticipated in some of the remarks on the Fancy and Imagination in the early part of this work. What is poetry?—is so nearly the same question with, what is a poet?—that the answer to the one is involved in the solution of the other. For it is a distinction resulting from the poetic genius itself, which sustains and modifies the images, thoughts, and emotions of the poet's own mind.

The poet, described in ideal perfection, brings the whole soul of man into activity, with the subordination of its faculties to each other according to their relative worth and dignity. He diffuses a tone and spirit of unity, that blends, and (as it were) fuses, each into each, by that synthetic and magical power, to which I would exclusively appropriate the name of Imagination. This power, first put in action by the will and understanding, and retained under their irremissive, though gentle and unnoticed, control, laxis effertur habenis, reveals "itself in the balance or reconcilement of opposite or discordant" qualities: of sameness, with difference; of the general with the concrete; the idea with the image; the individual with the representative; the sense of novelty and freshness with old and familiar objects; a more than usual state of emotion with more than usual order; judgment ever awake and steady self-possession with enthusiasm and feeling profound or vehement; and while it blends and harmonizes the natural and the artificial, still subordinates art to nature; the manner to the matter; and our admiration of the poet to our sympathy with the poetry. Doubtless, as Sir John Davies observes of the soul—(and his words may with slight alteration be applied, and even more appropriately, to the poetic Imagination)—

Doubtless this could not be, but that she turns
Bodies to spirit by sublimation strange,
As fire converts to fire the things it burns,
As we our food into our nature change.

From their gross matter she abstracts their forms,
And draws a kind of quintessence from things;
Which to her proper nature she transforms
To bear them light on her celestial wings.

Thus does she, when from individual states
She doth abstract the universal kinds;
Which then re-clothed in divers names and fates
Steal access through the senses to our minds.

Finally, Good Sense is the Body of poetic genius, Fancy its Drapery, Motion its Life, and Imagination the Soul that is everywhere, and in each; and forms all into one graceful and intelligent whole.

CHAPTER XV

The specific symptoms of poetic power elucidated in a critical analysis of Shakespeare's VENUS AND ADONIS, and RAPE of LUCRECE.

In the application of these principles to purposes of practical criticism, as employed in the appraisement of works more or less imperfect, I have endeavoured to discover what the qualities in a poem are, which may be deemed promises and specific symptoms of poetic power, as distinguished from general talent determined to poetic composition by accidental motives, by an act of the will, rather than by the inspiration of a genial and productive nature. In this investigation, I could not, I thought, do better, than keep before me the earliest work of the greatest genius, that perhaps human nature has yet produced, our myriad-minded [61] Shakespeare. I mean the VENUS AND ADONIS, and the LUCRECE; works which give at once strong promises of the strength, and yet obvious proofs of the immaturity, of his genius. From these I abstracted the following marks, as characteristics of original poetic genius in general.

1. In the VENUS AND ADONIS, the first and most obvious excellence is the perfect sweetness of the versification; its adaptation to the subject; and the power displayed in varying the march of the words without passing into a loftier and more majestic rhythm than was demanded by the thoughts, or permitted by the propriety of preserving a sense of melody predominant. The delight in richness and sweetness of sound, even to a faulty excess, if it be evidently original, and not the result of an easily imitable mechanism, I regard as a highly favourable promise in the compositions of a young man. The man that hath not music in his soul can indeed never be a genuine poet. Imagery,—(even taken from nature, much more when transplanted from books, as travels, voyages, and works of natural history),—affecting incidents, just thoughts, interesting personal or domestic feelings, and with these the art of their combination or intertexture in the form of a poem,— may all by incessant effort be acquired as a trade, by a man of talent and much reading, who, as I once before observed, has mistaken an intense desire of poetic reputation for a natural poetic genius; the love of the arbitrary end for a possession of the peculiar means. But the sense of musical delight, with the power of producing it, is a gift of imagination; and this together with the power of reducing multitude into unity of effect, and modifying a series of thoughts by some one predominant thought or feeling, may be cultivated and improved, but can never be learned. It is in these that "poeta nascitur non fit."

2. A second promise of genius is the choice of subjects very remote from the private interests and circumstances of the writer himself. At least I have found, that where the subject is taken immediately from the author's personal sensations and experiences, the excellence of a particular poem is but an equivocal mark, and often a fallacious pledge, of genuine poetic power. We may perhaps remember the tale of the statuary, who had acquired considerable reputation for the legs of his goddesses, though the rest of the statue accorded but indifferently with ideal beauty; till his wife, elated by her husband's praises, modestly acknowledged that she had been his constant model. In the VENUS AND ADONIS this proof of poetic power exists even to excess. It is throughout as if a superior spirit more intuitive, more intimately conscious, even than the characters themselves, not only of every outward look and act, but of the flux and reflux of the mind in all its subtlest thoughts and feelings, were placing the whole before our view; himself meanwhile unparticipating in the passions, and actuated only by that pleasurable excitement, which had resulted from the energetic fervour of his own spirit in so vividly exhibiting what it had so accurately and profoundly contemplated. I think, I should have conjectured from these poems, that even then the great instinct, which impelled the poet to the drama, was secretly working in him, prompting him—by a series and never broken chain of imagery, always vivid and, because unbroken, often minute; by the highest effort of the picturesque in words, of which words are capable, higher perhaps than was ever realized by any other poet, even Dante not excepted; to provide a substitute for that visual language, that constant intervention and running comment by tone, look and gesture, which in his dramatic works he was entitled to expect from the players. His Venus and Adonis seem at once the characters themselves, and the whole representation of those characters by the most consummate actors. You seem to be told nothing, but to see and hear everything. Hence it is, from the perpetual activity of attention required on the part of the reader; from the rapid flow, the quick change, and the playful nature of the thoughts and images; and above all from the alienation, and, if I may hazard such an expression, the utter aloofness of the poet's own feelings, from those of which he is at once the painter and the analyst; that though the very subject cannot but detract from the pleasure of a delicate mind, yet never was poem less dangerous on a moral account. Instead of doing as Ariosto, and as, still more offensively, Wieland has done, instead of degrading and deforming passion into appetite, the trials of love into the struggles of concupiscence; Shakespeare has here represented the animal impulse itself, so as to preclude all sympathy with it, by dissipating the reader's notice among the thousand outward images, and now beautiful, now fanciful circumstances, which form its dresses and its scenery; or by diverting our attention from the main subject by those frequent witty or profound

reflections, which the poet's ever active mind has deduced from, or connected with, the imagery and the incidents. The reader is forced into too much action to sympathize with the merely passive of our nature. As little can a mind thus roused and awakened be brooded on by mean and indistinct emotion, as the low, lazy mist can creep upon the surface of a lake, while a strong gale is driving it onward in waves and billows.

3. It has been before observed that images, however beautiful, though faithfully copied from nature, and as accurately represented in words, do not of themselves characterize the poet. They become proofs of original genius only as far as they are modified by a predominant passion; or by associated thoughts or images awakened by that passion; or when they have the effect of reducing multitude to unity, or succession to an instant; or lastly, when a human and intellectual life is transferred to them from the poet's own spirit,

Which shoots its being through earth, sea, and air.

In the two following lines for instance, there is nothing objectionable, nothing which would preclude them from forming, in their proper place, part of a descriptive poem:

Behold yon row of pines, that shorn and bow'd
Bend from the sea-blast, seen at twilight eve.

But with a small alteration of rhythm, the same words would be equally in their place in a book of topography, or in a descriptive tour. The same image will rise into semblance of poetry if thus conveyed:

Yon row of bleak and visionary pines,
By twilight glimpse discerned, mark! how they flee
From the fierce sea-blast, all their tresses wild
Streaming before them.

I have given this as an illustration, by no means as an instance, of that particular excellence which I had in view, and in which Shakespeare even in his earliest, as in his latest, works surpasses all other poets. It is by this, that he still gives a dignity and a passion to the objects which he presents. Unaided by any previous excitement, they burst upon us at once in life and in power,—

"*Full many a glorious morning have I seen*
Flatter the mountain tops with sovereign eye."

"*Not mine own fears, nor the prophetic soul*
Of the wide world dreaming on things to come—

* * * * * *
* * * * * *

The mortal moon hath her eclipse endured,
And the sad augurs mock their own presage;
Incertainties now crown themselves assur'd,
And Peace proclaims olives of endless age.
Now with the drops of this most balmy time
My love looks fresh, and Death to me subscribes,
Since spite of him, I'll live in this poor rhyme,
While he insults o'er dull and speechless tribes.
And thou in this shalt find thy monument,
When tyrants' crests, and tombs of brass are spent."

As of higher worth, so doubtless still more characteristic of poetic genius does the imagery become, when it moulds and colours itself to the circumstances, passion, or character, present and foremost in the mind. For unrivalled instances of this excellence, the reader's own memory will refer him to the LEAR, OTHELLO, in short to which not of the "great, ever living, dead man's" dramatic works? Inopem em copia fecit. How true it is to nature, he has himself finely expressed in the instance of love in his 98th Sonnet.

From you have I been absent in the spring,
When proud-pied April drest in all its trim,
Hath put a spirit of youth in every thing;
That heavy Saturn laugh'd and leap'd with him.
Yet nor the lays of birds, nor the sweet smell
Of different flowers in odour and in hue,
Could make me any summer's story tell,
Or from their proud lap pluck them, where they grew
Nor did I wonder at the lilies white,
Nor praise the deep vermilion in the rose;
They were, tho' sweet, but figures of delight,
Drawn after you, you pattern of all those.
Yet seem'd it winter still, and, you away,
As with your shadow, I with these did play!"

Scarcely less sure, or if a less valuable, not less indispensable mark

Gonimon men poiaetou―――
―――hostis rhaema gennaion lakoi,

will the imagery supply, when, with more than the power of the painter, the poet gives us the liveliest image of succession with the feeling of simultaneousness:—

- 135 -

With this, he breaketh from the sweet embrace
Of those fair arms, which bound him to her breast,
And homeward through the dark laund runs apace;—

* * * * * *

Look! how a bright star shooteth from the sky,
So glides he in the night from Venus' eye.

4. The last character I shall mention, which would prove indeed but little, except as taken conjointly with the former;—yet without which the former could scarce exist in a high degree, and (even if this were possible) would give promises only of transitory flashes and a meteoric power;—is depth, and energy of thought. No man was ever yet a great poet, without being at the same time a profound philosopher. For poetry is the blossom and the fragrancy of all human knowledge, human thoughts, human passions, emotions, language. In Shakespeare's poems the creative power and the intellectual energy wrestle as in a war embrace. Each in its excess of strength seems to threaten the extinction of the other. At length in the drama they were reconciled, and fought each with its shield before the breast of the other. Or like two rapid streams, that, at their first meeting within narrow and rocky banks, mutually strive to repel each other and intermix reluctantly and in tumult; but soon finding a wider channel and more yielding shores blend, and dilate, and flow on in one current and with one voice. The VENUS AND ADONIS did not perhaps allow the display of the deeper passions. But the story of Lucretia seems to favour and even demand their intensest workings. And yet we find in Shakespeare's management of the tale neither pathos, nor any other dramatic quality. There is the same minute and faithful imagery as in the former poem, in the same vivid colours, inspirited by the same impetuous vigour of thought, and diverging and contracting with the same activity of the assimilative and of the modifying faculties; and with a yet larger display, a yet wider range of knowledge and reflection; and lastly, with the same perfect dominion, often domination, over the whole world of language. What then shall we say? even this; that Shakespeare, no mere child of nature; no automaton of genius; no passive vehicle of inspiration, possessed by the spirit, not possessing it; first studied patiently, meditated deeply, understood minutely, till knowledge, become habitual and intuitive, wedded itself to his habitual feelings, and at length gave birth to that stupendous power, by which he stands alone, with no equal or second in his own class; to that power which seated him on one of the two glory-smitten summits of the poetic mountain, with Milton as his compeer not rival. While the former darts himself forth, and passes into all the forms of human character and passion, the one Proteus of the fire and the flood; the other attracts all forms and things to himself, into the unity of his own ideal. All things and modes of

action shape themselves anew in the being of Milton; while Shakespeare becomes all things, yet for ever remaining himself. O what great men hast thou not produced, England, my country!—Truly indeed—

We must be free or die, who speak the tongue,
Which Shakespeare spake; the faith and morals hold,
Which Milton held. In everything we are sprung
Of earth's first blood, have titles manifold.

CHAPTER XVI

Striking points of difference between the Poets of the present age and those of the fifteenth and sixteenth centuries—Wish expressed for the union of the characteristic merits of both.

Christendom, from its first settlement on feudal rights, has been so far one great body, however imperfectly organized, that a similar spirit will be found in each period to have been acting in all its members. The study of Shakespeare's poems—(I do not include his dramatic works, eminently as they too deserve that title)—led me to a more careful examination of the contemporary poets both in England and in other countries. But my attention was especially fixed on those of Italy, from the birth to the death of Shakespeare; that being the country in which the fine arts had been most sedulously, and hitherto most successfully cultivated. Abstracted from the degrees and peculiarities of individual genius, the properties common to the good writers of each period seem to establish one striking point of difference between the poetry of the fifteenth and sixteenth centuries, and that of the present age. The remark may perhaps be extended to the sister art of painting. At least the latter will serve to illustrate the former. In the present age the poet—(I would wish to be understood as speaking generally, and without allusion to individual names)—seems to propose to himself as his main object, and as that which is the most characteristic of his art, new and striking images; with incidents that interest the affections or excite the curiosity. Both his characters and his descriptions he renders, as much as possible, specific and individual, even to a degree of portraiture. In his diction and metre, on the other hand, he is comparatively careless. The measure is either constructed on no previous system, and acknowledges no justifying principle but that of the writer's convenience; or else some mechanical movement is adopted, of which one couplet or stanza is so far an adequate specimen, as that the occasional differences appear evidently to arise from accident, or the qualities of the language itself, not from meditation and an intelligent purpose. And the language from Pope's translation of Homer, to Darwin's Temple of Nature [62], may, notwithstanding some illustrious exceptions, be too faithfully characterized, as claiming to be poetical for no better reason, than that it would be intolerable in conversation or in prose. Though alas! even our prose writings, nay even the style of our more set discourses, strive to be in the fashion, and trick themselves out in the soiled and over-worn finery of the meretricious muse. It is true that of late a great improvement in this respect is observable in our most popular writers. But it is equally true, that this recurrence to plain sense and genuine mother English is far from being general; and that the composition of our novels, magazines, public harangues, and the like is commonly as trivial in thought, and yet enigmatic in expression, as if Echo and Sphinx had laid their heads together to construct it. Nay, even of those who have most rescued themselves from this contagion, I should plead inwardly guilty to the charge of duplicity or cowardice, if I withheld my conviction, that few have guarded the purity of their native tongue with that jealous care, which the sublime Dante in his tract De la volgare Eloquenza, declares to be the first duty of a poet. For language is the armoury of the human mind; and at once contains the trophies of its past, and the weapons of its future conquests. Animadverte, says Hobbes, quam sit ab improprietate verborum pronum hominihus prolabi in errores circa ipsas res! Sat [vero], says Sennertus, in hac vitae brevitate et naturae obscuritate, rerum est, quibus cognoscendis tempus impendatur, ut [confusis et multivotis] sermonibus intelligendis illud consumere opus non sit. [Eheu! quantas strages paravere verba nubila, quae tot dicunt ut nihil dicunt;—nubes potius, e quibus et in rebus politicis et in ecclesia turbines et tonitrua erumpunt!] Et proinde recte dictum putamus a Platone in Gorgia: os an ta onomata eidei, eisetai kai ta pragmata: et ab Epicteto, archae paideuseos hae ton onomaton episkepsis: et prudentissime Galenus scribit, hae ton onomaton chraesis tarachtheisa kai taen ton pragmaton epitarattei gnosin.

Egregie vero J. C. Scaliger, in Lib. I. de Plantis: Est primum, inquit, sapientis officium, bene sentire, ut sibi vivat: proximum, bene loqui, ut patriae vivat.

Something analogous to the materials and structure of modern poetry I seem to have noticed—(but here I beg to be understood as speaking with the utmost diffidence)—in our common landscape painters. Their foregrounds and intermediate distances are comparatively unattractive: while the main interest of the landscape is thrown into the background, where mountains and torrents and castles forbid the eye to proceed, and nothing tempts it to trace its way back again. But in the works of the great Italian and Flemish masters, the front and middle objects of the landscape are the most obvious and determinate, the interest gradually dies away in the background, and the charm and peculiar worth of the picture consists, not so much in the specific objects which it conveys to the understanding in a visual language formed by the substitution of figures for words, as in the beauty and harmony of the colours, lines, and expression, with which the objects are represented. Hence novelty of subject was rather avoided than sought for. Superior excellence in the manner of treating the same subjects was the trial and test of the artist's merit.

Not otherwise is it with the more polished poets of the fifteenth and sixteenth centuries, especially those of Italy. The imagery is almost always general: sun, moon, flowers, breezes, murmuring streams, warbling songsters, delicious shades, lovely damsels cruel as fair, nymphs, naiads, and goddesses, are the materials which are common to all, and which each shaped and arranged according to his judgment or fancy, little solicitous to add or to particularize. If we make an honourable exception in favour of some English poets, the thoughts too are as little novel as the images; and the fable of their narrative poems, for the most part drawn from mythology, or sources of equal notoriety, derive their chief attractions from the manner of treating them; from impassioned flow, or picturesque arrangement. In opposition to the present age, and perhaps in as faulty an extreme, they placed the essence of poetry in the art. The excellence, at which they aimed, consisted in the exquisite polish of the diction, combined with perfect simplicity. This their prime object they attained by the avoidance of every word, which a gentleman would not use in dignified conversation, and of every word and phrase, which none but a learned man would use; by the studied position of words and phrases, so that not only each part should be melodious in itself, but contribute to the harmony of the whole, each note referring and conducting to the melody of all the foregoing and following words of the same period or stanza; and lastly with equal labour, the greater because unbetrayed, by the variation and various harmonies of their metrical movement. Their measures, however, were not indebted for their variety to the introduction of new metres, such as have been attempted of late in the Alonzo and Imogen, and others borrowed from the German, having in their very mechanism a specific overpowering tune, to which the generous reader humours his voice and emphasis, with more indulgence to the author than attention to the meaning or quantity of the words; but which, to an ear familiar with the numerous sounds of the Greek and Roman poets, has an effect not unlike that of galloping over a paved road in a German stage-waggon without springs. On the contrary, the elder bards both of Italy and England produced a far greater as well as more charming variety by countless modifications, and subtle balances of sound in the common metres of their country. A lasting and enviable reputation awaits that man of genius, who should attempt and realize a union;—who should recall the high finish, the appropriateness, the facility, the delicate proportion, and above all, the perfusive and omnipresent grace, which have preserved, as in a shrine of precious amber, the Sparrow of Catullus, the Swallow, the Grasshopper, and all the other little loves of Anacreon; and which, with bright, though diminished glories, revisited the youth and early manhood of Christian Europe, in the vales of [63] Arno, and the groves of Isis and of Cam; and who with these should combine the keener interest, deeper pathos, manlier reflection, and the fresher and more various imagery, which give a value and a name that will not pass away to the poets who have done honour to our own times, and to those of our immediate predecessors.

CHAPTER XVII

Examination of the tenets peculiar to Mr. Wordsworth—Rustic life (above all, low and rustic life) especially unfavourable to the formation of a human diction—The best parts of language the product of philosophers, not of clowns or shepherds—Poetry essentially ideal and generic—The language of Milton as much the language of real life, yea, incomparably more so than that of the cottager.

As far then as Mr. Wordsworth in his preface contended, and most ably contended, for a reformation in our poetic diction, as far as he has evinced the truth of passion, and the dramatic propriety of those figures and metaphors in the original poets, which, stripped of their justifying reasons, and converted into mere artifices of connection or ornament, constitute the characteristic falsity in the poetic style of the moderns; and as far as he has, with equal acuteness and clearness, pointed out the process by which this change was effected, and the resemblances between that state into which the reader's mind is thrown by the pleasurable confusion of thought from an unaccustomed train of words and images; and that state which is induced by the natural language of impassioned feeling; he undertook a useful task, and deserves all praise, both for the attempt and for the execution. The provocations to this remonstrance in behalf of truth and nature were still of perpetual recurrence before and after the publication of this preface. I cannot likewise but add, that the comparison of such poems of merit, as have been given to the public within the last ten or twelve years, with the majority of those produced previously to the appearance of that preface, leave no doubt on my mind, that Mr. Wordsworth is fully justified in believing his efforts to have been by no means ineffectual. Not only in the verses of those who have professed their admiration of his genius, but even of those who have distinguished themselves by hostility to his theory, and depreciation of his writings, are the impressions of his principles plainly visible. It is possible, that with these principles others may have been blended, which are not equally evident; and some which are unsteady and subvertible from the narrowness or imperfection of their basis. But it is more than possible, that these errors of defect or exaggeration, by kindling and feeding the controversy, may have conduced not only to the wider propagation of the accompanying truths, but that, by their frequent presentation to the mind in an excited state, they may have won for them a more permanent and practical result. A man will borrow a part from his opponent the more easily, if he feels himself justified in continuing to reject a part. While there remain important points in which he can still feel himself in the right, in which he still finds firm footing for continued resistance, he will gradually adopt those opinions, which were the least remote from his own convictions, as not less congruous with his own theory than with that which he reprobates. In like manner with a kind of instinctive prudence, he will abandon by little and little his weakest posts, till at length he seems to forget that they had ever belonged to him, or affects to consider them at most as accidental and "petty annexments," the removal of which leaves the citadel unhurt and unendangered.

My own differences from certain supposed parts of Mr. Wordsworth's theory ground themselves on the assumption, that his words had been rightly interpreted, as purporting that the proper diction for poetry in general consists altogether in a language taken, with due exceptions, from the mouths of men in real life, a language which actually constitutes the natural conversation of men under the influence of natural feelings. My objection is, first, that in any sense this rule is applicable only to certain classes of poetry; secondly, that even to these classes it is not applicable, except in such a sense, as hath never by any one (as far as I know or have read,) been denied or doubted; and lastly, that as far as, and in that degree in which it is practicable, it is yet as a rule useless, if not injurious, and therefore either need not, or ought not to be practised. The poet informs his reader, that he had generally chosen low and rustic life; but not as low and rustic, or in order to repeat that pleasure of doubtful moral effect, which persons of elevated rank and of superior refinement oftentimes derive from a happy imitation of the rude unpolished manners and discourse of their inferiors. For the pleasure so derived may be traced to three exciting causes. The first is the naturalness, in fact, of the things represented. The second is the apparent naturalness of the representation, as raised and qualified by an imperceptible infusion of the author's own knowledge and talent, which infusion does, indeed, constitute it an imitation as distinguished from a mere copy. The third cause may be found in the reader's conscious feeling of his superiority awakened by the contrast presented to him; even as for the same purpose the kings and great barons of yore retained, sometimes actual clowns and fools, but more frequently shrewd and witty fellows in that character. These, however, were not Mr. Wordsworth's objects. He chose low and rustic life, "because in that condition the essential passions of the heart find a better soil, in which they can attain their maturity, are less under restraint, and speak a plainer and more emphatic language; because in that condition of life our elementary feelings coexist in a state of greater simplicity, and consequently may be more accurately contemplated, and more forcibly communicated; because the manners of rural life germinate from those elementary feelings; and from the necessary character of rural occupations are more easily comprehended, and are more durable; and lastly, because in that condition the passions of men are incorporated with the beautiful and permanent forms of nature."

Now it is clear to me, that in the most interesting of the poems, in which the author is more or less dramatic, as THE BROTHERS, MICHAEL, RUTH, THE MAD MOTHER, and others, the persons introduced are by no means taken from low or rustic life in the common acceptation of those words! and it is not less clear, that the sentiments and language, as far as they can be conceived to have been really transferred from the minds and conversation of such persons, are attributable to causes and circumstances not necessarily connected with "their occupations and abode." The thoughts, feelings, language, and manners of the shepherd-farmers in the vales of Cumberland and Westmoreland, as far as they are actually adopted in those poems, may be accounted for from causes, which will and do produce the same results in every state of life, whether in town or country. As the two principal I rank that independence, which raises a man above servitude, or daily toil for the profit of others, yet not above the necessity of industry and a frugal simplicity of domestic life; and the accompanying unambitious, but solid and religious, education, which has rendered few books familiar, but the Bible, and the Liturgy or Hymn book. To this latter cause, indeed, which is so far accidental, that it is the blessing of particular countries and a particular age, not the product of particular places or employments, the poet owes the show of probability, that his personages might really feel, think, and talk with any tolerable resemblance to his representation. It is an excellent remark of Dr. Henry More's, that "a man of confined education, but of good parts, by constant reading of the Bible will naturally form a more winning and commanding rhetoric than those that are learned: the intermixture of tongues and of artificial phrases debasing their style."

It is, moreover, to be considered that to the formation of healthy feelings, and a reflecting mind, negations involve impediments not less formidable than sophistication and vicious intermixture. I am convinced, that for the human soul to prosper in rustic life a certain vantage-ground is prerequisite. It is not every man that is likely to be improved by a country life or by country labours. Education, or original sensibility, or both, must pre-exist, if the changes, forms, and incidents of nature are to prove a sufficient stimulant. And where these are not sufficient, the mind contracts and hardens by want of stimulants: and the man becomes selfish, sensual, gross, and hard-hearted. Let the management of the Poor Laws in Liverpool, Manchester, or Bristol be compared with the ordinary dispensation of the poor rates in agricultural villages, where the farmers are the overseers and guardians of the poor. If my own experience have not been particularly unfortunate, as well as that of the many respectable country clergymen with whom I have conversed on the subject, the result would engender more than scepticism concerning the desirable influences of low and rustic life in and for itself. Whatever may be concluded on the other side, from the stronger local attachments and enterprising spirit of the Swiss, and other mountaineers, applies to a particular mode of pastoral life, under forms of property that permit and beget manners truly republican, not to rustic life in general, or to the absence of artificial cultivation. On the contrary the mountaineers, whose manners have been so often eulogized, are in general better educated and greater readers than men of equal rank elsewhere. But where this is not the case, as among the peasantry of North Wales, the ancient mountains, with all their terrors and all their glories, are pictures to the blind, and music to the deaf.

I should not have entered so much into detail upon this passage, but here seems to be the point, to which all the lines of difference converge as to their source and centre;—I mean, as far as, and in whatever respect, my poetic creed does differ from the doctrines promulgated in this preface. I adopt with full faith, the principle of Aristotle, that poetry, as poetry, is essentially ideal, that it avoids and excludes all accident; that its apparent individualities of rank, character, or occupation must be representative of a class; and that the persons of poetry must be clothed with generic attributes, with the common attributes of the class: not with such as one gifted individual might possibly possess, but such as from his situation it is most probable before-hand that he would possess. If my premises are right and my deductions legitimate, it follows that there can be no poetic medium between the swains of Theocritus and those of an imaginary golden age.

The characters of the vicar and the shepherd-mariner in the poem of THE BROTHERS, and that of the shepherd of Green-head Ghyll in the MICHAEL, have all the verisimilitude and representative quality, that the purposes of poetry can require. They are persons of a known and abiding class, and their manners and sentiments the natural product of circumstances common to the class. Take Michael for instance:

An old man stout of heart, and strong of limb.
His bodily frame had been from youth to age
Of an unusual strength: his mind was keen,
Intense, and frugal, apt for all affairs,
And in his shepherd's calling he was prompt
And watchful more than ordinary men.
Hence he had learned the meaning of all winds,
Of blasts of every tone; and oftentimes
When others heeded not, He heard the South
Make subterraneous music, like the noise

Of bagpipers on distant Highland hills.
The Shepherd, at such warning, of his flock
Bethought him, and he to himself would say,
'The winds are now devising work for me!'
And truly, at all times, the storm, that drives
The traveller to a shelter, summoned him
Up to the mountains: he had been alone
Amid the heart of many thousand mists,
That came to him and left him on the heights.
So lived he, until his eightieth year was past.
And grossly that man errs, who should suppose
That the green valleys, and the streams and rocks,
Were things indifferent to the Shepherd's thoughts.
Fields, where with cheerful spirits he had breathed
The common air; the hills, which he so oft
Had climbed with vigorous steps; which had impressed
So many incidents upon his mind
Of hardship, skill or courage, joy or fear;
Which, like a book, preserved the memory
Of the dumb animals, whom he had saved,
Had fed or sheltered, linking to such acts,
So grateful in themselves, the certainty
Of honourable gain; these fields, these hills
Which were his living Being, even more
Than his own blood—what could they less? had laid
Strong hold on his affections, were to him
A pleasurable feeling of blind love,
The pleasure which there is in life itself.

On the other hand, in the poems which are pitched in a lower key, as the HARRY GILL, and THE IDIOT BOY, the feelings are those of human nature in general; though the poet has judiciously laid the scene in the country, in order to place himself in the vicinity of interesting images, without the necessity of ascribing a sentimental perception of their beauty to the persons of his drama. In THE IDIOT BOY, indeed, the mother's character is not so much the real and native product of a "situation where the essential passions of the heart find a better soil, in which they can attain their maturity and speak a plainer and more emphatic language," as it is an impersonation of an instinct abandoned by judgment. Hence the two following charges seem to me not wholly groundless: at least, they are the only plausible objections, which I have heard to that fine poem. The one is, that the author has not, in the poem itself, taken sufficient care to preclude from the reader's fancy the disgusting images of ordinary morbid idiocy, which yet it was by no means his intention to represent. He was even by the "burr, burr, burr," uncounteracted by any preceding description of the boy's beauty, assisted in recalling them. The other is, that the idiocy of the boy is so evenly balanced by the folly of the mother, as to present to the general reader rather a laughable burlesque on the blindness of anile dotage, than an analytic display of maternal affection in its ordinary workings.

In THE THORN, the poet himself acknowledges in a note the necessity of an introductory poem, in which he should have portrayed the character of the person from whom the words of the poem are supposed to proceed: a superstitious man moderately imaginative, of slow faculties and deep feelings, "a captain of a small trading vessel, for example, who, being past the middle age of life, had retired upon an annuity, or small independent income, to some village or country town of which he was not a native, or in which he had not been accustomed to live. Such men having nothing to do become credulous and talkative from indolence." But in a poem, still more in a lyric poem—and the Nurse in ROMEO AND JULIET alone prevents me from extending the remark even to dramatic poetry, if indeed even the Nurse can be deemed altogether a case in point—it is not possible to imitate truly a dull and garrulous discourser, without repeating the effects of dullness and garrulity. However this may be, I dare assert, that the parts— (and these form the far larger portion of the whole)—which might as well or still better have proceeded from the poet's own imagination, and have been spoken in his own character, are those which have given, and which will continue to give, universal delight; and that the passages exclusively appropriate to the supposed narrator, such as the last couplet of the third stanza [64]; the seven last lines of the tenth [65]; and the five following stanzas, with the exception of the four admirable lines at the commencement of the fourteenth, are felt by many unprejudiced and unsophisticated hearts, as sudden and unpleasant sinkings from the height to which the poet had previously lifted them, and to which he again re-elevates both himself and his reader.

If then I am compelled to doubt the theory, by which the choice of characters was to be directed, not only a priori, from grounds of reason, but both from the few instances in which the poet himself need be supposed to have been governed by it, and from the comparative inferiority of those instances; still more must I hesitate in my assent to the sentence which immediately follows the former citation; and which I can neither admit as particular fact, nor as general rule. "The language, too, of these men has been adopted (purified indeed from what appear to be its real defects, from all lasting and rational causes of dislike or disgust) because such men hourly communicate with the best objects from which the best part of language is originally derived; and because, from their rank in society and the sameness and narrow circle of their intercourse, being less under the action of social vanity, they convey their feelings and notions in simple and unelaborated expressions." To this I reply; that a rustic's language, purified from all provincialism and grossness, and so far reconstructed as to be made consistent with the rules of grammar—(which are in essence no other than the laws of universal logic, applied to psychological materials)—will not differ from the language of any other man of common sense, however learned or refined he may be, except as far as the notions, which the rustic has to convey, are fewer and more indiscriminate. This will become still clearer, if we add the consideration—(equally important though less obvious)—that the rustic, from the more imperfect development of his faculties, and from the lower state of their cultivation, aims almost solely to convey insulated facts, either those of his scanty experience or his traditional belief; while the educated man chiefly seeks to discover and express those connections of things, or those relative bearings of fact to fact, from which some more or less general law is deducible. For facts are valuable to a wise man, chiefly as they lead to the discovery of the indwelling law, which is the true being of things, the sole solution of their modes of existence, and in the knowledge of which consists our dignity and our power.

As little can I agree with the assertion, that from the objects with which the rustic hourly communicates the best part of language is formed. For first, if to communicate with an object implies such an acquaintance with it, as renders it capable of being discriminately reflected on, the distinct knowledge of an uneducated rustic would furnish a very scanty vocabulary. The few things and modes of action requisite for his bodily conveniences would alone be individualized; while all the rest of nature would be expressed by a small number of confused general terms. Secondly, I deny that the words and combinations of words derived from the objects, with which the rustic is familiar, whether with distinct or confused knowledge, can be justly said to form the best part of language. It is more than probable, that many classes of the brute creation possess discriminating sounds, by which they can convey to each other notices of such objects as concern their food, shelter, or safety. Yet we hesitate to call the aggregate of such sounds a language, otherwise than metaphorically. The best part of human language, properly so called, is derived from reflection on the acts of the mind itself. It is formed by a voluntary appropriation of fixed symbols to internal acts, to processes and results of imagination, the greater part of which have no place in the consciousness of uneducated man; though in civilized society, by imitation and passive remembrance of what they hear from their religious instructors and other superiors, the most uneducated share in the harvest which they neither sowed, nor reaped. If the history of the phrases in hourly currency among our peasants were traced, a person not previously aware of the fact would be surprised at finding so large a number, which three or four centuries ago were the exclusive property of the universities and the schools; and, at the commencement of the Reformation, had been transferred from the school to the pulpit, and thus gradually passed into common life. The extreme difficulty, and often the impossibility, of finding words for the simplest moral and intellectual processes of the languages of uncivilized tribes has proved perhaps the weightiest obstacle to the progress of our most zealous and adroit missionaries. Yet these tribes are surrounded by the same nature as our peasants are; but in still more impressive forms; and they are, moreover, obliged to particularize many more of them. When, therefore, Mr. Wordsworth adds, "accordingly, such a language"—(meaning, as before, the language of rustic life purified from provincialism)—"arising out of repeated experience and regular feelings, is a more permanent, and a far more philosophical language, than that which is frequently substituted for it by Poets, who think that they are conferring honour upon themselves and their art in proportion as they indulge in arbitrary and capricious habits of expression;" it may be answered, that the language, which he has in view, can be attributed to rustics with no greater right, than the style of Hooker or Bacon to Tom Brown or Sir Roger L'Estrange. Doubtless, if what is peculiar to each were omitted in each, the result must needs be the same. Further, that the poet, who uses an illogical diction, or a style fitted to excite only the low and changeable pleasure of wonder by means of groundless novelty, substitutes a language of folly and vanity, not for that of the rustic, but for that of good sense and natural feeling.

Here let me be permitted to remind the reader, that the positions, which I controvert, are contained in the sentences—"a selection of the real language of men;"—"the language of these men" (that is, men in low and rustic life) "has been adopted; I have proposed to myself to imitate, and, as far as is possible, to adopt the very language of men."

"Between the language of prose and that of metrical composition, there neither is, nor can be, any essential difference:" it is against these exclusively that my opposition is directed.

I object, in the very first instance, to an equivocation in the use of the word "real." Every man's language varies, according to the extent of his knowledge, the activity of his faculties, and the depth or quickness of his feelings. Every man's language has, first, its individualities; secondly, the common properties of the class to which he belongs; and thirdly, words and phrases of universal use. The language of Hooker, Bacon, Bishop Taylor, and Burke differs from the common language of the learned class only by the superior number and novelty of the thoughts and relations which they had to convey. The language of Algernon Sidney differs not at all from that, which every well-educated gentleman would wish to write, and (with due allowances for the undeliberateness, and less connected train, of thinking natural and proper to conversation) such as he would wish to talk. Neither one nor the other differ half as much from the general language of cultivated society, as the language of Mr. Wordsworth's homeliest composition differs from that of a common peasant. For "real" therefore, we must substitute ordinary, or lingua communis. And this, we have proved, is no more to be found in the phraseology of low and rustic life than in that of any other class. Omit the peculiarities of each and the result of course must be common to all. And assuredly the omissions and changes to be made in the language of rustics, before it could be transferred to any species of poem, except the drama or other professed imitation, are at least as numerous and weighty, as would be required in adapting to the same purpose the ordinary language of tradesmen and manufacturers. Not to mention, that the language so highly extolled by Mr. Wordsworth varies in every county, nay in every village, according to the accidental character of the clergyman, the existence or non-existence of schools; or even, perhaps, as the exciteman, publican, and barber happen to be, or not to be, zealous politicians, and readers of the weekly newspaper pro bono publico. Anterior to cultivation the lingua communis of every country, as Dante has well observed, exists every where in parts, and no where as a whole.

Neither is the case rendered at all more tenable by the addition of the words, "in a state of excitement." For the nature of a man's words, where he is strongly affected by joy, grief, or anger, must necessarily depend on the number and quality of the general truths, conceptions and images, and of the words expressing them, with which his mind had been previously stored. For the property of passion is not to create; but to set in increased activity. At least, whatever new connections of thoughts or images, or—(which is equally, if not more than equally, the appropriate effect of strong excitement)—whatever generalizations of truth or experience the heat of passion may produce; yet the terms of their conveyance must have pre-existed in his former conversations, and are only collected and crowded together by the unusual stimulation. It is indeed very possible to adopt in a poem the unmeaning repetitions, habitual phrases, and other blank counters, which an unfurnished or confused understanding interposes at short intervals, in order to keep hold of his subject, which is still slipping from him, and to give him time for recollection; or, in mere aid of vacancy, as in the scanty companies of a country stage the same player pops backwards and forwards, in order to prevent the appearance of empty spaces, in the procession of Macbeth, or Henry VIII. But what assistance to the poet, or ornament to the poem, these can supply, I am at a loss to conjecture. Nothing assuredly can differ either in origin or in mode more widely from the apparent tautologies of intense and turbulent feeling, in which the passion is greater and of longer endurance than to be exhausted or satisfied by a single representation of the image or incident exciting it. Such repetitions I admit to be a beauty of the highest kind; as illustrated by Mr. Wordsworth himself from the song of Deborah. At her feet he bowed, he fell, he lay down: at her feet he bowed, he fell: where he bowed, there he fell down dead. Judges v. 27.

CHAPTER XVIII

Language of metrical composition, why and wherein essentially different from that of prose—Origin and elements of metre—Its necessary consequences, and the conditions thereby imposed on the metrical writer in the choice of his diction.

I conclude, therefore, that the attempt is impracticable; and that, were it not impracticable, it would still be useless. For the very power of making the selection implies the previous possession of the language selected. Or where can the poet have lived? And by what rules could he direct his choice, which would not have enabled him to select and arrange his words by the light of his own judgment? We do not adopt the language of a class by the mere adoption of such words exclusively, as that class would use, or at least understand; but likewise by following the order, in which the words of such men are wont to succeed each other. Now this order, in the intercourse of uneducated men, is distinguished from the diction of their superiors in knowledge and power, by the greater disjunction and separation in the component parts of that, whatever it be, which they wish to communicate. There is a want of that prospectiveness of mind, that surview, which enables a man to foresee the whole of what he is to convey, appertaining to any one point; and by this means so to subordinate and arrange the different parts according to their relative importance, as to convey it at once, and as an organized whole.

Now I will take the first stanza, on which I have chanced to open, in the Lyrical Ballads. It is one the most simple and the least peculiar in its language.

"In distant countries have I been,
And yet I have not often seen
A healthy man, a man full grown,
Weep in the public roads, alone.
But such a one, on English ground,
And in the broad highway, I met;
Along the broad highway he came,
His cheeks with tears were wet
Sturdy he seemed, though he was sad;
And in his arms a lamb he had."

The words here are doubtless such as are current in all ranks of life; and of course not less so in the hamlet and cottage than in the shop, manufactory, college, or palace. But is this the order, in which the rustic would have placed the words? I am grievously deceived, if the following less compact mode of commencing the same tale be not a far more faithful copy. "I have been in a many parts, far and near, and I don't know that I ever saw before a man crying by himself in the public road; a grown man I mean, that was neither sick nor hurt," etc., etc. But when I turn to the following stanza in The Thorn:

"At all times of the day and night
This wretched woman thither goes;
And she is known to every star,
And every wind that blows
And there, beside the Thorn, she sits,
When the blue day-light's in the skies,
And when the whirlwind's on the hill,
Or frosty air is keen and still,
And to herself she cries,
Oh misery! Oh misery!
Oh woe is me! Oh misery!"

and compare this with the language of ordinary men; or with that which I can conceive at all likely to proceed, in real life, from such a narrator, as is supposed in the note to the poem; compare it either in the succession of the images or of the sentences; I am reminded of the sublime prayer and hymn of praise, which Milton, in opposition to an established liturgy, presents as a fair specimen of common extemporary devotion, and such as we might expect to hear from every self-inspired minister of a conventicle! And I reflect with delight, how little a mere theory, though of his own workmanship, interferes with the processes of genuine imagination in a man of true poetic genius, who possesses, as Mr. Wordsworth, if ever man did, most assuredly does possess,

"The Vision and the Faculty divine."

One point then alone remains, but that the most important; its examination having been, indeed, my chief inducement for the preceding inquisition. "There neither is nor can be any essential difference between the language of prose and metrical composition." Such is Mr. Wordsworth's assertion. Now prose itself, at least in all argumentative and consecutive works, differs, and ought to differ, from the language of conversation; even as [66] reading ought to differ from talking. Unless therefore the difference denied be that of the mere words, as materials common to all styles of writing, and not of the style itself in the universally admitted sense of the term, it might be naturally presumed that there must exist a still greater between the ordonnance of poetic composition and that of prose, than is expected to distinguish prose from ordinary conversation.

There are not, indeed, examples wanting in the history of literature, of apparent paradoxes that have summoned the public wonder as new and startling truths, but which, on examination, have shrunk into tame and harmless truisms; as the eyes of a cat, seen in the dark, have been mistaken for flames of fire. But Mr. Wordsworth is among the last men, to whom a delusion of this kind would be attributed by anyone, who had enjoyed the slightest opportunity of understanding his mind and character. Where an objection has been anticipated by such an author as natural, his answer to it must needs be interpreted in some sense which either is, or has been, or is capable of being controverted. My object then must be to discover some other meaning for the term "essential difference" in this place, exclusive of the indistinction and community of the words themselves. For whether there ought to exist a class of words in the English, in any degree resembling the poetic dialect of the Greek and Italian, is a question of very subordinate importance. The number of such words would be small indeed, in our language; and even in the Italian and Greek, they consist not so much of different words, as of slight differences in the forms of declining and conjugating the same words; forms, doubtless, which having been, at some period more or less remote, the common grammatic flexions of some tribe or province, had been accidentally appropriated to poetry by the general admiration of certain master intellects, the first established lights of inspiration, to whom that dialect happened to be native.

Essence, in its primary signification, means the principle of individuation, the inmost principle of the possibility of any thing, as that particular thing. It is equivalent to the idea of a thing, whenever we use the word, idea, with philosophic precision. Existence, on the other hand, is distinguished from essence, by the superinduction of reality. Thus we speak of the essence, and essential properties of a circle; but we do not therefore assert, that any thing, which really exists, is mathematically circular. Thus too, without any tautology we contend for the existence of the Supreme Being; that is, for a reality correspondent to the idea. There is, next, a secondary use of the word essence, in which it signifies the point or ground of contra-distinction between two modifications of the same substance or subject. Thus we should be allowed to say, that the style of architecture of Westminster Abbey is essentially different from that of St. Paul, even though both had been built with blocks cut into the same form, and from the same quarry. Only in this latter sense of the term must it have been denied by Mr. Wordsworth (for in this sense alone is it affirmed by the general opinion) that the language of poetry (that is the formal construction, or architecture, of the words and phrases) is essentially different from that of prose. Now the burden of the proof lies with the oppugner, not with the supporters of the common belief. Mr. Wordsworth, in consequence, assigns as the proof of his position, "that not only the language of a large portion of every good poem, even of the most elevated character, must necessarily, except with reference to the metre, in no respect differ from that of good prose, but likewise that some of the most interesting parts of the best poems will be found to be strictly the language of prose, when prose is well written. The truth of this assertion might be demonstrated by innumerable passages from almost all the poetical writings, even of Milton himself." He then quotes Gray's sonnet—

"In vain to me the smiling mornings shine,
And reddening Phoebus lifts his golden fire;
The birds in vain their amorous descant join,
Or cheerful fields resume their green attire.
These ears, alas! for other notes repine;
A different object do these eyes require;
My lonely anguish melts no heart but mine;
And in my breast the imperfect joys expire.
Yet morning smiles the busy race to cheer,
And new-born pleasure brings to happier men;
The fields to all their wonted tribute bear;
To warm their little loves the birds complain:
I fruitless mourn to him that cannot hear,
And weep the more, because I weep in vain."

and adds the following remark:—"It will easily be perceived, that the only part of this Sonnet which is of any value, is the lines printed in italics; it is equally obvious, that, except in the rhyme, and in the use of the single word 'fruitless' for fruitlessly, which is so far a defect, the language of these lines does in no respect differ from that of prose."

An idealist defending his system by the fact, that when asleep we often believe ourselves awake, was well answered by his plain neighbour, "Ah, but when awake do we ever believe ourselves asleep?" Things identical must be convertible. The preceding passage seems to rest on a similar sophism. For the question is not, whether there may not occur in prose an order of words, which would be equally proper in a poem; nor whether there are not beautiful lines and sentences of frequent occurrence in good poems, which would be equally becoming as well as beautiful in good prose; for neither the one nor the other has ever been either denied or doubted by any one. The true question must be, whether there are not modes of expression, a construction, and an order of sentences, which are in their fit and natural place in a serious prose composition, but would be disproportionate and heterogeneous in metrical poetry; and, vice versa, whether in the language of a serious poem there may not be an arrangement both of words and sentences, and a use and selection of (what are called) figures of speech, both as to their kind, their frequency, and their occasions, which on a subject of equal weight would be vicious and alien in correct and manly prose. I contend, that in both cases this unfitness of each for the place of the other frequently will and ought to exist.

And first from the origin of metre. This I would trace to the balance in the mind effected by that spontaneous effort which strives to hold in check the workings of passion. It might be easily explained likewise in what manner this salutary antagonism is assisted by the very state, which it counteracts; and how this balance of antagonists became organized into metre (in the usual acceptation of that term), by a supervening act of the will and judgment, consciously and for the foreseen purpose of pleasure. Assuming these principles, as the data of our argument, we deduce from them two legitimate conditions, which the critic is entitled to expect in every metrical work. First, that, as the elements of metre owe their existence to a state of increased excitement, so the metre itself should be accompanied by the natural language of excitement. Secondly, that as these elements are formed into metre artificially, by a voluntary act, with the design and for the purpose of blending delight with emotion, so the traces of present volition should throughout the metrical language be proportionately discernible. Now these two conditions must be reconciled and co- present. There must be not only a partnership, but a union; an interpenetration of passion and of will, of spontaneous impulse and of voluntary purpose. Again, this union can be manifested only in a frequency of forms and figures of speech, (originally the offspring of passion, but now the adopted children of power), greater than would be desired or endured, where the emotion is not voluntarily encouraged and kept up for the sake of that pleasure, which such emotion, so tempered and mastered by the will, is found capable of communicating. It not only dictates, but of itself tends to produce a more frequent employment of picturesque and vivifying language, than would be natural in any other case, in which there did not exist, as there does in the present, a previous and well understood, though tacit, compact between the poet and his reader, that the latter is entitled to expect, and the former bound to supply this species and degree of pleasurable excitement. We may in some measure apply to this union the answer of Polixenes, in the Winter's Tale, to Perdita's neglect of the streaked gilliflowers, because she had heard it said,

"There is an art, which, in their piedness, shares
With great creating nature.
POL. Say there be;
Yet nature is made better by no mean,
But nature makes that mean; so, o'er that art,
Which, you say, adds to nature, is an art,
That nature makes. You see, sweet maid, we marry

A gentler scion to the wildest stock;
And make conceive a bark of baser kind
By bud of nobler race. This is an art,
Which does mend nature,—change it rather; but
The art itself is nature."

Secondly, I argue from the effects of metre. As far as metre acts in and for itself, it tends to increase the vivacity and susceptibility both of the general feelings and of the attention. This effect it produces by the continued excitement of surprise, and by the quick reciprocations of curiosity still gratified and still re-excited, which are too slight indeed to be at any one moment objects of distinct consciousness, yet become considerable in their aggregate influence. As a medicated atmosphere, or as wine during animated conversation, they act powerfully, though themselves unnoticed. Where, therefore, correspondent food and appropriate matter are not provided for the attention and feelings thus roused there must needs be a disappointment felt; like that of leaping in the dark from the last step of a stair-case, when we had prepared our muscles for a leap of three or four.

The discussion on the powers of metre in the preface is highly ingenious and touches at all points on truth. But I cannot find any statement of its powers considered abstractly and separately. On the contrary Mr. Wordsworth seems always to estimate metre by the powers, which it exerts during, (and, as I think, in consequence of) its combination with other elements of poetry. Thus the previous difficulty is left unanswered, what the elements are, with which it must be combined, in order to produce its own effects to any pleasurable purpose. Double and tri-syllable rhymes, indeed, form a lower species of wit, and, attended to exclusively for their own sake, may become a source of momentary amusement; as in poor Smart's distich to the Welsh Squire who had promised him a hare:

"Tell me, thou son of great Cadwallader!
Hast sent the hare? or hast thou swallow'd her?"

But for any poetic purposes, metre resembles, (if the aptness of the simile may excuse its meanness), yeast, worthless or disagreeable by itself, but giving vivacity and spirit to the liquor with which it is proportionally combined.

The reference to THE CHILDREN IN THE WOOD by no means satisfies my judgment. We all willingly throw ourselves back for awhile into the feelings of our childhood. This ballad, therefore, we read under such recollections of our own childish feelings, as would equally endear to us poems, which Mr. Wordsworth himself would regard as faulty in the opposite extreme of gaudy and technical ornament. Before the invention of printing, and in a still greater degree, before the introduction of writing, metre, especially alliterative metre, (whether alliterative at the beginning of the words, as in PIERCE PLOUMAN, or at the end, as in rhymes) possessed an independent value as assisting the recollection, and consequently the preservation, of any series of truths or incidents. But I am not convinced by the collation of facts, that THE CHILDREN IN THE WOOD owes either its preservation, or its popularity, to its metrical form. Mr. Marshal's repository affords a number of tales in prose inferior in pathos and general merit, some of as old a date, and many as widely popular. TOM HICKATHRIFT, JACK THE GIANT-KILLER, GOODY TWO-SHOES, and LITTLE RED RIDING-HOOD are formidable rivals. And that they have continued in prose, cannot be fairly explained by the assumption, that the comparative meanness of their thoughts and images precluded even the humblest forms of metre. The scene of GOODY TWO-SHOES in the church is perfectly susceptible of metrical narration; and, among the thaumata thaumastotata even of the present age, I do not recollect a more astonishing image than that of the "whole rookery, that flew out of the giant's beard," scared by the tremendous voice, with which this monster answered the challenge of the heroic TOM HICKATHRIFT!

If from these we turn to compositions universally, and independently of all early associations, beloved and admired; would the MARIA, THE MONK, or THE POOR MAN'S ASS of Sterne, be read with more delight, or have a better chance of immortality, had they without any change in the diction been composed in rhyme, than in their present state? If I am not grossly mistaken, the general reply would be in the negative. Nay, I will confess, that, in Mr. Wordsworth's own volumes, the ANECDOTE FOR FATHERS, SIMON LEE, ALICE FELL, BEGGARS, and THE SAILOR'S MOTHER, notwithstanding the beauties which are to be found in each of them where the poet interposes the music of his own thoughts, would have been more delightful to me in prose, told and managed, as by Mr. Wordsworth they would have been, in a moral essay or pedestrian tour.

Metre in itself is simply a stimulant of the attention, and therefore excites the question: Why is the attention to be thus stimulated? Now the question cannot be answered by the pleasure of the metre itself; for this we have shown to be conditional, and dependent on the appropriateness of the thoughts and expressions, to which the metrical form is superadded. Neither can I conceive any other answer that can be rationally given, short of this: I write in metre, because I am about to use a language different from that of prose. Besides, where the language is not such, how interesting soever the reflections are, that are capable of being drawn by a philosophic mind from the thoughts or incidents of the poem, the metre itself must often become feeble. Take the last three stanzas of THE SAILOR'S MOTHER, for instance. If I could for a moment abstract from the effect produced on the author's feelings, as a man, by the incident at the time of its real occurrence, I would dare appeal to his own judgment, whether in the metre itself he found a sufficient reason for their being written metrically?

And, thus continuing, she said,
"I had a Son, who many a day
Sailed on the seas; but he is dead;
In Denmark he was cast away;
And I have travelled far as Hull to see
What clothes he might have left, or other property.

The Bird and Cage they both were his
'Twas my Son's Bird; and neat and trim
He kept it: many voyages
This Singing-bird hath gone with him;
When last he sailed he left the Bird behind;
As it might be, perhaps, from bodings of his mind.

He to a Fellow-lodger's care
Had left it, to be watched and fed,
Till he came back again; and there
I found it when my Son was dead;
And now, God help me for my little wit!
I trail it with me, Sir! he took so much delight in it."

If disproportioning the emphasis we read these stanzas so as to make the rhymes perceptible, even tri-syllable rhymes could scarcely produce an equal sense of oddity and strangeness, as we feel here in finding rhymes at all in sentences so exclusively colloquial. I would further ask whether, but for that visionary state, into which the figure of the woman and the susceptibility of his own genius had placed the poet's imagination,—(a state, which spreads its influence and colouring over all, that co-exists with the exciting cause, and in which

"The simplest, and the most familiar things
Gain a strange power of spreading awe around them,") [67]

I would ask the poet whether he would not have felt an abrupt downfall in these verses from the preceding stanza?

"The ancient spirit is not dead;
Old times, thought I, are breathing there;
Proud was I that my country bred
Such strength, a dignity so fair:

*She begged an alms, like one in poor estate;
I looked at her again, nor did my pride abate."*

It must not be omitted, and is besides worthy of notice, that those stanzas furnish the only fair instance that I have been able to discover in all Mr. Wordsworth's writings, of an actual adoption, or true imitation, of the real and very language of low and rustic life, freed from provincialisms.

Thirdly, I deduce the position from all the causes elsewhere assigned, which render metre the proper form of poetry, and poetry imperfect and defective without metre. Metre, therefore, having been connected with poetry most often and by a peculiar fitness, whatever else is combined with metre must, though it be not itself essentially poetic, have nevertheless some property in common with poetry, as an intermedium of affinity, a sort, (if I may dare borrow a well-known phrase from technical chemistry), of mordaunt between it and the super-added metre. Now poetry, Mr. Wordsworth truly affirms, does always imply passion: which word must be here understood in its most general sense, as an excited state of the feelings and faculties. And as every passion has its proper pulse, so will it likewise have its characteristic modes of expression. But where there exists that degree of genius and talent which entitles a writer to aim at the honours of a poet, the very act of poetic composition itself is, and is allowed to imply and to produce, an unusual state of excitement, which of course justifies and demands a correspondent difference of language, as truly, though not perhaps in as marked a degree, as the excitement of love, fear, rage, or jealousy. The vividness of the descriptions or declamations in Donne or Dryden, is as much and as often derived from the force and fervour of the describer, as from the reflections, forms or incidents, which constitute their subject and materials. The wheels take fire from the mere rapidity of their motion. To what extent, and under what modifications, this may be admitted to act, I shall attempt to define in an after remark on Mr. Wordsworth's reply to this objection, or rather on his objection to this reply, as already anticipated in his preface.

Fourthly, and as intimately connected with this, if not the same argument in a more general form, I adduce the high spiritual instinct of the human being impelling us to seek unity by harmonious adjustment, and thus establishing the principle that all the parts of an organized whole must be assimilated to the more important and essential parts. This and the preceding arguments may be strengthened by the reflection, that the composition of a poem is among the imitative arts; and that imitation, as opposed to copying, consists either in the interfusion of the same throughout the radically different, or of the different throughout a base radically the same.

Lastly, I appeal to the practice of the best poets, of all countries and in all ages, as authorizing the opinion, (deduced from all the foregoing,) that in every import of the word essential, which would not here involve a mere truism, there may be, is, and ought to be an essential difference between the language of prose and of metrical composition.

In Mr. Wordsworth's criticism of Gray's Sonnet, the reader's sympathy with his praise or blame of the different parts is taken for granted rather perhaps too easily. He has not, at least, attempted to win or compel it by argumentative analysis. In my conception at least, the lines rejected as of no value do, with the exception of the two first, differ as much and as little from the language of common life, as those which he has printed in italics as possessing genuine excellence. Of the five lines thus honourably distinguished, two of them differ from prose even more widely, than the lines which either precede or follow, in the position of the words.

"A different object do these eyes require;
My lonely anguish melts no heart but mine;
And in my breast the imperfect joys expire."

But were it otherwise, what would this prove, but a truth, of which no man ever doubted?—videlicet, that there are sentences, which would be equally in their place both in verse and prose. Assuredly it does not prove the point, which alone requires proof; namely, that there are not passages, which would suit the one and not suit the other. The first line of this sonnet is distinguished from the ordinary language of men by the epithet to morning. For we will set aside, at present, the consideration, that the particular word "smiling" is hackneyed, and, as it involves a sort of personification, not quite congruous with the common and material attribute of "shining." And, doubtless, this adjunction of epithets for the purpose of additional description, where no particular attention is demanded for the quality of the thing, would be noticed as giving a poetic cast to a man's conversation. Should the sportsman exclaim, "Come boys! the rosy morning calls you up:" he will be supposed to have some song in his head. But no one suspects this, when he says, "A wet morning shall not confine us to our beds." This then is either a defect in poetry, or it is not. Whoever should decide in the affirmative, I would request him to re-peruse any one poem, of any confessedly great poet from Homer to Milton, or from Aeschylus to Shakespeare; and to strike out, (in thought I mean), every instance of this kind. If the number of these fancied erasures did not startle him; or if he continued to deem the work improved by their total omission; he must advance reasons of no ordinary strength and evidence, reasons grounded in the essence of human nature. Otherwise, I should not hesitate to consider him as a man not so much proof against all authority, as dead to it.

The second line,

"And reddening Phoebus lifts his golden fire;—"

has indeed almost as many faults as words. But then it is a bad line, not because the language is distinct from that of prose; but because it conveys incongruous images; because it confounds the cause and the effect; the real thing with the personified representative of the thing; in short, because it differs from the language of good sense! That the "Phoebus" is hackneyed, and a school-boy image, is an accidental fault, dependent on the age in which the author wrote, and not deduced from the nature of the thing. That it is part of an exploded mythology, is an objection more deeply grounded. Yet when the torch of ancient learning was re-kindled, so cheering were its beams, that our eldest poets, cut off by Christianity from all accredited machinery, and deprived of all acknowledged guardians and symbols of the great objects of nature, were naturally induced to adopt, as a poetic language, those fabulous personages, those forms of the [68]supernatural in nature, which had given them such dear delight in the poems of their great masters. Nay, even at this day what scholar of genial taste will not so far sympathize with them, as to read with pleasure in Petrarch, Chaucer, or Spenser, what he would perhaps condemn as puerile in a modern poet?

I remember no poet, whose writings would safelier stand the test of Mr. Wordsworth's theory, than Spenser. Yet will Mr. Wordsworth say, that the style of the following stanza is either undistinguished from prose, and the language of ordinary life? Or that it is vicious, and that the stanzas are blots in THE FAERY QUEEN?

*"By this the northern wagoner had set
His sevenfold teme behind the stedfast starre,
That was in ocean waves yet never wet,
But firme is fixt and sendeth light from farre
To all that in the wild deep wandering arre
And chearfull chaunticlere with his note shrill
Had warned once that Phoebus' fiery carre
In hast was climbing up the easterne hill,
Full envious that night so long his roome did fill."*

*"At last the golden orientall gate
Of greatest heaven gan to open fayre,
And Phoebus fresh, as brydegrome to his mate,
Came dauncing forth, shaking his deawie hayre,
And hurl'd his glist'ring beams through gloomy ayre:
Which when the wakeful elfe perceived, streightway*

He started up, and did him selfe prepayre
In sun-bright armes and battailous array;
For with that pagan proud he combat will that day."

On the contrary to how many passages, both in hymn books and in blank verse poems, could I, (were it not invidious), direct the reader's attention, the style of which is most unpoetic, because, and only because, it is the style of prose? He will not suppose me capable of having in my mind such verses, as

"I put my hat upon my head
And walk'd into the Strand;
And there I met another man,
Whose hat was in his hand."

To such specimens it would indeed be a fair and full reply, that these lines are not bad, because they are unpoetic; but because they are empty of all sense and feeling; and that it were an idle attempt to prove that "an ape is not a Newton, when it is self-evident that he is not a man." But the sense shall be good and weighty, the language correct and dignified, the subject interesting and treated with feeling; and yet the style shall, notwithstanding all these merits, be justly blamable as prosaic, and solely because the words and the order of the words would find their appropriate place in prose, but are not suitable to metrical composition. The CIVIL WARS of Daniel is an instructive, and even interesting work; but take the following stanzas, (and from the hundred instances which abound I might probably have selected others far more striking):

"And to the end we may with better ease
Discern the true discourse, vouchsafe to shew
What were the times foregoing near to these,
That these we may with better profit know.
Tell how the world fell into this disease;
And how so great distemperature did grow;
So shall we see with what degrees it came;
How things at full do soon wax out of frame."

"Ten kings had from the Norman Conqu'ror reign'd
With intermix'd and variable fate,
When England to her greatest height attain'd
Of power, dominion, glory, wealth, and state;
After it had with much ado sustain'd
The violence of princes, with debate
For titles and the often mutinies
Of nobles for their ancient liberties."

"For first, the Norman, conqu'ring all by might,
By might was forc'd to keep what he had got;
Mixing our customs and the form of right
With foreign constitutions, he had brought;
Mast'ring the mighty, humbling the poorer wight,
By all severest means that could be wrought;
And, making the succession doubtful, rent
His new-got state, and left it turbulent."

Will it be contended on the one side, that these lines are mean and senseless? Or on the other, that they are not prosaic, and for that reason unpoetic? This poet's well-merited epithet is that of the "well-languaged Daniel;" but likewise, and by the consent of his contemporaries no less than of all succeeding critics, "the prosaic Daniel." Yet those, who thus designate this wise and amiable writer from the frequent incorrespondency of his diction to his metre in the majority of his compositions, not only deem them valuable and interesting on other accounts; but willingly admit, that there are to be found throughout his poems, and especially in his EPISTLES and in his HYMEN'S TRIUMPH, many and exquisite specimens of that style which, as the neutral ground of prose and verse, is common to both. A fine and almost faultless extract, eminent as for other beauties, so for its perfection in this species of diction, may be seen in Lamb's DRAMATIC SPECIMENS, a work of various interest from the nature of the selections themselves, (all from the plays of Shakespeare's contemporaries),—and deriving a high additional value from the notes, which are full of just and original criticism, expressed with all the freshness of originality.

Among the possible effects of practical adherence to a theory, that aims to identify the style of prose and verse,—(if it does not indeed claim for the latter a yet nearer resemblance to the average style of men in the viva voce intercourse of real life)—we might anticipate the following as not the least likely to occur. It will happen, as I have indeed before observed, that the metre itself, the sole acknowledged difference, will occasionally become metre to the eye only. The existence of prosaisms, and that they detract from the merit of a poem, must at length be conceded, when a number of successive lines can be rendered, even to the most delicate ear, unrecognizable as verse, or as having even been intended for verse, by simply transcribing them as prose; when if the poem be in blank verse, this can be effected without any alteration, or at most by merely restoring one or two words to their proper places, from which they have been transplanted [69] for no assignable cause or reason but that of the author's convenience; but if it be in rhyme, by the mere exchange of the final word of each line for some other of the same meaning, equally appropriate, dignified and euphonic.

The answer or objection in the preface to the anticipated remark "that metre paves the way to other distinctions," is contained in the following words. "The distinction of rhyme and metre is regular and uniform, and not, like that produced by (what is usually called) poetic diction, arbitrary, and subject to infinite caprices, upon which no calculation whatever can be made. In the one case the reader is utterly at the mercy of the poet respecting what imagery or diction he may choose to connect with the passion." But is this a poet, of whom a poet is speaking? No surely! rather of a fool or madman: or at best of a vain or ignorant phantast! And might not brains so wild and so deficient make just the same havoc with rhymes and metres, as they are supposed to effect with modes and figures of speech? How is the reader at the mercy of such men? If he continue to read their nonsense, is it not his own fault? The ultimate end of criticism is much more to establish the principles of writing, than to furnish rules how to pass judgment on what has been written by others; if indeed it were possible that the two could be separated. But if it be asked, by what principles the poet is to regulate his own style, if he do not adhere closely to the sort and order of words which he hears in the market, wake, high-road, or plough-field? I reply; by principles, the ignorance or neglect of which would convict him of being no poet, but a silly or presumptuous usurper of the name. By the principles of grammar, logic, psychology. In one word by such a knowledge of the facts, material and spiritual, that most appertain to his art, as, if it have been governed and applied by good sense, and rendered instinctive by habit, becomes the representative and reward of our past conscious reasonings, insights, and conclusions, and acquires the name of Taste. By what rule that does not leave the reader at the poet's mercy, and the poet at his own, is the latter to distinguish between the language suitable to suppressed, and the language, which is characteristic of indulged, anger? Or between that of rage and that of jealousy? Is it obtained by wandering about in search of angry or jealous people in uncultivated society, in order to copy their words? Or not far rather by the power of imagination proceeding upon the all in each of human nature? By meditation, rather than by observation? And by the latter in consequence only of the former? As eyes, for which the former has pre-determined their field of vision, and to which, as to its organ, it communicates a microscopic power? There is not, I firmly believe, a man now living, who has, from his own inward experience, a clearer intuition, than Mr. Wordsworth himself, that the last mentioned are the true sources of genial discrimination. Through the same process and by the same creative agency will the poet distinguish the degree and kind of the excitement produced by the very act of poetic composition. As intuitively will he know, what differences of style it at once inspires and justifies; what intermixture of conscious volition is natural to that state; and in what instances such figures and colours of speech degenerate into mere creatures of an arbitrary purpose, cold technical artifices of ornament or connection. For, even as truth is its own light and evidence, discovering at once itself and falsehood, so is it the prerogative of poetic genius to distinguish by parental instinct its proper offspring from the changelings, which the gnomes of vanity or the fairies of fashion may have laid in its cradle or called by its names. Could a rule be given from without, poetry would cease to be poetry, and sink into a mechanical art. It would be morphosis, not poiaesis. The rules of the Imagination are themselves the very powers of growth and production. The words to which they are reducible, present only the outlines and external appearance of the fruit. A deceptive counterfeit of the superficial form and colours may be elaborated; but the marble peach feels cold and heavy, and children only put it to their mouths. We find no difficulty in admitting as excellent, and the legitimate language of poetic fervour self-impassioned, Donne's apostrophe to the Sun in the second stanza of his PROGRESS OF THE SOUL.

"Thee, eye of heaven! this great Soul envies not;
By thy male force is all, we have, begot.
In the first East thou now beginn'st to shine,
Suck'st early balm and island spices there,
And wilt anon in thy loose-rein'd career
At Tagus, Po, Seine, Thames, and Danow dine,
And see at night this western world of mine:
Yet hast thou not more nations seen than she,
Who before thee one day began to be,
And, thy frail light being quench'd, shall long, long outlive thee."

Or the next stanza but one:

"Great Destiny, the commissary of God,
That hast mark'd out a path and period
For every thing! Who, where we offspring took,
Our ways and ends see'st at one instant: thou
Knot of all causes! Thou, whose changeless brow
Ne'er smiles nor frowns! O! vouchsafe thou to look,
And shew my story in thy eternal book," etc.

As little difficulty do we find in excluding from the honours of unaffected warmth and elevation the madness prepense of pseudopoesy, or the startling hysteric of weakness over-exerting itself, which bursts on the unprepared reader in sundry odes and apostrophes to abstract terms. Such are the Odes to jealousy, to Hope, to Oblivion, and the like, in Dodsley's collection and the magazines of that day, which seldom fail to remind me of an Oxford copy of verses on the two SUTTONS, commencing with

"Inoculation, heavenly maid! descend!"

It is not to be denied that men of undoubted talents, and even poets of true, though not of first-rate, genius, have from a mistaken theory deluded both themselves and others in the opposite extreme. I once read to a company of sensible and well-educated women the introductory period of Cowley's preface to his "Pindaric Odes," written in imitation of the style and manner of the odes of Pindar. "If," (says Cowley), "a man should undertake to translate Pindar, word for word, it would be thought that one madman had translated another as may appear, when he, that understands not the original, reads the verbal traduction of him into Latin prose, than which nothing seems more raving." I then proceeded with his own free version of the second Olympic, composed for the charitable purpose of rationalizing the Theban Eagle.

"Queen of all harmonious things,
Dancing words and speaking strings,
What god, what hero, wilt thou sing?
What happy man to equal glories bring?
Begin, begin thy noble choice,
And let the hills around reflect the image of thy voice.
Pisa does to Jove belong,
Jove and Pisa claim thy song.
The fair first-fruits of war, th' Olympic games,
Alcides, offer'd up to Jove;
Alcides, too, thy strings may move,
But, oh! what man to join with these can worthy prove?
Join Theron boldly to their sacred names;
Theron the next honour claims;
Theron to no man gives place,
Is first in Pisa's and in Virtue's race;
Theron there, and he alone,
Ev'n his own swift forefathers has outgone."

One of the company exclaimed, with the full assent of the rest, that if the original were madder than this, it must be incurably mad. I then translated the ode from the Greek, and as nearly as possible, word for word; and the impression was, that in the general movement of the periods, in the form of the connections and transitions, and in the sober majesty of lofty sense, it appeared to them to approach more nearly, than any other poetry they had heard, to the style of our Bible, in the prophetic books. The first strophe will suffice as a specimen:

"Ye harp-controlling hymns! (or) ye hymns the sovereigns of harps!
What God? what Hero?
What Man shall we celebrate?
Truly Pisa indeed is of Jove,
But the Olympiad (or the Olympic games) did Hercules establish,
The first-fruits of the spoils of war.
But Theron for the four-horsed car,
That bore victory to him,
It behoves us now to voice aloud:
The Just, the Hospitable,
The Bulwark of Agrigentum,
Of renowned fathers
The Flower, even him
Who preserves his native city erect and safe."

But are such rhetorical caprices condemnable only for their deviation from the language of real life? and are they by no other means to be precluded, but by the rejection of all distinctions between prose and verse, save that of metre? Surely good sense, and a moderate insight into the constitution of the human mind, would be amply sufficient to prove, that such language and such combinations are the native product neither of the fancy nor of the imagination; that their operation consists in the excitement of surprise by the juxta-position and apparent reconciliation of widely different or incompatible things. As when, for instance, the hills are made to reflect the image of a voice. Surely, no unusual taste is requisite to see clearly, that this compulsory juxtaposition is not produced by the presentation of impressive or delightful forms to the inward vision, nor by any sympathy with the modifying powers with which the genius of the poet had united and inspirited all the objects of his thought; that it is therefore a species of wit, a pure work of the will, and implies a leisure and self-possession both of thought and of feeling, incompatible with the steady fervour of a mind possessed and filled with the grandeur of its subject. To sum up the whole in one sentence. When a poem, or a part of a poem, shall be adduced, which is evidently vicious in the figures and centexture of its style, yet for the condemnation of which no reason can be assigned, except that it differs from the style in which men actually converse, then, and not till then, can I hold this theory to be either plausible, or practicable, or capable of furnishing either rule, guidance, or precaution, that might not, more easily and more safely, as well as more naturally, have been deduced in the author's own mind from considerations of grammar, logic, and the truth and nature of things, confirmed by the authority of works, whose fame is not of one country nor of one age.

CHAPTER XIX

Continuation—Concerning the real object which, it is probable, Mr. Wordsworth had before him in his critical preface—Elucidation and application of this.

It might appear from some passages in the former part of Mr. Wordsworth's preface, that he meant to confine his theory of style, and the necessity of a close accordance with the actual language of men, to those particular subjects from low and rustic life, which by way of experiment he had purposed to naturalize as a new species in our English poetry. But from the train of argument that follows; from the reference to Milton; and from the spirit of his critique on Gray's sonnet; those sentences appear to have been rather courtesies of modesty, than actual limitations of his system. Yet so groundless does this system appear on a close examination; and so strange and overwhelming [70] in its consequences, that I cannot, and I do not, believe that the poet did ever himself adopt it in the unqualified sense, in which his expressions have been understood by others, and which, indeed, according to all the common laws of interpretation they seem to bear. What then did he mean? I apprehend, that in the clear perception, not unaccompanied with disgust or contempt, of the gaudy affectations of a style which passed current with too many for poetic diction, (though in truth it had as little pretensions to poetry, as to logic or common sense,) he narrowed his view for the time; and feeling a justifiable preference for the language of nature and of good sense, even in its humblest and least ornamented forms, he suffered himself to express, in terms at once too large and too exclusive, his predilection for a style the most remote possible from the false and showy splendour which he wished to explode. It is possible, that this predilection, at first merely comparative, deviated for a time into direct partiality. But the real object which he had in view, was, I doubt not, a species of excellence which had been long before most happily characterized by the judicious and amiable Garve, whose works are so justly beloved and esteemed by the Germans, in his remarks on Gellert, from which the following is literally translated. "The talent, that is required in order to make, excellent verses, is perhaps greater than the philosopher is ready to admit, or would find it in his power to acquire: the talent to seek only the apt expression of the thought, and yet to find at the same time with it the rhyme and the metre. Gellert possessed this happy gift, if ever any one of our poets possessed it; and nothing perhaps contributed more to the great and universal impression which his fables made on their first publication, or conduces more to their continued popularity. It was a strange and curious phaenomenon, and such as in Germany had been previously unheard of, to read verses in which everything was expressed just as one would wish to talk, and yet all dignified, attractive, and interesting; and all at the same time perfectly correct as to the measure of the syllables and the rhyme. It is certain, that poetry when it has attained this excellence makes a far greater impression than prose. So much so indeed, that even the gratification which the very rhymes afford, becomes then no longer a contemptible or trifling gratification." [71]

However novel this phaenomenon may have been in Germany at the time of Gellert, it is by no means new, nor yet of recent existence in our language. Spite of the licentiousness with which Spenser occasionally compels the orthography of his words into a subservience to his rhymes, the whole FAIRY QUEEN is an almost continued instance of this beauty. Waller's song GO, LOVELY ROSE, is doubtless familiar to most of my readers; but if I had happened to have had by me the Poems of Cotton, more but far less deservedly celebrated as the author of the VIRGIL TRAVESTIED, I should have indulged myself, and I think have gratified many, who are not acquainted with his serious works, by selecting some admirable specimens of this style. There are not a few poems in that volume, replete with every excellence of thought, image, and passion, which we expect or desire in the poetry of the milder muse; and yet so worded, that the reader sees no one reason either in the selection or the order of the words, why he might not have said the very same in an appropriate conversation, and cannot conceive how indeed he could have expressed such thoughts otherwise without loss or injury to his meaning.

But in truth our language is, and from the first dawn of poetry ever has been, particularly rich in compositions distinguished by this excellence. The final e, which is now mute, in Chaucer's age was either sounded or dropt indifferently. We ourselves still use either "beloved" or "belov'd" according as the rhyme, or measure, or the purpose of more or less solemnity may require. Let the reader then only adopt the pronunciation of the poet and of the court, at which he lived, both with respect to the final e and to the accentuation of the last syllable; I would then venture to ask, what even in the colloquial language of elegant and unaffected women, (who are the peculiar mistresses of "pure English and undefiled,") what could we hear more natural, or seemingly more unstudied, than the following stanzas from Chaucer's TROILUS AND CRESEIDE.

"And after this forth to the gate he wente,
Ther as Creseide out rode a ful gode pass,
And up and doun there made he many' a wente,
And to himselfe ful oft he said, Alas!
Fro hennis rode my blisse and my solas

As woulde blisful God now for his joie,
I might her sene agen come in to Troie!
And to the yondir hil I gan her Bide,
Alas! and there I toke of her my leve
And yond I saw her to her fathir ride;
For sorow of whiche mine hert shall to-cleve;
And hithir home I came whan it was eve,
And here I dwel, out-cast from ally joie,
And steal, til I maie sene her efte in Troie.
"And of himselfe imaginid he ofte
To ben defaitid, pale and woxin lesse
Than he was wonte, and that men saidin softe,
What may it be? who can the sothe gesse,
Why Troilus hath al this hevinesse?
And al this n' as but his melancolie,
That he had of himselfe suche fantasie.
Anothir time imaginin he would
That every wight, that past him by the wey,
Had of him routhe, and that thei saien should,
I am right sory, Troilus wol dey!
And thus he drove a daie yet forth or twey,
As ye have herde: suche life gan he to lede
As he that stode betwixin hope and drede:
For which him likid in his songis shewe
Th' encheson of his wo as he best might,
And made a songe of words but a fewe,
Somwhat his woful herte for to light,
And whan he was from every mann'is sight
With softe voice he of his lady dere,
That absent was, gan sing as ye may here:

* * * * * *

This song, when he thus songin had, ful Bone
He fil agen into his sighis olde
And every night, as was his wonte to done;
He stode the bright moone to beholde
And all his sorowe to the moone he tolde,
And said: I wis, whan thou art hornid newe,
I shall be glad, if al the world be trewe!"

Another exquisite master of this species of style, where the scholar and the poet supplies the material, but the perfect well-bred gentleman the expressions and the arrangement, is George Herbert. As from the nature of the subject, and the too frequent quaintness of the thoughts, his TEMPLE; or SACRED POEMS AND PRIVATE EJACULATIONS are Comparatively but little known, I shall extract two poems. The first is a sonnet, equally admirable for the weight, number, and expression of the thoughts, and for the simple dignity of the language. Unless, indeed, a fastidious taste should object to the latter half of the sixth line. The second is a poem of greater length, which I have chosen not only for the present purpose, but likewise as a striking example and illustration of an assertion hazarded in a former page of these sketches namely, that the characteristic fault of our elder poets is the reverse of that, which distinguishes too many of our more recent versifiers; the one conveying the most fantastic thoughts in the most correct and natural language; the other in the most fantastic language conveying the most trivial thoughts. The latter is a riddle of words; the former an enigma of thoughts. The one reminds me of an odd passage in Drayton's IDEAS

As other men, so I myself do muse,
Why in this sort I wrest invention so;
And why these giddy metaphors I use,
Leaving the path the greater part do go;
I will resolve you: I am lunatic! [72]

The other recalls a still odder passage in THE SYNAGOGUE: or THE SHADOW OF THE TEMPLE, a connected series of poems in imitation of Herbert's TEMPLE, and, in some editions, annexed to it.

O how my mind
Is gravell'd!
Not a thought,
That I can find,
But's ravell'd
All to nought!
Short ends of threds,
And narrow shreds
Of lists,
Knots, snarled ruffs,
Loose broken tufts
Of twists,
Are my torn meditations ragged clothing,
Which, wound and woven, shape a suit for nothing:
One while I think, and then I am in pain
To think how to unthink that thought again.

Immediately after these burlesque passages I cannot proceed to the extracts promised, without changing the ludicrous tone of feeling by the interposition of the three following stanzas of Herbert's.

VIRTUE.

Sweet day, so cool, so calm, so bright,
The bridal of the earth and sky,
The dew shall weep thy fall to-night;
For thou must die.

Sweet rose, whose hue angry and brave
Bids the rash gazer wipe his eye
Thy root is ever in its grave,
And thou must die.

Sweet spring, full of sweet days and roses,
A box, where sweets compacted lie
My music shews, ye have your closes,
And all must die.

THE BOSOM SIN:
A SONNET BY GEORGE HERBERT.

Lord, with what care hast thou begirt us round,
Parents first season us; then schoolmasters
Deliver us to laws; they send us bound
To rules of reason, holy messengers,
Pulpits and Sundays, sorrow dogging sin,
Afflictions sorted, anguish of all sizes,
Fine nets and stratagems to catch us in,
Bibles laid open, millions of surprises;
Blessings beforehand, ties of gratefulness,
The sound of Glory ringing in our ears
Without, our shame; within, our consciences;
Angels and grace, eternal hopes and fears.
Yet all these fences and their whole array
One cunning bosom-sin blows quite away.

LOVE UNKNOWN.

Dear friend, sit down, the tale is long and sad
And in my faintings, I presume, your love
Will more comply than help. A Lord I had,
And have, of whom some grounds, which may improve,

I hold for two lives, and both lives in me.
To him I brought a dish of fruit one day,
And in the middle placed my heart. But he
(I sigh to say)
Look'd on a servant, who did know his eye,
Better than you know me, or (which is one)
Than I myself. The servant instantly,
Quitting the fruit, seiz'd on my heart alone,
And threw it in a font, wherein did fall
A stream of blood, which issued from the side
Of a great rock: I well remember all,
And have good cause: there it was dipt and dyed,
And wash'd, and wrung: the very wringing yet
Enforceth tears. "Your heart was foul, I fear."
Indeed 'tis true. I did and do commit
Many a fault, more than my lease will bear;
Yet still ask'd pardon, and was not denied.
But you shall hear. After my heart was well,
And clean and fair, as I one eventide
(I sigh to tell)
Walk'd by myself abroad, I saw a large
And spacious furnace flaming, and thereon
A boiling caldron, round about whose verge
Was in great letters set AFFLICTION.
The greatness shew'd the owner. So I went
To fetch a sacrifice out of my fold,
Thinking with that, which I did thus present,
To warm his love, which I did fear, grew cold.
But as my heart did tender it, the man
Who was to take it from me, slipt his hand,
And threw my heart into the scalding pan;
My heart that brought it (do you understand?)
The offerer's heart. "Your heart was hard, I fear."
Indeed 'tis true. I found a callous matter
Began to spread and to expatiate there:
But with a richer drug than scalding water
I bath'd it often, ev'n with holy blood,
Which at a board, while many drank bare wine,
A friend did steal into my cup for good,
Ev'n taken inwardly, and most divine
To supple hardnesses. But at the length
Out of the caldron getting, soon I fled
Unto my house, where to repair the strength

Which I had lost, I hasted to my bed:
But when I thought to sleep out all these faults,
(I sigh to speak)
I found that some had stuff'd the bed with thoughts,
I would say thorns. Dear, could my heart not break,
When with my pleasures ev'n my rest was gone?
Full well I understood who had been there:
For I had given the key to none but one:
It must be he. "Your heart was dull, I fear."
Indeed a slack and sleepy state of mind
Did oft possess me; so that when I pray'd,
Though my lips went, my heart did stay behind.
But all my scores were by another paid,
Who took my guilt upon him. "Truly, Friend,
"For aught I hear, your Master shews to you
"More favour than you wot of. Mark the end.
"The font did only what was old renew
"The caldron suppled what was grown too hard:
"The thorns did quicken what was grown too dull:
"All did but strive to mend what you had marr'd.
"Wherefore be cheer'd, and praise him to the full
"Each day, each hour, each moment of the week
"Who fain would have you be new, tender quick."

CHAPTER XX

The former subject continued—The neutral style, or that common to Prose and Poetry, exemplified by specimens from Chaucer, Herbert, and others.

I have no fear in declaring my conviction, that the excellence defined and exemplified in the preceding chapter is not the characteristic excellence of Mr. Wordsworth's style; because I can add with equal sincerity, that it is precluded by higher powers. The praise of uniform adherence to genuine, logical English is undoubtedly his; nay, laying the main emphasis on the word uniform, I will dare add that, of all contemporary poets, it is his alone. For, in a less absolute sense of the word, I should certainly include Mr. Bowies, Lord Byron, and, as to all his later writings, Mr. Southey, the exceptions in their works being so few and unimportant. But of the specific excellence described in the quotation from Garve, I appear to find more, and more undoubted specimens in the works of others; for instance, among the minor poems of Mr. Thomas Moore, and of our illustrious Laureate. To me it will always remain a singular and noticeable fact; that a theory, which would establish this lingua communis, not only as the best, but as the only commendable style, should have proceeded from a poet, whose diction, next to that of Shakespeare and Milton, appears to me of all others the most individualized and characteristic. And let it be remembered too, that I am now interpreting the controverted passages of Mr. Wordsworth's critical preface by the purpose and object, which he may be supposed to have intended, rather than by the sense which the words themselves must convey, if they are taken without this allowance.

A person of any taste, who had but studied three or four of Shakespeare's principal plays, would without the name affixed scarcely fail to recognise as Shakespeare's a quotation from any other play, though but of a few lines. A similar peculiarity, though in a less degree, attends Mr. Wordsworth's style, whenever he speaks in his own person; or whenever, though under a feigned name, it is clear that he himself is still speaking, as in the different dramatis personae of THE RECLUSE. Even in the other poems, in which he purposes to be most dramatic, there are few in which it does not occasionally burst forth. The reader might often address the poet in his own words with reference to the persons introduced:

"It seems, as I retrace the ballad line by line
That but half of it is theirs, and the better half is thine."

Who, having been previously acquainted with any considerable portion of Mr. Wordsworth's publications, and having studied them with a full feeling of the author's genius, would not at once claim as Wordsworthian the little poem on the rainbow?

"The Child is father of the Man, etc."

Or in the LUCY GRAY?

"No mate, no comrade Lucy knew;
She dwelt on a wide moor;
The sweetest thing that ever grew
Beside a human door."

Or in the IDLE SHEPHERD-BOYS?

"Along the river's stony marge
The sand-lark chants a joyous song;
The thrush is busy in the wood,
And carols loud and strong.
A thousand lambs are on the rocks,
All newly born! both earth and sky
Keep jubilee, and more than all,
Those boys with their green coronal;
They never hear the cry,
That plaintive cry! which up the hill
Comes from the depth of Dungeon-Ghyll."

Need I mention the exquisite description of the Sea-Loch in THE BLIND HIGHLAND BOY. Who but a poet tells a tale in such language to the little ones by the fire-side as—

"Yet had he many a restless dream;
Both when he heard the eagle's scream,
And when he heard the torrents roar,
And heard the water beat the shore
Near where their cottage stood.

Beside a lake their cottage stood,
Not small like our's, a peaceful flood;
But one of mighty size, and strange;
That, rough or smooth, is full of change,
And stirring in its bed.

For to this lake, by night and day,
The great Sea-water finds its way
Through long, long windings of the hills,
And drinks up all the pretty rills
And rivers large and strong:

*Then hurries back the road it came
Returns on errand still the same;
This did it when the earth was new;
And this for evermore will do,
As long as earth shall last.
And, with the coming of the tide,
Come boats and ships that sweetly ride,
Between the woods and lofty rocks;
And to the shepherds with their flocks
Bring tales of distant lands."*

I might quote almost the whole of his RUTH, but take the following stanzas:

*But, as you have before been told,
This Stripling, sportive, gay, and bold,
And, with his dancing crest,
So beautiful, through savage lands
Had roamed about with vagrant bands
Of Indians in the West.*

*The wind, the tempest roaring high,
The tumult of a tropic sky,
Might well be dangerous food
For him, a Youth to whom was given
So much of earth—so much of heaven,
And such impetuous blood.*

*Whatever in those climes he found
Irregular in sight or sound
Did to his mind impart
A kindred impulse, seemed allied
To his own powers, and justified
The workings of his heart.*

*Nor less, to feed voluptuous thought,
The beauteous forms of nature wrought,
Fair trees and lovely flowers;
The breezes their own languor lent;
The stars had feelings, which they sent
Into those magic bowers.*

Yet in his worst pursuits, I ween,

*That sometimes there did intervene
Pure hopes of high intent
For passions linked to forms so fair
And stately, needs must have their share
Of noble sentiment."*

But from Mr. Wordsworth's more elevated compositions, which already form three-fourths of his works; and will, I trust, constitute hereafter a still larger proportion;—from these, whether in rhyme or blank verse, it would be difficult and almost superfluous to select instances of a diction peculiarly his own, of a style which cannot be imitated without its being at once recognised, as originating in Mr. Wordsworth. It would not be easy to open on any one of his loftier strains, that does not contain examples of this; and more in proportion as the lines are more excellent, and most like the author. For those, who may happen to have been less familiar with his writings, I will give three specimens taken with little choice. The first from the lines on the BOY OF WINANDER-MERE,—who

*"Blew mimic hootings to the silent owls,
That they might answer him.—And they would shout
Across the watery vale, and shout again,
With long halloos, and screams, and echoes loud
Redoubled and redoubled; concourse wild
Of mirth and jocund din! And when it chanced,
That pauses of deep silence mocked his skill,
Then sometimes in that silence, while he hung
Listening, a gentle shock of mild surprise
Has carried far into his heart the voice
Of mountain-torrents; or the visible scene [73]
Would enter unawares into his mind
With all its solemn imagery, its rocks,
Its woods, and that uncertain heaven, received
Into the bosom of the steady lake."*

The second shall be that noble imitation of Drayton [74] (if it was not rather a coincidence) in the lines TO JOANNA.

*—'When I had gazed perhaps two minutes' space,
Joanna, looking in my eyes, beheld
That ravishment of mine, and laughed aloud.
The Rock, like something starting from a sleep,
Took up the Lady's voice, and laughed again!
That ancient woman seated on Helm-crag
Was ready with her cavern; Hammar-scar
And the tall Steep of Silver-How sent forth*

A noise of laughter; southern Loughrigg heard,
And Fairfield answered with a mountain tone.
Helvellyn far into the clear blue sky
Carried the lady's voice!—old Skiddaw blew
His speaking trumpet!—back out of the clouds
From Glaramara southward came the voice:
And Kirkstone tossed it from its misty head!"

The third, which is in rhyme, I take from the SONG AT THE FEAST OF BROUGHAM CASTLE, upon the restoration of Lord Clifford, the Shepherd, to the Estates and Honours of his Ancestors.

————"Now another day is come,
Fitter hope, and nobler doom;
He hath thrown aside his crook,
And hath buried deep his book;
Armour rusting in his halls
On the blood of Clifford calls,—
'Quell the Scot,' exclaims the Lance!
Bear me to the heart of France,
Is the longing of the Shield—
Tell thy name, thou trembling Field!—
Field of death, where'er thou be,
Groan thou with our victory!
Happy day, and mighty hour,
When our Shepherd, in his power,
Mailed and horsed, with lance and sword,
To his ancestors restored,
Like a re-appearing Star,
Like a glory from afar,
First shall head the flock of war!"

"Alas! the fervent harper did not know,
That for a tranquil Soul the Lay was framed,
Who, long compelled in humble walks to go,
Was softened into feeling, soothed, and tamed.

Love had he found in huts where poor men lie;
His daily teachers had been woods and rills,
The silence that is in the starry sky,
The sleep that is among the lonely hills."

The words themselves in the foregoing extracts, are, no doubt, sufficiently common for the greater part.—But in what poem are they not so, if we except a few misadventurous attempts to translate the arts and sciences into verse? In THE EXCURSION the number of polysyllabic (or what the common people call, dictionary) words is more than usually great. And so must it needs be, in proportion to the number and variety of an author's conceptions, and his solicitude to express them with precision.—But are those words in those places commonly employed in real life to express the same thought or outward thing? Are they the style used in the ordinary intercourse of spoken words? No! nor are the modes of connections; and still less the breaks and transitions. Would any but a poet—at least could any one without being conscious that he had expressed himself with noticeable vivacity—have described a bird singing loud by, "The thrush is busy in the wood?"—or have spoken of boys with a string of club-moss round their rusty hats, as the boys "with their green coronal?"—or have translated a beautiful May-day into "Both earth and sky keep jubilee!"—or have brought all the different marks and circumstances of a sealoch before the mind, as the actions of a living and acting power? Or have represented the reflection of the sky in the water, as "That uncertain heaven received into the bosom of the steady lake?" Even the grammatical construction is not unfrequently peculiar; as "The wind, the tempest roaring high, the tumult of a tropic sky, might well be dangerous food to him, a youth to whom was given, etc." There is a peculiarity in the frequent use of the asymartaeton (that is, the omission of the connective particle before the last of several words, or several sentences used grammatically as single words, all being in the same case and governing or governed by the same verb) and not less in the construction of words by apposition ("to him, a youth"). In short, were there excluded from Mr. Wordsworth's poetic compositions all, that a literal adherence to the theory of his preface would exclude, two thirds at least of the marked beauties of his poetry must be erased. For a far greater number of lines would be sacrificed than in any other recent poet; because the pleasure received from Wordsworth's poems being less derived either from excitement of curiosity or the rapid flow of narration, the striking passages form a larger proportion of their value. I do not adduce it as a fair criterion of comparative excellence, nor do I even think it such; but merely as matter of fact. I affirm, that from no contemporary writer could so many lines be quoted, without reference to the poem in which they are found, for their own independent weight or beauty. From the sphere of my own experience I can bring to my recollection three persons of no every-day powers and acquirements, who had read the poems of others with more and more unallayed pleasure, and had thought more highly of their authors, as poets; who yet have confessed to me, that from no modern work had so many passages started up anew in their minds at different times, and as different occasions had awakened a meditative mood.

CHAPTER XXI

Remarks on the present mode of conducting critical journals.

Long have I wished to see a fair and philosophical inquisition into the character of Wordsworth, as a poet, on the evidence of his published works; and a positive, not a comparative, appreciation of their characteristic excellencies, deficiencies, and defects. I know no claim that the mere opinion of any individual can have to weigh down the opinion of the author himself; against the probability of whose parental partiality we ought to set that of his having thought longer and more deeply on the subject. But I should call that investigation fair and philosophical in which the critic announces and endeavours to establish the principles, which he holds for the foundation of poetry in general, with the specification of these in their application to the different classes of poetry. Having thus prepared his canons of criticism for praise and condemnation, he would proceed to particularize the most striking passages to which he deems them applicable, faithfully noticing the frequent or infrequent recurrence of similar merits or defects, and as faithfully distinguishing what is characteristic from what is accidental, or a mere flagging of the wing. Then if his premises be rational, his deductions legitimate, and his conclusions justly applied, the reader, and possibly the poet himself, may adopt his judgment in the light of judgment and in the independence of free-agency. If he has erred, he presents his errors in a definite place and tangible form, and holds the torch and guides the way to their detection.

I most willingly admit, and estimate at a high value, the services which the EDINBURGH REVIEW, and others formed afterwards on the same plan, have rendered to society in the diffusion of knowledge. I think the commencement of the EDINBURGH REVIEW an important epoch in periodical criticism; and that it has a claim upon the gratitude of the literary republic, and indeed of the reading public at large, for having originated the scheme of reviewing those books only, which are susceptible and deserving of argumentative criticism. Not less meritorious, and far more faithfully and in general far more ably executed, is their plan of supplying the vacant place of the trash or mediocrity, wisely left to sink into oblivion by its own weight, with original essays on the most interesting subjects of the time, religious, or political; in which the titles of the books or pamphlets prefixed furnish only the name and occasion of the disquisition. I do not arraign the keenness, or asperity of its damnatory style, in and for itself, as long as the author is addressed or treated as the mere impersonation of the work then under trial. I have no quarrel with them on this account, as long as no personal allusions are admitted, and no re-commitment (for new trial) of juvenile performances, that were published, perhaps forgotten, many years before the commencement of the review: since for the forcing back of such works to public notice no motives are easily assignable, but such as are furnished to the critic by his own personal malignity; or what is still worse, by a habit of malignity in the form of mere wantonness.

"No private grudge they need, no personal spite
The viva sectio is its own delight!
All enmity, all envy, they disclaim,
Disinterested thieves of our good name:
Cool, sober murderers of their neighbour's fame!"
S. T. C.

Every censure, every sarcasm respecting a publication which the critic, with the criticised work before him, can make good, is the critic's right. The writer is authorized to reply, but not to complain. Neither can anyone prescribe to the critic, how soft or how hard; how friendly, or how bitter, shall be the phrases which he is to select for the expression of such reprehension or ridicule. The critic must know, what effect it is his object to produce; and with a view to this effect must he weigh his words. But as soon as the critic betrays, that he knows more of his author, than the author's publications could have told him; as soon as from this more intimate knowledge, elsewhere obtained, he avails himself of the slightest trait against the author; his censure instantly becomes personal injury, his sarcasms personal insults. He ceases to be a critic, and takes on him the most contemptible character to which a rational creature can be degraded, that of a gossip, backbiter, and pasquillant: but with this heavy aggravation, that he steals the unquiet, the deforming passions of the world into the museum; into the very place which, next to the chapel and oratory, should be our sanctuary, and secure place of refuge; offers abominations on the altar of the Muses; and makes its sacred paling the very circle in which he conjures up the lying and profane spirit.

This determination of unlicensed personality, and of permitted and legitimate censure, (which I owe in part to the illustrious Lessing, himself a model of acute, spirited, sometimes stinging, but always argumentative and honourable, criticism) is beyond controversy the true one: and though I would not myself exercise all the rights of the latter, yet, let but the former be excluded, I submit myself to its exercise in the hands of others, without complaint and without resentment.

Let a communication be formed between any number of learned men in the various branches of science and literature; and whether the president and central committee be in London, or Edinburgh, if only they previously lay aside their individuality, and pledge themselves inwardly, as well as ostensibly, to administer judgment according to a constitution and code of laws; and if by grounding this code on the two-fold basis of universal morals and philosophic reason, independent of all foreseen application to particular works and authors, they obtain the right to speak each as the representative of their body corporate; they shall have honour and good wishes from me, and I shall accord to them their fair dignities, though self-assumed, not less cheerfully than if I could inquire concerning them in the herald's office, or turn to them in the book of peerage. However loud may be the outcries for prevented or subverted reputation, however numerous and impatient the complaints of merciless severity and insupportable despotism, I shall neither feel, nor utter aught but to the defence and justification of the critical machine. Should any literary Quixote find himself provoked by its sounds and regular movements, I should admonish him with Sancho Panza, that it is no giant but a windmill; there it stands on its own place, and its own hillock, never goes out of its way to attack anyone, and to none and from none either gives or asks assistance. When the public press has poured in any part of its produce between its mill-stones, it grinds it off, one man's sack the same as another, and with whatever wind may happen to be then blowing. All the two-and-thirty winds are alike its friends. Of the whole wide atmosphere it does not desire a single finger-breadth more than what is necessary for its sails to turn round in. But this space must be left free and unimpeded. Gnats, beetles, wasps, butterflies, and the whole tribe of ephemerals and insignificants, may flit in and out and between; may hum, and buzz, and jar; may shrill their tiny pipes, and wind their puny horns, unchastised and unnoticed. But idlers and bravadoes of larger size and prouder show must beware, how they place themselves within its sweep. Much less may they presume to lay hands on the sails, the strength of which is neither greater nor less than as the wind is, which drives them round. Whomsoever the remorseless arm slings aloft, or whirls along with it in the air, he has himself alone to blame; though, when the same arm throws him from it, it will more often double than break the force of his fall.

Putting aside the too manifest and too frequent interference of national party, and even personal predilection or aversion; and reserving for deeper feelings those worse and more criminal intrusions into the sacredness of private life, which not seldom merit legal rather than literary chastisement, the two principal objects and occasions which I find for blame and regret in the conduct of the review in question are first, its unfaithfulness to its own announced and excellent plan, by subjecting to criticism works neither indecent nor immoral, yet of such trifling importance even in point of size and, according to the critic's own verdict, so devoid of all merit, as must excite in the most candid mind the suspicion, either that dislike or vindictive feelings were at work; or that there was a cold prudential pre-determination to increase the sale of the review by flattering the malignant passions of human nature. That I may not myself become subject to the charge, which I am bringing against others, by an accusation without proof, I refer to the article on Dr. Rennell's sermon in the very first number of the EDINBURGH REVIEW as an illustration of my meaning. If in looking through all the succeeding volumes the reader should find this a solitary instance, I must submit to that painful forfeiture of esteem, which awaits a groundless or exaggerated charge.

The second point of objection belongs to this review only in common with all other works of periodical criticism: at least, it applies in common to the general system of all, whatever exception there may be in favour of particular articles. Or if it attaches to THE EDINBURGH REVIEW, and to its only corrival (THE QUARTERLY), with any peculiar force, this results from the superiority of talent, acquirement, and information which both have so undeniably displayed; and which doubtless deepens the regret though not the blame. I am referring to the substitution of assertion for argument; to the frequency of arbitrary and sometimes petulant verdicts, not seldom unsupported even by a single quotation from the work condemned, which might at least have explained the critic's meaning, if it did not prove the justice of his sentence. Even where this is not the case, the extracts are too often made without reference to any general grounds or rules from which the faultiness or inadmissibility of the qualities attributed may be deduced; and without any attempt to show, that the qualities are attributable to the passage extracted. I have met with such extracts from Mr. Wordsworth's poems, annexed to such assertions, as led me to imagine, that the reviewer, having written his critique before he had read the work, had then pricked with a pin for passages, wherewith to illustrate the various branches of his preconceived opinions. By what principle of rational choice can we suppose a critic to have been directed (at least in a Christian country, and himself, we hope, a Christian) who gives the following lines, portraying the fervour of solitary devotion excited by the magnificent display of the Almighty's works, as a proof and example of an author's tendency to downright ravings, and absolute unintelligibility?

"*O then what soul was his, when on the tops*
Of the high mountains he beheld the sun
Rise up, and bathe the world in light! He looked—
Ocean and earth, the solid frame of earth,
And ocean's liquid mass, beneath him lay
In gladness and deep joy. The clouds were touched,
And in their silent faces did he read
Unutterable love. Sound needed none,

Nor any voice of joy: his spirit drank
The spectacle! sensation, soul, and form,
All melted into him; they swallowed up
His animal being; in them did he live,
And by them did he live: they were his life."

Can it be expected, that either the author or his admirers, should be induced to pay any serious attention to decisions which prove nothing but the pitiable state of the critic's own taste and sensibility? On opening the review they see a favourite passage, of the force and truth of which they had an intuitive certainty in their own inward experience confirmed, if confirmation it could receive, by the sympathy of their most enlightened friends; some of whom perhaps, even in the world's opinion, hold a higher intellectual rank than the critic himself would presume to claim. And this very passage they find selected, as the characteristic effusion of a mind deserted by reason!—as furnishing evidence that the writer was raving, or he could not have thus strung words together without sense or purpose! No diversity of taste seems capable of explaining such a contrast in judgment.

That I had over-rated the merit of a passage or poem, that I had erred concerning the degree of its excellence, I might be easily induced to believe or apprehend. But that lines, the sense of which I had analysed and found consonant with all the best convictions of my understanding; and the imagery and diction of which had collected round those convictions my noblest as well as my most delightful feelings; that I should admit such lines to be mere nonsense or lunacy, is too much for the most ingenious arguments to effect. But that such a revolution of taste should be brought about by a few broad assertions, seems little less than impossible. On the contrary, it would require an effort of charity not to dismiss the criticism with the aphorism of the wise man, *in animam malevolam sapientia haud intrare potest*.

What then if this very critic should have cited a large number of single lines and even of long paragraphs, which he himself acknowledges to possess eminent and original beauty? What if he himself has owned, that beauties as great are scattered in abundance throughout the whole book? And yet, though under this impression, should have commenced his critique in vulgar exultation with a prophecy meant to secure its own fulfilment? With a "This won't do!" What? if after such acknowledgments extorted from his own judgment he should proceed from charge to charge of tameness and raving; flights and flatness; and at length, consigning the author to the house of incurables, should conclude with a strain of rudest contempt evidently grounded in the distempered state of his own moral associations? Suppose too all this done without a single leading principle established or even announced, and without any one attempt at argumentative deduction, though the poet had presented a more than usual opportunity for it, by having previously made public his own principles of judgment in poetry, and supported them by a connected train of reasoning!

The office and duty of the poet is to select the most dignified as well as

"The gayest, happiest attitude of things."

The reverse, for in all cases a reverse is possible, is the appropriate business of burlesque and travesty, a predominant taste for which has been always deemed a mark of a low and degraded mind. When I was at Rome, among many other visits to the tomb of Julius II. I went thither once with a Prussian artist, a man of genius and great vivacity of feeling. As we were gazing on Michael Angelo's MOSES, our conversation turned on the horns and beard of that stupendous statue; of the necessity of each to support the other; of the super-human effect of the former, and the necessity of the existence of both to give a harmony and integrity both to the image and the feeling excited by it. Conceive them removed, and the statue would become un-natural, without being super-natural. We called to mind the horns of the rising sun, and I repeated the noble passage from Taylor's HOLY DYING. That horns were the emblem of power and sovereignty among the Eastern nations, and are still retained as such in Abyssinia; the Achelous of the ancient Greeks; and the probable ideas and feelings, that originally suggested the mixture of the human and the brute form in the figure, by which they realized the idea of their mysterious Pan, as representing intelligence blended with a darker power, deeper, mightier, and more universal than the conscious intellect of man; than intelligence;—all these thoughts and recollections passed in procession before our minds. My companion who possessed more than his share of the hatred, which his countrymen bore to the French, had just observed to me, "a Frenchman, Sir! is the only animal in the human shape, that by no possibility can lift itself up to religion or poetry:" when, lo! two French officers of distinction and rank entered the church! "Mark you," whispered the Prussian, "the first thing which those scoundrels will notice—(for they will begin by instantly noticing the statue in parts, without one moment's pause of admiration impressed by the whole)—will be the horns and the beard. And the associations, which they will immediately connect with them will be those of a he-goat and a cuckold." Never did man guess more luckily. Had he inherited a portion of the great legislator's prophetic powers, whose statue we had been contemplating, he could scarcely have uttered words more coincident with the result: for even as he had said, so it came to pass.

In THE EXCURSION the poet has introduced an old man, born in humble but not abject circumstances, who had enjoyed more than usual advantages of education, both from books and from the more awful discipline of nature. This person he represents, as having been driven by the restlessness of fervid feelings, and from a craving intellect to an itinerant life; and as having in consequence passed the larger portion of his time, from earliest manhood, in villages and hamlets from door to door,

"A vagrant Merchant bent beneath his load."

Now whether this be a character appropriate to a lofty didactick poem, is perhaps questionable. It presents a fair subject for controversy; and the question is to be determined by the congruity or incongruity of such a character with what shall be proved to be the essential constituents of poetry. But surely the critic who, passing by all the opportunities which such a mode of life would present to such a man; all the advantages of the liberty of nature, of solitude, and of solitary thought; all the varieties of places and seasons, through which his track had lain, with all the varying imagery they bring with them; and lastly, all the observations of men,

"Their manners, their enjoyments, and pursuits, Their passions and their feelings="

which the memory of these yearly journeys must have given and recalled to such a mind—the critic, I say, who from the multitude of possible associations should pass by all these in order to fix his attention exclusively on the pin-papers, and stay-tapes, which might have been among the wares of his pack; this critic, in my opinion, cannot be thought to possess a much higher or much healthier state of moral feeling, than the Frenchmen above recorded.

CHAPTER XXII

The characteristic defects of Wordsworth's poetry, with the principles from which the judgment, that they are defects, is deduced—Their proportion to the beauties—For the greatest part characteristic of his theory only.

If Mr. Wordsworth have set forth principles of poetry which his arguments are insufficient to support, let him and those who have adopted his sentiments be set right by the confutation of those arguments, and by the substitution of more philosophical principles. And still let the due credit be given to the portion and importance of the truths, which are blended with his theory; truths, the too exclusive attention to which had occasioned its errors, by tempting him to carry those truths beyond their proper limits. If his mistaken theory have at all influenced his poetic compositions, let the effects be pointed out, and the instances given. But let it likewise be shown, how far the influence has acted; whether diffusively, or only by starts; whether the number and importance of the poems and passages thus infected be great or trifling compared with the sound portion; and lastly, whether they are inwoven into the texture of his works, or are loose and separable. The result of such a trial would evince beyond a doubt, what it is high time to announce decisively and aloud, that the supposed characteristics of Mr. Wordsworth's poetry, whether admired or reprobated; whether they are simplicity or simpleness; faithful adherence to essential nature, or wilful selections from human nature of its meanest forms and under the least attractive associations; are as little the real characteristics of his poetry at large, as of his genius and the constitution of his mind.

In a comparatively small number of poems he chose to try an experiment; and this experiment we will suppose to have failed. Yet even in these poems it is impossible not to perceive that the natural tendency of the poet's mind is to great objects and elevated conceptions. The poem entitled FIDELITY is for the greater part written in language, as unraised and naked as any perhaps in the two volumes. Yet take the following stanza and compare it with the preceding stanzas of the same poem.

"There sometimes doth a leaping fish
Send through the tarn a lonely cheer;
The crags repeat the raven's croak,
In symphony austere;
Thither the rainbow comes—the cloud—
And mists that spread the flying shroud;
And sun-beams; and the sounding blast,

That, if it could, would hurry past;
But that enormous barrier holds it fast."

Or compare the four last lines of the concluding stanza with the former half.

"Yes, proof was plain that, since the day
On which the Traveller thus had died,
The Dog had watched about the spot,
Or by his Master's side:
How nourish'd here through such long time
He knows, who gave that love sublime,—
And gave that strength of feeling, great
Above all human estimate!"

Can any candid and intelligent mind hesitate in determining, which of these best represents the tendency and native character of the poet's genius? Will he not decide that the one was written because the poet would so write, and the other because he could not so entirely repress the force and grandeur of his mind, but that he must in some part or other of every composition write otherwise? In short, that his only disease is the being out of his element; like the swan, that, having amused himself, for a while, with crushing the weeds on the river's bank, soon returns to his own majestic movements on its reflecting and sustaining surface. Let it be observed that I am here supposing the imagined judge, to whom I appeal, to have already decided against the poet's theory, as far as it is different from the principles of the art, generally acknowledged.

I cannot here enter into a detailed examination of Mr. Wordsworth's works; but I will attempt to give the main results of my own judgment, after an acquaintance of many years, and repeated perusals. And though, to appreciate the defects of a great mind it is necessary to understand previously its characteristic excellences, yet I have already expressed myself with sufficient fulness, to preclude most of the ill effects that might arise from my pursuing a contrary arrangement. I will therefore commence with what I deem the prominent defects of his poems hitherto published.

The first characteristic, though only occasional defect, which I appear to myself to find in these poems is the inconstancy of the style. Under this name I refer to the sudden and unprepared transitions from lines or sentences of peculiar felicity—(at all events striking and original)—to a style, not only unimpassioned but undistinguished. He sinks too often and too abruptly to that style, which I should place in the second division of language, dividing it into the three species; first, that which is peculiar to poetry; second, that which is only proper in prose; and third, the neutral or common to both. There have been works, such as Cowley's Essay on

Cromwell, in which prose and verse are intermixed (not as in the Consolation of Boetius, or the ARGENIS of Barclay, by the insertion of poems supposed to have been spoken or composed on occasions previously related in prose, but) the poet passing from one to the other, as the nature of the thoughts or his own feelings dictated. Yet this mode of composition does not satisfy a cultivated taste. There is something unpleasant in the being thus obliged to alternate states of feeling so dissimilar, and this too in a species of writing, the pleasure from which is in part derived from the preparation and previous expectation of the reader. A portion of that awkwardness is felt which hangs upon the introduction of songs in our modern comic operas; and to prevent which the judicious Metastasio (as to whose exquisite taste there can be no hesitation, whatever doubts may be entertained as to his poetic genius) uniformly placed the aria at the end of the scene, at the same time that he almost always raises and impassions the style of the recitative immediately preceding. Even in real life, the difference is great and evident between words used as the arbitrary marks of thought, our smooth market-coin of intercourse, with the image and superscription worn out by currency; and those which convey pictures either borrowed from one outward object to enliven and particularize some other; or used allegorically to body forth the inward state of the person speaking; or such as are at least the exponents of his peculiar turn and unusual extent of faculty. So much so indeed, that in the social circles of private life we often find a striking use of the latter put a stop to the general flow of conversation, and by the excitement arising from concentred attention produce a sort of damp and interruption for some minutes after. But in the perusal of works of literary art, we prepare ourselves for such language; and the business of the writer, like that of a painter whose subject requires unusual splendour and prominence, is so to raise the lower and neutral tints, that what in a different style would be the commanding colours, are here used as the means of that gentle degradation requisite in order to produce the effect of a whole. Where this is not achieved in a poem, the metre merely reminds the reader of his claims in order to disappoint them; and where this defect occurs frequently, his feelings are alternately startled by anticlimax and hyperclimax.

I refer the reader to the exquisite stanzas cited for another purpose from THE BLIND HIGHLAND BOY; and then annex, as being in my opinion instances of this disharmony in style, the two following:

"And one, the rarest, was a shell,
Which he, poor child, had studied well:
The shell of a green turtle, thin
And hollow;—you might sit therein,
It was so wide, and deep."

> "Our Highland Boy oft visited
> The house which held this prize; and, led
> By choice or chance, did thither come
> One day, when no one was at home,
> And found the door unbarred."

Or page 172, vol. I.

> "'Tis gone forgotten, let me do
> My best. There was a smile or two—
> I can remember them, I see
> The smiles worth all the world to me.
> Dear Baby! I must lay thee down:
> Thou troublest me with strange alarms;
> Smiles hast thou, sweet ones of thine own;
> I cannot keep thee in my arms;
> For they confound me: as it is,
> I have forgot those smiles of his!"

Or page 269, vol. I.

> "Thou hast a nest, for thy love and thy rest
> And though little troubled with sloth
> Drunken lark! thou would'st be loth
> To be such a traveller as I.
> Happy, happy liver!
> With a soul as strong as a mountain river
> Pouring out praise to th' Almighty giver,
> Joy and jollity be with us both!
> Hearing thee or else some other,
> As merry a brother
> I on the earth will go plodding on
> By myself cheerfully till the day is done."

The incongruity, which I appear to find in this passage, is that of the two noble lines in italics with the preceding and following. So vol. II. page 30.

> "Close by a Pond, upon the further side,
> He stood alone; a minute's space I guess,
> I watch'd him, he continuing motionless
> To the Pool's further margin then I drew;
> He being all the while before me full in view."

Compare this with the repetition of the same image, the next stanza but two.

*"And, still as I drew near with gentle pace,
Beside the little pond or moorish flood
Motionless as a Cloud the Old Man stood,
That heareth not the loud winds when they call;
And moveth altogether, if it move at all."*

Or lastly, the second of the three following stanzas, compared both with the first and the third.

*"My former thoughts returned; the fear that kills;
And hope that is unwilling to be fed;
Cold, pain, and labour, and all fleshly ills;
And mighty Poets in their misery dead.
But now, perplex'd by what the Old Man had said,
My question eagerly did I renew,
'How is it that you live, and what is it you do?'*

*"He with a smile did then his words repeat;
And said, that gathering Leeches far and wide
He travell'd; stirring thus about his feet
The waters of the Ponds where they abide.
'Once I could meet with them on every side;
'But they have dwindled long by slow decay;
'Yet still I persevere, and find them where I may.'*

*While he was talking thus, the lonely place,
The Old Man's shape, and speech, all troubled me
In my mind's eye I seemed to see him pace
About the weary moors continually,
Wandering about alone and silently."*

Indeed this fine poem is especially characteristic of the author. There is scarce a defect or excellence in his writings of which it would not present a specimen. But it would be unjust not to repeat that this defect is only occasional. From a careful reperusal of the two volumes of poems, I doubt whether the objectionable passages would amount in the whole to one hundred lines; not the eighth part of the number of pages. In THE EXCURSION the feeling of incongruity is seldom excited by the diction of any passage considered in itself, but by the sudden superiority of some other passage forming the context.

The second defect I can generalize with tolerable accuracy, if the reader will pardon an uncouth and new-coined word. There is, I should say, not seldom a matter-of-factness in certain poems. This may be divided into, first, a laborious minuteness and fidelity in the representation of objects, and their positions, as they appeared to the poet himself; secondly, the insertion of accidental circumstances, in order to the full explanation of his living characters, their dispositions and actions; which circumstances might be necessary to establish the probability of a statement in real life, where nothing is taken for granted by the hearer; but appear superfluous in poetry, where the reader is willing to believe for his own sake. To this actidentality I object, as contravening the essence of poetry, which Aristotle pronounces to be spoudaiotaton kai philosophotaton genos, the most intense, weighty and philosophical product of human art; adding, as the reason, that it is the most catholic and abstract. The following passage from Davenant's prefatory letter to Hobbes well expresses this truth. "When I considered the actions which I meant to describe; (those inferring the persons), I was again persuaded rather to choose those of a former age, than the present; and in a century so far removed, as might preserve me from their improper examinations, who know not the requisites of a poem, nor how much pleasure they lose, (and even the pleasures of heroic poesy are not unprofitable), who take away the liberty of a poet, and fetter his feet in the shackles of an historian. For why should a poet doubt in story to mend the intrigues of fortune by more delightful conveyances of probable fictions, because austere historians have entered into bond to truth? An obligation, which were in poets as foolish and unnecessary, as is the bondage of false martyrs, who lie in chains for a mistaken opinion. But by this I would imply, that truth, narrative and past, is the idol of historians, (who worship a dead thing), and truth operative, and by effects continually alive, is the mistress of poets, who hath not her existence in matter, but in reason."

For this minute accuracy in the painting of local imagery, the lines in THE EXCURSION, pp. 96, 97, and 98, may be taken, if not as a striking instance, yet as an illustration of my meaning. It must be some strong motive—(as, for instance, that the description was necessary to the intelligibility of the tale)—which could induce me to describe in a number of verses what a draughtsman could present to the eye with incomparably greater satisfaction by half a dozen strokes of his pencil, or the painter with as many touches of his brush. Such descriptions too often occasion in the mind of a reader, who is determined to understand his author, a feeling of labour, not very dissimilar to that, with which he would construct a diagram, line by line, for a long geometrical proposition. It seems to be like taking the pieces of a dissected map out of its box. We first look at one part, and then at another, then join and dove-tail them; and when the successive acts of attention have been completed, there is a retrogressive effort of mind to behold it as a whole. The poet should paint to the imagination, not to the fancy; and I know no happier case to exemplify the distinction between these two faculties. Master-pieces of the former mode of poetic painting abound in the writings of Milton, for example:

"The fig-tree; not that kind for fruit renown'd,
"But such as at this day, to Indians known,
"In Malabar or Decan spreads her arms
"Branching so broad and long, that in the ground
"The bended twigs take root, and daughters grow
"About the mother tree, a pillar'd shade
"High over-arch'd and ECHOING WALKS BETWEEN;
"There oft the Indian herdsman, shunning heat,
"Shelters in cool, and tends his pasturing herds
"At hoop-holes cut through thickest shade."

This is creation rather than painting, or if painting, yet such, and with such co-presence of the whole picture flashed at once upon the eye, as the sun paints in a camera obscura. But the poet must likewise understand and command what Bacon calls the vestigia communia of the senses, the latency of all in each, and more especially as by a magical penny duplex, the excitement of vision by sound and the exponents of sound. Thus, "The echoing walks between," may be almost said to reverse the fable in tradition of the head of Memnon, in the Egyptian statue. Such may be deservedly entitled the creative words in the world of imagination.

The second division respects an apparent minute adherence to matter-of-fact in character and Incidents; a biographical attention to probability, and an anxiety of explanation and retrospect. Under this head I shall deliver, with no feigned diffidence, the results of my best reflection on the great point of controversy between Mr. Wordsworth and his objectors; namely, on the choice of his characters. I have already declared, and, I trust justified, my utter dissent from the mode of argument which his critics have hitherto employed. To their question, "Why did you choose such a character, or a character from such a rank of life?"—the poet might in my opinion fairly retort: why with the conception of my character did you make wilful choice of mean or ludicrous associations not furnished by me, but supplied from your own sickly and fastidious feelings? How was it, indeed, probable, that such arguments could have any weight with an author, whose plan, whose guiding principle, and main object it was to attack and subdue that state of association, which leads us to place the chief value on those things on which man differs from man, and to forget or disregard the high dignities, which belong to Human Nature, the sense and the feeling, which may be, and ought to be, found in all ranks? The feelings with which, as Christians, we contemplate a mixed congregation rising or kneeling before their common Maker, Mr. Wordsworth would have us entertain at all times, as men, and as readers; and by the excitement of this lofty, yet prideless impartiality in poetry, he might hope to have encouraged its continuance in real life. The praise of good men be his! In real life, and, I trust, even in my imagination, I honour a virtuous and wise man, without reference to the presence or absence of artificial advantages. Whether in the person of an armed baron, a laurelled bard, or of an old Pedlar, or still older Leech-gatherer, the same qualities of head and heart must claim the same reverence. And even in poetry I am not conscious, that I have ever suffered my feelings to be disturbed or offended by any thoughts or images, which the poet himself has not presented.

But yet I object, nevertheless, and for the following reasons. First, because the object in view, as an immediate object, belongs to the moral philosopher, and would be pursued, not only more appropriately, but in my opinion with far greater probability of success, in sermons or moral essays, than in an elevated poem. It seems, indeed, to destroy the main fundamental distinction, not only between a poem and prose, but even between philosophy and works of fiction, inasmuch as it proposes truth for its immediate object, instead of pleasure. Now till the blessed time shall come, when truth itself shall be pleasure, and both shall be so united, as to be distinguishable in words only, not in feeling, it will remain the poet's office to proceed upon that state of association, which actually exists as general; instead of attempting first to make it what it ought to be, and then to let the pleasure follow. But here is unfortunately a small hysteron-proteron. For the communication of pleasure is the introductory means by which alone the poet must expect to moralize his readers. Secondly: though I were to admit, for a moment, this argument to be groundless: yet how is the moral effect to be produced, by merely attaching the name of some low profession to powers which are least likely, and to qualities which are assuredly not more likely, to be found in it? The Poet, speaking in his own person, may at once delight and improve us by sentiments, which teach us the independence of goodness, of wisdom, and even of genius, on the favours of fortune. And having made a due reverence before the throne of Antonine, he may bow with equal awe before Epictetus among his fellow-slaves

———*"and rejoice*
In the plain presence of his dignity."

Who is not at once delighted and improved, when the Poet Wordsworth himself exclaims,

"Oh! many are the Poets that are sown
By Nature; men endowed with highest gifts
The vision and the faculty divine,
Yet wanting the accomplishment of verse,
Nor having e'er, as life advanced, been led
By circumstance to take unto the height

The measure of themselves, these favoured Beings,
All but a scattered few, live out their time,
Husbanding that which they possess within,
And go to the grave, unthought of. Strongest minds
Are often those of whom the noisy world
Hears least."

To use a colloquial phrase, such sentiments, in such language, do one's heart good; though I for my part, have not the fullest faith in the truth of the observation. On the contrary I believe the instances to be exceedingly rare; and should feel almost as strong an objection to introduce such a character in a poetic fiction, as a pair of black swans on a lake, in a fancy landscape. When I think how many, and how much better books than Homer, or even than Herodotus, Pindar or Aeschylus, could have read, are in the power of almost every man, in a country where almost every man is instructed to read and write; and how restless, how difficultly hidden, the powers of genius are; and yet find even in situations the most favourable, according to Mr. Wordsworth, for the formation of a pure and poetic language; in situations which ensure familiarity with the grandest objects of the imagination; but one Burns, among the shepherds of Scotland, and not a single poet of humble life among those of English lakes and mountains; I conclude, that Poetic Genius is not only a very delicate but a very rare plant.

But be this as it may, the feelings with which,

"I think of Chatterton, the marvellous Boy,
The sleepless Soul, that perished in his pride;
Of Burns, who walk'd in glory and in joy
Behind his plough, upon the mountain-side"—

are widely different from those with which I should read a poem, where the author, having occasion for the character of a poet and a philosopher in the fable of his narration, had chosen to make him a chimney-sweeper; and then, in order to remove all doubts on the subject, had invented an account of his birth, parentage and education, with all the strange and fortunate accidents which had concurred in making him at once poet, philosopher, and sweep! Nothing, but biography, can justify this. If it be admissible even in a novel, it must be one in the manner of De Foe's, that were meant to pass for histories, not in the manner of Fielding's: In THE LIFE OF MOLL FLANDERS, Or COLONEL JACK, not in a TOM JONES, or even a JOSEPH ANDREWS. Much less then can it be legitimately introduced in a poem, the characters of which, amid the strongest individualization, must still remain representative. The precepts of Horace, on this point, are grounded on the nature both of poetry and of the human mind. They are not more peremptory, than wise and prudent. For in the first place a deviation from them perplexes the reader's feelings, and all the circumstances which are feigned in order to make such accidents less improbable, divide and disquiet his faith, rather than aid and support it. Spite of all attempts, the fiction will appear, and unfortunately not as fictitious but as false. The reader not only knows, that the sentiments and language are the poet's own, and his own too in his artificial character, as poet; but by the fruitless endeavours to make him think the contrary, he is not even suffered to forget it. The effect is similar to that produced by an Epic Poet, when the fable and the characters are derived from Scripture history, as in THE MESSIAH of Klopstock, or in CUMBERLAND'S CALVARY; and not merely suggested by it as in the PARADISE LOST of Milton. That illusion, contradistinguished from delusion, that negative faith, which simply permits the images presented to work by their own force, without either denial or affirmation of their real existence by the judgment, is rendered impossible by their immediate neighbourhood to words and facts of known and absolute truth. A faith, which transcends even historic belief, must absolutely put out this mere poetic analogon of faith, as the summer sun is said to extinguish our household fires, when it shines full upon them. What would otherwise have been yielded to as pleasing fiction, is repelled as revolting falsehood. The effect produced in this latter case by the solemn belief of the reader, is in a less degree brought about in the instances, to which I have been objecting, by the balked attempts of the author to make him believe.

Add to all the foregoing the seeming uselessness both of the project and of the anecdotes from which it is to derive support. Is there one word, for instance, attributed to the pedlar in THE EXCURSION, characteristic of a Pedlar? One sentiment, that might not more plausibly, even without the aid of any previous explanation, have proceeded from any wise and beneficent old man, of a rank or profession in which the language of learning and refinement are natural and to be expected? Need the rank have been at all particularized, where nothing follows which the knowledge of that rank is to explain or illustrate? When on the contrary this information renders the man's language, feelings, sentiments, and information a riddle, which must itself be solved by episodes of anecdote? Finally when this, and this alone, could have induced a genuine Poet to inweave in a poem of the loftiest style, and on subjects the loftiest and of most universal interest, such minute matters of fact, (not unlike those furnished for the obituary of a magazine by the friends of some obscure "ornament of society lately deceased" in some obscure town,) as

*"Among the hills of Athol he was born
There, on a small hereditary Farm,*

An unproductive slip of rugged ground,
His Father dwelt; and died in poverty;
While He, whose lowly fortune I retrace,
The youngest of three sons, was yet a babe,
A little One—unconscious of their loss.
But ere he had outgrown his infant days
His widowed Mother, for a second Mate,
Espoused the teacher of the Village School;
Who on her offspring zealously bestowed
Needful instruction."

"From his sixth year, the Boy of whom I speak,
In summer tended cattle on the Hills;
But, through the inclement and the perilous days
Of long-continuing winter, he repaired
To his Step-father's School,"-etc.

For all the admirable passages interposed in this narration, might, with trifling alterations, have been far more appropriately, and with far greater verisimilitude, told of a poet in the character of a poet; and without incurring another defect which I shall now mention, and a sufficient illustration of which will have been here anticipated.

Third; an undue predilection for the dramatic form in certain poems, from which one or other of two evils result. Either the thoughts and diction are different from that of the poet, and then there arises an incongruity of style; or they are the same and indistinguishable, and then it presents a species of ventriloquism, where two are represented as talking, while in truth one man only speaks.

The fourth class of defects is closely connected with the former; but yet are such as arise likewise from an intensity of feeling disproportionate to such knowledge and value of the objects described, as can be fairly anticipated of men in general, even of the most cultivated classes; and with which therefore few only, and those few particularly circumstanced, can be supposed to sympathize: In this class, I comprise occasional prolixity, repetition, and an eddying, instead of progression, of thought. As instances, see pages 27, 28, and 62 of the Poems, vol. I. and the first eighty lines of the VIth Book of THE EXCURSION.

Fifth and last; thoughts and images too great for the subject. This is an approximation to what might be called mental bombast, as distinguished from verbal: for, as in the latter there is a disproportion of the expressions to the thoughts so in this there is a disproportion of thought to the circumstance and occasion. This, by the bye, is a fault of which none but a man of genius is capable. It is the awkwardness and strength of Hercules with the distaff of Omphale.

It is a well-known fact, that bright colours in motion both make and leave the strongest impressions on the eye. Nothing is more likely too, than that a vivid image or visual spectrum, thus originated, may become the link of association in recalling the feelings and images that had accompanied the original impression. But if we describe this in such lines, as

"They flash upon that inward eye,
Which is the bliss of solitude!"

in what words shall we describe the joy of retrospection, when the images and virtuous actions of a whole well-spent life, pass before that conscience which is indeed the inward eye: which is indeed "the bliss of solitude?" Assuredly we seem to sink most abruptly, not to say burlesquely, and almost as in a medley, from this couplet to—

"And then my heart with pleasure fills, And dances with the daffodils." Vol. I. p. 328.

The second instance is from vol. II. page 12, where the poet having gone out for a day's tour of pleasure, meets early in the morning with a knot of Gipsies, who had pitched their blanket-tents and straw-beds, together with their children and asses, in some field by the road-side. At the close of the day on his return our tourist found them in the same place. "Twelve hours," says he,

"Twelve hours, twelve bounteous hours are gone, while I
Have been a traveller under open sky,
Much witnessing of change and cheer,
Yet as I left I find them here!"

Whereat the poet, without seeming to reflect that the poor tawny wanderers might probably have been tramping for weeks together through road and lane, over moor and mountain, and consequently must have been right glad to rest themselves, their children and cattle, for one whole day; and overlooking the obvious truth, that such repose might be quite as necessary for them, as a walk of the same continuance was pleasing or healthful for the more fortunate poet; expresses his indignation in a series of lines, the diction and imagery of which would have been rather above, than below the mark, had they been applied to the immense empire of China improgressive for thirty centuries:

"The weary Sun betook himself to rest:—
—Then issued Vesper from the fulgent west,
Outshining, like a visible God,

The glorious path in which he trod.
And now, ascending, after one dark hour,
And one night's diminution of her power,
Behold the mighty Moon! this way
She looks, as if at them—but they
Regard not her:—oh, better wrong and strife,
Better vain deeds or evil than such life!
The silent Heavens have goings on
The stars have tasks!—but these have none!"

The last instance of this defect,(for I know no other than these already cited) is from the Ode, page 351, vol. II., where, speaking of a child, "a six years' Darling of a pigmy size," he thus addresses him:

"Thou best Philosopher, who yet dost keep
Thy heritage, thou Eye among the blind,
That, deaf and silent, read'st the eternal deep,
Haunted for ever by the Eternal Mind,—
Mighty Prophet! Seer blest!
On whom those truths do rest,
Which we are toiling all our lives to find!
Thou, over whom thy Immortality
Broods like the Day, a Master o'er a Slave,
A Present which is not to be put by!"

Now here, not to stop at the daring spirit of metaphor which connects the epithets "deaf and silent," with the apostrophized eye: or (if we are to refer it to the preceding word, "Philosopher"), the faulty and equivocal syntax of the passage; and without examining the propriety of making a "Master brood o'er a Slave," or "the Day" brood at all; we will merely ask, what does all this mean? In what sense is a child of that age a Philosopher? In what sense does he read "the eternal deep?" In what sense is he declared to be "for ever haunted" by the Supreme Being? or so inspired as to deserve the splendid titles of a Mighty Prophet, a blessed Seer? By reflection? by knowledge? by conscious intuition? or by any form or modification of consciousness? These would be tidings indeed; but such as would pre-suppose an immediate revelation to the inspired communicator, and require miracles to authenticate his inspiration. Children at this age give us no such information of themselves; and at what time were we dipped in the Lethe, which has produced such utter oblivion of a state so godlike? There are many of us that still possess some remembrances, more or less distinct, respecting themselves at six years old; pity that the worthless straws only should float, while treasures, compared with which all the mines of Golconda and Mexico were but straws, should be absorbed by some unknown gulf into some unknown abyss.

But if this be too wild and exorbitant to be suspected as having been the poet's meaning; if these mysterious gifts, faculties, and operations, are not accompanied with consciousness; who else is conscious of them? or how can it be called the child, if it be no part of the child's conscious being? For aught I know, the thinking Spirit within me may be substantially one with the principle of life, and of vital operation. For aught I know, it might be employed as a secondary agent in the marvellous organization and organic movements of my body. But, surely, it would be strange language to say, that I construct my heart! or that I propel the finer influences through my nerves! or that I compress my brain, and draw the curtains of sleep round my own eyes! Spinoza and Behmen were, on different systems, both Pantheists; and among the ancients there were philosophers, teachers of the EN KAI PAN, who not only taught that God was All, but that this All constituted God. Yet not even these would confound the part, as a part, with the whole, as the whole. Nay, in no system is the distinction between the individual and God, between the Modification, and the one only Substance, more sharply drawn, than in that of Spinoza. Jacobi indeed relates of Lessing, that, after a conversation with him at the house of the Poet, Gleim, (the Tyrtaeus and Anacreon of the German Parnassus,) in which conversation Lessing had avowed privately to Jacobi his reluctance to admit any personal existence of the Supreme Being, or the possibility of personality except in a finite Intellect, and while they were sitting at table, a shower of rain came on unexpectedly. Gleim expressed his regret at the circumstance, because they had meant to drink their wine in the garden: upon which Lessing in one of his half-earnest, half-joking moods, nodded to Jacobi, and said, "It is I, perhaps, that am doing that," i.e. raining!—and Jacobi answered, "or perhaps I;" Gleim contented himself with staring at them both, without asking for any explanation.

So with regard to this passage. In what sense can the magnificent attributes, above quoted, be appropriated to a child, which would not make them equally suitable to a bee, or a dog, or a field of corn: or even to a ship, or to the wind and waves that propel it? The omnipresent Spirit works equally in them, as in the child; and the child is equally unconscious of it as they. It cannot surely be, that the four lines, immediately following, are to contain the explanation?

"To whom the grave
Is but a lonely bed without the sense or sight
Of day or the warm light,
A place of thought where we in waiting lie;"—

Surely, it cannot be that this wonder-rousing apostrophe is but a comment on the little poem, "We are Seven?"—that the whole meaning of the passage is reducible to the assertion, that a child, who by the bye at six years old would have been better instructed in most Christian families, has no other notion of death than that of lying in a dark, cold place? And still, I hope, not as in a place of thought! not the frightful notion of lying awake in his grave! The analogy between death and sleep is too simple, too natural, to render so horrid a belief possible for children; even had they not been in the habit, as all Christian children are, of hearing the latter term used to express the former. But if the child's belief be only, that "he is not dead, but sleepeth:" wherein does it differ from that of his father and mother, or any other adult and instructed person? To form an idea of a thing's becoming nothing; or of nothing becoming a thing; is impossible to all finite beings alike, of whatever age, and however educated or uneducated. Thus it is with splendid paradoxes in general. If the words are taken in the common sense, they convey an absurdity; and if, in contempt of dictionaries and custom, they are so interpreted as to avoid the absurdity, the meaning dwindles into some bald truism. Thus you must at once understand the words contrary to their common import, in order to arrive at any sense; and according to their common import, if you are to receive from them any feeling of sublimity or admiration.

Though the instances of this defect in Mr. Wordsworth's poems are so few, that for themselves it would have been scarcely just to attract the reader's attention toward them; yet I have dwelt on it, and perhaps the more for this very reason. For being so very few, they cannot sensibly detract from the reputation of an author, who is even characterized by the number of profound truths in his writings, which will stand the severest analysis; and yet few as they are, they are exactly those passages which his blind admirers would be most likely, and best able, to imitate. But Wordsworth, where he is indeed Wordsworth, may be mimicked by copyists, he may be plundered by plagiarists; but he cannot be imitated, except by those who are not born to be imitators. For without his depth of feeling and his imaginative power his sense would want its vital warmth and peculiarity; and without his strong sense, his mysticism would become sickly—mere fog, and dimness!

To these defects which, as appears by the extracts, are only occasional, I may oppose, with far less fear of encountering the dissent of any candid and intelligent reader, the following (for the most part correspondent) excellencies. First, an austere purity of language both grammatically and logically; in short a perfect appropriateness of the words to the meaning. Of how high value I deem this, and how particularly estimable I hold the example at the present day, has been already stated: and in part too the reasons on which I ground both the moral and intellectual importance of habituating ourselves to a strict accuracy of expression. It is noticeable, how limited an acquaintance with the masterpieces of art will suffice to form a correct and even a sensitive taste, where none but master-pieces have been seen and admired: while on the other hand, the most correct notions, and the widest acquaintance with the works of excellence of all ages and countries, will not perfectly secure us against the contagious familiarity with the far more numerous offspring of tastelessness or of a perverted taste. If this be the case, as it notoriously is, with the arts of music and painting, much more difficult will it be, to avoid the infection of multiplied and daily examples in the practice of an art, which uses words, and words only, as its instruments. In poetry, in which every line, every phrase, may pass the ordeal of deliberation and deliberate choice, it is possible, and barely possible, to attain that ultimatum which I have ventured to propose as the infallible test of a blameless style; namely: its untranslatableness in words of the same language without injury to the meaning. Be it observed, however, that I include in the meaning of a word not only its correspondent object, but likewise all the associations which it recalls. For language is framed to convey not the object alone but likewise the character, mood and intentions of the person who is representing it. In poetry it is practicable to preserve the diction uncorrupted by the affectations and misappropriations, which promiscuous authorship, and reading not promiscuous only because it is disproportionally most conversant with the compositions of the day, have rendered general. Yet even to the poet, composing in his own province, it is an arduous work: and as the result and pledge of a watchful good sense of fine and luminous distinction, and of complete self-possession, may justly claim all the honour which belongs to an attainment equally difficult and valuable, and the more valuable for being rare. It is at all times the proper food of the understanding; but in an age of corrupt eloquence it is both food and antidote.

In prose I doubt whether it be even possible to preserve our style wholly unalloyed by the vicious phraseology which meets us everywhere, from the sermon to the newspaper, from the harangue of the legislator to the speech from the convivial chair, announcing a toast or sentiment. Our chains rattle, even while we are complaining of them. The poems of Boetius rise high in our estimation when we compare them with those of his contemporaries, as Sidonius Apollinaris, and others. They might even be referred to a purer age, but that the prose, in which they are set, as jewels in a crown of lead or iron, betrays the true age of the writer. Much however may be effected by education. I believe not only from grounds of reason, but from having in great measure assured myself of the fact by actual though limited experience, that, to a youth led from his first boyhood to investigate the meaning of every word and the reason of its choice and position, logic presents itself as an old acquaintance under new names.

On some future occasion, more especially demanding such disquisition, I shall attempt to prove the close connection between veracity and habits of mental accuracy; the beneficial after-effects of verbal precision in the preclusion of fanaticism, which masters the feelings more especially by indistinct watch-words; and to display the advantages which language alone, at least which language with incomparably greater ease and certainty than any other means, presents to the instructor of impressing modes of intellectual energy so constantly, so imperceptibly, and as it were by such elements and atoms, as to secure in due time the formation of a second nature. When we reflect, that the cultivation of the judgment is a positive command of the moral law, since the reason can give the principle alone, and the conscience bears witness only to the motive, while the application and effects must depend on the judgment when we consider, that the greater part of our success and comfort in life depends on distinguishing the similar from the same, that which is peculiar in each thing from that which it has in common with others, so as still to select the most probable, instead of the merely possible or positively unfit, we shall learn to value earnestly and with a practical seriousness a mean, already prepared for us by nature and society, of teaching the young mind to think well and wisely by the same unremembered process and with the same never forgotten results, as those by which it is taught to speak and converse. Now how much warmer the interest is, how much more genial the feelings of reality and practicability, and thence how much stronger the impulses to imitation are, which a contemporary writer, and especially a contemporary poet, excites in youth and commencing manhood, has been treated of in the earlier pages of these sketches. I have only to add, that all the praise which is due to the exertion of such influence for a purpose so important, joined with that which must be claimed for the infrequency of the same excellence in the same perfection, belongs in full right to Mr. Wordsworth. I am far however from denying that we have poets whose general style possesses the same excellence, as Mr. Moore, Lord Byron, Mr. Bowles, and, in all his later and more important works, our laurel-honouring Laureate. But there are none, in whose works I do not appear to myself to find more exceptions, than in those of Wordsworth. Quotations or specimens would here be wholly out of place, and must be left for the critic who doubts and would invalidate the justice of this eulogy so applied.

The second characteristic excellence of Mr. Wordsworth's work is: a correspondent weight and sanity of the Thoughts and Sentiments,—won, not from books; but—from the poet's own meditative observation. They are fresh and have the dew upon them. His muse, at least when in her strength of wing, and when she hovers aloft in her proper element,

Makes audible a linked lay of truth,
Of truth profound a sweet continuous lay,
Not learnt, but native, her own natural notes!

Even throughout his smaller poems there is scarcely one, which is not rendered valuable by some just and original reflection.

See page 25, vol. II.: or the two following passages in one of his humblest compositions.

"O Reader! had you in your mind
Such stores as silent thought can bring,
O gentle Reader! you would find
A tale in every thing;"

and

"I've heard of hearts unkind, kind deeds
With coldness still returning;
Alas! the gratitude of men
Has oftener left me mourning;"

or in a still higher strain the six beautiful quatrains, page 134.

"Thus fares it still in our decay:
And yet the wiser mind
Mourns less for what age takes away
Than what it leaves behind.

The Blackbird in the summer trees,
The Lark upon the hill,
Let loose their carols when they please,
Are quiet when they will.

With Nature never do they wage
A foolish strife; they see
A happy youth, and their old age
Is beautiful and free!

But we are pressed by heavy laws;
And often glad no more,
We wear a face of joy, because
We have been glad of yore.

If there is one, who need bemoan
His kindred laid in earth,
The household hearts that were his own,
It is the man of mirth.

My days, my Friend, are almost gone,

My life has been approved,
And many love me; but by none
Am I enough beloved;"

or the sonnet on Buonaparte, page 202, vol. II. or finally (for a volume would scarce suffice to exhaust the instances,) the last stanza of the poem on the withered Celandine, vol. II. p. 312.

"*To be a Prodigal's Favorite—then, worse truth,*
A Miser's Pensioner—behold our lot!
O Man! That from thy fair and shining youth
Age might but take the things Youth needed not."

Both in respect of this and of the former excellence, Mr. Wordsworth strikingly resembles Samuel Daniel, one of the golden writers of our golden Elizabethan age, now most causelessly neglected: Samuel Daniel, whose diction bears no mark of time, no distinction of age which has been, and as long as our language shall last, will be so far the language of the to-day and for ever, as that it is more intelligible to us, than the transitory fashions of our own particular age. A similar praise is due to his sentiments. No frequency of perusal can deprive them of their freshness. For though they are brought into the full day-light of every reader's comprehension; yet are they drawn up from depths which few in any age are privileged to visit, into which few in any age have courage or inclination to descend. If Mr. Wordsworth is not equally with Daniel alike intelligible to all readers of average understanding in all passages of his works, the comparative difficulty does not arise from the greater impurity of the ore, but from the nature and uses of the metal. A poem is not necessarily obscure, because it does not aim to be popular. It is enough, if a work be perspicuous to those for whom it is written, and

"*Fit audience find, though few.*"

To the "Ode on the Intimations of Immortality from Recollections of early Childhood" the poet might have prefixed the lines which Dante addresses to one of his own Canzoni—

"*Canzone, i' credo, che saranno radi*
Color, che tua ragione intendan bene,
Tanto lor sei faticoso ed alto."

"*O lyric song, there will be few, I think,*
Who may thy import understand aright:
Thou art for them so arduous and so high!"

But the ode was intended for such readers only as had been accustomed to watch the flux and reflux of their inmost nature, to venture at times into the twilight realms of consciousness, and to feel a deep interest in modes of inmost being, to which they know that the attributes of time and space are inapplicable and alien, but which yet can not be conveyed, save in symbols of time and space. For such readers the sense is sufficiently plain, and they will be as little disposed to charge Mr. Wordsworth with believing the Platonic pre-existence in the ordinary interpretation of the words, as I am to believe, that Plato himself ever meant or taught it.

Polla oi ut' ankonos
okea belae
endon enti pharetras
phonanta synetoisin; es
de to pan hermaeneon
chatizei; sophos o polla
eidos phua;
mathontes de labroi
panglossia, korakes os,
akranta garueton
Dios pros ornicha theion.

Third (and wherein he soars far above Daniel) the sinewy strength and originality of single lines and paragraphs: the frequent curiosa felicitas of his diction, of which I need not here give specimens, having anticipated them in a preceding page. This beauty, and as eminently characteristic of Wordsworth's poetry, his rudest assailants have felt themselves compelled to acknowledge and admire.

Fourth; the perfect truth of nature in his images and descriptions as taken immediately from nature, and proving a long and genial intimacy with the very spirit which gives the physiognomic expression to all the works of nature. Like a green field reflected in a calm and perfectly transparent lake, the image is distinguished from the reality only by its greater softness and lustre. Like the moisture or the polish on a pebble, genius neither distorts nor false-colours its objects; but on the contrary brings out many a vein and many a tint, which escape the eye of common observation, thus raising to the rank of gems what had been often kicked away by the hurrying foot of the traveller on the dusty high road of custom.

Let me refer to the whole description of skating, vol. I. page 42 to 47, especially to the lines

"So through the darkness and the cold we flew,
And not a voice was idle. with the din
Meanwhile the precipices rang aloud;
The leafless trees and every icy crag
Tinkled like iron; while the distant hills

*Into the tumult sent an alien sound
Of melancholy, not unnoticed, while the stars,
Eastward, were sparkling clear, and in the west
The orange sky of evening died away."*

Or to the poem on THE GREEN LINNET, vol. I. page 244. What can be more accurate yet more lovely than the two concluding stanzas?

*"Upon yon tuft of hazel trees,
That twinkle to the gusty breeze,
Behold him perched in ecstasies,
Yet seeming still to hover;
There! where the flutter of his wings
Upon his back and body flings
Shadows and sunny glimmerings,
That cover him all over.*

*While thus before my eyes he gleams,
A Brother of the Leaves he seems;
When in a moment forth he teems
His little song in gushes
As if it pleased him to disdain
And mock the Form which he did feign
While he was dancing with the train
Of Leaves among the bushes."*

Or the description of the blue-cap, and of the noontide silence, page 284; or the poem to the cuckoo, page 299; or, lastly, though I might multiply the references to ten times the number, to the poem, so completely Wordsworth's, commencing

"Three years she grew in sun and shower"—

Fifth: a meditative pathos, a union of deep and subtle thought with sensibility; a sympathy with man as man; the sympathy indeed of a contemplator, rather than a fellow-sufferer or co-mate, (spectator, haud particeps) but of a contemplator, from whose view no difference of rank conceals the sameness of the nature; no injuries of wind or weather, or toil, or even of ignorance, wholly disguise the human face divine. The superscription and the image of the Creator still remain legible to him under the dark lines, with which guilt or calamity had cancelled or cross-barred it. Here the Man and the Poet lose and find themselves in each other, the one as glorified, the latter as substantiated. In this mild and philosophic pathos, Wordsworth appears to me without a compeer. Such as he is: so he writes. See vol. I. page 134 to 136, or that most affecting composition, THE AFFLICTION OF MARGARET —— OF ——, page

165 to 168, which no mother, and, if I may judge by my own experience, no parent can read without a tear. Or turn to that genuine lyric, in the former edition, entitled, THE MAD MOTHER, page 174 to 178, of which I cannot refrain from quoting two of the stanzas, both of them for their pathos, and the former for the fine transition in the two concluding lines of the stanza, so expressive of that deranged state, in which, from the increased sensibility, the sufferer's attention is abruptly drawn off by every trifle, and in the same instant plucked back again by the one despotic thought, bringing home with it, by the blending, fusing power of Imagination and Passion, the alien object to which it had been so abruptly diverted, no longer an alien but an ally and an inmate.

"Suck, little babe, oh suck again!
It cools my blood; it cools my brain;
Thy lips, I feel them, baby! They
Draw from my heart the pain away.
Oh! press me with thy little hand;
It loosens something at my chest
About that tight and deadly band
I feel thy little fingers prest.
The breeze I see is in the tree!
It comes to cool my babe and me."

"Thy father cares not for my breast,
'Tis thine, sweet baby, there to rest;
'Tis all thine own!—and if its hue
Be changed, that was so fair to view,
'Tis fair enough for thee, my dove!
My beauty, little child, is flown,
But thou wilt live with me in love;
And what if my poor cheek be brown?
'Tis well for me, thou canst not see
How pale and wan it else would be."

Last, and pre-eminently, I challenge for this poet the gift of Imagination in the highest and strictest sense of the word. In the play of fancy, Wordsworth, to my feelings, is not always graceful, and sometimes recondite. The likeness is occasionally too strange, or demands too peculiar a point of view, or is such as appears the creature of predetermined research, rather than spontaneous presentation. Indeed his fancy seldom displays itself, as mere and unmodified fancy. But in imaginative power, he stands nearest of all modern writers to Shakespeare and Milton; and yet in a kind perfectly unborrowed and his own. To employ his own words, which are at once an instance and an illustration, he does indeed to all thoughts and to all objects—

"————*add the gleam,*
The light that never was, on sea or land,
The consecration, and the Poet's dream."

I shall select a few examples as most obviously manifesting this faculty; but if I should ever be fortunate enough to render my analysis of Imagination, its origin and characters, thoroughly intelligible to the reader, he will scarcely open on a page of this poet's works without recognising, more or less, the presence and the influences of this faculty. From the poem on the YEW TREES, vol. I. page 303, 304.

"But worthier still of note
Are those fraternal Four of Borrowdale,
Joined in one solemn and capacious grove;
Huge trunks!—and each particular trunk a growth
Of intertwisted fibres serpentine
Up-coiling, and inveterately convolved;
Not uninformed with phantasy, and looks
That threaten the profane;—a pillared shade,
Upon whose grassless floor of red-brown hue,
By sheddings from the pinal umbrage tinged
Perennially—beneath whose sable roof
Of boughs, as if for festal purpose, decked
With unrejoicing berries—ghostly shapes
May meet at noontide; FEAR and trembling HOPE,
SILENCE and FORESIGHT; DEATH, the Skeleton,
And TIME, the Shadow; there to celebrate,
As in a natural temple scattered o'er
With altars undisturbed of mossy stone,
United worship; or in mute repose
To lie, and listen to the mountain flood
Murmuring from Glazamara's inmost caves."

The effect of the old man's figure in the poem of RESOLUTION AND INDEPENDENCE, vol. II. page 33.

"While he was talking thus, the lonely place,
The Old Man's shape, and speech, all troubled me
In my mind's eye I seemed to see him pace
About the weary moors continually,
Wandering about alone and silently."

Or the 8th, 9th, 19th, 26th, 31st, and 33rd, in the collection of miscellaneous sonnets—the sonnet on the subjugation of Switzerland, page 210, or the last ode, from which I especially select the two following stanzas or paragraphs, page 349 to 350.

"Our birth is but a sleep and a forgetting:
The Soul that rises with us, our life's Star,
Hath had elsewhere its setting,
And cometh from afar.
Not in entire forgetfulness,
And not in utter nakedness,
But trailing clouds of glory do we come
From God, who is our home:
Heaven lies about us in our infancy!
Shades of the prison-house begin to close
Upon the growing Boy;
But He beholds the light, and whence it flows,
He sees it in his joy!
The Youth who daily further from the East
Must travel, still is Nature's Priest,
And by the vision splendid
Is on his way attended;
At length the Man perceives it die away,
And fade into the light of common day."

And page 352 to 354 of the same ode.

"O joy! that in our embers
Is something that doth live,
That nature yet remembers
What was so fugitive!
The thought of our past years in me doth breed
Perpetual benedictions: not indeed
For that which is most worthy to be blest;
Delight and liberty, the simple creed
Of Childhood, whether busy or at rest,
With new-fledged hope still fluttering in his breast:—
Not for these I raise
The song of thanks and praise;
But for those obstinate questionings
Of sense and outward things,
Fallings from us, vanishings;
Blank misgivings of a Creature
Moving about in worlds not realized,
High instincts, before which our mortal Nature

Did tremble like a guilty Thing surprised!
But for those first affections,
Those shadowy recollections,
Which, be they what they may,
Are yet the fountain light of all our day,
Are yet a master light of all our seeing;
Uphold us—cherish—and have power to make
Our noisy years seem moments in the being
Of the eternal Silence; truths that wake
To perish never;
Which neither listlessness, nor mad endeavour,
Nor Man nor Boy,
Nor all that is at enmity with joy,
Can utterly abolish or destroy!
Hence, in a season of calm weather,
Though inland far we be,
Our Souls have sight of that immortal sea
Which brought us hither;
Can in a moment travel thither,—
And see the children sport upon the shore,
And hear the mighty waters rolling evermore."

And since it would be unfair to conclude with an extract, which, though highly characteristic, must yet, from the nature of the thoughts and the subject, be interesting or perhaps intelligible, to but a limited number of readers; I will add, from the poet's last published work, a passage equally Wordsworthian; of the beauty of which, and of the imaginative power displayed therein, there can be but one opinion, and one feeling. See White Doe, page 5.

"Fast the church-yard fills;—anon
Look again and they all are gone;
The cluster round the porch, and the folk
Who sate in the shade of the Prior's Oak!
And scarcely have they disappeared
Ere the prelusive hymn is heard;—
With one consent the people rejoice,
Filling the church with a lofty voice!
They sing a service which they feel:
For 'tis the sun-rise now of zeal;
And faith and hope are in their prime
In great Eliza's golden time."

"*A moment ends the fervent din,*

And all is hushed, without and within;
For though the priest, more tranquilly,
Recites the holy liturgy,
The only voice which you can hear
Is the river murmuring near.
—When soft!—the dusky trees between,
And down the path through the open green,
Where is no living thing to be seen;
And through yon gateway, where is found,
Beneath the arch with ivy bound,
Free entrance to the church-yard ground—
And right across the verdant sod,
Towards the very house of God;
Comes gliding in with lovely gleam,
Comes gliding in serene and slow,
Soft and silent as a dream.
A solitary Doe!
White she is as lily of June,
And beauteous as the silver moon
When out of sight the clouds are driven
And she is left alone in heaven!
Or like a ship some gentle day
In sunshine sailing far away
A glittering ship that hath the plain
Of ocean for her own domain."

* * * * * *

"What harmonious pensive changes
Wait upon her as she ranges
Round and through this Pile of state
Overthrown and desolate!
Now a step or two her way
Is through space of open day,
Where the enamoured sunny light
Brightens her that was so bright;
Now doth a delicate shadow fall,
Falls upon her like a breath,
From some lofty arch or wall,
As she passes underneath."

The following analogy will, I am apprehensive, appear dim and fantastic, but in reading Bartram's Travels I could not help transcribing the following lines as a sort of allegory, or connected simile and metaphor of

Wordsworth's intellect and genius.—"The soil is a deep, rich, dark mould, on a deep stratum of tenacious clay; and that on a foundation of rocks, which often break through both strata, lifting their backs above the surface. The trees which chiefly grow here are the gigantic, black oak; magnolia grandi-flora; fraximus excelsior; platane; and a few stately tulip trees." What Mr. Wordsworth will produce, it is not for me to prophesy but I could pronounce with the liveliest convictions what he is capable of producing. It is the FIRST GENUINE PHILOSOPHIC POEM.

The preceding criticism will not, I am aware, avail to overcome the prejudices of those, who have made it a business to attack and ridicule Mr. Wordsworth's compositions.

Truth and prudence might be imaged as concentric circles. The poet may perhaps have passed beyond the latter, but he has confined himself far within the bounds of the former, in designating these critics, as "too petulant to be passive to a genuine poet, and too feeble to grapple with him;——men of palsied imaginations, in whose minds all healthy action is languid;——who, therefore, feed as the many direct them, or with the many are greedy after vicious provocatives."

So much for the detractors from Wordsworth's merits. On the other hand, much as I might wish for their fuller sympathy, I dare not flatter myself, that the freedom with which I have declared my opinions concerning both his theory and his defects, most of which are more or less connected with his theory, either as cause or effect, will be satisfactory or pleasing to all the poet's admirers and advocates. More indiscriminate than mine their admiration may be: deeper and more sincere it cannot be. But I have advanced no opinion either for praise or censure, other than as texts introductory to the reasons which compel me to form it. Above all, I was fully convinced that such a criticism was not only wanted; but that, if executed with adequate ability, it must conduce, in no mean degree, to Mr. Wordsworth's reputation. His fame belongs to another age, and can neither be accelerated nor retarded. How small the proportion of the defects are to the beauties, I have repeatedly declared; and that no one of them originates in deficiency of poetic genius. Had they been more and greater, I should still, as a friend to his literary character in the present age, consider an analytic display of them as pure gain; if only it removed, as surely to all reflecting minds even the foregoing analysis must have removed, the strange mistake, so slightly grounded, yet so widely and industriously propagated, of Mr. Wordsworth's turn for simplicity! I am not half as much irritated by hearing his enemies abuse him for vulgarity of style, subject, and conception, as I am disgusted with the gilded side of the same meaning, as displayed by some affected admirers, with whom he is, forsooth, a "sweet, simple poet!" and so natural, that little master Charles and his younger sister are so charmed with them, that they play at "Goody Blake," or at "Johnny and Betty Foy!"

Were the collection of poems, published with these biographical sketches, important enough, (which I am not vain enough to believe,) to deserve such a distinction; even as I have done, so would I be done unto.

For more than eighteen months have the volume of Poems, entitled SIBYLLINE LEAVES, and the present volume, up to this page, been printed, and ready for publication. But, ere I speak of myself in the tones, which are alone natural to me under the circumstances of late years, I would fain present myself to the Reader as I was in the first dawn of my literary life:

When Hope grew round me, like the climbing vine,
And fruits, and foliage, not my own, seem'd mine!

For this purpose I have selected from the letters, which I wrote home from Germany, those which appeared likely to be most interesting, and at the same time most pertinent to the title of this work.

SATYRANE'S LETTERS

LETTER I

On Sunday morning, September 16, 1798, the Hamburg packet set sail from Yarmouth; and I, for the first time in my life, beheld my native land retiring from me. At the moment of its disappearance—in all the kirks, churches, chapels, and meeting-houses, in which the greater number, I hope, of my countrymen were at that time assembled, I will dare question whether there was one more ardent prayer offered up to heaven, than that which I then preferred for my country. "Now then," (said I to a gentleman who was standing near me,) "we are out of our country." "Not yet, not yet!" he replied, and pointed to the sea; "This, too, is a Briton's country." This bon mot gave a fillip to my spirits, I rose and looked round on my fellow-passengers, who were all on the deck. We were eighteen in number, videlicet, five Englishmen, an English lady, a French gentleman and his servant, an Hanoverian and his servant, a Prussian, a Swede, two Danes, and a Mulatto boy, a German tailor and his wife, (the smallest couple I ever beheld,) and a Jew. We were all on the deck; but in a short time I observed marks of dismay. The lady retired to the cabin in some confusion, and many of the faces round me assumed a very doleful and frog-coloured appearance; and within an hour the number of those on deck was lessened by one half. I was giddy, but not sick, and the giddiness soon went away, but left a feverishness and want of appetite, which I attributed, in great measure, to the saeva Mephitis of the bilge-water; and it was certainly not decreased by the exportations from the cabin. However, I was well enough to join the able-bodied passengers, one of whom observed not inaptly, that Momus might have discovered an easier way to see a man's inside, than by placing a window in his breast. He needed only have taken a saltwater trip in a packet-boat.

I am inclined to believe, that a packet is far superior to a stage- coach, as a means of making men open out to each other. In the latter the uniformity of posture disposes to dozing, and the definitiveness of the period, at which the company will separate, makes each individual think more of those to whom he is going, than of those with whom he is going. But at sea, more curiosity is excited, if only on this account, that the pleasant or unpleasant qualities of your companions are of greater importance to you, from the uncertainty how long you may be obliged to house with them. Besides, if you are countrymen, that now begins to form a distinction and a bond of brotherhood; and if of different countries, there are new incitements of conversation, more to ask and more to communicate. I found that I had interested the Danes in no common degree. I had crept into the boat on the deck and fallen asleep; but was awakened by one of them, about three o'clock in the afternoon, who told me that they had been seeking me in every hole and corner, and insisted that I should join their party and drink with them. He talked English with such fluency, as left me wholly unable to account for the singular and even ludicrous incorrectness with which he spoke it. I went, and found some excellent wines and a dessert of grapes with a pine-apple. The Danes had christened me Doctor Teology, and dressed as I was all in black, with large shoes and black worsted stockings, I might certainly have passed very well for a Methodist missionary. However I disclaimed my title. What then may you be? A man of fortune? No!—A merchant? No!—A merchant's traveller? No!—A clerk? No!—Un Philosophe, perhaps? It was at that time in my life, in which of all possible names and characters I had the greatest disgust to that of "un Philosophe." But I was weary of being questioned, and rather than be nothing, or at best only the abstract idea of a man, I submitted by a bow, even to the aspersion implied in the word "un Philosophe."—The Dane then informed me, that all in the present party were Philosophers likewise. Certes we were not of the Stoick school. For we drank and talked and sung, till we talked and sung all together; and then we rose and danced on the deck a set of dances, which in one sense of the word at least, were very intelligibly and appropriately entitled reels. The passengers, who lay in the cabin below in all the agonies of sea- sickness, must have found our bacchanalian merriment

————a   tune
Harsh and of dissonant mood from their complaint.

I thought so at the time; and, (by way, I suppose, of supporting my newly assumed philosophical character,) I thought too, how closely the greater number of our virtues are connected with the fear of death, and how little sympathy we bestow on pain, where there is no danger.

The two Danes were brothers. The one was a man with a clear white complexion, white hair, and white eyebrows; looked silly, and nothing that he uttered gave the lie to his looks. The other, whom, by way of eminence I have called the Dane, had likewise white hair, but was much shorter than his brother, with slender limbs, and a very thin face slightly pockfretten. This man convinced me of the justice of an old remark, that many a faithful portrait in our novels and farces has been rashly censured for an outrageous caricature, or perhaps nonentity. I had retired to my station in the boat—he came and seated himself by my side, and appeared not a little tipsy. He commenced the conversation in the most magnific style, and, as a sort of pioneering to his own vanity, he flattered me with such grossness! The parasites of the old comedy were modest in the comparison. His language and accentuation were so exceedingly singular, that I determined for once in my life to take notes of a conversation. Here it follows, somewhat abridged, indeed, but in all other respects as accurately as my memory permitted.

THE DANE. Vat imagination! vat language! vat vast science! and vat eyes! vat a milk-vite forehead! O my heafen! vy, you're a Got!

ANSWER. You do me too much honour, Sir.

THE DANE. O me! if you should dink I is flattering you!—No, no, no! I haf ten tousand a year—yes, ten tousand a year—yes, ten tousand pound a year! Vel—and vat is dhat? a mere trifle! I 'ouldn't gif my sincere heart for ten times dhe money. Yes, you're a Got! I a mere man! But, my dear friend! dhink of me, as a man! Is, is—I mean to ask you now, my dear friend—is I not very eloquent? Is I not speak English very fine?

ANSWER. Most admirably! Believe me, Sir! I have seldom heard even a native talk so fluently.

THE DANE. (Squeezing my hand with great vehemence.) My dear friend! vat an affection and fidelity ve have for each odher! But tell me, do tell me,—Is I not, now and den, speak some fault? Is I not in some wrong?

ANSWER. Why, Sir! perhaps it might be observed by nice critics in the English language, that you occasionally use the word "is" instead of "am." In our best companies we generally say I am, and not I is or I'se. Excuse me, Sir! it is a mere trifle.

THE DANE. O!—is, is, am, am, am. Yes, yes—I know, I know.

ANSWER. I am, thou art, he is, we are, ye are, they are.

THE DANE. Yes, yes,—I know, I know—Am, am, am, is dhe praesens, and is is dhe perfectum—yes, yes—and are is dhe plusquam perfectum.

ANSWER. And art, Sir! is—?

THE DANE. My dear friend! it is dhe plusquam perfectum, no, no—dhat is a great lie; are is dhe plusquam perfectum—and art is dhe plasquam plue-perfectum—(then swinging my hand to and fro, and cocking his little bright hazel eyes at me, that danced with vanity and wine)—You see, my dear friend that I too have some lehrning?

ANSWER. Learning, Sir? Who dares suspect it? Who can listen to you for a minute, who can even look at you, without perceiving the extent of it?

THE DANE. My dear friend!—(then with a would-be humble look, and in a tone of voice as if he was reasoning) I could not talk so of prawns and imperfectum, and futurum and plusquamplue perfectum, and all dhat, my dear friend! without some lehrning?

ANSWER. Sir! a man like you cannot talk on any subject without discovering the depth of his information.

THE DANE. Dhe grammatic Greek, my friend; ha! ha! Ha! (laughing, and swinging my hand to and fro—then with a sudden transition to great solemnity) Now I will tell you, my dear friend! Dhere did happen about me vat de whole historia of Denmark record no instance about nobody else. Dhe bishop did ask me all dhe questions about all dhe religion in dhe Latin grammar.

ANSWER. The grammar, Sir? The language, I presume—

THE DANE. (A little offended.) Grammar is language, and language is grammar—

ANSWER. Ten thousand pardons!

THE DANE. Vell, and I was only fourteen years—

ANSWER. Only fourteen years old?

THE DANE. No more. I vas fourteen years old—and he asked me all questions, religion and philosophy, and all in dhe Latin language—and I answered him all every one, my dear friend! all in dhe Latin language.

ANSWER. A prodigy! an absolute prodigy!

THE DANE. No, no, no! he was a bishop, a great superintendent.

ANSWER. Yes! a bishop.

THE DANE. A bishop—not a mere predicant, not a prediger.

ANSWER. My dear Sir! we have misunderstood each other. I said that your answering in Latin at so early an age was a prodigy, that is, a thing that is wonderful; that does not often happen.

THE DANE. Often! Dhere is not von instance recorded in dhe whole historia of Denmark.

ANSWER. And since then, Sir—?

THE DANE. I was sent ofer to dhe Vest Indies—to our Island, and dhere I had no more to do vid books. No! no! I put my genius anodher way—and I haf made ten tousand pound a year. Is not dhat ghenius, my dear friend?—But vat is money?—I dhink dhe poorest man alive my equal. Yes, my dear friend; my little fortune is pleasant to my generous heart, because I can do good—no man with so little a fortune ever did so much generosity—no person—no man person, no woman person ever denies it. But we are all Got's children.

Here the Hanoverian interrupted him, and the other Dane, the Swede, and the Prussian, joined us, together with a young Englishman who spoke the German fluently, and interpreted to me many of the Prussian's jokes. The Prussian was a travelling merchant, turned of threescore, a hale man, tall, strong, and stout, full of stories, gesticulations, and buffoonery, with the soul as well as the look of a mountebank, who, while he is making you laugh, picks your pocket. Amid all his droll looks and droll gestures, there remained one look untouched by laughter; and that one look was the true face, the others were but its mask. The Hanoverian was a pale, fat, bloated young man, whose father had made a large fortune in London, as an army-contractor. He seemed to emulate the manners of young Englishmen of fortune. He was a good-natured fellow, not without information or literature; but a most egregious coxcomb. He had been in the habit of attending the House of Commons, and had once spoken, as he informed me, with great applause in a debating society. For this he appeared to have qualified himself with laudable industry: for he was perfect in Walker's Pronouncing Dictionary, and with an accent, which forcibly reminded me of the Scotchman in Roderic Random, who professed to teach the English pronunciation, he was constantly deferring to my superior judgment, whether or no I had pronounced this or that word with propriety, or "the true delicacy." When he spoke, though it were only half a dozen sentences, he always rose: for which I could detect no other motive, than his partiality to that elegant phrase so liberally introduced in the orations of our British legislators, "While I am on my legs." The Swede, whom for reasons that will soon appear, I shall distinguish by the name of Nobility, was a strong-featured, scurvy-faced man, his complexion resembling in colour, a red hot poker beginning to cool. He appeared miserably dependent on the Dane; but was, however, incomparably the best informed and most rational of the party. Indeed his manners and conversation discovered him to be both a man of the world and a gentleman. The Jew was in the hold: the French gentleman was lying on the deck so ill, that I could observe nothing concerning him, except the affectionate attentions of his servant to him. The poor fellow was very sick himself, and every now and then ran to the side of the vessel, still keeping his eye on his master, but returned in a moment and seated himself again by him, now supporting his head, now wiping his forehead and talking to him all the while in the most soothing tones. There had been a matrimonial squabble of a very ludicrous kind in the cabin, between the little German tailor and his little wife. He had secured two beds, one for himself and one for her. This had struck the little woman as a very cruel action; she insisted upon their having but one, and assured the mate in the most piteous tones, that she was his lawful wife.

The mate and the cabin boy decided in her favour, abused the little man for his want of tenderness with much humour, and hoisted him into the same compartment with his sea-sick wife. This quarrel was interesting to me, as it procured me a bed, which I otherwise should not have had.

In the evening, at seven o'clock, the sea rolled higher, and the Dane, by means of the greater agitation, eliminated enough of what he had been swallowing to make room for a great deal more. His favourite potation was sugar and brandy, i.e. a very little warm water with a large quantity of brandy, sugar, and nutmeg His servant boy, a black-eyed Mulatto, had a good-natured round face, exactly the colour of the skin of the walnut-kernel. The Dane and I were again seated, tete-a-tete, in the ship's boat. The conversation, which was now indeed rather an oration than a dialogue, became extravagant beyond all that I ever heard. He told me that he had made a large fortune in the island of Santa Cruz, and was now returning to Denmark to enjoy it. He expatiated on the style in which he meant to live, and the great undertakings which he proposed to himself to commence, till, the brandy aiding his vanity, and his vanity and garrulity aiding the brandy, he talked like a madman—entreated me to accompany him to Denmark—there I should see his influence with the government, and he would introduce me to the king, etc., etc. Thus he went on dreaming aloud, and then passing with a very lyrical transition to the subject of general politics, he declaimed, like a member of the Corresponding Society, about, (not concerning,) the Rights of Man, and assured me that, notwithstanding his fortune, he thought the poorest man alive his equal. "All are equal, my dear friend! all are equal! Ve are all Got's children. The poorest man haf the same rights with me. Jack! Jack! some more sugar and brandy. Dhere is dhat fellow now! He is a Mulatto—but he is my equal.—That's right, Jack! (taking the sugar and brandy.) Here you Sir! shake hands with dhis gentleman! Shake hands with me, you dog! Dhere, dhere!—We are all equal my dear friend! Do I not speak like Socrates, and Plato, and Cato—they were all philosophers, my dear philosophe! all very great men!—and so was Homer and Virgil—but they were poets. Yes, yes! I know all about it!—But what can anybody say more than this? We are all equal, all Got's children. I haf ten tousand a year, but I am no more dhan de meanest man alive. I haf no pride; and yet, my dear friend! I can say, do! and it is done. Ha! ha! ha! my dear friend! Now dhere is dhat gentleman (pointing to Nobility) he is a Swedish baron—you shall see. Ho! (calling to the Swede) get me, will you, a bottle of wine from the cabin. SWEDE.—Here, Jack! go and get your master a bottle of wine from the cabin. DANE. No, no, no! do you go now—you go yourself you go now! SWEDE. Pah!—DANE. Now go! Go, I pray you." And the Swede went!!

After this the Dane commenced an harangue on religion, and mistaking me for un philosophe in the continental sense of the word, he talked of Deity in a declamatory style, very much resembling the devotional rants of that rude blunderer, Mr. Thomas Paine, in his Age of Reason, and whispered in my ear, what damned hypocrism all Jesus Christ's business was. I dare aver, that few men have less reason to charge themselves with indulging in persiflage than myself. I should hate it, if it were only that it is a Frenchman's vice, and feel a pride in avoiding it, because our own language is too honest to have a word to express it by. But in this instance the temptation had been too powerful, and I have placed it on the list of my offences. Pericles answered one of his dearest friends, who had solicited him on a case of life and death, to take an equivocal oath for his preservation: Debeo amicis opitulari, sed usque ad Deos [75]. Friendship herself must place her last and boldest step on this side the altar. What Pericles would not do to save a friend's life, you may be assured, I would not hazard merely to mill the chocolate-pot of a drunken fool's vanity till it frothed over. Assuming a serious look, I professed myself a believer, and sunk at once an hundred fathoms in his good graces. He retired to his cabin, and I wrapped myself up in my great coat, and looked at the water. A beautiful white cloud of foam at momently intervals coursed by the side of the vessel with a roar, and little stars of flame danced and sparkled and went out in it: and every now and then light detachments of this white cloud-like foam darted off from the vessel's side, each with its own small constellation, over the sea, and scoured out of sight like a Tartar troop over a wilderness.

It was cold, the cabin was at open war with my olfactories, and I found reason to rejoice in my great coat, a weighty high-caped, respectable rug, the collar of which turned over, and played the part of a night-cap very passably. In looking up at two or three bright stars, which oscillated with the motion of the sails, I fell asleep, but was awakened at one o'clock, Monday morning, by a shower of rain. I found myself compelled to go down into the cabin, where I slept very soundly, and awoke with a very good appetite at breakfast time, my nostrils, the most placable of all the senses, reconciled to, or indeed insensible of the mephitis.

Monday, September 17th, I had a long conversation with the Swede, who spoke with the most poignant contempt of the Dane, whom he described as a fool, purse-mad; but he confirmed the boasts of the Dane respecting the largeness of his fortune, which he had acquired in the first instance as an advocate, and afterwards as a planter. From the Dane and from himself I collected that he was indeed a Swedish nobleman, who had squandered a fortune, that was never very large, and had made over his property to the Dane, on whom he was now utterly dependent. He seemed to suffer very little pain from the Dane's insolence. He was in a high degree humane and attentive to the English lady, who suffered most fearfully, and for whom he performed many little offices with a tenderness and delicacy which seemed to prove real goodness of heart. Indeed his general manners and conversation were not only pleasing, but even interesting; and I struggled to believe his insensibility respecting the Dane philosophical fortitude. For though the Dane was now quite sober, his character oozed out of him at every pore. And after dinner, when he was again flushed with wine, every quarter of an hour or perhaps oftener he would shout out to the Swede, "Ho! Nobility, go—do such a thing! Mr. Nobility!—tell the gentlemen such a story, and so forth;" with an insolence which must have excited disgust and detestation, if his vulgar rants on the sacred rights of equality, joined to his wild havoc of general grammar no less than of the English language, had not rendered it so irresistibly laughable.

At four o'clock I observed a wild duck swimming on the waves, a single solitary wild duck. It is not easy to conceive, how interesting a thing it looked in that round objectless desert of waters. I had associated such a feeling of immensity with the ocean, that I felt exceedingly disappointed, when I was out of sight of all land, at the narrowness and nearness, as it were, of the circle of the horizon. So little are images capable of satisfying the obscure feelings connected with words. In the evening the sails were lowered, lest we should run foul of the land, which can be seen only at a small distance. And at four o'clock, on Tuesday morning, I was awakened by the cry of "land! land!" It was an ugly island rock at a distance on our left, called Heiligeland, well known to many passengers from Yarmouth to Hamburg, who have been obliged by stormy weather to pass weeks and weeks in weary captivity on it, stripped of all their money by the exorbitant demands of the wretches who inhabit it. So at least the sailors informed me.—About nine o'clock we saw the main land, which seemed scarcely able to hold its head above water, low, flat, and dreary, with lighthouses and land-marks which seemed to give a character and language to the dreariness. We entered the mouth of the Elbe, passing Neu-werk; though as yet the right bank only of the river was visible to us. On this I saw a church, and thanked God for my safe voyage, not without affectionate thoughts of those I had left in England. At eleven o'clock on the same morning we arrived at Cuxhaven, the ship dropped anchor, and the boat was hoisted out, to carry the Hanoverian and a few others on shore. The captain agreed to take us, who remained, to Hamburg for ten guineas, to which the Dane contributed so largely, that the other passengers paid but half a guinea each. Accordingly we hauled anchor, and passed gently up the river. At Cuxhaven both sides of the river may be seen in clear weather; we could now see the right bank only. We passed a multitude of English traders that had been waiting many weeks for a wind. In a short time both banks became visible, both flat and evidencing the labour of human hands by their extreme neatness. On the left bank I saw a church or two in the distance; on the right bank we passed by steeple and windmill and cottage, and windmill and single house, windmill and windmill, and neat single house, and steeple. These were the objects and in the succession. The shores were very green and planted with trees not inelegantly. Thirty-five miles from Cuxhaven the night came on us, and, as the navigation of the Elbe is perilous, we dropped anchor.

Over what place, thought I, does the moon hang to your eye, my dearest friend? To me it hung over the left bank of the Elbe. Close above the moon was a huge volume of deep black cloud, while a very thin fillet crossed the middle of the orb, as narrow and thin and black as a ribbon of crape. The long trembling road of moonlight, which lay on the water and reached to the stern of our vessel, glimmered dimly and obscurely. We saw two or three lights from the right bank, probably from bed-rooms. I felt the striking contrast between the silence of this majestic stream, whose banks are populous with men and women and children, and flocks and herds— between the silence by night of this peopled river, and the ceaseless noise, and uproar, and loud agitations of the desolate solitude of the ocean. The passengers below had all retired to their beds; and I felt the interest of this quiet scene the more deeply from the circumstance of having just quitted them. For the Prussian had during the whole of the evening displayed all his talents to captivate the Dane, who had admitted him into the train of his dependents. The young Englishman continued to interpret the Prussian's jokes to me. They were all without exception profane and abominable, but some sufficiently witty, and a few incidents, which he related in his own person, were valuable as illustrating the manners of the countries in which they had taken place.

Five o'clock on Wednesday morning we hauled the anchor, but were soon obliged to drop it again in consequence of a thick fog, which our captain feared would continue the whole day; but about nine it cleared off, and we sailed slowly along, close by the shore of a very beautiful island, forty miles from Cuxhaven, the wind continuing slack. This holm or island is about a mile and a half in length, wedge-shaped, well wooded, with glades of the liveliest green, and rendered more interesting by the remarkably neat farm-house on it. It seemed made for retirement without solitude—a place that would allure one's friends, while it precluded the impertinent calls of mere visitors. The shores of the Elbe now became more beautiful, with rich meadows and trees running like a low wall along the river's edge; and peering over them, neat houses and, (especially on the right bank,) a profusion of steeple-spires, white, black, or red. An instinctive taste teaches men to build their churches in flat countries with spire-steeples, which, as they cannot be referred to any other object, point, as with silent finger, to the sky and stars, and sometimes, when they reflect the brazen light of a rich though rainy sun-set, appear like a pyramid of flame burning heavenward. I remember once, and once only, to have seen a spire in a narrow valley of a mountainous country. The effect was not only mean but ludicrous, and reminded me against my will of an extinguisher; the close neighbourhood of the high mountain, at the foot of which it stood, had so completely dwarfed it, and deprived it of all connection with the sky or clouds. Forty-six English miles from Cuxhaven, and sixteen from Hamburg, the Danish village Veder ornaments the left bank with its black steeple, and close by it is the wild and pastoral hamlet of Schulau. Hitherto both the right and left bank, green to the very brink, and level with the river, resembled the shores of a park canal. The trees and houses were alike low, sometimes the low trees over-topping the yet lower houses, sometimes the low houses rising above the yet lower trees. But at Schulau the left bank rises at once forty or fifty feet, and stares on the river with its perpendicular facade of sand, thinly patched with tufts of green. The Elbe continued to present a more and more lively spectacle from the multitude of fishing boats and the flocks of sea gulls wheeling round them, the clamorous rivals and companions of the fishermen; till we came to Blankaness, a most interesting village scattered amid scattered trees, over three hills in three divisions. Each of the three hills stares upon the river, with faces of bare sand, with which the boats with their bare poles, standing in files along the banks, made a sort of fantastic harmony. Between each facade lies a green and woody dell, each deeper than the other. In short it is a large village made up of individual cottages, each cottage in the centre of its own little wood or orchard, and each with its own separate path: a village with a labyrinth of paths, or rather a neighbourhood of houses! It is inhabited by fishermen and boat-makers, the Blankanese boats being in great request through the whole navigation of the Elbe. Here first we saw the spires of Hamburg, and from hence, as far as Altona, the left bank of the Elbe is uncommonly pleasing, considered as the vicinity of an industrious and republican city—in that style of beauty, or rather prettiness, that might tempt the citizen into the country, and yet gratify the taste which he had acquired in the town. Summer-houses and Chinese show-work are everywhere scattered along the high and green banks; the boards of the farm-houses left unplastered and gaily painted with green and yellow; and scarcely a tree not cut into shapes and made to remind the human being of his own power and intelligence instead of the wisdom of nature. Still, however, these are links of connection between town and country, and far better than the affectation of tastes and enjoyments for which men's habits have disqualified them. Pass them by on Saturdays and Sundays with the burghers of Hamburg smoking their pipes, the women and children feasting in the alcoves of box and yew, and it becomes a nature of its own. On Wednesday, four o'clock, we left the vessel, and passing with trouble through the huge masses of shipping that seemed to choke the wide Elbe from Altona upward, we were at length landed at the Boom House, Hamburg.

LETTER II

To a lady.

RATZEBURG.

Meine liebe Freundinn,

See how natural the German comes from me, though I have not yet been six weeks in the country!—almost as fluently as English from my neighbour the Amtsschreiber, (or public secretary,) who as often as we meet, though it should be half a dozen times in the same day, never fails to greet me with—"——ddam your ploot unt eyes, my dearest Englander! vhee goes it!"—which is certainly a proof of great generosity on his part, these words being his whole stock of English. I had, however, a better reason than the desire of displaying my proficiency: for I wished to put you in good humour with a language, from the acquirement of which I have promised myself much edification and the means too of communicating a new pleasure to you and your sister, during our winter readings. And how can I do this better than by pointing out its gallant attention to the ladies? Our English affix, ess, is, I believe, confined either to words derived from the Latin, as actress, directress, etc., or from the French, as mistress, duchess, and the like. But the German, inn, enables us to designate the sex in every possible relation of life. Thus the Amtmann's lady is the Frau Amtmanninn—the secretary's wife, (by the bye, the handsomest woman I have yet seen in Germany,) is die allerliebste Frau Amtsschreiberinn—the colonel's lady, die Frau Obristinn or Colonellinn—and even the parson's wife, die Frau Pastorinn. But I am especially pleased with their Freundinn, which, unlike the amica of the Romans, is seldom used but in its best and purest sense. Now, I know it will be said, that a friend is already something more than a friend, when a man feels an anxiety to express to himself that this friend is a female; but this I deny—in that sense at least in which the objection will be made. I would hazard the impeachment of heresy, rather than abandon my belief that there is a sex in our souls as well as in their perishable garments; and he who does not feel it, never truly loved a sister—nay, is not capable even of loving a wife as she deserves to be loved, if she indeed be worthy of that holy name.

Now I know, my gentle friend, what you are murmuring to yourself—"This is so like him! running away after the first bubble, that chance has blown off from the surface of his fancy; when one is anxious to learn where he is and what he has seen." Well then! that I am settled at Ratzeburg, with my motives and the particulars of my journey hither, will inform you. My first letter to him, with which doubtless he has edified your whole fireside, left me safely landed at Hamburg on the Elbe Stairs, at the Boom House. While standing on the stairs, I was amused by the contents of the passage-boat which crosses the river once or twice a day from Hamburg to Haarburg. It was stowed close with all people of all nations, in all sorts of dresses; the men all with pipes in their mouths, and these pipes of all shapes and fancies—straight and wreathed, simple and complex, long and short, cane, clay, porcelain, wood, tin, silver, and ivory; most of them with silver chains and silver bole-covers. Pipes and boots are the first universal characteristic of the male Hamburgers that would strike the eye of a raw traveller. But I forget my promise of journalizing as much as possible.—Therefore, Septr. 19th Afternoon. My companion, who, you recollect, speaks the French language with unusual propriety, had formed a kind of confidential acquaintance with the emigrant, who appeared to be a man of sense, and whose manners were those of a perfect gentleman. He seemed about fifty or rather more. Whatever is unpleasant in French manners from excess in the degree, had been softened down by age or affliction; and all that is delightful in the kind, alacrity and delicacy in little attentions, etc., remained, and without bustle, gesticulation, or disproportionate eagerness. His demeanour exhibited the minute philanthropy of a polished Frenchman, tempered by the sobriety of the English character disunited from its reserve. There is something strangely attractive in the character of a gentleman when you apply the word emphatically, and yet in that sense of the term which it is easy to feel than to define. It neither includes the possession of high moral excellence, nor of necessity even the ornamental graces of manner. I have now in my mind's eye a person whose life would scarcely stand scrutiny even in the court of honour, much less in that of conscience; and his manners, if nicely observed, would of the two excite an idea of awkwardness rather than of elegance: and yet every one who conversed with him felt and acknowledged the gentleman. The secret of the matter, I believe to be this—we feel the gentlemanly character present to us, whenever, under all the circumstances of social intercourse, the trivial not less than the important, through the whole detail of his manners and deportment, and with the ease of a habit, a person shows respect to others in such a way, as at the same time implies in his own feelings an habitual and assured anticipation of reciprocal respect from them to himself. In short, the gentlemanly character arises out of the feeling of Equality acting, as a Habit, yet flexible to the varieties of Rank, and modified without being disturbed or superseded by them. This description will perhaps explain to you the ground of one of your own remarks, as I was englishing to you the interesting dialogue concerning the causes of the corruption of eloquence. "What perfect gentlemen these old Romans must have been! I was impressed, I remember, with the same feeling at the time I was reading a translation of Cicero's philosophical dialogues and of his epistolary correspondence: while in Pliny's Letters I seemed to have a different feeling—he gave me the notion of a very fine gentleman." You uttered the words as if you had felt that the adjunct had injured the substance and the increased degree altered the kind. Pliny was the courtier of an absolute monarch—Cicero an aristocratic republican. For this reason the character of gentleman, in the sense to which I have confined it, is frequent in England, rare in France, and found, where it is found, in age or the latest period of manhood; while in Germany the character is almost unknown. But the proper antipode of a gentleman is to be sought for among the Anglo-American democrats.

I owe this digression, as an act of justice to this amiable Frenchman, and of humiliation for myself. For in a little controversy between us on the subject of French poetry, he made me feel my own ill behaviour by the silent reproof of contrast, and when I afterwards apologized to him for the warmth of my language, he answered me with a cheerful expression of surprise, and an immediate compliment, which a gentleman might both make with dignity and receive with pleasure. I was pleased therefore to find it agreed on, that we should, if possible, take up our quarters in the same house. My friend went with him in search of an hotel, and I to deliver my letters of recommendation.

I walked onward at a brisk pace, enlivened not so much by anything I actually saw, as by the confused sense that I was for the first time in my life on the continent of our planet. I seemed to myself like a liberated bird that had been hatched in an aviary, who now, after his first soar of freedom, poises himself in the upper air. Very naturally I began to wonder at all things, some for being so like and some for being so unlike the things in England—Dutch women with large umbrella hats shooting out half a yard before them, with a prodigal plumpness of petticoat behind—the women of Hamburg with caps plaited on the caul with silver, or gold, or both, bordered round with stiffened lace, which stood out before their eyes, but not lower, so that the eyes sparkled through it—the Hanoverian with the fore part of the head bare, then a stiff lace standing up like a wall perpendicular on the cap, and the cap behind tailed with an enormous quantity of ribbon which lies or tosses on the back:

"Their visnomies seem'd like a goodly banner
Spread in defiance of all enemies."

The ladies all in English dresses, all rouged, and all with bad teeth: which you notice instantly from their contrast to the almost animal, too glossy mother-of-pearl whiteness and the regularity of the teeth of the laughing, loud-talking country-women and servant-girls, who with their clean white stockings and with slippers without heel quarters, tripped along the dirty streets, as if they were secured by a charm from the dirt: with a lightness too, which surprised me, who had always considered it as one of the annoyances of sleeping in an Inn, that I had to clatter up stairs in a pair of them. The streets narrow; to my English nose sufficiently offensive, and explaining at first sight the universal use of boots; without any appropriate path for the foot-passengers; the gable ends of the houses all towards the street, some in the ordinary triangular form and entire as the botanists say; but the greater number notched and scolloped with more than Chinese grotesqueness. Above all, I was struck with the profusion of windows, so large and so many, that the houses look all glass. Mr. Pitt's window tax, with its pretty little additionals sprouting out from it like young toadlets on the back of a Surinam toad, would certainly improve the appearance of the Hamburg houses, which have a slight summer look, not in keeping with their size, incongruous with the climate, and precluding that feeling of retirement and self-content, which one wishes to associate with a house in a noisy city. But a conflagration would, I fear, be the previous requisite to the production of any architectural beauty in Hamburg: for verily it is a filthy town. I moved on and crossed a multitude of ugly bridges, with huge black deformities of water wheels close by them. The water intersects the city everywhere, and would have furnished to the genius of Italy the capabilities of all that is most beautiful and magnificent in architecture. It might have been the rival of Venice, and it is huddle and ugliness, stench and stagnation. The Jungfer Stieg, (that is, Young Ladies' Walk), to which my letters directed me, made an exception. It was a walk or promenade planted with treble rows of elm trees, which, being yearly pruned and cropped, remain slim and dwarf-like. This walk occupies one side of a square piece of water, with many swans on it perfectly tame, and, moving among the swans, shewy pleasure-boats with ladies in them, rowed by their husbands or lovers.———

(Some paragraphs have been here omitted.)————thus embarrassed by sad and solemn politeness still more than by broken English, it sounded like the voice of an old friend when I heard the emigrant's servant inquiring after me. He had come for the purpose of guiding me to our hotel. Through streets and streets I pressed on as happy as a child, and, I doubt not, with a childish expression of wonderment in my busy eyes, amused by the wicker waggons with movable benches across them, one behind the other, (these were the hackney coaches;) amused by the sign-boards of the shops, on which all the articles sold within are painted, and that too very exactly, though in a grotesque confusion, (a useful substitute for language in this great mart of nations;) amused with the incessant tinkling of the shop and house door bells, the bell hanging over each door and struck with a small iron rod at every entrance and exit;—and finally, amused by looking in at the windows, as I passed along; the ladies and gentlemen drinking coffee or playing cards, and the gentlemen all smoking. I wished myself a painter, that I might have sent you a sketch of one of the card parties. The long pipe of one gentleman rested on the table, its bole half a yard from his mouth, fuming like a censer by the fish-pool—the other gentleman, who was dealing the cards, and of course had both hands employed, held his pipe in his teeth, which hanging down between his knees, smoked beside his ancles. Hogarth himself never drew a more ludicrous distortion both of attitude and physiognomy, than this effort occasioned nor was there wanting beside it one of those beautiful female faces which the same Hogarth, in whom the satirist never extinguished that love of beauty which belonged to him as a poet, so often and so gladly introduces, as the central figure, in a crowd of humorous deformities, which figures, (such is the power of true genius!) neither acts, nor is meant to act as a contrast; but diffuses through all, and over each of the group, a spirit of reconciliation and human kindness; and, even when the attention is no longer consciously directed to the cause of this feeling, still blends its tenderness with our laughter: and thus prevents the instructive merriment at the whims of nature or the foibles or humours of our fellow-men from degenerating into the heart-poison of contempt or hatred.

Our hotel DIE WILDE MAN, (the sign of which was no bad likeness of the landlord, who had ingrafted on a very grim face a restless grin, that was at every man's service, and which indeed, like an actor rehearsing to himself, he kept playing in expectation of an occasion for it)—neither our hotel, I say, nor its landlord were of the genteelest class. But it has one great advantage for a stranger, by being in the market place, and the next neighbour of the huge church of St. Nicholas: a church with shops and houses built up against it, out of which wens and warts its high massy steeple rises, necklaced near the top with a round of large gilt balls. A better pole-star could scarcely be desired. Long shall I retain the impression made on my mind by the awful echo, so loud and long and tremulous, of the deep-toned clock within this church, which awoke me at two in the morning from a distressful dream, occasioned, I believe, by the feather bed, which is used here instead of bed-clothes. I will rather carry my blanket about with me like a wild Indian, than submit to this abominable custom. Our emigrant acquaintance was, we found, an intimate friend of the celebrated Abbe de Lisle: and from the large fortune which he possessed under the monarchy, had rescued sufficient not only for independence, but for respectability. He had offended some of his fellow-emigrants in

London, whom he had obliged with considerable sums, by a refusal to make further advances, and in consequence of their intrigues had received an order to quit the kingdom. I thought it one proof of his innocence, that he attached no blame either to the alien act, or to the minister who had exerted it against him; and a still greater, that he spoke of London with rapture, and of his favourite niece, who had married and settled in England, with all the fervour and all the pride of a fond parent. A man sent by force out of a country, obliged to sell out of the stocks at a great loss, and exiled from those pleasures and that style of society which habit had rendered essential to his happiness, whose predominant feelings were yet all of a private nature, resentment for friendship outraged, and anguish for domestic affections interrupted—such a man, I think, I could dare warrant guiltless of espionnage in any service, most of all in that of the present French Directory. He spoke with ecstasy of Paris under the Monarchy: and yet the particular facts, which made up his description, left as deep a conviction on my mind, of French worthlessness, as his own tale had done of emigrant ingratitude. Since my arrival in Germany, I have not met a single person, even among those who abhor the Revolution, that spoke with favour, or even charity of the French emigrants. Though the belief of their influence in the organization of this disastrous war (from the horrors of which, North Germany deems itself only reprieved, not secured,) may have some share in the general aversion with which they are regarded: yet I am deeply persuaded that the far greater part is owing to their own profligacy, to their treachery and hardheartedness to each other, and the domestic misery or corrupt principles which so many of them have carried into the families of their protectors. My heart dilated with honest pride, as I recalled to mind the stern yet amiable characters of the English patriots, who sought refuge on the Continent at the Restoration! O let not our civil war under the first Charles be paralleled with the French Revolution! In the former, the character overflowed from excess of principle; in the latter from the fermentation of the dregs! The former, was a civil war between the virtues and virtuous prejudices of the two parties; the latter, between the vices. The Venetian glass of the French monarchy shivered and flew asunder with the working of a double poison.

Sept. 20th. I was introduced to Mr. Klopstock, the brother of the poet, who again introduced me to Professor Ebeling, an intelligent and lively man, though deaf: so deaf, indeed, that it was a painful effort to talk with him, as we were obliged to drop our pearls into a huge ear-trumpet. From this courteous and kind-hearted man of letters, (I hope, the German literati in general may resemble this first specimen), I heard a tolerable Italian pun, and an interesting anecdote. When Buonaparte was in Italy, having been irritated by some instance of perfidy, he said in a loud and vehement tone, in a public company—"'tis a true proverb, gli Italiani tutti ladroni"—(that is, the Italians all plunderers.) A lady had the courage to reply, "Non tutti; ma BUONA PARTE," (not all, but a good part, or Buonaparte.) This, I confess, sounded to my ears, as one of the many good things that might have been said. The anecdote is more valuable; for it instances the ways and means of French insinuation. Hoche had received much information concerning the face of the country from a map of unusual fulness and accuracy, the maker of which, he heard, resided at Duesseldorf. At the storming of Duesseldorf by the French army, Hoche previously ordered, that the house and property of this man should be preserved, and intrusted the performance of the order to an officer on whose troop he could rely. Finding afterwards, that the man had escaped before the storming commenced, Hoche exclaimed, "HE had no reason to flee! It is for such men, not against them, that the French nation makes war, and consents to shed the blood of its children." You remember Milton's sonnet—

*"The great Emathian conqueror bid spare
The house of Pindarus when temple and tower
Went to the ground"*———

Now though the Duesseldorf map-maker may stand in the same relation to the Theban bard, as the snail, that marks its path by lines of film on the wall it creeps over, to the eagle that soars sunward and beats the tempest with its wings; it does not therefore follow, that the Jacobin of France may not be as valiant a general and as good a politician, as the madman of Macedon.

From Professor Ebeling's Mr. Klopstock accompanied my friend and me to his own house, where I saw a fine bust of his brother. There was a solemn and heavy greatness in his countenance, which corresponded to my preconceptions of his style and genius.—I saw there, likewise, a very fine portrait of Lessing, whose works are at present the chief object of my admiration. His eyes were uncommonly like mine, if anything, rather larger and more prominent. But the lower part of his face and his nose—O what an exquisite expression of elegance and sensibility!—There appeared no depth, weight, or comprehensiveness in the forehead.—The whole face seemed to say, that Lessing was a man of quick and voluptuous feelings; of an active but light fancy; acute; yet acute not in the observation of actual life, but in the arrangements and management of the ideal world, that is, in taste, and in metaphysics. I assure you, that I wrote these very words in my memorandum-book with the portrait before my eyes, and when I knew nothing of Lessing but his name, and that he was a German writer of eminence.

We consumed two hours and more over a bad dinner, at the table d'hote. "Patience at a German ordinary, smiling at time." The Germans are the worst cooks in Europe. There is placed for every two persons a bottle of common wine—Rhenish and Claret alternately; but in the houses of the opulent, during the many and long intervals of the dinner, the servants hand round glasses of richer wines. At the Lord of Culpin's they came in this order. Burgundy—Madeira—Port—Frontiniac—Pacchiaretti—Old Hock—Mountain—Champagne—Hock again—Bishop, and lastly, Punch. A tolerable quantum, methinks! The last dish at the ordinary, viz. slices of roast pork, (for all the larger dishes are brought in, cut up, and first handed round and then set on the table,) with stewed prunes and other sweet fruits, and this followed by cheese and butter, with plates of apples, reminded me of Shakespeare [76], and Shakespeare put it in my head to go to the French comedy.

Bless me! why it is worse than our modern English plays! The first act informed me, that a court martial is to be held on a Count Vatron, who had drawn his sword on the Colonel, his brother-in-law. The officers plead in his behalf—in vain! His wife, the Colonel's sister, pleads with most tempestuous agonies—in vain! She falls into hysterics and faints away, to the dropping of the inner curtain! In the second act sentence of death is passed on the Count—his wife, as frantic and hysterical as before: more so (good industrious creature!) she could not be. The third and last act, the wife still frantic, very frantic indeed!—the soldiers just about to fire, the handkerchief actually dropped; when reprieve! reprieve! is heard from behind the scenes: and in comes Prince Somebody, pardons the Count, and the wife is still frantic, only with joy; that was all!

O dear lady! this is one of the cases, in which laughter is followed by melancholy: for such is the kind of drama, which is now substituted every where for Shakespeare and Racine. You well know, that I offer violence to my own feelings in joining these names. But however meanly I may think of the French serious drama, even in its most perfect specimens; and with whatever right I may complain of its perpetual falsification of the language, and of the connections and transitions of thought, which Nature has appropriated to states of passion; still, however, the French tragedies are consistent works of art, and the offspring of great intellectual power. Preserving a fitness in the parts, and a harmony in the whole, they form a nature of their own, though a false nature. Still they excite the minds of the spectators to active thought, to a striving after ideal excellence. The soul is not stupefied into mere sensations by a worthless sympathy with our own ordinary sufferings, or an empty curiosity for the surprising, undignified by the language or the situations which awe and delight the imagination. What, (I would ask of the crowd, that press forward to the pantomimic tragedies and weeping comedies of Kotzebue and his imitators), what are you seeking? Is it comedy? But in the comedy of Shakespeare and Moliere the more accurate my knowledge, and the more profoundly I think, the greater is the satisfaction that mingles with my laughter. For though the qualities which these writers pourtray are ludicrous indeed, either from the kind or the excess, and exquisitely ludicrous, yet are they the natural growth of the human mind and such as, with more or less change in the drapery, I can apply to my own heart, or at least to whole classes of my fellow-creatures. How often are not the moralist and the metaphysician obliged for the happiest illustrations of general truths and the subordinate laws of human thought and action to quotations, not only from the tragic characters, but equally from the Jaques, Falstaff, and even from the fools and clowns of Shakespeare, or from the Miser, Hypochondriast, and Hypocrite, of Moliere! Say not, that I am recommending abstractions: for these class-characteristics, which constitute the instructiveness of a character, are so modified and particularized in each person of the Shakesperian Drama, that life itself does not excite more distinctly that sense of individuality which belongs to real existence. Paradoxical as it may sound, one of the essential properties of geometry is not less essential to dramatic excellence, and, (if I may mention his name without pedantry to a lady,) Aristotle has accordingly required of the poet an involution of the universal in the individual. The chief differences are, that in geometry it is the universal truth itself, which is uppermost in the consciousness, in poetry the individual form in which the truth is clothed. With the ancients, and not less with the elder dramatists of England and France, both comedy and tragedy were considered as kinds of poetry. They neither sought in comedy to make us laugh merely, much less to make us laugh by wry faces, accidents of jargon, slang phrases for the day, or the clothing of commonplace morals in metaphors drawn from the shops or mechanic occupations of their characters; nor did they condescend in tragedy to wheedle away the applause of the spectators, by representing before them fac-similes of their own mean selves in all their existing meanness, or to work on their sluggish sympathies by a pathos not a whit more respectable than the maudlin tears of drunkenness. Their tragic scenes were meant to affect us indeed, but within the bounds of pleasure, and in union with the activity both of our understanding and imagination. They wished to transport the mind to a sense of its possible greatness, and to implant the germs of that greatness during the temporary oblivion of the worthless "thing, we are" and of the peculiar state, in which each man happens to be; suspending our individual recollections and lulling them to sleep amid the music of nobler thoughts.

Hold!—(methinks I hear the spokesman of the crowd reply, and we will listen to him. I am the plaintiff, and he the defendant.)

DEFENDANT. Hold! are not our modern sentimental plays filled with the best Christian morality?

PLAINTIFF. Yes! just as much of it, and just that part of it, which you can exercise without a single Christian virtue—without a single sacrifice that is really painful to you!—just as much as flatters you, sends you away pleased with your own hearts, and quite reconciled to your vices, which can never be thought very ill of, when they keep such good company, and walk hand in hand with so much compassion and generosity; adulation so loathsome, that you would spit in the man's face who dared offer it to you in a private company, unless you interpreted it as insulting irony, you appropriate with infinite satisfaction, when you share the garbage with the whole stye, and gobble it out of a common trough. No Caesar must pace your boards—no Antony, no royal Dane, no Orestes, no Andromache!

D. No: or as few of them as possible. What has a plain citizen of London, or Hamburg, to do with your kings and queens, and your old school-boy Pagan heroes? Besides, every body knows the stories; and what curiosity can we feel——

P. What, Sir, not for the manner?—not for the delightful language of the poet?—not for the situations, the action and reaction of the passions?

D. You are hasty, Sir! the only curiosity, we feel, is in the story: and how can we be anxious concerning the end of a play, or be surprised by it, when we know how it will turn out?

P. Your pardon, for having interrupted you! we now understand each other. You seek then, in a tragedy, which wise men of old held for the highest effort of human genius, the same gratification, as that you receive from a new novel, the last German romance, and other dainties of the day, which can be enjoyed but once. If you carry these feelings to the sister art of Painting, Michael Angelo's Sixtine Chapel, and the Scripture Gallery of Raphael can expect no favour from you. You know all about them beforehand; and are, doubtless, more familiar with the subjects of those paintings, than with the tragic tales of the historic or heroic ages. There is a consistency, therefore, in your preference of contemporary writers: for the great men of former times, those at least who were deemed great by our ancestors, sought so little to gratify this kind of curiosity, that they seemed to have regarded the story in a not much higher light, than the painter regards his canvass: as that on, not by, which they were to display their appropriate excellence. No work, resembling a tale or romance, can well show less variety of invention in the incidents, or less anxiety in weaving them together, than the DON QUIXOTE of Cervantes. Its admirers feel the disposition to go back and re-peruse some preceding chapter, at least ten times for once that they find any eagerness to hurry forwards: or open the book on those parts which they best recollect, even as we visit those friends oftenest whom we love most, and with whose characters and actions we are the most intimately acquainted. In the divine Ariosto, (as his countrymen call this, their darling poet,) I question whether there be a single tale of his own invention, or the elements of which, were not familiar to the readers of "old romance." I will pass by the ancient Greeks, who thought it even necessary to the fable of a tragedy, that its substance should be previously known. That there had been at least fifty tragedies with the same title, would be one of the motives which determined Sophocles and Euripides, in the choice of Electra as a subject. But Milton—

D. Aye Milton, indeed!—but do not Dr. Johnson and other great men tell us, that nobody now reads Milton but as a task?

P. So much the worse for them, of whom this can be truly said! But why then do you pretend to admire Shakespeare? The greater part, if not all, of his dramas were, as far as the names and the main incidents are concerned, already stock plays. All the stories, at least, on which they are built, pre-existed in the chronicles, ballads, or translations of contemporary or preceding English writers. Why, I repeat, do you pretend to admire Shakespeare? Is it, perhaps, that you only pretend to admire him? However, as once for all, you have dismissed the well-known events and personages of history, or the epic muse, what have you taken in their stead? Whom has your tragic muse armed with her bowl and dagger? the sentimental muse I should have said, whom you have seated in the throne of tragedy? What heroes has she reared on her buskins?

D. O! our good friends and next-door neighbours—honest tradesmen, valiant tars, high-spirited half-pay officers, philanthropic Jews, virtuous courtezans, tender-hearted braziers, and sentimental rat-catchers!—(a little bluff or so, but all our very generous, tender-hearted characters are a little rude or misanthropic, and all our misanthropes very tender-hearted.)

P. But I pray you, friend, in what actions great or interesting, can such men be engaged?

D. They give away a great deal of money; find rich dowries for young men and maidens who have all other good qualities; they brow-beat lords, baronets, and justices of the peace, (for they are as bold as Hector!)—they rescue stage coaches at the instant they are falling down precipices; carry away infants in the sight of opposing armies; and some of our performers act a muscular able-bodied man to such perfection, that our dramatic poets, who always have the actors in their eye, seldom fail to make their favourite male character as strong as Samson. And then they take such prodigious leaps!! And what is done on the stage is more striking even than what is acted. I once remember such a deafening explosion, that I could not hear a word of the play for half an act after it: and a little real gunpowder being set fire to at the same time, and smelt by all the spectators, the naturalness of the scene was quite astonishing!

P. But how can you connect with such men and such actions that dependence of thousands on the fate of one, which gives so lofty an interest to the personages of Shakespeare, and the Greek Tragedians? How can you connect with them that sublimest of all feelings, the power of destiny and the controlling might of heaven, which seems to elevate the characters which sink beneath its irresistible blow?

D. O mere fancies! We seek and find on the present stage our own wants and passions, our own vexations, losses, and embarrassments.

P. It is your own poor pettifogging nature then, which you desire to have represented before you?—not human nature in its height and vigour? But surely you might find the former with all its joys and sorrows, more conveniently in your own houses and parishes.

D. True! but here comes a difference. Fortune is blind, but the poet has his eyes open, and is besides as complaisant as fortune is capricious. He makes every thing turn out exactly as we would wish it. He gratifies us by representing those as hateful or contemptible whom we hate and wish to despise.

P. (aside.) That is, he gratifies your envy by libelling your superiors.

D. He makes all those precise moralists, who affect to be better than their neighbours, turn out at last abject hypocrites, traitors, and hard-hearted villains; and your men of spirit, who take their girl and their glass with equal freedom, prove the true men of honour, and, (that no part of the audience may remain unsatisfied,) reform in the last scene, and leave no doubt in the minds of the ladies, that they will make most faithful and excellent husbands: though it does seem a pity, that they should be obliged to get rid of qualities which had made them so interesting! Besides, the poor become rich all at once; and in the final matrimonial choice the opulent and high-born themselves are made to confess; that VIRTUE IS THE ONLY TRUE NOBILITY, AND THAT A LOVELY WOMAN IS A DOWRY OF HERSELF!!

P. Excellent! But you have forgotten those brilliant flashes of loyalty, those patriotic praises of the King and Old England, which, especially if conveyed in a metaphor from the ship or the shop, so often solicit and so unfailingly receive the public plaudit! I give your prudence credit for the omission. For the whole system of your drama is a moral and intellectual Jacobinism of the most dangerous kind, and those common-place rants of loyalty are no better than hypocrisy in your playwrights, and your own sympathy with them a gross self-delusion. For the whole secret of dramatic popularity consists with you in the confusion and subversion of the natural order of things, their causes and their effects; in the excitement of surprise, by representing the qualities of liberality, refined feeling, and a nice sense of honour, (those things rather which pass among you for such), in persons and in classes of life where experience teaches us least to expect them; and in rewarding with all the sympathies, that are the dues of virtue, those criminals whom law, reason, and religion have excommunicated from our esteem!

And now—good night! Truly! I might have written this last sheet without having gone to Germany; but I fancied myself talking to you by your own fireside, and can you think it a small pleasure to me to forget now and then, that I am not there? Besides, you and my other good friends have made up your minds to me as I am, and from whatever place I write you will expect that part of my "Travels" will consist of excursions in my own mind.

LETTER III

RATZEBURG.

No little fish thrown back again into the water, no fly unimprisoned from a child's hand, could more buoyantly enjoy its element, than I this clean and peaceful house, with this lovely view of the town, groves, and lake of Ratzeburg, from the window at which I am writing. My spirits certainly, and my health I fancied, were beginning to sink under the noise, dirt, and unwholesome air of our Hamburg hotel. I left it on Sunday, Sept. 23rd, with a letter of introduction from the poet Klopstock, to the Amtmann of Ratzeburg. The Amtmann received me with kindness, and introduced me to the worthy pastor, who agreed to board and lodge me for any length of time not less than a month. The vehicle, in which I took my place, was considerably larger than an English stage-coach, to which it bore much the same proportion and rude resemblance, that an elephant's ear does to the human. Its top was composed of naked boards of different colours, and seeming to have been parts of different wainscots. Instead of windows there were leathern curtains with a little eye of glass in each: they perfectly answered the purpose of keeping out the prospect and letting in the cold. I could observe little therefore, but the inns and farmhouses at which we stopped. They were all alike, except in size: one great room, like a barn, with a hay-loft over it, the straw and hay dangling in tufts through the boards which formed the ceiling of the room, and the floor of the loft. From this room, which is paved like a street, sometimes one, sometimes two smaller ones, are enclosed at one end. These are commonly floored. In the large room the cattle, pigs, poultry, men, women, and children, live in amicable community; yet there was an appearance of cleanliness and rustic comfort. One of these houses I measured. It was an hundred feet in length.

The apartments were taken off from one corner. Between these and the stalls there was a small interspace, and here the breadth was forty-eight feet, but thirty-two where the stalls were; of course, the stalls were on each side eight feet in depth. The faces of the cows, etc. were turned towards the room; indeed they were in it, so that they had at least the comfort of seeing each other's faces. Stall-feeding is universal in this part of Germany, a practice concerning which the agriculturist and the poet are likely to entertain opposite opinions—or at least, to have very different feelings. The woodwork of these buildings on the outside is left unplastered, as in old houses among us, and, being painted red and green, it cuts and tesselates the buildings very gaily. From within three miles of Hamburg almost to Molln, which is thirty miles from it, the country, as far as I could see it, was a dead flat, only varied by woods. At Molln it became more beautiful. I observed a small lake nearly surrounded with groves, and a palace in view belonging to the King of Great Britain, and inhabited by the Inspector of the Forests. We were nearly the same time in travelling the thirty-five miles from Hamburg to Ratzeburg, as we had been in going from London to Yarmouth, one hundred and twenty-six miles.

The lake of Ratzeburg runs from south to north, about nine miles in length, and varying in breadth from three miles to half a mile. About a mile from the southernmost point it is divided into two, of course very unequal, parts by an island, which, being connected by a bridge and a narrow slip of land with the one shore, and by another bridge of immense length with the other shore, forms a complete isthmus. On this island the town of Ratzeburg is built. The pastor's house or vicarage, together with the Amtmann's Amtsschreiber's, and the church, stands near the summit of a hill, which slopes down to the slip of land and the little bridge, from which, through a superb military gate, you step into the island-town of Ratzeburg. This again is itself a little hill, by ascending and descending which, you arrive at the long bridge, and so to the other shore. The water to the south of the town is called the Little Lake, which however almost engrosses the beauties of the whole the shores being just often enough green and bare to give the proper effect to the magnificent groves which occupy the greater part of their circumference. From the turnings, windings, and indentations of the shore, the views vary almost every ten steps, and the whole has a sort of majestic beauty, a feminine grandeur. At the north of the Great Lake, and peeping over it, I see the seven church towers of Luebec, at the distance of twelve or thirteen miles, yet as distinctly as if they were not three. The only defect in the view is, that Ratzeburg is built entirely of red bricks, and all the houses roofed with red tiles. To the eye, therefore, it presents a clump of brick-dust red. Yet this evening, Oct. 10th, twenty minutes past five, I saw the town perfectly beautiful, and the whole softened down into complete keeping, if I may borrow a term from the painters. The sky over Ratzeburg and all the east was a pure evening blue, while over the west it was covered with light sandy clouds. Hence a deep red light spread over the whole prospect, in undisturbed harmony with the red town, the brown-red woods, and the yellow-red reeds on the skirts of the lake. Two or three boats, with single persons paddling them, floated up and down in the rich light, which not only was itself in harmony with all, but brought all into harmony.

I should have told you that I went back to Hamburg on Thursday (Sept. 27th) to take leave of my friend, who travels southward, and returned hither on the Monday following. From Empfelde, a village half way from Ratzeburg, I walked to Hamburg through deep sandy roads and a dreary flat: the soil everywhere white, hungry, and excessively pulverised; but the approach to the city is pleasing. Light cool country houses, which you can look through and see the gardens behind them, with arbours and trellis work, and thick vegetable walls, and trees in cloisters and piazzas, each house with neat rails before it, and green seats within the rails. Every object, whether the growth of nature or the work of man, was neat and artificial. It pleased me far better, than if the houses and gardens, and pleasure fields, had been in a nobler taste: for this nobler taste would have been mere apery. The busy, anxious, money-loving merchant of Hamburg could only have adopted, he could not have enjoyed the simplicity of nature. The mind begins to love nature by imitating human conveniences in nature; but this is a step in intellect, though a low one—and were it not so, yet all around me spoke of innocent enjoyment and sensitive comforts, and I entered with unscrupulous sympathy into the enjoyments and comforts even of the busy, anxious, money-loving merchants of Hamburg. In this charitable and catholic mood I reached the vast ramparts of the city. These are huge green cushions, one rising above the other, with trees growing in the interspaces, pledges and symbols of a long peace. Of my return I have nothing worth communicating, except that I took extra post, which answers to posting in England. These north German post chaises are uncovered wicker carts. An English dust-cart is a piece of finery, a chef d'auvre of mechanism, compared with them and the horses!—a savage might use their ribs instead of his fingers for a numeration table. Wherever we stopped, the postilion fed his cattle with the brown rye bread of which he eat himself, all breakfasting together; only the horses had no gin to their water, and the postilion no water to his gin. Now and henceforward for subjects of more interest to you, and to the objects in search of which I left you: namely, the literati and literature of Germany.

Believe me, I walked with an impression of awe on my spirits, as W—— and myself accompanied Mr. Klopstock to the house of his brother, the poet, which stands about a quarter of a mile from the city gate. It is one of a row of little common-place summer-houses, (for so they looked,) with four or five rows of young meagre elm trees before the windows, beyond which is a green, and then a dead flat intersected with several roads. Whatever beauty, (thought I,) may be before the poet's eyes at present, it must certainly be purely of his own creation. We waited a few minutes in a neat little parlour, ornamented with the figures of two of the Muses and with prints, the subjects of which were from Klopstock's odes. The poet entered. I was much disappointed in his countenance, and recognised in it no likeness to the bust. There was no comprehension in the forehead, no weight over the eye-brows, no expression of peculiarity, moral or intellectual, on the eyes, no massiveness in the general countenance. He is, if anything, rather below the middle size. He wore very large half-boots, which his legs filled, so fearfully were they swollen. However, though neither W—— nor myself could discover any indications of sublimity or enthusiasm in his physiognomy, we were both equally impressed with his liveliness, and his kind and ready courtesy. He talked in French with my friend, and with difficulty spoke a few sentences to me in English. His enunciation was not in the least affected by the entire want of his upper teeth. The conversation began on his part by the expression of his rapture at the surrender of the detachment of French troops under General Humbert. Their proceedings in Ireland with regard to the committee which they had appointed, with the rest of their organizing system, seemed to have given the poet great entertainment. He then declared his sanguine belief in Nelson's victory, and anticipated its confirmation with a keen and triumphant pleasure. His words, tones, looks, implied the most vehement Anti-Gallicanism. The subject changed to literature, and I inquired in Latin concerning the history of German poetry and the elder German poets. To my great astonishment he confessed, that he knew very little on the subject. He had indeed occasionally read one or two of their elder writers, but not so as to enable him to speak of their merits. Professor Ebeling, he said, would probably give me every information of this kind: the subject had not particularly excited his curiosity. He then talked of Milton and Glover, and thought Glover's blank verse superior to Milton's. W—— and myself expressed our surprise: and my friend gave his definition and notion of harmonious verse, that it consisted, (the English iambic blank verse above all,) in the apt arrangement of pauses and cadences, and the sweep of whole paragraphs,

*"with many a winding bout
Of linked sweetness long drawn out,"*

and not in the even flow, much less in the prominence of antithetic vigour, of single lines, which were indeed injurious to the total effect, except where they were introduced for some specific purpose. Klopstock assented, and said that he meant to confine Glover's superiority to single lines. He told us that he had read Milton, in a prose translation, when he was fourteen [77]. I understood him thus myself, and W---- interpreted Klopstock's French as I had already construed it. He appeared to know very little of Milton or indeed of our poets in general. He spoke with great indignation of the English prose translation of his MESSIAH. All the translations had been bad, very bad--but the English was no translation--there were pages on pages not in the original--and half the original was not to be found in the translation. W---- told him that I intended to translate a few of his odes as specimens of German lyrics--he then said to me in English, "I wish you would render into English some select passages of THE MESSIAH, and revenge me of your countryman!". It was the liveliest thing which he produced in the whole conversation. He told us, that his first ode was fifty years older than his last. I looked at him with much emotion--I considered him as the venerable father of German poetry; as a good man; as a Christian; seventy-four years old; with legs enormously swollen; yet active, lively, cheerful, and kind, and communicative. My eyes felt as if a tear were swelling into them. In the portrait of Lessing there was a toupee periwig, which enormously injured the effect of his physiognomy--Klopstock wore the same, powdered and frizzled. By the bye, old men ought never to wear powder--the contrast between a large snow-white wig and the colour of an old man's skin is disgusting, and wrinkles in such a neighbourhood appear only channels for dirt. It is an honour to poets and great men, that you think of them as parts of nature; and anything of trick and fashion wounds you in them, as much as when you see venerable yews clipped into miserable peacocks.--The author of THE MESSIAH should have worn his own grey hair.--His powder and periwig were to the eye what Mr. Virgil would be to the ear.

Klopstock dwelt much on the superior power which the German language possessed of concentrating meaning. He said, he had often translated parts of Homer and Virgil, line by line, and a German line proved always sufficient for a Greek or Latin one. In English you cannot do this. I answered, that in English we could commonly render one Greek heroic line in a line and a half of our common heroic metre, and I conjectured that this line and a half would be found to contain no more syllables than one German or Greek hexameter. He did not understand me [78]: and I, who wished to hear his opinions, not to correct them, was glad that he did not.

We now took our leave. At the beginning of the French Revolution Klopstock wrote odes of congratulation. He received some honorary presents from the French Republic, (a golden crown I believe), and, like our Priestley, was invited to a seat in the legislature, which he declined. But when French liberty metamorphosed herself into a fury, he sent back these presents with a palinodia, declaring his abhorrence of their proceedings: and since then he has been perhaps more than enough an Anti-Gallican. I mean, that in his just contempt and detestation of the crimes and follies of the Revolutionists, he suffers himself to forget that the revolution itself is a process of the Divine Providence; and that as the folly of men is the wisdom of God, so are their iniquities instruments of his goodness. From Klopstock's house we walked to the ramparts, discoursing together on the poet and his conversation, till our attention was diverted to the beauty and singularity of the sunset and its effects on the objects around us. There were woods in the distance. A rich sandy light, (nay, of a much deeper colour than sandy,) lay over these woods that blackened in the blaze. Over that part of the woods which lay immediately under the intenser light, a brassy mist floated. The trees on the ramparts, and the people moving to and fro between them, were cut or divided into equal segments of deep shade and brassy light. Had the trees, and the bodies of the men and women, been divided into equal segments by a rule or pair of compasses, the portions could not have been more regular. All else was obscure. It was a fairy scene!—and to increase its romantic character, among the moving objects, thus divided into alternate shade and brightness, was a beautiful child, dressed with the elegant simplicity of an English child, riding on a stately goat, the saddle, bridle, and other accoutrements of which were in a high degree costly and splendid. Before I quit the subject of Hamburg, let me say, that I remained a day or two longer than I otherwise should have done, in order to be present at the feast of St. Michael, the patron saint of Hamburg, expecting to see the civic pomp of this commercial Republic. I was however disappointed. There were no processions, two or three sermons were preached to two or three old women in two or three churches, and St. Michael and his patronage wished elsewhere by the higher classes, all places of entertainment, theatre, etc. being shut up on this day. In Hamburg, there seems to be no religion at all; in Luebec it is confined to the women. The men seemed determined to be divorced from their wives in the other world, if they cannot in this. You will not easily conceive a more singular sight, than is presented by the vast aisle of the principal church at Luebec, seen from the organ loft: for being filled with female servants and persons in the same class of life, and all their caps having gold and silver cauls, it appears like a rich pavement of gold and silver.

I will conclude this letter with the mere transcription of notes, which my friend W—— made of his conversations with Klopstock, during the interviews that took place after my departure. On these I shall make but one remark at present, and that will appear a presumptuous one, namely, that Klopstock's remarks on the venerable sage of Koenigsburg are to my own knowledge injurious and mistaken; and so far is it from being true, that his system is now given up, that throughout the Universities of Germany there is not a single professor who is not either a Kantean or a disciple of Fichte, whose system is built on the Kantean, and presupposes its truth; or lastly who, though an antagonist of Kant, as to his theoretical work, has not embraced wholly or in part his moral system, and adopted part of his nomenclature. "Klopstock having wished to see the CALVARY of Cumberland, and asked what was thought of it in England, I went to Remnant's (the English bookseller) where I procured the Analytical Review, in which is contained the review of Cumberland's CALVARY. I remembered to have read there some specimens of a blank verse translation of THE MESSIAH. I had mentioned this to Klopstock, and he had a great desire to see them. I walked over to his house and put the book into his hands. On adverting to his own poem, he told me he began THE MESSIAH when he was seventeen; he devoted three entire years to the plan without composing a single line. He was greatly at a loss in what manner to execute his work. There were no successful specimens of versification in the German language before this time. The first three cantos he wrote in a species of measured or numerous prose. This, though done with much labour and some success, was far from satisfying him. He had composed hexameters both Latin and Greek as a school exercise, and there had been also in the German language attempts in that style of versification. These were only of very moderate merit.—One day he was struck with the idea of what could be done in this way—he kept his room a whole day, even went without his dinner, and found that in the evening he had written twenty-three hexameters, versifying a part of what he had before written in prose. From that time, pleased with his efforts, he composed no more in prose. Today he informed me that he had finished his plan before he read Milton. He was enchanted to see an author who before him had trod the same path. This is a contradiction of what he said before. He did not wish to speak of his poem to any one till it was finished: but some of his friends who had seen what he had finished, tormented him till he had consented to publish a few books in a journal. He was then, I believe, very young, about twenty-five. The rest was printed at different periods, four books at a time. The reception given to the first specimens was highly flattering. He was nearly thirty years in finishing the whole poem, but of these thirty years not more than two were employed in the composition. He only composed in favourable moments; besides he had other occupations. He values himself upon the plan of his odes, and accuses the modern lyrical writers of gross deficiency in this respect. I laid the same accusation against Horace: he would not hear of it—but waived the discussion. He called Rousseau's ODE TO FORTUNE a moral dissertation in stanzas. I spoke of Dryden's ST. CECILIA; but he did not seem familiar with our writers. He wished to know the distinctions between our dramatic and epic blank verse. He recommended me to read his HERMANN before I read either THE

MESSIAH or the odes. He flattered himself that some time or other his dramatic poems would be known in England. He had not heard of Cowper. He thought that Voss in his translation of THE ILIAD had done violence to the idiom of the Germans, and had sacrificed it to the Greeks, not remembering sufficiently that each language has its particular spirit and genius. He said Lessing was the first of their dramatic writers. I complained of NATHAN as tedious. He said there was not enough of action in it; but that Lessing was the most chaste of their writers. He spoke favourably of Goethe; but said that his SORROWS OF WERTER was his best work, better than any of his dramas: he preferred the first written to the rest of Goethe's dramas. Schiller's ROBBERS he found so extravagant, that he could not read it. I spoke of the scene of the setting sun. He did not know it. He said Schiller could not live. He thought DON CARLOS the best of his dramas; but said that the plot was inextricable.—It was evident he knew little of Schiller's works: indeed, he said, he could not read them. Buerger, he said, was a true poet, and would live; that Schiller, on the contrary, must soon be forgotten; that he gave himself up to the imitation of Shakespeare, who often was extravagant, but that Schiller was ten thousand times more so. He spoke very slightingly of Kotzebue, as an immoral author in the first place, and next, as deficient in power. At Vienna, said he, they are transported with him; but we do not reckon the people of Vienna either the wisest or the wittiest people of Germany. He said Wieland was a charming author, and a sovereign master of his own language: that in this respect Goethe could not be compared to him, nor indeed could any body else. He said that his fault was to be fertile to exuberance. I told him the OBERON had just been translated into English. He asked me if I was not delighted with the poem. I answered, that I thought the story began to flag about the seventh or eighth book; and observed, that it was unworthy of a man of genius to make the interest of a long poem turn entirely upon animal gratification. He seemed at first disposed to excuse this by saying, that there are different subjects for poetry, and that poets are not willing to be restricted in their choice. I answered, that I thought the passion of love as well suited to the purposes of poetry as any other passion; but that it was a cheap way of pleasing to fix the attention of the reader through a long poem on the mere appetite. Well! but, said he, you see, that such poems please every body. I answered, that it was the province of a great poet to raise people up to his own level, not to descend to theirs. He agreed, and confessed, that on no account whatsoever would he have written a work like the OBERON. He spoke in raptures of Wieland's style, and pointed out the passage where Retzia is delivered of her child, as exquisitely beautiful. I said that I did not perceive any very striking passages; but that I made allowance for the imperfections of a translation. Of the thefts of Wieland, he said, they were so exquisitely managed, that the greatest writers might be proud to steal as he did. He considered the books and fables of old romance writers in the light of the ancient mythology, as a sort of common property, from which a man was free to take whatever he could make a good use of. An Englishman had presented him with the odes of Collins, which he had read with pleasure. He knew little or nothing of Gray, except his ELEGY written in a country CHURCH-YARD. He complained of the fool in LEAR. I observed that he seemed to give a terrible wildness to the distress; but still he complained. He asked whether it was not allowed, that Pope had written rhymed poetry with more skill than any of our writers—I said I preferred Dryden, because his couplets had greater variety in their movement. He thought my reason a good one; but asked whether the rhyme of Pope were not more exact. This question I understood as applying to the final terminations, and observed to him that I believed it was the case; but that I thought it was easy to excuse some inaccuracy in the final sounds, if the general sweep of the verse was superior. I told him that we were not so exact with regard to the final endings of the lines as the French. He did not seem to know that we made no distinction between masculine and feminine (i.e. single or double,) rhymes: at least he put inquiries to me on this subject. He seemed to think that no language could be so far formed as that it might not be enriched by idioms borrowed from another tongue. I said this was a very dangerous practice; and added, that I thought Milton had often injured both his prose and verse by taking this liberty too frequently. I recommended to him the prose works of Dryden as models of pure and native English. I was treading upon tender ground, as I have reason to suppose that he has himself liberally indulged in the practice."

The same day I dined at Mr. Klopstock's, where I had the pleasure of a third interview with the poet. We talked principally about indifferent things. I asked him what he thought of Kant. He said that his reputation was much on the decline in Germany. That for his own part he was not surprised to find it so, as the works of Kant were to him utterly incomprehensible—that he had often been pestered by the Kanteans; but was rarely in the practice of arguing with them. His custom was to produce the book, open it and point to a passage, and beg they would explain it. This they ordinarily attempted to do by substituting their own ideas. I do not want, I say, an explanation of your own ideas, but of the passage which is before us. In this way I generally bring the dispute to an immediate conclusion. He spoke of Wolfe as the first Metaphysician they had in Germany. Wolfe had followers; but they could hardly be called a sect, and luckily till the appearance of Kant, about fifteen years ago, Germany had not been pestered by any sect of philosophers whatsoever; but that each man had separately pursued his inquiries uncontrolled by the dogmas of a master. Kant had appeared ambitious to be the founder of a sect; that he had succeeded: but that the Germans were now coming to their senses again. That Nicolai and Engel had in different ways contributed to disenchant the nation; but above all the incomprehensibility of the philosopher and his philosophy. He seemed pleased to hear, that as yet Kant's doctrines had not met with many admirers in England—did not doubt but that we had too much wisdom to be duped by a writer who set at defiance the common sense and common understandings of men. We talked of tragedy. He seemed to rate highly the power of exciting tears—I said that nothing was more easy than to deluge an audience, that it was done every day by the meanest writers.

I must remind you, my friend, first, that these notes are not intended as specimens of Klopstock's intellectual power, or even "colloquial prowess," to judge of which by an accidental conversation, and this with strangers, and those too foreigners, would be not only unreasonable, but calumnious. Secondly, I attribute little other interest to the remarks than what is derived from the celebrity of the person who made them. Lastly, if you ask me, whether I have read THE MESSIAH, and what I think of it? I answer—as yet the first four books only: and as to my opinion—(the reasons of which hereafter)—you may guess it from what I could not help muttering to myself, when the good pastor this morning told me, that Klopstock was the German Milton—"a very German Milton indeed!!!"

Heaven preserve you, and S. T. COLERIDGE.

CHAPTER XXIII

Quid quod praefatione praemunierim libellum, qua conor omnem offendiculi ansam praecidere? [79] Neque quicquam addubito, quin ea candidis omnibus faciat satis. Quid autem facias istis, qui vel ob ingenii pertinaciam sibi satisfieri nolint, vel stupidiores sint, quam ut satisfactionem intelligant? Nam quemadmodum Simonides dixit, Thessalos hebetiores esse, quam ut possint a se decipi, ita quosdam videas stupidiores, quam ut placari queant. Adhaec, non mirum est invenire quod calumnietur, qui nihil aliud quaerit, nisi quod calumnietur. ERASMUS ad Dorpium, Theologum.

In the rifacimento of THE FRIEND, I have inserted extracts from the CONCIONES AD POPULUM, printed, though scarcely published, in the year 1795, in the very heat and height of my anti-ministerial enthusiasm: these in proof that my principles of politics have sustained no change.--In the present chapter, I have annexed to my Letters from Germany, with particular reference to that, which contains a disquisition on the modern drama, a critique on the Tragedy of BERTRAM, written within the last twelve months: in proof, that I have been as falsely charged with any fickleness in my principles of taste.--The letter was written to a friend: and the apparent abruptness with which it begins, is owing to the omission of the introductory sentences.

You remember, my dear Sir, that Mr. Whitbread, shortly before his death, proposed to the assembled subscribers of Drury Lane Theatre, that the concern should be farmed to some responsible individual under certain conditions and limitations: and that his proposal was rejected, not without indignation, as subversive of the main object, for the attainment of which the enlightened and patriotic assemblage of philodramatists had been induced to risk their subscriptions. Now this object was avowed to be no less than the redemption of the British stage not only from horses, dogs, elephants, and the like zoological rarities, but also from the more pernicious barbarisms and Kotzebuisms in morals and taste. Drury Lane was to be restored to its former classical renown; Shakespeare, Jonson, and Otway, with the expurgated muses of Vanbrugh, Congreve, and Wycherley, were to be reinaugurated in their rightful dominion over British audiences; and the Herculean process was to commence, by exterminating the speaking monsters imported from the banks of the Danube, compared with which their mute relations, the emigrants from Exeter 'Change, and Polito (late Pidcock's) show-carts, were tame and inoffensive. Could an heroic project, at once so refined and so arduous, be consistently entrusted to, could its success be rationally expected from, a mercenary manager, at whose critical quarantine the lucri bonus odor would conciliate a bill of health to the plague in person? No! As the work proposed, such must be the workmasters. Rank, fortune, liberal education, and (their natural accompaniments, or consequences) critical discernment, delicate tact, disinterestedness, unsuspected morals, notorious patriotism, and tried Maecenasship, these were the recommendations that influenced the votes of the proprietary subscribers of Drury Lane Theatre, these the motives that occasioned the election of its Supreme Committee of Management. This circumstance alone would have excited a strong interest in the public mind, respecting the first production of the Tragic Muse which had been announced under such auspices, and had passed the ordeal of such judgments: and the tragedy, on which you have requested my judgment, was the work on which the great expectations, justified by so many causes, were doomed at length to settle.

But before I enter on the examination of BERTRAM, or THE CASTLE OF ST. ALDOBRAND, I shall interpose a few words, on the phrase German Drama, which I hold to be altogether a misnomer. At the time of Lessing, the German stage, such as it was, appears to have been a flat and servile copy of the French. It was Lessing who first introduced the name and the works of Shakespeare to the admiration of the Germans; and I should not perhaps go too far, if I add, that it was Lessing who first proved to all thinking men, even to Shakespeare's own countrymen, the true nature of his apparent irregularities. These, he demonstrated, were deviations only from the accidents of the Greek tragedy; and from such accidents as hung a heavy weight on the wings of the Greek poets, and narrowed their flight within the limits of what we may call the heroic opera. He proved, that, in all the essentials of art, no less than in the truth of nature, the Plays of Shakespeare were incomparably more coincident with the principles of Aristotle, than the productions of Corneille and Racine, notwithstanding the boasted regularity of the latter. Under these convictions were Lessing's own dramatic works composed. Their deficiency is in depth and imagination: their excellence is in the construction of the plot; the good sense of the sentiments; the sobriety of the morals; and the high polish of the diction and dialogue. In short, his dramas are the very antipodes of all those which it has been the fashion of late years at once to abuse and enjoy, under the name of the German drama. Of this latter, Schiller's ROBBERS was the earliest specimen; the first fruits of his youth, (I had almost said of his boyhood), and as such, the pledge, and promise of no ordinary genius. Only as such, did the maturer judgment of the author tolerate the Play. During his whole life he expressed himself concerning this production with more than needful asperity, as a monster not less offensive to good taste, than to sound morals; and, in his latter years, his indignation at the unwonted popularity of the ROBBERS seduced him into the contrary extremes, viz. a studied feebleness of interest, (as far as the interest was to be derived from incidents and the excitement of curiosity); a diction elaborately metrical; the affectation of rhymes; and the pedantry of the chorus.

But to understand the true character of the ROBBERS, and of the countless imitations which were its spawn, I must inform you, or at least call to your recollection, that, about that time, and for some years before it, three of the most popular books in the German language were, the translations Of YOUNG'S NIGHT THOUGHTS, HERVEY'S MEDITATIONS, and RICHARDSON'S CLARISSA HARLOW. Now we have only to combine the bloated style and peculiar rhythm of Hervey, which is poetic only on account of its utter unfitness for prose, and might as appropriately be called prosaic, from its utter unfitness for poetry; we have only, I repeat, to combine these Herveyisms with the strained thoughts, the figurative metaphysics and solemn epigrams of Young on the one hand; and with the loaded sensibility, the minute detail, the morbid consciousness of every thought and feeling in the whole flux and reflux of the mind, in short the self-involution and dreamlike continuity of Richardson on the other hand; and then to add the horrific incidents, and mysterious villains, (geniuses of supernatural intellect, if you will take the authors' words for it, but on a level with the meanest ruffians of the condemned cells, if we are to judge by their actions and contrivances)--to add the ruined castles, the dungeons, the trap-doors, the skeletons, the flesh-and-blood ghosts, and the perpetual moonshine of a modern author, (themselves the literary brood of the CASTLE OF OTRANTO, the translations of which, with the imitations and improvements aforesaid, were about that time beginning to make as much noise in Germany as their originals were making in England),--and as the compound of these ingredients duly mixed, you will recognize the so-called German drama. The olla podrida thus cooked up, was denounced, by the best critics in Germany, as the mere cramps of weakness, and orgasms of a sickly imagination on the part of the author, and the lowest provocation of torpid feeling on that of the readers. The old blunder, however, concerning the irregularity and wildness of Shakespeare, in which the German did but echo the French, who again were but the echoes of our own critics, was still in vogue, and Shakespeare was quoted as authority for the most anti-Shakespearean drama. We have indeed two poets who wrote as one, near the age of Shakespeare, to whom, (as the worst characteristic of their writings), the Coryphaeus of the present drama may challenge the honour of being a poor relation, or impoverished descendant. For if we would charitably consent to forget the comic humour, the wit, the felicities of style, in other words, all the poetry, and nine-tenths of all the genius of Beaumont and Fletcher, that which would remain becomes a Kotzebue.

The so-called German drama, therefore, is English in its origin, English in its materials, and English by re-adoption; and till we can prove that Kotzebue, or any of the whole breed of Kotzebues, whether dramatists or romantic writers, or writers of romantic dramas, were ever admitted to any other shelf in the libraries of well-educated Germans than were occupied by their originals, and apes' apes in their mother country, we should submit to carry our own brat on our own shoulders; or rather consider it as a lack-grace returned from transportation with such improvements only in growth and manners as young transported convicts usually come home with.

I know nothing that contributes more to a clearer insight into the true nature of any literary phaenomenon, than the comparison of it with some elder production, the likeness of which is striking, yet only apparent, while the difference is real. In the present case this opportunity is furnished us, by the old Spanish play, entitled Atheista Fulminato, formerly, and perhaps still, acted in the churches and monasteries of Spain, and which, under various names (Don Juan, the Libertine, etc.) has had its day of favour in every country throughout Europe. A popularity so extensive, and of a work so grotesque and extravagant, claims and merits philosophical attention and investigation. The first point to be noticed is, that the play is throughout imaginative. Nothing of it belongs to the real world, but the names of the places and persons. The comic parts, equally with the tragic; the living, equally with the defunct characters, are creatures of the brain; as little amenable to the rules of ordinary probability, as the Satan Of PARADISE LOST, or the Caliban of THE TEMPEST, and therefore to be understood and judged of as impersonated abstractions. Rank, fortune, wit, talent, acquired knowledge, and liberal accomplishments, with beauty of person, vigorous health, and constitutional hardihood,--all these advantages, elevated by the habits and sympathies of noble birth and national character, are supposed to have combined in Don Juan, so as to give him the means of carrying into all its practical consequences the doctrine of a godless nature, as the sole ground and efficient cause not only of all things, events, and appearances, but likewise of all our thoughts, sensations, impulses and actions. Obedience to nature is the only virtue: the gratification of the passions and appetites her only dictate: each individual's self-will the sole organ through which nature utters her commands, and

"Self-contradiction is the only wrong!
For, by the laws of spirit, in the right
Is every individual character
That acts in strict consistence with itself."

That speculative opinions, however impious and daring they may be, are not always followed by correspondent conduct, is most true, as well as that they can scarcely in any instance be systematically realized, on account of their unsuitableness to human nature and to the institutions of society. It can be hell, only where it is all hell: and a separate world of devils is necessary for the existence of any one complete devil. But on the other hand it is no less clear, nor, with the biography of Carrier and his fellow atheists before us, can it be denied without wilful blindness, that the (so called) system of nature (that is, materialism, with the utter rejection of moral responsibility, of a present Providence, and of both present and future retribution) may influence the characters and actions of individuals, and even of communities, to a degree that almost does away the distinction between men and devils, and will make the page of the future historian resemble the narration of a madman's dreams. It is not the wickedness of Don Juan, therefore, which constitutes the character an abstraction, and removes it from the rules of probability; but the rapid succession of the correspondent acts and incidents, his intellectual superiority, and the splendid accumulation of his gifts and desirable qualities, as co-existent with entire wickedness in one and the same person. But this likewise is the very circumstance which gives to this strange play its charm and universal interest. Don Juan is, from beginning to end, an intelligible character: as much so as the Satan of Milton. The poet asks only of the reader, what, as a poet, he is privileged to ask: namely, that sort of negative faith in the existence of such a being, which we willingly give to productions professedly ideal, and a disposition to the same state of feeling, as that with which we contemplate the idealized figures of the Apollo Belvidere, and the Farnese Hercules. What the Hercules is to the eye in corporeal strength, Don Juan is to the mind in strength of character. The ideal consists in the happy balance of the generic with the individual. The former makes the character representative and symbolical, therefore instructive; because, mutatis mutandis, it is applicable to whole classes of men. The latter gives it living interest; for nothing lives or is real, but as definite and individual. To understand this completely, the reader need only recollect the specific state of his feelings, when in looking at a picture of the historic (more properly of the poetic or heroic) class, he objects to a particular figure as being too much of a portrait; and this interruption of his complacency he feels without the least reference to, or the least acquaintance with, any person in real life whom he might recognise in this figure. It is enough that such a figure is not ideal: and therefore not ideal, because one of the two factors or elements of the ideal is in excess. A similar and more powerful objection he would feel towards a set of figures which were mere abstractions, like those of Cipriani, and what have been called Greek forms and faces, that is, outlines drawn according to a recipe. These again are not ideal; because in these the other element is in excess. "Forma formans per formam formatam translucens," [80] is the definition and perfection of ideal art.

This excellence is so happily achieved in the Don Juan, that it is capable of interesting without poetry, nay, even without words, as in our pantomime of that name. We see clearly how the character is formed; and the very extravagance of the incidents, and the super-human entireness of Don Juan's agency, prevents the wickedness from shocking our minds to any painful degree. We do not believe it enough for this effect; no, not even with that kind of temporary and negative belief or acquiescence which I have described above. Meantime the qualities of his character are too desirable, too flattering to our pride and our wishes, not to make up on this side as much additional faith as was lost on the other. There is no danger (thinks the spectator or reader) of my becoming such a monster of iniquity as Don Juan! I never shall be an atheist! I shall never disallow all distinction between right and wrong! I have not the least inclination to be so outrageous a drawcansir in my love affairs! But to possess such a power of captivating and enchanting the affections of the other sex!—to be capable of inspiring in a charming and even a virtuous woman, a love so deep, and so entirely personal to me!—that even my worst vices, (if I were vicious), even my cruelty and perfidy, (if I were cruel and perfidious), could not eradicate the passion!—to be so loved for my own self, that even with a distinct knowledge of my character, she yet died to save me!—this, sir, takes hold of two sides of our nature, the better and the worse. For the heroic disinterestedness, to which love can transport a woman, can not be contemplated without an honourable emotion of reverence towards womanhood: and, on the other hand, it is among the miseries, and abides in the dark ground-work of our nature, to crave an outward confirmation of that something within us, which is our very self, that something, not made up of our qualities and relations, but itself the supporter and substantial basis of all these. Love me, and not my qualities, may be a vicious and an insane wish, but it is not a wish wholly without a meaning.

Without power, virtue would be insufficient and incapable of revealing its being. It would resemble the magic transformation of Tasso's heroine into a tree, in which she could only groan and bleed. Hence power is necessarily an object of our desire and of our admiration. But of all power, that of the mind is, on every account, the grand desideratum of human ambition. We shall be as Gods in knowledge, was and must have been the first temptation: and the coexistence of great intellectual lordship with guilt has never been adequately represented without exciting the strongest interest, and for this reason, that in this bad and heterogeneous co-ordination we can contemplate the intellect of man more exclusively as a separate self-subsistence, than in its proper state of subordination to his own conscience, or to the will of an infinitely superior being.

This is the sacred charm of Shakespeare's male characters in general. They are all cast in the mould of Shakespeare's own gigantic intellect; and this is the open attraction of his Richard, Iago, Edmund, and others in particular. But again; of all intellectual power, that of superiority to the fear of the invisible world is the most dazzling. Its influence is abundantly proved by the one circumstance, that it can bribe us into a voluntary submission of our better knowledge, into suspension of all our judgment derived from constant experience, and enable us to peruse with the liveliest interest the wildest tales of ghosts, wizards, genii, and secret talismans. On this propensity, so deeply rooted in our nature, a specific dramatic probability may be raised by a true poet, if the whole of his work be in harmony: a dramatic probability, sufficient for dramatic pleasure, even when the component characters and incidents border on impossibility. The poet does not require us to be awake and believe; he solicits us only to yield ourselves to a dream; and this too with our eyes open, and with our judgment perdue behind the curtain, ready to awaken us at the first motion of our will: and meantime, only, not to disbelieve. And in such a state of mind, who but must be impressed with the cool intrepidity of Don john on the appearance of his father's ghost:

"*GHOST.—Monster! behold these wounds!*

"*D. JOHN.—I do! They were well meant and well performed, I see.*

"*GHOST.———Repent, repent of all thy villanies.*
My clamorous blood to heaven for vengeance cries,
Heaven will pour out his judgments on you all.
Hell gapes for you, for you each fiend doth call,
And hourly waits your unrepenting fall.
You with eternal horrors they'll torment,
Except of all your crimes you suddenly repent. (Ghost sinks.)

"*D. JOHN.—Farewell, thou art a foolish ghost. Repent, quoth he! what could this mean? Our senses are all in a mist sure.*

"*D. ANTONIO.—(one of D. Juan's reprobate companions.) They are not! Twas a ghost.*

"*D. LOPEZ.—(another reprobate.) I ne'er believed those foolish tales before.*

"*D. JOHN.—Come! Tis no matter. Let it be what it will, it must be natural.*

"*D. ANT.—And nature is unalterable in us too.*

"*D. JOHN.—'Tis true! The nature of a ghost can not change our's.*"

Who also can deny a portion of sublimity to the tremendous consistency with which he stands out the last fearful trial, like a second Prometheus?

"*Chorus of Devils.*

"*STATUE-GHOST.—Will you not relent and feel remorse?*

"*D. JOHN.—Could'st thou bestow another heart on me I might. But with this heart I have, I can not.*

"*D. LOPEZ.—These things are prodigious.*

"*D. ANTON.—I have a sort of grudging to relent, but something holds me back.*

"*D. LOP.—If we could, 'tis now too late. I will not.*

"*D. ANT.—We defy thee!*

"*GHOST.—Perish ye impious wretches, go and find the punishments laid up in store for you!*

(Thunder and lightning. D. Lop. and D. Ant. are swallowed up.)

"*GHOST To D. JOHN.—Behold their dreadful fates, and know that thy last moment's come!*

"*D. JOHN.—Think not to fright me, foolish ghost; I'll break your marble body in pieces and pull down your horse.*
(Thunder and lightning—chorus of devils, etc.)

"*D. JOHN.—These things I see with wonder, but no fear.*
Were all the elements to be confounded,
And shuffled all into their former chaos;
Were seas of sulphur flaming round about me,
And all mankind roaring within those fires,
I could not fear, or feel the least remorse.
To the last instant I would dare thy power.
Here I stand firm, and all thy threats contemn.
Thy murderer (to the ghost of one whom he had murdered)

Stands here! Now do thy worst!"
(He is swallowed up in a cloud of fire.)

In fine the character of Don John consists in the union of every thing desirable to human nature, as means, and which therefore by the well known law of association becomes at length desirable on their own account. On their own account, and, in their own dignity, they are here displayed, as being employed to ends so unhuman, that in the effect, they appear almost as means without an end. The ingredients too are mixed in the happiest proportion, so as to uphold and relieve each other—more especially in that constant interpoise of wit, gaiety, and social generosity, which prevents the criminal, even in his most atrocious moments, from sinking into the mere ruffian, as far at least, as our imagination sits in judgment. Above all, the fine suffusion through the whole, with the characteristic manners and feelings, of a highly bred gentleman gives life to the drama. Thus having invited the statue-ghost of the governor, whom he had murdered, to supper, which invitation the marble ghost accepted by a nod of the head, Don John has prepared a banquet.

"*D. JOHN.—Some wine, sirrah! Here's to Don Pedro's ghost—he should have been welcome.*

"*D. LOP.—The rascal is afraid of you after death.*
(One knocks hard at the door.)
"*D. JOHN.—(to the servant)—Rise and do your duty.*

"*SERV.—Oh the devil, the devil! (Marble ghost enters.)*

"*D. JOHN.—Ha! 'tis the ghost! Let's rise and receive him! Come, Governour, you are welcome, sit there; if we had thought you would have come, we would have staid for you.*

* * * * * *

Here, Governour, your health! Friends, put it about! Here's excellent meat, taste of this ragout. Come, I'll help you, come eat, and let old quarrels be forgotten. (The ghost threatens him with vengeance.)

"*D. JOHN.—We are too much confirmed—curse on this dry discourse. Come, here's to your mistress, you had one when you were living: not forgetting your sweet sister. (devils enter.)*

"*D. JOHN.—Are these some of your retinue? Devils, say you? I'm *sorry I have no burnt brandy to treat 'em with, that's drink fit for devils,"* etc.

Nor is the scene from which we quote interesting, in dramatic probability alone; it is susceptible likewise of a sound moral; of a moral that has more than common claims on the notice of a too numerous class, who are ready to receive the qualities of gentlemanly courage, and scrupulous honour, (in all the recognised laws of honour,) as the substitutes of virtue, instead of its ornaments. This, indeed, is the moral value of the play at large, and that which places it at a world's distance from the spirit of modern jacobinism. The latter introduces to us clumsy copies of these showy instrumental qualities, in order to reconcile us to vice and want of principle; while the Atheista Fulminato presents an exquisite portraiture of the same qualities, in all their gloss and glow, but presents them for the sole purpose of displaying their hollowness, and in order to put us on our guard by demonstrating their utter indifference to vice and virtue, whenever these and the like accomplishments are contemplated for themselves alone.

Eighteen years ago I observed, that the whole secret of the modern jacobinical drama, (which, and not the German, is its appropriate designation,) and of all its popularity, consists in the confusion and subversion of the natural order of things in their causes and effects: namely, in the excitement of surprise by representing the qualities of liberality, refined feeling, and a nice sense of honour (those things rather which pass amongst us for such) in persons and in classes where experience teaches us least to expect them; and by rewarding with all the sympathies which are the due of virtue, those criminals whom law, reason, and religion have excommunicated from our esteem.

This of itself would lead me back to BERTRAM, or the CASTLE OF ST. ALDOBRAND; but, in my own mind, this tragedy was brought into connection with THE LIBERTINE, (Shadwell's adaptation of the Atheista Fulminato to the English stage in the reign of Charles the Second,) by the fact, that our modern drama is taken, in the substance of it, from the first scene of the third act of THE LIBERTINE. But with what palpable superiority of judgment in the original! Earth and hell, men and spirits are up in arms against Don John; the two former acts of the play have not only prepared us for the supernatural, but accustomed us to the prodigious. It is, therefore, neither more nor less than we anticipate when the Captain exclaims: "In all the dangers I have been, such horrors I never knew. I am quite unmanned:" and when the Hermit says, that he had "beheld the ocean in wildest rage, yet ne'er before saw a storm so dreadful, such horrid flashes of lightning, and such claps of thunder, were never in my remembrance." And Don John's burst of startling impiety is equally intelligible in its motive, as dramatic in its effect.

But what is there to account for the prodigy of the tempest at Bertram's shipwreck? It is a mere supernatural effect, without even a hint of any supernatural agency; a prodigy, without any circumstance mentioned that is prodigious; and a miracle introduced without a ground, and ending without a result. Every event and every scene of the play might have taken place as well if Bertram and his vessel had been driven in by a common hard gale, or from want of provisions. The first act would have indeed lost its greatest and most sonorous picture; a scene for the sake of a scene, without a word spoken; as such, therefore, (a rarity without a precedent), we must take it, and be thankful! In the opinion of not a few, it was, in every sense of the word, the best scene in the play. I am quite certain it was the most innocent: and the steady, quiet uprightness of the flame of the wax-candles, which the monks held over the roaring billows amid the storm of wind and rain, was really miraculous.

The Sicilian sea coast: a convent of monks: night: a most portentous, unearthly storm: a vessel is wrecked contrary to all human expectation, one man saves himself by his prodigious powers as a swimmer, aided by the peculiarity of his destination—

"PRIOR.————*All, all did perish*

FIRST MONK.—*Change, change those drenched weeds*—

PRIOR.—*I wist not of them—every soul did perish—*
Enter third Monk hastily.

"THIRD MONK.—*No, there was one did battle with the storm*
With careless desperate force; full many times
His life was won and lost, as tho' he recked not—
No hand did aid him, and he aided none—
Alone he breasted the broad wave, alone
That man was saved."

Well! This man is led in by the monks, supposed dripping wet, and to very natural inquiries he either remains silent, or gives most brief and surly answers, and after three or four of these half-line courtesies, "dashing off the monks" who had saved him, he exclaims in the true sublimity of our modern misanthropic heroism—

"*Off! ye are men—there's poison in your touch.*
But I must yield, for this" (what?) "*hath left me strengthless.*"

So end the three first scenes. In the next (the Castle of St. Aldobrand,) we find the servants there equally frightened with this unearthly storm, though wherein it differed from other violent storms we are not told, except that Hugo informs us, page 9—

"PIET.—*Hugo, well met. Does e'en thy age bear*
Memory of so terrible a storm?

HUGO.—*They have been frequent lately.*

PIET.—*They are ever so in Sicily.*

HUGO.—*So it is said. But storms when I was young*
Would still pass o'er like Nature's fitful fevers,
And rendered all more wholesome. Now their rage,
Sent thus unseasonable and profitless,
Speaks like the threats of heaven."

A most perplexing theory of Sicilian storms is this of old Hugo! and what is very remarkable, not apparently founded on any great familiarity of his own with this troublesome article. For when Pietro asserts the "ever more frequency" of tempests in Sicily, the old man professes to know nothing more of the fact, but by hearsay. "So it is said."—But why he assumed this storm to be unseasonable, and on what he grounded his prophecy, (for the storm is still in full fury), that it would be profitless, and without the physical powers common to all other violent sea-winds in purifying the atmosphere, we are left in the dark; as well concerning the particular points in which he knew it, during its continuance, to differ from those that he had been acquainted with in his youth. We are at length introduced to the Lady Imogine, who, we learn, had not rested "through" the night; not on account of the tempest, for

"Long ere the storm arose, her restless gestures
Forbade all hope to see her blest with sleep."

Sitting at a table, and looking at a portrait, she informs us—First, that portrait-painters may make a portrait from memory,

"The limner's art may trace the absent feature."

For surely these words could never mean, that a painter may have a person sit to him who afterwards may leave the room or perhaps the country? Secondly, that a portrait-painter can enable a mourning lady to possess a good likeness of her absent lover, but that the portrait- painter cannot, and who shall—

"Restore the scenes in which they met and parted?"

The natural answer would have been—Why the scene-painter to be sure! But this unreasonable lady requires in addition sundry things to be painted that have neither lines nor colours—

*"The thoughts, the recollections, sweet and bitter,
Or the Elysian dreams of lovers when they loved."*

Which last sentence must be supposed to mean; when they were present, and making love to each other.—Then, if this portrait could speak, it would "acquit the faith of womankind." How? Had she remained constant? No, she has been married to another man, whose wife she now is. How then? Why, that, in spite of her marriage vow, she had continued to yearn and crave for her former lover—

*"This has her body, that her mind:
Which has the better bargain?"*

The lover, however, was not contented with this precious arrangement, as we shall soon find. The lady proceeds to inform us that during the many years of their separation, there have happened in the different parts of the world, a number of "such things;" even such, as in a course of years always have, and till the Millennium, doubtless always will happen somewhere or other. Yet this passage, both in language and in metre, is perhaps amongst the best parts of the play. The lady's love companion and most esteemed attendant, Clotilda, now enters and explains this love and esteem by proving herself a most passive and dispassionate listener, as well as a brief and lucky querist, who asks by chance, questions that we should have thought made for the very sake of the answers. In short, she very much reminds us of those puppet-heroines, for whom the showman contrives to dialogue without any skill in ventriloquism. This, notwithstanding, is the best scene in the Play, and though crowded with solecisms, corrupt diction, and offences against metre, would possess merits sufficient to out-weigh them, if we could suspend the moral sense during the perusal. It tells well and passionately the preliminary circumstances, and thus overcomes the main difficulty of most first acts, to wit, that of retrospective narration. It tells us of her having been honourably addressed by a noble youth, of rank and fortune vastly superior to her own: of their mutual love, heightened on her part by gratitude; of his loss of his sovereign's favour; his disgrace; attainder; and flight; that he (thus degraded) sank into a vile ruffian, the chieftain of a murderous banditti; and that from the habitual indulgence of the most reprobate habits and ferocious passions, he had become so changed, even in appearance, and features,

*"That she who bore him had recoiled from him,
Nor known the alien visage of her child,
Yet still she (Imogine) lov'd him."*

She is compelled by the silent entreaties of a father, perishing with "bitter shameful want on the cold earth," to give her hand, with a heart thus irrecoverably pre-engaged, to Lord Aldobrand, the enemy of her lover, even to the very man who had baffled his ambitious schemes, and was, at the present time, entrusted with the execution of the sentence of death which had been passed on Bertram. Now, the proof of "woman's love," so industriously held forth for the sympathy, if not for the esteem of the audience, consists in this, that, though Bertram had become a robber and a murderer by trade, a ruffian in manners, yea, with form and features at which his own mother could not but "recoil," yet she (Lady Imogine) "the wife of a most noble, honoured Lord," estimable as a man, exemplary and affectionate as a husband, and the fond father of her only child—that she, notwithstanding all this, striking her heart, dares to say to it—

"But thou art Bertram's still, and Bertram's ever."

A Monk now enters, and entreats in his Prior's name for the wonted hospitality, and "free noble usage" of the Castle of St. Aldobrand for some wretched shipwrecked souls, and from this we learn, for the first time, to our infinite surprise, that notwithstanding the supernaturalness of the storm aforesaid, not only Bertram, but the whole of his gang, had been saved, by what means we are left to conjecture, and can only conclude that they had all the same desperate swimming powers, and the same saving destiny as the hero, Bertram himself. So ends the first act, and with it the tale of the events, both those with which the tragedy begins, and those which had occurred previous to the date of its commencement. The second displays Bertram in disturbed sleep, which the Prior, who hangs over him, prefers calling a "starting trance," and with a strained voice, that would have awakened one of the seven sleepers, observes to the audience—

"How the lip works! How the bare teeth do grind!
And beaded drops course [81] down his writhen brow!"

The dramatic effect of which passage we not only concede to the admirers of this tragedy, but acknowledge the further advantages of preparing the audience for the most surprising series of wry faces, proflated mouths, and lunatic gestures that were ever "launched" on an audience to "sear the sense."[82]

"PRIOR.—I will awake him from this horrid trance. This is no natural sleep! Ho, wake thee, stranger!"

This is rather a whimsical application of the verb reflex we must confess, though we remember a similar transfer of the agent to the patient in a manuscript tragedy, in which the Bertram of the piece, prostrating a man with a single blow of his fist, exclaims—"Knock me thee down, then ask thee if thou liv'st." Well; the stranger obeys, and whatever his sleep might have been, his waking was perfectly natural; for lethargy itself could not withstand the scolding Stentorship of Mr. Holland, the Prior. We next learn from the best authority, his own confession, that the misanthropic hero, whose destiny was incompatible with drowning, is Count Bertram, who not only reveals his past fortunes, but avows with open atrocity, his Satanic hatred of Imogine's lord, and his frantick thirst of revenge; and so the raving character raves, and the scolding character scolds—and what else? Does not the Prior act? Does he not send for a posse of constables or thief-takers to handcuff the villain, or take him either to Bedlam or Newgate? Nothing of the kind; the author preserves the unity of character, and the scolding Prior from first to last does nothing but scold, with the exception indeed of the last scene of the last act, in which, with a most surprising revolution, he whines, weeps, and kneels to the condemned blaspheming assassin out of pure affection to the high-hearted man, the sublimity of whose angel-sin rivals the star-bright apostate, (that is, who was as proud as Lucifer, and as wicked as the Devil), and, "had thrilled him," (Prior Holland aforesaid), with wild admiration.

Accordingly in the very next scene, we have this tragic Macheath, with his whole gang, in the Castle of St. Aldobrand, without any attempt on the Prior's part either to prevent him, or to put the mistress and servants of the Castle on their guard against their new inmates; though he (the Prior) knew, and confesses that he knew, that Bertram's "fearful mates" were assassins so habituated and naturalized to guilt, that—

*"When their drenched hold forsook both gold and gear,
They griped their daggers with a murderer's instinct;"*

and though he also knew, that Bertram was the leader of a band whose trade was blood. To the Castle however he goes, thus with the holy Prior's consent, if not with his assistance; and thither let us follow him.

No sooner is our hero safely housed in the Castle of St. Aldobrand, than he attracts the notice of the lady and her confidante, by his "wild and terrible dark eyes," "muffled form," "fearful form," [83] "darkly wild," "proudly stern," and the like common-place indefinites, seasoned by merely verbal antitheses, and at best, copied with very slight change, from the Conrade of Southey's JOAN OF ARC. The lady Imogine, who has been, (as is the case, she tells us, with all soft and solemn spirits,) worshipping the moon on a terrace or rampart within view of the Castle, insists on having an interview with our hero, and this too tete-a-tete. Would the reader learn why and wherefore the confidante is excluded, who very properly remonstrates against such "conference, alone, at night, with one who bears such fearful form;" the reason follows—"why, therefore send him!" I say, follows, because the next line, "all things of fear have lost their power over me," is separated from the former by a break or pause, and besides that it is a very poor answer to the danger, is no answer at all to the gross indelicacy of this wilful exposure. We must therefore regard it as a mere after-thought, that a little softens the rudeness, but adds nothing to the weight, of that exquisite woman's reason aforesaid. And so exit Clotilda and enter Bertram, who "stands without looking at her," that is, with his lower limbs forked, his arms akimbo, his side to the lady's front, the whole figure resembling an inverted Y. He is soon however roused from the state surly to the state frantick, and then follow raving, yelling, cursing, she fainting, he relenting, in runs Imogine's child, squeaks "mother!" He snatches it up, and with a "God bless thee, child! Bertram has kissed thy child,"—the curtain drops. The third act is short, and short be our account of it. It introduces Lord St. Aldobrand on his road homeward, and next Imogine in the convent, confessing the foulness of her heart to the Prior, who first indulges his old humour with a fit of senseless scolding, then leaves her alone with her ruffian paramour, with whom she makes at once an infamous appointment, and the curtain drops, that it may be carried into act and consummation.

I want words to describe the mingled horror and disgust with which I witnessed the opening of the fourth act, considering it as a melancholy proof of the depravation of the public mind. The shocking spirit of jacobinism seemed no longer confined to politics. The familiarity with atrocious events and characters appeared to have poisoned the taste, even where it had not directly disorganized the moral principles, and left the feelings callous to all the mild appeals, and craving alone for the grossest and most outrageous stimulants. The very fact then present to our senses, that a British audience could remain passive under such an insult to common decency, nay, receive with a thunder of applause, a human being supposed to have come reeking from the consummation of this complex foulness and baseness, these and the like reflections so pressed as with the weight of lead upon my heart, that actor, author, and tragedy would have been forgotten, had it not been for a plain elderly man sitting beside me, who, with a very serious face, that at once expressed surprise and aversion, touched my elbow, and, pointing to the actor, said to me in a half-whisper—"Do you see that little fellow there? he has just been committing adultery!" Somewhat relieved by the laugh which this droll address occasioned, I forced back my attention to the stage sufficiently to learn, that Bertram is recovered from a transient fit of remorse by the information, that St. Aldobrand was commissioned (to do, what every honest man must have done without commission, if he did his duty) to seize him and deliver him to the just vengeance of the law; an information which, (as he had long known himself to be an attainted traitor and proclaimed outlaw, and not only a trader in blood himself, but notoriously the Captain of a gang of thieves, pirates, and assassins), assuredly could not have been new to him. It is this, however, which alone and instantly restores him to his accustomed state of raving, blasphemy, and nonsense. Next follows Imogine's constrained interview with her injured husband, and his sudden departure again, all in love and kindness, in order to attend the feast of St. Anselm at the convent. This was, it must be owned, a very strange engagement for so tender a husband to make within a few minutes after so long an absence. But first his lady has told him that she has "a vow on her," and wishes "that black perdition may gulf her perjured soul,"—(Note: she is lying at the very time)—if she ascends his bed, till her penance is accomplished. How, therefore, is the poor husband to amuse himself in this interval of her penance? But do not be distressed, reader, on account of the St. Aldobrand's absence! As the author has contrived to send him out of the house, when a husband would be in his, and the lover's way, so he will doubtless not be at a loss to bring him back again as soon as he is wanted. Well! the husband gone in on the one side, out pops the lover from the other, and for the fiendish purpose of harrowing up the soul of his wretched accomplice in guilt, by announcing to her, with most brutal and blasphemous execrations, his fixed and deliberate resolve to assassinate her husband; all this too is for no discoverable purpose on the part of the author, but that of introducing a series of super-tragic starts, pauses, screams, struggling, dagger-throwing, falling on the ground, starting up again wildly, swearing, outcries for help, falling again on the ground, rising again, faintly tottering towards the door, and, to end the scene, a most convenient fainting fit of our lady's, just in time to give Bertram an opportunity of seeking the object of his hatred, before she alarms the house, which indeed she has had full time to have done before, but that the author rather chose she should amuse herself and the audience by the above-described ravings and startings. She recovers slowly, and to her enter, Clotilda, the confidante and mother confessor; then commences, what in theatrical language is called the madness, but which the author more accurately entitles, delirium, it appearing indeed a sort of intermittent fever with fits of lightheadedness off and on, whenever occasion and stage effect happen to call for it. A convenient return of the storm, (we told the reader before-hand how it would be), had changed—

"The rivulet, that bathed the convent walls,
Into a foaming flood: upon its brink
The Lord and his small train do stand appalled.
With torch and bell from their high battlements
The monks do summon to the pass in vain;
He must return to-night."

Talk of the Devil, and his horns appear, says the proverb and sure enough, within ten lines of the exit of the messenger, sent to stop him, the arrival of Lord St. Aldobrand is announced. Bertram's ruffian band now enter, and range themselves across the stage, giving fresh cause for Imogine's screams and madness. St. Aldobrand, having received his mortal wound behind the scenes, totters in to welter in his blood, and to die at the feet of this double-damned adultress.

Of her, as far as she is concerned in this fourth act, we have two additional points to notice: first, the low cunning and Jesuitical trick with which she deludes her husband into words of forgiveness, which he himself does not understand; and secondly, that everywhere she is made the object of interest and sympathy, and it is not the author's fault, if, at any moment, she excites feelings less gentle, than those we are accustomed to associate with the self-accusations of a sincere religious penitent. And did a British audience endure all this?—They received it with plaudits, which, but for the rivalry of the carts and hackney coaches, might have disturbed the evening-prayers of the scanty week day congregation at St. Paul's cathedral.

Tempora mutantur, nos et mutamur in illis.

Of the fifth act, the only thing noticeable, (for rant and nonsense, though abundant as ever, have long before the last act become things of course,) is the profane representation of the high altar in a chapel, with all the vessels and other preparations for the holy sacrament. A hymn is actually sung on the stage by the chorister boys! For the rest, Imogine, who now and then talks deliriously, but who is always light-headed as far as her gown and hair can make her so, wanders about in dark woods with cavern-rocks and precipices in the back-scene; and a number of mute dramatis personae move in and out continually, for whose presence, there is always at least this reason, that they afford something to be seen, by that very large part of a Drury Lane audience who have small chance of hearing a word. She had, it appears, taken her child with her, but what becomes of the child, whether she murdered it or not, nobody can tell, nobody can learn; it was a riddle at the representation, and after a most attentive perusal of the Play, a riddle it remains.

"No more I know, I wish I did,
And I would tell it all to you;
For what became of this poor child
There's none that ever knew."

Our whole information [84] is derived from the following words--

"PRIOR.--Where is thy child?

CLOTIL.--*(Pointing to the cavern into which she has looked)*
Oh he lies cold! within his cavern-tomb!
Why dost thou urge her with the horrid theme?

PRIOR.--*(who will not, the reader may observe, be disappointed of his dose of scolding)*
It was to make (query wake) one living cord o' th' heart,
And I will try, tho' my own breaks at it.
Where is thy child?

IMOG.--*(with a frantic laugh) The forest fiend hath snatched him--*
He (who? the fiend or the child?) rides the night-mare thro' the wizard woods."

Now these two lines consist in a senseless plagiarism from the counterfeited madness of Edgar in Lear, who, in imitation of the gypsy incantations, puns on the old word mair, a hag; and the no less senseless adoption of Dryden's forest fiend, and the wisard stream by which Milton, in his Lycidas, so finely characterizes the spreading Deva, fabulosus amnis. Observe too these images stand unique in the speeches of Imogine, without the slightest resemblance to anything she says before or after. But we are weary. The characters in this act frisk about, here, there, and every where, as teasingly as the Jack o' Lantern-lights which mischievous boys, from across a narrow street, throw with a looking-glass on the faces of their opposite neighbours. Bertram disarmed, outheroding Charles de Moor in the Robbers, befaces the collected knights of St. Anselm, (all in complete armour) and so, by pure dint of black looks, he outdares them into passive poltroons. The sudden revolution in the Prior's manners we have before noticed, and it is indeed so outre, that a number of the audience imagined a great secret was to come out, viz.: that the Prior was one of the many instances of a youthful sinner metamorphosed into an old scold, and that this Bertram would appear at last to be his son. Imogine re-appears at the convent, and dies of her own accord. Bertram stabs himself, and dies by her side, and that the play may conclude as it began, to wit, in a superfetation of blasphemy upon nonsense, because he had snatched a sword from a despicable coward, who retreats in terror when it is pointed towards him in sport; this felo de se, and thief-captain--this loathsome and leprous confluence of robbery, adultery, murder, and cowardly assassination,--this monster, whose best deed is, the having saved his betters from the degradation of hanging him, by turning Jack Ketch to himself; first recommends the charitable Monks and holy Prior to pray for his soul, and then has the folly and impudence to exclaim--

"I die no felon's death,
A warriour's weapon freed a warriour's soul!"

CHAPTER XXIV

CONCLUSION

It sometimes happens that we are punished for our faults by incidents, in the causation of which these faults had no share: and this I have always felt the severest punishment. The wound indeed is of the same dimensions; but the edges are jagged, and there is a dull underpain that survives the smart which it had aggravated. For there is always a consolatory feeling that accompanies the sense of a proportion between antecedents and consequents. The sense of Before and After becomes both intelligible and intellectual when, and only when, we contemplate the succession in the relations of Cause and Effect, which, like the two poles of the magnet manifest the being and unity of the one power by relative opposites, and give, as it were, a substratum of permanence, of identity, and therefore of reality, to the shadowy flux of Time. It is Eternity revealing itself in the phaenomena of Time: and the perception and acknowledgment of the proportionality and appropriateness of the Present to the Past, prove to the afflicted Soul, that it has not yet been deprived of the sight of God, that it can still recognise the effective presence of a Father, though through a darkened glass and a turbid atmosphere, though of a Father that is chastising it. And for this cause, doubtless, are we so framed in mind, and even so organized in brain and nerve, that all confusion is painful. It is within the experience of many medical practitioners, that a patient, with strange and unusual symptoms of disease, has been more distressed in mind, more wretched, from the fact of being unintelligible to himself and others, than from the pain or danger of the disease: nay, that the patient has received the most solid comfort, and resumed a genial and enduring cheerfulness, from some new symptom or product, that had at once determined the name and nature of his complaint, and rendered it an intelligible effect of an intelligible cause: even though the discovery did at the same moment preclude all hope of restoration. Hence the mystic theologians, whose delusions we may more confidently hope to separate from their actual intuitions, when we condescend to read their works without the presumption that whatever our fancy, (always the ape, and too often the adulterator and counterfeit of our memory,) has not made or cannot make a picture of, must be nonsense,—hence, I say, the Mystics have joined in representing the state of the reprobate spirits as a dreadful dream in which there is no sense of reality, not even of the pangs they are enduring—an eternity without time, and as it were below it—God present without manifestation of his presence. But these are depths, which we dare not linger over. Let us turn to an instance more on a level with the ordinary sympathies of mankind. Here then, and in this same healing influence of Light and distinct Beholding, we may detect the final cause of that instinct which, in the great majority of instances, leads, and almost compels the Afflicted to communicate their sorrows. Hence too flows the alleviation that results from "opening out our griefs:" which are thus presented in distinguishable forms instead of the mist, through which whatever is shapeless becomes magnified and (literally) enormous. Casimir, in the fifth Ode of his third Book, has happily [85] expressed this thought.

Me longus silendi
Edit amor, facilesque luctus
Hausit medullas. Fugerit ocyus,
Simul negantem visere jusseris
Aures amicorum, et loquacem
Questibus evacuaris iram.
Olim querendo desinimus queri,
Ipsoque fletu lacryma perditur
Nec fortis [86] *aeque, si per omnes*
Cura volat residetque ramos.
Vires amicis perdit in auribus,
Minorque semper dividitur dolor,
Per multa permissus vagari
Pectora.—

I shall not make this an excuse, however, for troubling my readers with any complaints or explanations, with which, as readers, they have little or no concern. It may suffice, (for the present at least,) to declare, that the causes that have delayed the publication of these volumes for so long a period after they had been printed off, were not connected with any neglect of my own; and that they would form an instructive comment on the chapter concerning authorship as a trade, addressed to young men of genius in the first volume of this work. I remember the ludicrous effect produced on my mind by the fast sentence of an auto-biography, which, happily for the writer, was as meagre in incidents as it is well possible for the life of an individual to be—"The eventful life which I am about to record, from the hour in which I rose into existence on this planet, etc." Yet when, notwithstanding this warning example of self-importance before me, I review my own life, I cannot refrain from applying the same epithet to it, and with more than ordinary emphasis—and no private feeling, that affected myself only, should prevent me from publishing the same, (for write it I assuredly shall, should life and leisure be granted me,) if continued reflection should strengthen my present belief, that my history would add its contingent to the enforcement of one important truth, to wit, that we must not only love our neighbours as ourselves, but ourselves likewise as our neighbours; and that we can do neither unless we love God above both.

Who lives, that's not
Depraved or depraves? Who dies, that bears
Not one spurn to the grave of their friends' gift?

Strange as the delusion may appear, yet it is most true, that three years ago I did not know or believe that I had an enemy in the world: and now even my strongest sensations of gratitude are mingled with fear, and I reproach myself for being too often disposed to ask,—Have I one friend?—During the many years which intervened between the composition and the publication of the CHRISTABEL, it became almost as well known among literary men as if it had been on common sale; the same references were made to it, and the same liberties taken with it, even to the very names of the imaginary persons in the poem. From almost all of our most celebrated poets, and from some with whom I had no personal acquaintance, I either received or heard of expressions of admiration that, (I can truly say,) appeared to myself utterly disproportionate to a work, that pretended to be nothing more than a common Faery Tale. Many, who had allowed no merit to my other poems, whether printed or manuscript, and who have frankly told me as much, uniformly made an exception in favour of the CHRISTABEL and the poem entitled LOVE. Year after year, and in societies of the most different kinds, I had been entreated to recite it and the result was still the same in all, and altogether different in this respect from the effect produced by the occasional recitation of any other poems I had composed.—This before the publication. And since then, with very few exceptions, I have heard nothing but abuse, and this too in a spirit of bitterness at least as disproportionate to the pretensions of the poem, had it been the most pitiably below mediocrity, as the previous eulogies, and far more inexplicable.—This may serve as a warning to authors, that in their calculations on the probable reception of a poem, they must subtract to a large amount from the panegyric, which may have encouraged them to publish it, however unsuspicious and however various the sources of this panegyric may have been. And, first, allowances must be made for private enmity, of the very existence of which they had perhaps entertained no suspicion—for personal enmity behind the mask of anonymous criticism: secondly for the necessity of a certain proportion of abuse and ridicule in a Review, in order to make it saleable, in consequence of which, if they have no friends behind the scenes, the chance must needs be against them; but lastly and chiefly, for the excitement and temporary sympathy of feeling, which the recitation of the poem by an admirer, especially if he be at once a warm admirer and a man of acknowledged celebrity, calls forth in the audience. For this is really a species of animal magnetism, in which the enkindling reciter, by perpetual comment of looks and tones, lends his own will and apprehensive faculty to his auditors. They live for the time within the dilated sphere of his intellectual being. It is equally possible, though not equally common, that a reader left to himself should sink below the poem, as that the poem left to itself should flag beneath the feelings of the reader.—But, in my own instance, I had the additional misfortune of having been gossiped about, as devoted to metaphysics, and worse than all, to a system incomparably nearer to the visionary flights of Plato, and even to the jargon of the Mystics, than to the established tenets of Locke. Whatever therefore appeared with my name was condemned beforehand, as predestined metaphysics. In a dramatic poem, which had been submitted by me to a gentleman of great influence in the theatrical world, occurred the following passage:—

"O we are querulous creatures! Little less
Than all things can suffice to make us happy:
And little more than nothing is enough
To make us wretched."

Aye, here now! (exclaimed the critic) here come Coleridge's metaphysics! And the very same motive (that is, not that the lines were unfit for the present state of our immense theatres; but that they were metaphysics [87]) was assigned elsewhere for the rejection of the two following passages. The first is spoken in answer to a usurper, who had rested his plea on the circumstance, that he had been chosen by the acclamations of the people.—

"What people? How convened? or, if convened,
Must not the magic power that charms together
Millions of men in council, needs have power
To win or wield them? Rather, O far rather
Shout forth thy titles to yon circling mountains,
And with a thousand-fold reverberation
Make the rocks flatter thee, and the volleying air,
Unbribed, shout back to thee, King Emerick!
By wholesome laws to embank the sovereign power,
To deepen by restraint, and by prevention
Of lawless will to amass and guide the flood
In its majestic channel, is man's task
And the true patriot's glory! In all else
Men safelier trust to Heaven, than to themselves
When least themselves: even in those whirling crowds
Where folly is contagious, and too oft

Even wise men leave their better sense at home,
To chide and wonder at them, when returned."

The second passage is in the mouth of an old and experienced courtier, betrayed by the man in whom he had most trusted.

"And yet Sarolta, simple, inexperienced,
Could see him as he was, and often warned me.
Whence learned she this?—O she was innocent!
And to be innocent is Nature's wisdom!
The fledge-dove knows the prowlers of the air,
Feared soon as seen, and flutters back to shelter.
And the young steed recoils upon his haunches,
The never-yet-seen adder's hiss first heard.
O surer than suspicion's hundred eyes
Is that fine sense, which to the pure in heart,
By mere oppugnancy of their own goodness,
Reveals the approach of evil."

As therefore my character as a writer could not easily be more injured by an overt act than it was already in consequence of the report, I published a work, a large portion of which was professedly metaphysical. A long delay occurred between its first annunciation and its appearance; it was reviewed therefore by anticipation with a malignity, so avowedly and exclusively personal, as is, I believe, unprecedented even in the present contempt of all common humanity that disgraces and endangers the liberty of the press. After its appearance, the author of this lampoon undertook to review it in the Edinburgh Review; and under the single condition, that he should have written what he himself really thought, and have criticised the work as he would have done had its author been indifferent to him, I should have chosen that man myself, both from the vigour and the originality of his mind, and from his particular acuteness in speculative reasoning, before all others.—I remembered Catullus's lines.

Desine de quoquam quicquam bene velle mereri,
Aut aliquem fieri posse putare pium.
Omnia sunt ingrata: nihil fecisse benigne est:
Immo, etiam taedet, taedet obestque magis;
Ut mihi, quem nemo gravius nec acerbius urget,
Quam modo qui me unum atque unicum amicum habuit.

But I can truly say, that the grief with which I read this rhapsody of predetermined insult, had the rhapsodist himself for its whole and sole object.

* * * * * *

I refer to this review at present, in consequence of information having been given me, that the inuendo of my "potential infidelity," grounded on one passage of my first Lay Sermon, has been received and propagated with a degree of credence, of which I can safely acquit the originator of the calumny. I give the sentences, as they stand in the sermon, premising only that I was speaking exclusively of miracles worked for the outward senses of men. "It was only to overthrow the usurpation exercised in and through the senses, that the senses were miraculously appealed to. REASON AND RELIGION ARE THEIR OWN EVIDENCE. The natural sun is in this respect a symbol of the spiritual. Ere he is fully arisen, and while his glories are still under veil, he calls up the breeze to chase away the usurping vapours of the night-season, and thus converts the air itself into the minister of its own purification: not surely in proof or elucidation of the light from heaven, but to prevent its interception."

"Wherever, therefore, similar circumstances co-exist with the same moral causes, the principles revealed, and the examples recorded, in the inspired writings, render miracles superfluous: and if we neglect to apply truths in expectation of wonders, or under pretext of the cessation of the latter, we tempt God, and merit the same reply which our Lord gave to the Pharisees on a like occasion."

In the sermon and the notes both the historical truth and the necessity of the miracles are strongly and frequently asserted. "The testimony of books of history (that is, relatively to the signs and wonders, with which Christ came) is one of the strong and stately pillars of the church: but it is not the foundation!" Instead, therefore, of defending myself, which I could easily effect by a series of passages, expressing the same opinion, from the Fathers and the most eminent Protestant Divines, from the Reformation to the Revolution, I shall merely state what my belief is, concerning the true evidences of Christianity. 1. Its consistency with right Reason, I consider as the outer court of the temple—the common area, within which it stands. 2. The miracles, with and through which the Religion was first revealed and attested, I regard as the steps, the vestibule, and the portal of the temple. 3. The sense, the inward feeling, in the soul of each believer of its exceeding desirableness—the experience, that he needs something, joined with the strong foretokening, that the redemption and the graces propounded to us in Christ are what he needs—this I hold to be the true foundation of the spiritual edifice. With the strong a priori probability that flows in from 1 and 3 on the correspondent historical evidence of 2, no man can refuse or neglect to make the experiment without guilt. But, 4, it is the experience derived from a practical conformity to the conditions of the Gospel—it is the opening eye; the dawning light: the terrors and the promises of spiritual growth; the blessedness of loving God as God, the nascent sense of sin hated as sin, and of the incapability of attaining to either without Christ; it is the sorrow that still rises up from beneath and the consolation that meets it from above; the bosom treacheries of the principal in the warfare and the exceeding faithfulness and long-suffering of the uninteresting ally;—in a word, it is the actual trial of the faith in Christ, with its accompaniments and results, that must form the arched roof, and the faith itself is the completing key-stone. In order to an efficient belief in Christianity, a man must have been a Christian, and this is the seeming argumentum in circulo, incident to all spiritual Truths, to every subject not presentable under the forms of Time and Space, as long as we attempt to master by the reflex acts of the Understanding what we can only know by the act of becoming. Do the will of my Father, and ye shall know whether I am of God. These four evidences I believe to have been and still to be, for the world, for the whole Church, all necessary, all equally necessary: but at present, and for the majority of Christians born in Christian countries, I believe the third and the fourth evidences to be the most operative, not as superseding but as involving a glad undoubting faith in the two former. Credidi, ideoque intellexi, appears to me the dictate equally of Philosophy and Religion, even as I believe Redemption to be the antecedent of Sanctification, and not its consequent. All spiritual predicates may be construed indifferently as modes of Action or as states of Being, Thus Holiness and Blessedness are the same idea, now seen in relation to act and now to existence. The ready belief which has been yielded to the slander of my "potential infidelity," I attribute in part to the openness with which I have avowed my doubts, whether the heavy interdict, under which the name of Benedict Spinoza lies, is merited on the whole or to the whole extent. Be this as it may, I wish, however, that I could find in the books of philosophy, theoretical or moral, which are alone recommended to the present students of theology in our established schools, a few passages as thoroughly Pauline, as completely accordant with the doctrines of the Established Church, as the following sentences in the concluding page of Spinoza's Ethics. Deinde quo mens hoc amore divino, seu beatitudine magis gaudet, eo plus intelligit, hoc est, eo majorem in affectus habet potentiam, et eo minus ab affectibus, qui mali sunt, patitur; atque adeo ex eo, quod mens hoc amore divino, seu beatitudine gaudet, potestatem habet libidines coercendi; et quia humana potentia ad coercendos affectus in solo intellectu consistit; ergo nemo beatitudine gaudet, quia affectus coercuit, sed contra potestas libidines coercendi ex ipsa beatitudine oritur.

With regard to the Unitarians, it has been shamelessly asserted, that I have denied them to be Christians. God forbid! For how should I know, what the piety of the heart may be, or what quantum of error in the understanding may consist with a saving faith in the intentions and actual dispositions of the whole moral being in any one individual? Never will

God reject a soul that sincerely loves him: be his speculative opinions what they may: and whether in any given instance certain opinions, be they unbelief, or misbelief, are compatible with a sincere love of God, God can only know.—But this I have said, and shall continue to say: that if the doctrines, the sum of which I believe to constitute the truth in Christ, be Christianity, then Unitarianism is not, and vice versa: and that, in speaking theologically and impersonally, i.e. of Psilanthropism and Theanthropism as schemes of belief, without reference to individuals, who profess either the one or the other, it will be absurd to use a different language as long as it is the dictate of common sense, that two opposites cannot properly be called by the same name. I should feel no offence if a Unitarian applied the same to me, any more than if he were to say, that two and two being four, four and four must be eight.

alla broton
ton men keneophrones auchai
ex agathon ebalon;
ton d' au katamemphthent' agan
ischun oikeion paresphalen kalon,
cheiros elkon opisso, thumos atolmos eon.

This has been my object, and this alone can be my defence—and O! that with this my personal as well as my LITERARY LIFE might conclude!—the unquenched desire I mean, not without the consciousness of having earnestly endeavoured to kindle young minds, and to guard them against the temptations of scorners, by showing that the scheme of Christianity, as taught in the liturgy and homilies of our Church, though not discoverable by human reason, is yet in accordance with it; that link follows link by necessary consequence; that Religion passes out of the ken of Reason only where the eye of Reason has reached its own horizon; and that Faith is then but its continuation: even as the day softens away into the sweet twilight, and twilight, hushed and breathless, steals into the darkness. It is night, sacred night! the upraised eye views only the starry heaven which manifests itself alone: and the outward beholding is fixed on the sparks twinkling in the awful depth, though suns of other worlds, only to preserve the soul steady and collected in its pure act of inward adoration to the great I AM, and to the filial WORD that re-affirmeth it from eternity to eternity, whose choral echo is the universe.

THEO, MONO, DOXA.

FOOTNOTES

1 (return)
[The authority of Milton and Shakespeare may be usefully pointed out to young authors. In the Comus and other early poems of Milton there is a superfluity of double epithets; while in the Paradise Lost we find very few, in the Paradise Regained scarce any. The same remark holds almost equally true of the Love's Labour Lost, Romeo and Juliet, Venus and Adonis, and Lucrece, compared with the Lear, Macbeth, Othello, and Hamlet of our great Dramatist. The rule for the admission of double epithets seems to be this: either that they should be already denizens of our language, such as blood-stained, terror-stricken, self-applauding: or when a new epithet, or one found in books only, is hazarded, that it, at least, be one word, not two words made one by mere virtue of the printers hyphen. A language which, like the English, is almost without cases, is indeed in its very genius unfitted for compounds. If a writer, every time a compounded word suggests itself to him, would seek for some other mode of expressing the same sense, the chances are always greatly in favour of his finding a better word. Ut tanquam scopulum sic fugias insolens verbum, is the wise advice of Caesar to the Roman Orators, and the precept applies with double force to the writers in our own language. But it must not be forgotten, that the same Caesar wrote a Treatise for the purpose of reforming the ordinary language by bringing it to a greater accordance with the principles of logic or universal grammar.]

2 (return)
[See the criticisms on the Ancient Mariner, in the Monthly and Critical Reviews of the first volume of the Lyrical Ballads.]

3 (return)
[This is worthy of ranking as a maxim, (regula maxima,) of criticism. Whatever is translatable in other and simpler words of the same language, without loss of sense or dignity, is bad. N.B.—By dignity I mean the absence of ludicrous and debasing associations.]

4 (return)
[The Christ's Hospital phrase, not for holidays altogether, but for those on which the boys are permitted to go beyond the precincts of the school.]

5 (return)
[I remember a ludicrous instance in the poem of a young tradesman:

"No more will I endure love's pleasing pain,
Or round my heart's leg tie his galling chain."]

6 (return)

[Cowper's Task was published some time before the Sonnets of Mr. Bowles; but I was not familiar with it till many years afterwards. The vein of satire which runs through that excellent poem, together with the sombre hue of its religious opinions, would probably, at that time, have prevented its laying any strong hold on my affections. The love of nature seems to have led Thomson to a cheerful religion; and a gloomy religion to have led Cowper to a love of nature. The one would carry his fellow-men along with him into nature; the other flies to nature from his fellow-men. In chastity of diction however, and the harmony of blank verse, Cowper leaves Thomson immeasurably below him; yet still I feel the latter to have been the born poet.]

7 (return)

[SONNET I

Pensive at eve, on the hard world I mused,
And m poor heart was sad; so at the Moon
I gazed and sighed, and sighed; for ah how soon
Eve saddens into night! mine eyes perused
With tearful vacancy the dampy grass
That wept and glitter'd in the paly ray
And I did pause me on my lonely way
And mused me on the wretched ones that pass
O'er the bleak heath of sorrow. But alas!
Most of myself I thought! when it befel,
That the soothe spirit of the breezy wood
Breath'd in mine ear: "All this is very well,
But much of one thing, is for no thing good."
Oh my poor heart's inexplicable swell!

SONNET II

Oh I do love thee, meek Simplicity!
For of thy lays the lulling simpleness
Goes to my heart, and soothes each small distress,
Distress the small, yet haply great to me.
'Tis true on Lady Fortune's gentlest pad
I amble on; and yet I know not why
So sad I am! but should a friend and I
Frown, pout and part, then I am very sad.
And then with sonnets and with sympathy
My dreamy bosom's mystic woes I pall:
Now of my false friend plaining plaintively,

Now raving at mankind in general;
But whether sad or fierce, 'tis simple all,
All very simple, meek Simplicity!

SONNET III

And this reft house is that, the which he built,
Lamented Jack! and here his malt he pil'd,
Cautious in vain! these rats, that squeak so wild,
Squeak not unconscious of their father's guilt.
Did he not see her gleaming thro' the glade!
Belike 'twas she, the maiden all forlorn.
What the she milk no cow with crumpled horn,
Yet, aye she haunts the dale where erst she stray'd:
And aye, beside her stalks her amorous knight
Still on his thighs their wonted brogues are worn,
And thro' those brogues, still tatter'd and betorn,
His hindward charms gleam an unearthly white.
Ah! thus thro' broken clouds at night's high noon
Peeps to fair fragments forth the full-orb'd harvest-moon!

The following anecdote will not be wholly out of place here, and may perhaps amuse the reader. An amateur performer in verse expressed to a common friend a strong desire to be introduced to me, but hesitated in accepting my friend's immediate offer, on the score that "he was, he must acknowledge, the author of a confounded severe epigram on my Ancient Mariner, which had given me great pain." I assured my friend that, if the epigram was a good one, it would only increase my desire to become acquainted with the author, and begged to hear it recited: when, to my no less surprise than amusement, it proved to be one which I had myself some time before written and inserted in the "Morning Post," to wit—

To the Author of the Ancient Mariner.

Your poem must eternal be,
Dear sir! it cannot fail,
For 'tis incomprehensible,
And without head or tail.]

8 (return)
[—
Of old things all are over old,
Of good things none are good enough;—
We'll show that we can help to frame

A world of other stuff.

*I too will have my kings, that take
From me the sign of life and death:
Kingdoms shall shift about, like clouds,
Obedient to my breath.
Wordsworth's Rob Roy.—Poet. Works, vol. III. p. 127.]*

9 (return)

[Pope was under the common error of his age, an error far from being sufficiently exploded even at the present day. It consists (as I explained at large, and proved in detail in my public lectures,) in mistaking for the essentials of the Greek stage certain rules, which the wise poets imposed upon themselves, in order to render all the remaining parts of the drama consistent with those, that had been forced upon them by circumstances independent of their will; out of which circumstances the drama itself arose. The circumstances in the time of Shakespeare, which it was equally out of his power to alter, were different, and such as, in my opinion, allowed a far wider sphere, and a deeper and more human interest. Critics are too apt to forget, that rules are but means to an end; consequently, where the ends are different, the rules must be likewise so. We must have ascertained what the end is, before we can determine what the rules ought to be. Judging under this impression, I did not hestitate to declare my full conviction, that the consummate judgment of Shakespeare, not only in the general construction, but in all the details, of his dramas, impressed me with greater wonder, than even the might of his genius, or the depth of his philosophy. The substance of these lectures I hope soon to publish; and it is but a debt of justice to myself and my friends to notice, that the first course of lectures, which differed from the following courses only, by occasionally varying the illustrations of the same thoughts, was addressed to very numerous, and I need not add, respectable audiences at the Royal institution, before Mr. Schlegel gave his lectures on the same subjects at Vienna.]

10 (return)

[In the course of one of my Lectures, I had occasion to point out the almost faultless position and choice of words, in Pope's original compositions, particularly in his Satires and moral Essays, for the purpose of comparing them with his translation of Homer, which, I do not stand alone in regarding, as the main source of our pseudo-poetic diction. And this, by the bye, is an additional confirmation of a remark made, I believe, by Sir Joshua Reynolds, that next to the man who forms and elevates the taste of the public, he that corrupts it, is commonly the greatest genius.

Among other passages, I analyzed sentence by sentence, and almost word by word, the popular lines,

As when the moon, refulgent lamp of night, etc.
(Iliad. B. viii.)

much in the same way as has been since done, in an excellent article on Chalmers's British Poets in the Quarterly Review. The impression on the audience in general was sudden and evident: and a number of enlightened and highly educated persons, who at different times afterwards addressed me on the subject, expressed their wonder, that truth so obvious should not have struck them before; but at the same time acknowledged—(so much had they been accustomed, in reading poetry, to receive pleasure from the separate images and phrases successively, without asking themselves whether the collective meaning was sense or nonsense)—that they might in all probability have read the same passage again twenty times with undiminished admiration, and without once reflecting, that

astra phaeinaen amphi selaenaen
phainet aritretea—

(that is, the stars around, or near the full moon, shine pre-eminently bright) conveys a just and happy image of a moonlight sky: while it is difficult to determine whether, in the lines,

Around her throne the vivid planets roll,
And stars unnumber'd gild the glowing pole,

the sense or the diction be the more absurd. My answer was; that, though I had derived peculiar advantages from my school discipline, and though my general theory of poetry was the same then as now, I had yet experienced the same sensations myself, and felt almost as if I had been newly couched, when, by Mr. Wordsworth's conversation, I had been induced to re-examine with impartial strictness Gray's celebrated Elegy. I had long before detected the defects in The Bard; but the Elegy I had considered as proof against all fair attacks; and to this day I cannot read either without delight, and a portion of enthusiasm. At all events, whatever pleasure I may have lost by the clearer perception of the faults in certain passages, has been more than repaid to me by the additional delight with which I read the remainder.

Another instance in confirmation of these remarks occurs to me in the Faithful Shepherdess. Seward first traces Fletcher's lines;

More foul diseases than e'er yet the hot
Sun bred thro' his burnings, while the dog
Pursues the raging lion, throwing the fog

And deadly vapour from his angry breath,
Filling the lower world with plague and death,

to Spenser's Shepherd's Calendar,

The rampant lion hunts he fast
With dogs of noisome breath;
Whose baleful barking brings, in haste,
Pine, plagues, and dreary death!

He then takes occasion to introduce Homer's simile of the appearance of Achilles' mail to Priam compared with the Dog Star; literally thus—

"For this indeed is most splendid, but it was made an evil sign, and brings many a consuming disease to wretched mortals." Nothing can be more simple as a description, or more accurate as a simile; which, (says Seward,) is thus finely translated by Mr. Pope

Terrific Glory! for his burning breath
Taints the red air with fevers, plagues, and death!

Now here—(not to mention the tremendous bombast)—the Dog Star, so called, is turned into a real dog, a very odd dog, a fire, fever, plague, and death-breathing, red, air-tainting dog: and the whole visual likeness is lost, while the likeness in the effects is rendered absurd by the exaggeration. In Spenser and Fletcher the thought is justifiable; for the images are at least consistent, and it was the intention of the writers to mark the seasons by this allegory of visualized puns.]

11 (return)
[Especially in this age of personality, this age of literary and political gossiping, when the meanest insects are worshipped with a sort of Egyptian superstition, if only the brainless head be atoned for by the sting of personal malignity in the tail;—when the most vapid satires have become the objects of a keen public interest, purely from the number of contemporary characters named in the patch-work notes, (which possess, however, the comparative merit of being more poetical than the text,) and because, to increase the stimulus, the author has sagaciously left his own name for whispers and conjectures.]

12 (return)
[If it were worth while to mix together, as ingredients, half the anecdotes which I either myself know to be true, or which I have received from men incapable of intentional falsehood, concerning the characters, qualifications, and motives of our anonymous critics, whose decisions are oracles for our reading public; I might safely borrow the words of the apocryphal Daniel; "Give me leave, O SOVEREIGN PUBLIC, and I shall slay this dragon

without sward or staff." For the compound would be as the "pitch, and fat, and hair, which Daniel took, and did seethe them together, and made lumps thereof; this he put in the dragon's mouth, and so the dragon burst in sunder; and Daniel said, LO, THESE ARE THE GODS YE WORSHIP."]

13 (return)

[This is one instance among many of deception, by the telling the half of a fact, and omitting the other half, when it is from their mutual counteraction and neutralization, that the whole truth arises, as a tertium aliquid different from either. Thus in Dryden's famous line

Great wit (meaning genius) to madness sure is near allied.

Now if the profound sensibility, which is doubtless one of the components of genius, were alone considered, single and unbalanced, it might be fairly described as exposing the individual to a greater chance of mental derangement; but then a more than usual rapidity of association, a more than usual power of passing from thought to thought, and image to image, is a component equally essential; and to the due modification of each by the other the genius itself consists; so that it would be just as fair to describe the earth, as in imminent danger of exorbitating, or of falling into the sun, according as the assertor of the absurdity confined his attention either to the projectile or to the attractive force exclusively.]

14 (return)

[For as to the devotees of the circulating libraries, I dare not compliment their pass-time, or rather kill-time, with the name of reading. Call it rather a sort of beggarly day-dreaming, during which the mind of the dreamer furnishes for itself nothing but laziness, and a little mawkish sensibility; while the whole materiel and imagery of the doze is supplied ab extra by a sort of mental camera obscura manufactured at the printing office, which pro tempore fixes, reflects, and transmits the moving phantasms of one mans delirium, so as to people the barrenness of a hundred other brains afflicted with the same trance or suspension of all common sense and all definite purpose. We should therefore transfer this species of amusement—(if indeed those can be said to retire a musis, who were never in their company, or relaxation be attributable to those, whose bows are never bent)—from the genus, reading, to that comprehensive class characterized by the power of reconciling the two contrary yet coexisting propensities of human nature, namely, indulgence of sloth, and hatred of vacancy. In addition to novels and tales of chivalry to prose or rhyme, (by which last I mean neither rhythm nor metre) this genus comprises as its species, gaming, swinging, or swaying on a chair or gate; spitting over a bridge; smoking; snuff-taking; tete-a-tete quarrels after dinner between husband

and wife; conning word by word all the advertisements of a daily newspaper in a public house on a rainy day, etc. etc. etc.]

15 (return)
[Ex. gr. Pediculos e capillis excerptos in arenam jacere incontusos; eating of unripe fruit; gazing on the clouds, and (in genere) on movable things suspended in the air; riding among a multitude of camels; frequent laughter; listening to a series of jests and humorous anecdotes,—as when (so to modernize the learned Saracen's meaning) one man's droll story of an Irishman inevitably occasions another's droll story of a Scotchman, which again, by the same sort of conjunction disjunctive, leads to some etourderie of a Welshman, and that again to some sly hit of a Yorkshireman;—the habit of reading tomb-stones in church-yards, etc. By the bye, this catalogue, strange as it may appear, is not insusceptible of a sound psychological commentary.]

16 (return)
[I have ventured to call it unique; not only because I know no work of the kind in our language, (if we except a few chapters of the old translation of Froissart)—none, which uniting the charms of romance and history, keeps the imagination so constantly on the wing, and yet leaves so much for after reflection; but likewise, and chiefly, because it is a compilation, which, in the various excellencies of translation, selection, and arrangement, required and proves greater genius in the compiler, as living in the present state of society, than in the original composers.]

17 (return)
[It is not easy to estimate the effects which the example of a young man as highly distinguished for strict purity of disposition and conduct, as for intellectual power and literary acquirements, may produce on those of the same age with himself, especially on those of similar pursuits and congenial minds. For many years, my opportunities of intercourse with Mr. Southey have been rare, and at long intervals; but I dwell with unabated pleasure on the strong and sudden, yet I trust not fleeting, influence, which my moral being underwent on my acquaintance with him at Oxford, whither I had gone at the commencement of our Cambridge vacation on a visit to an old school-fellow. Not indeed on my moral or religious principles, for they had never been contaminated; but in awakening the sense of the duty and dignity of making my actions accord with those principles, both in word and deed. The irregularities only not universal among the young men of my standing, which I always knew to be wrong, I then learned to feel as degrading; learned to know that an opposite conduct, which was at that time considered by us as the easy virtue of cold and selfish prudence, might originate in the noblest emotions, in views the most disinterested and imaginative. It is not however from grateful recollections only, that I have

been impelled thus to leave these my deliberate sentiments on record; but in some sense as a debt of justice to the man, whose name has been so often connected with mine for evil to which he is a stranger. As a specimen I subjoin part of a note, from The Beauties of the Anti-jacobin, in which, having previously informed the public that I had been dishonoured at Cambridge for preaching Deism, at a time when, for my youthful ardour in defence of Christianity, I was decried as a bigot by the proselytes of French phi-(or to speak more truly psi-)-losophy, the writer concludes with these words; "since this time he has left his native country, commenced citizen of the world, left his poor children fatherless, and his wife destitute. Ex his disce his friends, LAMB and SOUTHEY." With severest truth it may be asserted, that it would not be easy to select two men more exemplary in their domestic affections than those whose names were thus printed at full length as in the same rank of morals with a denounced infidel and fugitive, who had left his children fatherless and his wife destitute! Is it surprising, that many good men remained longer than perhaps they otherwise would have done adverse to a party, which encouraged and openly rewarded the authors of such atrocious calumnies? Qualis es, nescio; sed per quales agis, scio et doleo.]

18   (return)
[In opinions of long continuance, and in which we have never before been molested by a single doubt, to be suddenly convinced of an error, is almost like being convicted of a fault. There is a state of mind, which is the direct antithesis of that, which takes place when we make a bull. The bull namely consists in the bringing her two incompatible thoughts, with the sensation, but without the sense, of their connection. The psychological condition, or that which constitutes the possibility, of this state, being such disproportionate vividness of two distant thoughts, as extinguishes or obscures the consciousness of the intermediate images or conceptions, or wholly abstracts the attention from them. Thus in the well known bull, "I was a fine child, but they changed me:" the first conception expressed in the word "I," is that of personal identity—Ego contemplans: the second expressed in the word "me," is the visual image or object by which the mind represents to itself its past condition, or rather, its personal identity under the form in which it imagined itself previously to have existed,—Ego contemplatus. Now the change of one visual image for another involves in itself no absurdity, and becomes absurd only by its immediate juxta-position with the fast thought, which is rendered possible by the whole attention being successively absorbed to each singly, so as not to notice the interjacent notion, changed, which by its incongruity, with the first thought, I, constitutes the bull. Add only, that this process is facilitated by the circumstance of the words I, and me, being sometimes equivalent, and sometimes having a distinct meaning; sometimes, namely, signifying the act

of self-consciousness, sometimes the external image in and by which the mind represents that act to itself, the result and symbol of its individuality. Now suppose the direct contrary state, and you will have a distinct sense of the connection between two conceptions, without that sensation of such connection which is supplied by habit. The man feels as if he were standing on his head though he cannot but see that he is truly standing on his feet. This, as a painful sensation, will of course have a tendency to associate itself with him who occasions it; even as persons, who have been by painful means restored from derangement, are known to feel an involuntary dislike towards their physician.]

19 (return)
[Without however the apprehensions attributed to the Pagan reformer of the poetic republic. If we may judge from the preface to the recent collection of his poems, Mr. W. would have answered with Xanthias—

su d' ouk edeisas ton huophon ton rhaematon,
kai tas apeilas; XAN, ou ma Di', oud' ephrontisa.—Ranae, 492-3.

And here let me hint to the authors of the numerous parodies, and pretended imitations of Mr. Wordsworth's style, that at once to conceal and convey wit and wisdom in the semblance of folly and dulness, as is done in the Clowns and Fools, nay even in the Dogberry, of our Shakespeare, is doubtless a proof of genius, or at all events of satiric talent; but that the attempt to ridicule a silly and childish poem, by writing another still sillier and still more childish, can only prove (if it prove any thing at all) that the parodist is a still greater blockhead than the original writer, and, what is far worse, a malignant coxcomb to boot. The talent for mimicry seems strongest where the human race are most degraded. The poor, naked half human savages of New Holland were found excellent mimics: and, in civilized society, minds of the very lowest stamp alone satirize by copying. At least the difference which must blend with and balance the likeness, in order to constitute a just imitation, existing here merely in caricature, detracts from the libeller's heart, without adding an iota to the credit of his understanding.]

20 (return)
[—

The Butterfly the ancient Grecians made
The soul's fair emblem, and its only name—
But of the soul, escaped the slavish trade
Of mortal life! For to this earthly frame
Ours is the reptile's lot, much toil, much blame,
Manifold motions making little speed,
And to deform and kill the things whereon we feed.]

21   (return)
[Mr. Wordsworth, even in his two earliest poems, The Evening Walk and the Descriptive Sketches, is more free from this latter defect than most of the young poets his contemporaries. It may however be exemplified, together with the harsh and obscure construction, in which he more often offended, in the following lines:—

"Mid stormy vapours ever driving by,
Where ospreys, cormorants, and herons cry;
Where hardly given the hopeless waste to cheer,
Denied the bread of life the foodful ear,
Dwindles the pear on autumn's latest spray,
And apple sickens pale in summer's ray;
Ev'n here content has fixed her smiling reign
With independence, child of high disdain."

I hope, I need not say, that I have quoted these lines for no other purpose than to make my meaning fully understood. It is to be regretted that Mr. Wordsworth has not republished these two poems entire.]

22   (return)
[This is effected either by giving to the one word a general, and to the other an exclusive use; as "to put on the back" and "to indorse;" or by an actual distinction of meanings, as "naturalist," and "physician;" or by difference of relation, as "I" and "Me" (each of which the rustics of our different provinces still use in all the cases singular of the first personal pronoun). Even the mere difference, or corruption, in the pronunciation of the same word, if it have become general, will produce a new word with a distinct signification; thus "property" and "propriety;" the latter of which, even to the time of Charles II was the written word for all the senses of both. There is a sort of minim immortal among the animalcula infusoria, which has not naturally either birth, or death, absolute beginning, or absolute end: for at a certain period a small point appears on its back, which deepens and lengthens till the creature divides into two, and the same process recommences in each of the halves now become integral. This may be a fanciful, but it is by no means a bad emblem of the formation of words, and may facilitate the conception, how immense a nomenclature may be organized from a few simple sounds by rational beings in a social state. For each new application, or excitement of the same sound, will call forth a different sensation, which cannot but affect the pronunciation. The after recollections of the sound, without the same vivid sensation, will modify it still further till at length all trace of the original likeness is worn away.]

23 (return)

[I ought to have added, with the exception of a single sheet which I accidentally met with at the printer's. Even from this scanty specimen, I found it impossible to doubt the talent, or not to admire the ingenuity, of the author. That his distinctions were for the greater part unsatisfactory to my mind, proves nothing against their accuracy; but it may possibly be serviceable to him, in case of a second edition, if I take this opportunity of suggesting the query; whether he may not have been occasionally misled, by having assumed, as to me he appears to have done, the non-existence of any absolute synonymes in our language? Now I cannot but think, that there are many which remain for our posterity to distinguish and appropriate, and which I regard as so much reversionary wealth in our mother tongue. When two distinct meanings are confounded under one or more words,—(and such must be the case, as sure as our knowledge is progressive and of course imperfect)—erroneous consequences will be drawn, and what is true in one sense of the word will be affirmed as true in toto. Men of research, startled by the consequences, seek in the things themselves—(whether in or out of the mind)—for a knowledge of the fact, and having discovered the difference, remove the equivocation either by the substitution of a new word, or by the appropriation of one of the two or more words, which had before been used promiscuously. When this distinction has been so naturalized and of such general currency that the language does as it were think for us—(like the sliding rule which is the mechanic's safe substitute for arithmetical knowledge)—we then say, that it is evident to common sense. Common sense, therefore, differs in different ages. What was born and christened in the Schools passes by degrees into the world at large, and becomes the property of the market and the tea-table. At least I can discover no other meaning of the term, common sense, if it is to convey any specific difference from sense and judgment in genere, and where it is not used scholastically for the universal reason. Thus in the reign of Charles II the philosophic world was called to arms by the moral sophisms of Hobbes, and the ablest writers exerted themselves in the detection of an error, which a school-boy would now be able to confute by the mere recollection, that compulsion and obligation conveyed two ideas perfectly disparate, and that what appertained to the one, had been falsely transferred to the other by a mere confusion of terms.]

24 (return)

[I here use the word idea in Mr. Hume's sense on account of its general currency amongst the English metaphysicians; though against my own judgment, for I believe that the vague use of this word has been the cause of much error and more confusion. The word, idea, in its original sense as used by Pindar, Aristophanes, and in the Gospel of St. Matthew, represented the visual abstraction of a distant object, when we see the whole without distinguishing its parts. Plato adopted it as a technical term, and as the antithesis to eidolon, or sensuous image; the transient and perishable emblem, or mental word, of the idea. Ideas themselves he considered as mysterious powers, living, seminal, formative, and exempt from time. In this sense the word Idea became the property of the Platonic school; and it seldom occurs in Aristotle, without some such phrase annexed to it, as according to Plato, or as Plato says. Our English writers to the end of the reign of Charles II or somewhat later, employed it either in the original sense, or Platonically, or in a sense nearly correspondent to our present use of the substantive, Ideal; always however opposing it, more or less to image, whether of present or absent objects. The reader will not be displeased with the following interesting exemplification from Bishop Jeremy Taylor. "St. Lewis the King sent Ivo Bishop of Chartres on an embassy, and he told, that he met a grave and stately matron on the way with a censer of fire in one band, and a vessel of water in the other; and observing her to have a melancholy, religious, and phantastic deportment and look, he asked her what those symbols meant, and what she meant to do with her fire and water; she answered, My purpose is with the fire to burn paradise, and with my water to quench the flames of hell, that men may serve God purely for the love of God. But we rarely meet with such spirits which love virtue so metaphysically as to abstract her from all sensible compositions, and love the purity of the idea." Des Cartes having introduced into his philosophy the fanciful hypothesis of material ideas, or certain configurations of the brain, which were as so many moulds to the influxes of the external world,—Locke adopted the term, but extended its signification to whatever is the immediate object of the mind's attention or consciousness. Hume, distinguishing those representations which are accompanied with a sense of a present object from those reproduced by the mind itself, designated the former by impressions, and confined the word idea to the latter.]

25 (return)

[I am aware, that this word occurs neither in Johnson's Dictionary nor in any classical writer. But the word, to intend, which Newton and others before him employ in this sense, is now so completely appropriated to another meaning, that I could not use it without ambiguity: while to paraphrase the sense, as by render intense, would often break up the sentence and destroy that harmony of the position of the words with the logical position of the thoughts, which is a beauty in all composition, and more especially desirable in a close philosophical investigation. I have therefore hazarded the word, intensify: though, I confess, it sounds uncouth to my own ear.]

26 (return)
[And Coxcombs vanquish Berkeley by a grin.]

27 (return)
[Videlicet; Quantity, Quality, Relation, and Mode, each consisting of three subdivisions. See Kritik der reinen Vernunft. See too the judicious remarks on Locke and Hume.]

28 (return)
[St. Luke x. 21.]

29 (return)
[An American Indian with little variety of images, and a still scantier stock of language, is obliged to turn his few words to many purposes, by likenesses so clear and analogies so remote as to give his language the semblance and character of lyric poetry interspersed with grotesques. Something not unlike this was the case of such men as Behmen and Fox with regard to the Bible. It was their sole armoury of expressions, their only organ of thought.]

30 (return)
[The following burlesque on the Fichtean Egoisnsus may, perhaps, be amusing to the few who have studied the system, and to those who are unacquainted with it, may convey as tolerable a likeness of Fichte's idealism as can be expected from an avowed caricature.

The Categorical Imperative, or the annunciation of the new Teutonic God, EGOENKAIPAN: a dithyrambic ode, by QUERKOPF VON KLUBSTICK, Grammarian, and Subrector in Gymmasic.

Eu! Dei vices gerens, ipse Divus,
(Speak English, Friend!) the God Imperativus,
Here on this market-cross aloud I cry:
I, I, I! I itself I!
The form and the substance, the what and the why,
The when and the where, and the low and the high,
The inside and outside, the earth and the sky,
I, you and he, and he, you and I,
All souls and all bodies are I itself I!
All I itself I!
(Fools! a truce with this starting!)
All my I! all my I!
He's a heretic dog who but adds Betty Martin!
Thus cried the God with high imperial tone;
In robe of stiffest state, that scoffed at beauty,
A pronoun-verb imperative he shone—

Then substantive and plural-singular grown
He thus spake on! Behold in I alone
(For ethics boast a syntax of their own)
Or if in ye, yet as I doth depute ye,
In O! I, you, the vocative of duty!
I of the world's whole Lexicon the root!
Of the whole universe of touch, sound, sight
The genitive and ablative to boot:
The accusative of wrong, the nominative of right,
And in all cases the case absolute!
Self-construed, I all other moods decline:
Imperative, from nothing we derive us;
Yet as a super-postulate of mine,
Unconstrued antecedence I assign
To X, Y, Z, the God Infinitivus!]

31 (return)

[It would be an act of high and almost criminal injustice to pass over in silence the name of Mr. Richard Saumarez, a gentleman equally well known as a medical man and as a philanthropist, but who demands notice on the present occasion as the author of "A new System of Physiology" in two volumes octavo, published 1797; and in 1812 of "An Examination of the natural and artificial Systems of Philosophy which now prevail" in one volume octavo, entitled, "The Principles of physiological and physical Science." The latter work is not quite equal to the former in style or arrangement; and there is a greater necessity of distinguishing the principles of the author's philosophy from his conjectures concerning colour, the atmospheric matter, comets, etc. which, whether just or erroneous, are by no means necessary consequences of that philosophy. Yet even in this department of this volume, which I regard as comparatively the inferior work, the reasonings by which Mr. Saumarez invalidates the immanence of an infinite power in any finite substance are the offspring of no common mind; and the experiment on the expansibility of the air is at least plausible and highly ingenious. But the merit, which will secure both to the book and to the writer a high and honourable name with posterity, consists in the masterly force of reasoning, and the copiousness of induction, with which he has assailed, and (in my opinion) subverted the tyranny of the mechanic system in physiology; established not only the existence of final causes, but their necessity and efficiency to every system that merits the name of philosophical; and, substituting life and progressive power for the contradictory inert force, has a right to be known and remembered as the first instaurator of the dynamic philosophy in England. The author's views, as far as concerns himself, are unborrowed and completely his own, as he neither possessed nor do his writings discover, the least acquaintance with the works of Kant, in which the germs of the philosophy exist: and his volumes were published many years before the full development of these germs by Schelling. Mr. Saumarez's detection of the Braunonian system was no light or ordinary service at the time; and I scarcely remember in any work on any subject a confutation so thoroughly satisfactory. It is sufficient at this time to have stated the fact; as in the preface to the work, which I have already announced on the Logos, I have exhibited in detail the merits of this writer, and genuine philosopher, who needed only have taken his foundation somewhat deeper and wider to have superseded a considerable part of my labours.]

32   (return)
[But for sundry notes on Shakespeare, and other pieces which have fallen in my way, I should have deemed it unnecessary to observe; that discourse here, or elsewhere does not mean what we now call discoursing; but the discursion of the mind, the processes of generalization and subsumption, of deduction and conclusion. Thus, Philosophy has hitherto been discursive; while Geometry is always and essentially intuitive.]

33   (return)
[Revelation xx. 3.]

34   (return)
[See Laing's History of Scotland.—Walter Scott's bards, ballads, etc.]

35   (return)
[Thus organization, and motion are regarded as from God, not in God.]

36   (return)
[Job, chap. xxviii.]

37   (return)
[Wherever A=B, and A is not=B, are equally demonstrable, the premise in each undeniable, the induction evident, and the conclusion legitimate—the result must be, either that contraries can both be true, (which is absurd,) or that the faculty and forms of reasoning employed are inapplicable to the subject—i.e. that there is a metabasis eis allo genos. Thus, the attributes of Space and time applied to Spirit are heterogeneous—and the proof of this is, that by admitting them explicite or implicite contraries may be demonstrated true—i.e. that the same, taken in the same sense, is true and not true.—That the world had a beginning in Time and a bound in Space; and That the world had not a beginning and has no limit;—That a self originating act is, and is not possible, are instances.]

38   (return)
[To those, who design to acquire the language of a country in the country itself, it may be useful, if I mention the incalculable advantage which I

derived from learning all the words, that could possibly be so learned, with the objects before me, and without the intermediation of the English terms. It was a regular part of my morning studies for the first six weeks of my residence at Ratzeburg, to accompany the good and kind old pastor, with whom I lived, from the cellar to the roof, through gardens, farmyard, etc. and to call every, the minutest, thing by its German name. Advertisements, farces, jest books, and the conversation of children while I was at play with them, contributed their share to a more home-like acquaintance with the language than I could have acquired from works of polite literature alone, or even from polite society. There is a passage of hearty sound sense in Luther's German Letter on interpretation, to the translation of which I shall prefix, for the sake of those who read the German, yet are not likely to have dipped often in the massive folios of this heroic reformer, the simple, sinewy, idiomatic words of the original. "Denn man muss nicht die Buchstaben in der Lateinischen Sprache fragen wie man soll Deutsch reden: sondern man muss die Mutter in Hause, die Kinder auf den Gassen, den gemeinen Mann auf dem Markte, darum fragen: und denselbigen auf das Maul sehen wie sie reden, und darnach dolmetschen. So verstehen sie es denn, und merken dass man Deutsch mit ihnen redet."

TRANSLATION:

For one must not ask the letters in the Latin tongue, how one ought to speak German; but one must ask the mother in the house, the children in the lanes and alleys, the common man in the market, concerning this; yea, and look at the moves of their mouths while they are talking, and thereafter interpret. They understand you then, and mark that one talks German with them.]

39 (return)

[This paraphrase, written about the time of Charlemagne, is by no means deficient in occasional passages of considerable poetic merit. There is a flow, and a tender enthusiasm in the following lines (at the conclusion of Chapter XI.) which, even in the translation will not, I flatter myself, fail to interest the reader. Ottfried is describing the circumstances immediately following the birth of our Lord.

She gave with joy her virgin breast;
She hid it not, she bared the breast,
Which suckled that divinest babe!
Blessed, blessed were the breasts
Which the Saviour infant kiss'd;
And blessed, blessed was the mother
Who wrapp'd his limbs in swaddling clothes,
Singing placed him on her lap,

Hung o'er him with her looks of love,
And sooth'd him with a lulling motion.
Blessed; for she shelter'd him
From the damp and chilling air;
Blessed, blessed! for she lay
With such a babe in one blest bed,
Close as babes and mothers lie!
Blessed, blessed evermore,
With her virgin lips she kiss'd,
With her arms, and to her breast
She embraced the babe divine,
Her babe divine the virgin mother!
There lives not on this ring of earth
A mortal, that can sing her praise.
Mighty mother, virgin pure,
In the darkness and the night
For us she bore the heavenly Lord!

Most interesting is it to consider the effect, when the feelings are wrought above the natural pitch by the belief of something mysterious, while all the images are purely natural. Then it is, that religion and poetry strike deepest.]

40 (return)

[Lord Grenville has lately re-asserted (in the House of Lords) the imminent danger of a revolution in the earlier part of the war against France. I doubt not, that his Lordship is sincere; and it must be flattering to his feelings to believe it. But where are the evidences of the danger, to which a future historian can appeal? Or must he rest on an assertion? Let me be permitted to extract a passage on the subject from The Friend. "I have said that to withstand the arguments of the lawless, the anti-Jacobins proposed to suspend the law, and by the interposition of a particular statute to eclipse the blessed light of the universal sun, that spies and informers might tyrannize and escape in the ominous darkness. Oh! if these mistaken men, intoxicated with alarm and bewildered by that panic of property, which they themselves were the chief agents in exciting, had ever lived in a country where there really existed a general disposition to change and rebellion! Had they ever travelled through Sicily; or through France at the first coming on of the revolution; or even alas! through too many of the provinces of a sister island; they could not but have shrunk from their own declarations concerning the state of feeling and opinion at that time predominant throughout Great Britain. There was a time—(Heaven grant that that time may have passed by!)—when by crossing a narrow strait, they might have learned the true symptoms of approaching danger, and have secured themselves from mistaking the meetings and idle rant of such sedition, as shrank appalled from the sight of a constable, for the dire murmuring and strange consternation which precedes the storm or earthquake of national discord. Not only in coffee-houses and public theatres, but even at the tables of the wealthy, they would have heard the advocates of existing Government defend their cause in the language and with the tone of men, who are conscious that they are in a minority. But in England, when the alarm was at its highest, there was not a city, no, not a town or village, in which a man suspected of holding democratic principles could move abroad without receiving some unpleasant proof of the hatred in which his supposed opinions were held by the great majority of the people; and the only instances of popular excess and indignation were on the side of the government and the established church. But why need I appeal to these invidious facts? Turn over the pages of history and seek for a single instance of a revolution having been effected without the concurrence of either the nobles, or the ecclesiastics, or the monied classes, in any country, in which the influences of property had ever been predominant, and where the interests of the proprietors were interlinked! Examine the revolution of the Belgic provinces under Philip II; the civil wars of France in the preceding generation; the history of the American revolution, or the yet more recent events in Sweden and in Spain; and it will be scarcely possible not to perceive that in England from 1791 to the peace of Amiens there were neither tendencies to confederacy nor actual confederacies, against which the existing laws had not provided both sufficient safeguards and an ample punishment. But alas! the panic of property had been struck in the first instance for party purposes; and when it became general, its propagators caught it themselves and ended in believing their own lie; even as our bulls to Borrowdale sometimes run mad with the echo of their own bellowing. The consequences were most injurious. Our attention was concentrated on a monster, which could not survive the convulsions, in which it had been brought forth,—even the enlightened Burke himself too often talking and reasoning, as if a perpetual and organized anarchy had been a possible thing! Thus while we were warring against French doctrines, we took little heed whether the means by which we attempted to overthrow them, were not likely to aid and augment the far more formidable evil of French ambition. Like children we ran away from the yelping of a cur, and took shelter at the heels of a vicious war horse." (Vol. II. Essay i. p. 21, 4th edit.)]

41 (return)
[I seldom think of the murder of this illustrious Prince without recollecting the lines of Valerius Flaccus:

————*super ipsius ingens*
Instat fama viri, virtusque haud laeta tyranno;

Ergo anteire metus, juvenemque exstinguere pergit.
Argonaut, I. 29.]

42 (return)
[—

Theara de kai ton chaena kai taen dorkada,
Kai ton lagoon, kai to ton tauron genos.
Manuel Phile, De Animal. Proprietat. sect. I. i. 12.]

43 (return)
[Paradise Regained. Book IV. I. 261.]

44 (return)
[Vita e Costumi di Dante.]

45 (return)
[TRANSLATION: "With the greatest possible solicitude avoid authorship. Too early or immoderately employed, it makes the head waste and the heart empty; even were there no other worse consequences. A person, who reads only to print, to all probability reads amiss; and he, who sends away through the pen and the press every thought, the moment it occurs to him, will in a short time have sent all away, and will become a mere journeyman of the printing-office, a compositor."

To which I may add from myself, that what medical physiologists affirm of certain secretions applies equally to our thoughts; they too must be taken up again into the circulation, and be again and again re-secreted to order to ensure a healthful vigour, both to the mind and to its intellectual offspring.]

46 (return)
[This distinction between transcendental and transcendent is observed by our elder divines and philosophers, whenever they express themselves scholastically. Dr. Johnson indeed has confounded the two words; but his own authorities do not bear him out. Of this celebrated dictionary I will venture to remark once for all, that I should suspect the man of a morose disposition who should speak of it without respect and gratitude as a most instructive and entertaining book, and hitherto, unfortunately, an indispensable book; but I confess, that I should be surprised at hearing from a philosophic and thorough scholar any but very qualified praises of it, as a dictionary. I am not now alluding to the number of genuine words omitted; for this is (and perhaps to a greater extent) true, as Mr. Wakefield has noticed, of our best Greek Lexicons, and this too after the successive labours of so many giants in learning. I refer at present both to omissions and commissions of a more important nature. What these are, me saltem judice, will be stated at full in The Friend, re-published and completed.

I had never heard of the correspondence between Wakefield and Fox till I saw the account of it this morning (16th September 1815) in the Monthly Review. I was not a little gratified at finding, that Mr. Wakefield had proposed to himself nearly the same plan for a Greek and English Dictionary, which I had formed, and began to execute, now ten years ago. But far, far more grieved am I, that he did not live to complete it. I cannot but think it a subject of most serious regret, that the same heavy expenditure, which is now employing in the republication of STEPHANUS augmented, had not been applied to a new Lexicon on a more philosophical plan, with the English, German, and French synonymes as well as the Latin. In almost every instance the precise individual meaning might be given in an English or German word; whereas in Latin we must too often be contented with a mere general and inclusive term. How indeed can it be otherwise, when we attempt to render the most copious language of the world, the most admirable for the fineness of its distinctions, into one of the poorest and most vague languages? Especially when we reflect on the comparative number of the works, still extant, written while the Greek and Latin were living languages. Were I asked what I deemed the greatest and most unmixed benefit, which a wealthy individual, or an association of wealthy individuals could bestow on their country and on mankind, I should not hesitate to answer, "a philosophical English dictionary; with the Greek, Latin, German, French, Spanish, and Italian synonymes, and with correspondent indexes." That the learned languages might thereby be acquired, better, in half the time, is but a part, and not the most important part, of the advantages which would accrue from such a work. O! if it should be permitted by Providence, that without detriment to freedom and independence our government might be enabled to become more than a committee for war and revenue! There was a time, when every thing was to be done by Government. Have we not flown off to the contrary extreme?]

47   (return)
[April, 1825. If I did not see it with my own eyes, I should not believe that I had been guilty of so many hydrostatic Bulls as bellow in this unhappy allegory or string of metaphors! How a river was to travel up hill from a vale far inward, over the intervening mountains, Morpheus, the Dream weaver, can alone unriddle. I am ashamed and humbled. S. T. Coleridge.]

48   (return)
[Ennead, III. 8. 3. The force of the Greek sunienai is imperfectly expressed by "understand;" our own idiomatic phrase "to go along with me" comes nearest to it. The passage, that follows, full of profound sense, appears to me evidently corrupt; and in fact no writer more wants, better deserves, or is less likely to obtain, a new and more correct edition-ti oun sunienai; oti to genomenon esti theama emon, siopaesis (mallem, theama, emon sioposaes,)

kai physei genomenon theoraema, kai moi genomenae ek theorias taes odi, taen physin echein philotheamona uparkei. (mallem, kai moi hae genomenae ek theorias autaes odis). "What then are we to understand? That whatever is produced is an intuition, I silent; and that, which is thus generated, is by its nature a theorem, or form of contemplation; and the birth; which results to me from this contemplation, attains to have a contemplative nature." So Synesius:

'Odis   hiera
'Arraeta gona

The after comparison of the process of the natura naturans with that of the geometrician is drawn from the very heart of philosophy.]

49   (return)
[This is happily effected in three lines by Synesius, in his THIRD HYMN:

'En kai Pan'ta—(taken by itself) is Spinozism.
'En d' 'Apan'ton—a mere Anima Mundi.
'En te pro panton—is mechanical Theism.

But unite all three, and the result is the Theism of Saint Paul and Christianity. Synesius was censured for his doctrine of the pre- existence of the soul; but never, that I can find, arraigned or deemed heretical for his Pantheism, though neither Giordano Bruno, nor Jacob Behmen ever avowed it more broadly.

Mystas de Noos,
Ta te kai ta legei,
Buthon arraeton
Amphichoreuon.
Su to tikton ephus, Su to tiktomenon;
Su to photizon,
Su to lampomenon;
Su to phainomenon,
Su to kryptomenon
Idiais augais.
'En kai panta,
'En kath' heauto,
Kai dia panton.

Pantheism is therefore not necessarily irreligious or heretical; though it may be taught atheistically. Thus Spinoza would agree with Synesius in calling God Physis en Noerois, the Nature in Intelligences; but he could not subscribe to the preceding Nous kai noeros, i.e. Himself Intelligence and intelligent.

In this biographical sketch of my literary life I may be excused, if I mention here, that I had translated the eight Hymns of Synesius from the Greek into English Anacreontics before my fifteenth year.]

50 (return)
[See Schell. Abhandl. zur Erlaeuter. des Id. der Wissenschafslehre.]

51 (return)
[Des Cartes, Diss. de Methodo.]

52 (return)
[The impossibility of an absolute thing (substantia unica) as neither genus, species, nor individuum: as well as its utter unfitness for the fundamental position of a philosophic system, will be demonstrated in the critique on Spinozism in the fifth treatise of my Logosophia.]

53 (return)
[It is most worthy of notice, that in the first revelation of himself, not confined to individuals; indeed in the very first revelation of his absolute being, Jehovah at the same time revealed the fundamental truth of all philosophy, which must either commence with the absolute, or have no fixed commencement; that is, cease to be philosophy. I cannot but express my regret, that in the equivocal use of the word that, for in that, or because, our admirable version has rendered the passage susceptible of a degraded interpretation in the mind of common readers or hearers, as if it were a mere reproof to an impertinent question, I am what I am, which might be equally affirmed of himself by any existent being.

The Cartesian Cogito ergo sum is objectionable, because either the Cogito is used extra gradum, and then it is involved to the sum and is tautological; or it is taken as a particular mode or dignity, and then it is subordinated to the sum as the species to the genus, or rather as a particular modification to the subject modified; and not pre- ordinated as the arguments seem to require. For Cogito is Sum Cogitans. This is clear by the inevidence of the converse. Cogitat, ergo est is true, because it is a mere application of the logical rule: Quicquid in genere est, est et in specie. Est (cogitans), ergo est. It is a cherry tree; therefore it is a tree. But, est ergo cogitat, is illogical: for quod est in specie, non NBCESSARIO in genere est. It may be true. I hold it to be true, that quicquid vere est, est per veram sui affirmationem; but it is a derivative, not an immediate truth. Here then we have, by anticipation, the distinction between the conditional finite! (which, as known in distinct consciousness by occasion of experience, is called by Kant's followers the empirical!) and the absolute I AM, and likewise the dependence or rather the inherence of the former in the latter; in whom "we live, and move, and have our being," as St. Paul divinely asserts, differing widely from the Theists of the mechanic school (as Sir J. Newton, Locke, and others) who must say from whom we had our being, and with it life and the powers of life.]

54 (return)
[TRANSLATION. "Hence it is clear, from what cause many reject the notion of the continuous and the infinite. They take, namely, the words irrepresentable and impossible in one and the same meaning; and, according to the forms of sensuous evidence, the notion of the continuous and the infinite is doubtless impossible. I am not now pleading the cause of these laws, which not a few schools have thought proper to explode, especially the former (the law of continuity). But it is of the highest importance to admonish the reader, that those, who adopt so perverted a mode of reasoning, are under a grievous error. Whatever opposes the formal principles of the understanding and the reason is confessedly impossible; but not therefore that, which is therefore not amenable to the forms of sensuous evidence, because it is exclusively an object of pure intellect. For this non-coincidence of the sensuous and the intellectual (the nature of which I shall presently lay open) proves nothing more, but that the mind cannot always adequately represent to the concrete, and transform into distinct images, abstract notions derived from the pure intellect. But this contradiction, which is in itself merely subjective (i.e. an incapacity in the nature of man), too often passes for an incongruity or impossibility in the object (i.e. the notions themselves), and seduces the incautious to mistake the limitations of the human faculties for the limits of things, as they really exist."

I take this occasion to observe, that here and elsewhere Kant uses the term intuition, and the verb active (intueri Germanice anschauen) for which we have unfortunately no correspondent word, exclusively for that which can be represented in space and time. He therefore consistently and rightly denies the possibility of intellectual intuitions. But as I see no adequate reason for this exclusive sense of the term, I have reverted to its wider signification, authorized by our elder theologians and metaphysicians, according to whom the term comprehends all truths known to us without a medium.

From Kant's Treatise De mundi sensibilis et intelligibilis forma et principiis. 1770.]

55 (return)
[Franc. Baconis de Verulam, NOVUM ORGANUM.]

56 (return)
[This phrase, a priori, is in common, most grossly misunderstood, and as absurdity burdened on it, which it does not deserve. By knowledge a priori, we do not mean, that we can know anything previously to experience,

which would be a contradiction in terms; but that having once known it by occasion of experience (that is, something acting upon us from without) we then know, that it must have existed, or the experience itself would have been impossible. By experience only now, that I have eyes; but then my reason convinces me, that I must have had eyes in order to the experience.]

57 (return)
[Jer. Taylor's Via Pacis.]

58 (return)
[Par. Lost. Book V. I. 469.]

59 (return)
[Leibnitz. Op. T. II. P. II. p. 53.—T. III. p. 321.]

60 (return)
[Synesii Episcop. Hymn. III. I. 231]

61 (return)
['Anaer morionous, a phrase which I have borrowed from a Greek monk, who applies it to a Patriarch of Constantinople. I might have said, that I have reclaimed, rather than borrowed, it: for it seems to belong to Shakespeare, de jure singulari, et ex privilegio naturae.]

62 (return)
[First published in 1803.]

63 (return)
[These thoughts were suggested to me during the perusal of the Madrigals of Giovambatista Strozzi published in Florence in May, 1593, by his sons Lorenzo and Filippo Strozzi, with a dedication to their paternal uncle, Signor Leone Strozzi, Generale delle battaglie di Santa Chiesa. As I do not remember to have seen either the poems or their author mentioned in any English work, or to have found them in any of the common collections of Italian poetry; and as the little work is of rare occurrence; I will transcribe a few specimens. I have seldom met with compositions that possessed, to my feelings, more of that satisfying entireness, that complete adequateness of the manner to the matter which so charms us in Anacreon, joined with the tenderness, and more than the delicacy of Catullus. Trifles as they are, they were probably elaborated with great care; yet to the perusal we refer them to a spontaneous energy rather than to voluntary effort. To a cultivated taste there is a delight in perfection for its own sake, independently of the material in which it is manifested, that none but a cultivated taste can understand or appreciate.

After what I have advanced, it would appear presumption to offer a translation; even if the attempt were not discouraged by the different genius of the English mind and language, which demands a denser body of thought as the condition of a high polish, than the Italian. I cannot but deem it likewise an advantage in the Italian tongue, in many other respects inferior to our own, that the language of poetry is more distinct from that of prose than with us. From the earlier appearance and established primacy of the Tuscan poets, concurring with the number of independent states, and the diversity of written dialects, the Italians have gained a poetic idiom, as the Greeks before them had obtained from the same causes with greater and more various discriminations, for example, the Ionic for their heroic verses; the Attic for their iambic; and the two modes of the Doric for the lyric or sacerdotal, and the pastoral, the distinctions of which were doubtless more obvious to the Greeks themselves than they are to us.

I will venture to add one other observation before I proceed to the transcription. I am aware that the sentiments which I have avowed concerning the points of difference between the poetry of the present age, and that of the period between 1500 and 1650, are the reverse of the opinion commonly entertained. I was conversing on this subject with a friend, when the servant, a worthy and sensible woman, coming in, I placed before her two engravings, the one a pinky-coloured plate of the day, the other a masterly etching by Salvator Rosa from one of his own pictures. On pressing her to tell us, which she preferred, after a little blushing and flutter of feeling, she replied "Why, that, Sir, to be sure! (pointing to the ware from the Fleet-street print shops);—it's so neat and elegant. T'other is such a scratchy slovenly thing." An artist, whose writings are scarcely less valuable than his pictures, and to whose authority more deference will be willingly paid, than I could even wish should be shown to mine, has told us, and from his own experience too, that good taste must be acquired, and like all other good things, is the result of thought and the submissive study of the best models. If it be asked, "But what shall I deem such?"—the answer is; presume those to be the best, the reputation of which has been matured into fame by the consent of ages. For wisdom always has a final majority, if not by conviction, yet by acquiescence. In addition to Sir J. Reynolds I may mention Harris of Salisbury; who in one of his philosophical disquisitions has written on the means of acquiring a just taste with the precision of Aristotle, and the elegance of Quinctilian.

MADRIGALI.

Gelido suo ruscel chiaro, e tranquillo
M'insegno Amor di state a mezzo'l giorno;
Ardean le solve, ardean le piagge, e i colli.
Ond' io, ch' al piu gran gielo ardo e sfavillo,
Subito corsi; ma si puro adorno

Girsene il vidi, che turbar no'l volli:
Sol mi specchiava, e'n dolce ombrosa sponda
Mi stava intento al mormorar dell' onda.

Aure dell' angoscioso viver mio
Refrigerio soave,
E dolce si, che piu non mi par grave
Ne'l ardor, ne'l morir, anz' il desio;
Deh voi l ghiaccio, e le nubi, e'l tempo rio
Discacciatene omai, che l'onda chiara,
E l'ombra non men cara
A scherzare, a cantar per suoi boschetti,
E prati festa et allegrezza alletti.

Pacifiche, ma spesso in amorosa
Guerra co' fiori, e l'erba
Alla stagione acerba
Verdi insegne del giglio e della rosa,
Movete, Aure, pian pian; che tregua o posa,
Se non pace, io ritrove;
E so ben dove:—Oh vago, a mansueto
Sguardo, oh labbra d'ambrosia, oh rider, lieto!

Hor come un scoglio stassi,
Hor come un rio se'n fugge,
Ed hor crud' orsa rugge,
Hor canta angelo pio: ma che non fassi!
E che non fammi, O sassi,
O rivi, o belue, o Dii, questa mia vaga
Non so, se ninfa, o magna,
Non so, se donna, o Dea,
Non so, se dolce o rea?

Piangendo mi baciaste,
E ridendo il negaste:
In doglia hebbivi pin,
In festa hebbivi ria:
Nacque gioia di pianti,
Dolor di riso: O amanti
Miseri, habbiate insieme
Ognor paura e speme.

Bel Fior, tu mi rimembri

La rugiadosa guancia del bel viso;
E si vera l'assembri,
Che'n te sovente, come in lei m'affiso:
Et hor del vago riso,
Hor del serene sguardo
Io pur cieco riguardo. Ma qual fugge,
O Rosa, il mattin lieve!
E chi te, come neve,
E'l mio cor teco, e la mia vita strugge!

Anna mia, Anna dolce, oh sempre nuovo
E piu chiaro concento,
Quanta dolcezza sento
In sol Anna dicendo? Io mi pur pruovo,
Ne qui tra noi ritruovo,
Ne tra cieli armonia,
Che del bel nome suo piu dolce sia:
Altro il Cielo, altro Amore,
Altro non suona l'Ecco del mio core.

Hor che'l prato, e la selva si scoiora,
Al tuo serena ombroso
Muovine, alto Riposo,
Deh ch'io riposi una sol notte, un hora:
Han le fere, e gi't augelli, ognun talora
Ha qualche pace; io quando,
Lasso! non vonne errando,
E non piango, e non grido? e qual pur forte?
Ma poiche, non sent' egli, odine, Morte.

Risi e piansi d'Amor; ne pero mai
Se non in fiamma, o'n onda, o'n vento scrissi
Spesso msrce trovai
Crudel; sempre in me morto, in altri vissi:
Hor da' piu scuri Abissi al ciel m'aizai,
Hor ne pur caddi giuso;
Stance al fin qui son chiuso.

64   (return)
[—

'I've measured it from side to side;
'Tis three feet long, and two feet wide."]

65

[—

"Nay, rack your brain— 'tis all in vain,
I'll tell you every thing I know;
But to the Thorn, and to the Pond
Which is a little step beyond,
I wish that you would go:
Perhaps, when you are at the place,
You something of her tale may trace.

I'll give you the best help I can
Before you up the mountain go,
Up to the dreary mountain-top,
I'll tell you all I know.
'Tis now some two-and-twenty years
Since she (her name is Martha Ray)
Gave, with a maiden's true good will,
Her company to Stephen Hill;
And she was blithe and gay,
And she was happy, happy still
Whene'er she thought of Stephen Hill.

And they had fixed the wedding-day,
The morning that must wed them both
But Stephen to another maid
Had sworn another oath;
And, with this other maid, to church
Unthinking Stephen went—
Poor Martha! on that woeful day
A pang of pitiless dismay
Into her soul was sent;
A fire was kindled in her breast,
Which might not burn itself to rest.

They say, full six months after this,
While yet the summer leaves were green,
She to the mountain-top would go,
And there was often seen;
'Tis said a child was in her womb,
As now to any eye was plain;
She was with child, and she was mad;
Yet often she was sober sad
From her exceeding pain.

Oh me! ten thousand times I'd rather
That he had died, that cruel father!

* * * *
* * * *
* * * *
* * * *

Last Christmas when they talked of this,
Old Farmer Simpson did maintain,
That in her womb the infant wrought
About its mother's heart, and brought
Her senses back again:
And, when at last her time drew near,
Her looks were calm, her senses clear.

No more I know, I wish I did,
And I would tell it all to you
For what became of this poor child
There's none that ever knew
And if a child was born or no,
There's no one that could ever tell;
And if 'twas born alive or dead,
There's no one knows, as I have said:
But some remember well,
That Martha Ray about this time
Would up the mountain often climb."]

66 (return)
[It is no less an error in teachers, than a torment to the poor children, to enforce the necessity of reading as they would talk. In order to cure them of singing as it is called, that is, of too great a difference, the child is made to repeat the words with his eyes from off the book; and then, indeed, his tones resemble talking, as far as his fears, tears and trembling will permit. But as soon as the eye is again directed to the printed page, the spell begins anew; for an instinctive sense tells the child's feelings, that to utter its own momentary thoughts, and to recite the written thoughts of another, as of another, and a far wiser than himself, are two widely different things; and as the two acts are accompanied with widely different feelings, so must they justify different modes of enunciation. Joseph Lancaster, among his other sophistications of the excellent Dr. Bell's invaluable system, cures this fault of singing, by hanging fetters and chains on the child, to the music of which one of his school-fellows, who walks before, dolefully chants out the child's last speech and confession, birth, parentage, and education. And this soul-

benumbing ignominy, this unholy and heart-hardening burlesque on the last fearful infliction of outraged law, in pronouncing the sentence to which the stern and familiarized judge not seldom bursts into tears, has been extolled as a happy and ingenious method of remedying—what? and how?—why, one extreme in order to introduce another, scarce less distant from good sense, and certainly likely to have worse moral effects, by enforcing a semblance of petulant ease and self-sufficiency, in repression and possible after-perversion of the natural feelings. I have to beg Dr. Bell's pardon for this connection of the two names, but he knows that contrast is no less powerful a cause of association than likeness.]

67 (return)
[Altered from the description of Night-Mair in the REMORSE.

"Oh Heaven! 'twas frightful! Now ran down and stared at
By hideous shapes that cannot be remembered;
Now seeing nothing and imagining nothing;
But only being afraid—stifled with fear!
While every goodly or familiar form
Had a strange power of spreading terror round me!"

N.B.—Though Shakespeare has, for his own all justifying purposes, introduced the Night-Mare with her own foals, yet Mair means a Sister, or perhaps a Hag.]

68 (return)
[But still more by the mechanical system of philosophy which has needlessly infected our theological opinions, and teaching us to consider the world in its relation to god, as of a building to its mason, leaves the idea of omnipresence a mere abstract notion in the stateroom of our reason.]

69 (return)
[As the ingenious gentleman under the influence of the Tragic Muse contrived to dislocate, "I wish you a good morning, Sir! Thank you, Sir, and I wish you the same," into two blank-verse heroics:—

To you a morning good, good Sir! I wish.
You, Sir! I thank: to you the same wish I.

In those parts of Mr. Wordsworth's works which I have thoroughly studied, I find fewer instances in which this would be practicable than I have met to many poems, where an approximation of prose has been sedulously and on system guarded against. Indeed excepting the stanzas already quoted from THE SAILOR'S MOTHER, I can recollect but one instance: that is to say, a short passage of four or five lines in THE BROTHERS, that model of English pastoral, which I never yet read with unclouded eye.—"James, pointing to its summit, over which they had all purposed to return together, informed them that he would wait for them there. They parted, and his comrades passed that way some two hours after, but they did not find him at the appointed place, *a circumstance of which they took no heed:* but one of them, going by chance into the house, which at this time was James's house, learnt *there,* that nobody had seen him all that day." The only change which has been made is in the position of the little word there in two instances, the position in the original being clearly such as is not adopted in ordinary conversation. The other words printed in italics were so marked because, though good and genuine English, they are not the phraseology of common conversation either in the word put in apposition, or in the connection by the genitive pronoun. Men in general would have said, "but that was a circumstance they paid no attention to, or took no notice of;" and the language is, on the theory of the preface, justified only by the narrator's being the Vicar. Yet if any ear could suspect, that these sentences were ever printed as metre, on those very words alone could the suspicion have been grounded.]

70 (return)
[I had in my mind the striking but untranslatable epithet, which the celebrated Mendelssohn applied to the great founder of the Critical Philosophy "Der alleszermalmende KANT," that is, the all-becrushing, or rather the all-to-nothing-crushing Kant. In the facility and force of compound epithets, the German from the number of its cases and inflections approaches to the Greek, that language so

"Bless'd in the happy marriage of sweet words."

It is in the woful harshness of its sounds alone that the German need shrink from the comparison.]

71 (return)
[Sammlung einiger Abhandlungen von Christian Garve.]

72 (return)
[Sonnet IX.]

73 (return)
[Mr. Wordsworth's having judiciously adopted "concourse wild" in this passage for "a wild scene" as it stood to the former edition, encourages me to hazard a remark, which I certainly should not have made in the works of a poet less austerely accurate in the use of words, than he is, to his own great honour. It respects the propriety of the word, "scene," even in the sentence in which it is retained. Dryden, and he only in his more careless verses, was the first, as far as my researches have discovered, who for the convenience of rhyme used this word in the vague sense, which has been since too current even in our best writers, and which (unfortunately, I

think) is given as its first explanation in Dr. Johnson's Dictionary and therefore would be taken by an incautious reader as its proper sense. In Shakespeare and Milton the word is never used without some clear reference, proper or metaphorical, to the theatre. Thus Milton:

"*Cedar, and pine, and fir, and branching palm*
A sylvan scene; and, as the ranks ascend
Shade above shade, a woody theatre
Of stateliest view."

I object to any extension of its meaning, because the word is already more equivocal than might be wished; inasmuch as to the limited use, which I recommend, it may still signify two different things; namely, the scenery, and the characters and actions presented on the stage during the presence of particular scenes. It can therefore be preserved from obscurity only by keeping the original signification full in the mind. Thus Milton again,

——— *"Prepare thee for another scene."*]

74 (return)
[——

Which Copland scarce had spoke, but quickly every hill,
Upon her verge that stands, the neighbouring vallies fill;
Helvillon from his height, it through the mountains threw,
From whom as soon again, the sound Dunbalrase drew,
From whose stone-trophied head, it on the Windross went,
Which tow'rds the sea again, resounded it to Dent.
That Brodwater, therewith within her banks astound,
In sailing to the sea, told it to Egremound,
Whose buildings, walks, and streets, with echoes loud and long,
Did mightily commend old Copland for her song.
Drayton's POLYOLBION: Song XXX.]

75 (return)
[Translation. It behoves me to side with my friends, but only as far as the gods.]

76 (return)
["Slender. I bruised my shin with playing with sword and dagger for a dish of stewed prunes, and by my troth I cannot abide the smell of hot meat since."—So again, Evans. "I will make an end of my dinner: there's pippins and cheese to come."]

77 (return)
[This was accidentally confirmed to me by an old German gentleman at Helmstadt, who had been Klopstock's school and bed-fellow. Among other

boyish anecdotes, he related that the young poet set a particular value on a translation of the PARADISE LOST, and always slept with it under his pillow.]

78 (return)
[Klopstock's observation was partly true and partly erroneous. In the literal sense of his words, and, if we confine the comparison to the average of space required for the expression of the same thought in the two languages, it is erroneous. I have translated some German hexameters into English hexameter; and find, that on the average three English lines will express four lines German. The reason is evident: our language abounds in monosyllables and dissyllables. The German, not less than the Greek, is a polysyllable language. But in another point of view the remark was not without foundation. For the German possessing the same unlimited privilege of forming compounds, both with prepositions and with epithets, as the Greek, it can express the richest single Greek word in a single German one, and is thus freed from the necessity of weak or ungraceful paraphrases. I will content myself with one at present, viz. the use of the prefixed participles ver, zer, ent, and weg: thus reissen to rend, verreissen to rend away, zerreissen to rend to pieces, entreissen to rend off or out of a thing, in the active sense: or schmelzen to melt—ver, zer, ent, schmelzen— and in like manner through all the verbs neuter and active. If you consider only how much we should feel the loss of the prefix be, as in bedropt, besprinkle, besot, especially in our poetical language, and then think that this same mode of composition is carved through all their simple and compound prepositions, and many of their adverbs; and that with most of these the Germans have the same privilege as we have of dividing them from the verb and placing them at the end of the sentence; you will have no difficulty in comprehending the reality and the cause of this superior power in the German of condensing meaning, in which its great poet exulted. It is impossible to read half a dozen pages of Wieland without perceiving that in this respect the German has no rival but the Greek. And yet I feel, that concentration or condensation is not the happiest mode of expressing this excellence, which seems to consist not so much in the less time required for conveying an impression, as in the unity and simultaneousness with which the impression is conveyed. It tends to make their language more picturesque: it depictures images better. We have obtained this power in part by our compound verbs derived from the Latin: and the sense of its great effect no doubt induced our Milton both to the use and the abuse of Latin derivatives. But still these prefixed particles, conveying no separate or separable meaning to the mere English reader, cannot possibly act on the mind with the force or liveliness of an original and homogeneous language such as the German is, and besides are confined to certain words.]

79 (return)
[Praecludere calumniam, in the original.]

80 (return)
[Better thus: Forma specifica per formam individualem translucens: or better yet—Species individualisata, sive Individuum cuilibet Speciei determinatae in omni parte correspondens et quasi versione quadam eam interpretans et repetens.]

81 (return)
[—

————"*The big round tears*
Cours'd one another down his innocent nose
In piteous chase,"

says Shakespeare of a wounded stag hanging its head over a stream: naturally, from the position of the head, and most beautifully, from the association of the preceding image, of the chase, in which "the poor sequester'd stag from the hunter's aim had ta'en a hurt." In the supposed position of Bertram, the metaphor, if not false, loses all the propriety of the original.]

82 (return)
[Among a number of other instances of words chosen without reason, Imogine in the first act declares, that thunder-storms were not able to intercept her prayers for "the desperate man, in desperate ways who dealt"——

"Yea, when the launched bolt did sear her sense,
Her soul's deep orisons were breathed for him;"

that is, when a red-hot bolt, launched at her from a thunder-cloud, had cauterized her sense, to plain English, burnt her eyes out of her head, she kept still praying on.

"Was not this love? Yea, thus doth woman love!"]

83 (return)
[This sort of repetition is one of this writers peculiarities, and there is scarce a page which does not furnish one or more instances—Ex. gr. in the first page or two. Act I, line 7th, "and deemed that I might sleep."—Line 10, "Did rock and quiver in the bickering glare."—Lines 14, 15, 16, "But by the momently gleams of sheeted blue, Did the pale marbles dare so sternly on me, I almost deemed they lived."—Line 37, "The glare of Hell."—Line 35, "O holy Prior, this is no earthly storm."—Line 38, "This is no earthly storm."—Line 42, "Dealing with us."—Line 43, "Deal thus sternly:"—Line 44, "Speak! thou hast something seen?"—"A fearful sight!"—Line 45,

"What hast thou seen! A piteous, fearful sight."—Line 48, "quivering gleams."—Line 50, "In the hollow pauses of the storm."—Line 61, "The pauses of the storm, etc."]

84 (return)
[The child is an important personage, for I see not by what possible means the author could have ended the second and third acts but for its timely appearance. How ungrateful then not further to notice its fate!]

85 (return)
[Classically too, as far as consists with the allegorizing fancy of the modern, that still striving to project the inward, contradistinguishes itself from the seeming ease with which the poetry of the ancients reflects the world without. Casimir affords, perhaps, the most striking instance of this characteristic difference.—For his style and diction are really classical: while Cowley, who resembles Casimir in many respects, completely barbarizes his Latinity, and even his metre, by the heterogeneous nature of his thoughts. That Dr. Johnson should have passed a contrary judgment, and have even preferred Cowley's Latin Poems to Milton's, is a caprice that has, if I mistake not, excited the surprise of all scholars. I was much amused last summer with the laughable affright, with which an Italian poet perused a page of Cowley's Davideis, contrasted with the enthusiasm with which he first ran through, and then read aloud, Milton's Mansus and Ad Patrem.]

86 (return)
[Flectit, or if the metre had allowed, premit would have supported the metaphor better.]

87 (return)
[Poor unlucky Metaphysicks! and what are they? A single sentence expresses the object and thereby the contents of this science. Gnothi seauton:

Nosce te ipsum,
Tuque Deum, quantum licet, inque Deo omnia noscas.]

Know thyself: and so shalt thou know God, as far as is permitted to a creature, and in God all things.—Surely, there is a strange—nay, rather too natural—aversion to many to know themselves.]